From

From Ronald to Donald

*How the Myth of Reagan
Became the Cult of Trump*

EDWIN G. OSWALD *and*
ALAN AXELROD

McFarland & Company, Inc., Publishers
Jefferson, North Carolina

LIBRARY OF CONGRESS CATALOGUING-IN-PUBLICATION DATA

Names: Oswald, Edwin G., author. | Axelrod, Alan, 1952– author.
Title: From Ronald to Donald : how the myth of Reagan became the cult of Trump /
    Edwin G. Oswald and Alan Axelrod.
Other titles: How the myth of Reagan became the cult of Trump
Description: Jefferson, North Carolina : McFarland & Company, Inc., Publishers, 2024 |
    Includes bibliographical references and index.
Identifiers: LCCN 2023051786 | ISBN 9781476690322 (print) ∞
    ISBN 9781476650623 (ebook)
Subjects: LCSH: Reagan, Ronald—Influence. | United States—Politics and
    government—1981–1989. | United States—Politics and government—1989– |
    Trump, Donald, 1946– | Presidents—United States—Public opinion. | Public
    opinion—United States. | BISAC: HISTORY / United States / 21st Century |
    POLITICAL SCIENCE / American Government / Executive Branch
Classification: LCC E877.2 .O89 2024 | DDC 973.9—dc23/eng/20231122
LC record available at https://lccn.loc.gov/2023051786

BRITISH LIBRARY CATALOGUING DATA ARE AVAILABLE

ISBN (print) 978-1-4766-9032-2
ISBN (ebook) 978-1-4766-5062-3

Front cover images: Official portrait of President Ronald Reagan in Oval Office
for 1985 (National Archives); Donald Trump speaking with supporters at a
campaign rally at Fountain Park in Fountain Hills, Arizona (Gage Skidmore Flickr).

Printed in the United States of America

McFarland & Company, Inc., Publishers
    Box 611, Jefferson, North Carolina 28640
    www.mcfarlandpub.com

Contents

Acknowledgments

To my wife Lisa, for her love, devotion and tireless support.
To my sons, Eddie and Nick, who give me boundless joy.
To my brothers, Stephen and John, for their encouragement.
Finally, I want to thank my co-author Alan Axelrod,
an ideal partner, whose expertise and sense of humor
kept this book project moving.
—*Edwin G. Oswald*

Thanks to Ed Oswald for inviting me
to contribute to his remarkable book,
a good, stiff belt of truth serum.
—*Alan Axelrod*

Preface

On November 4, 1980, 50.7 percent of the national electorate gave Ronald Reagan a forty-four-state Electoral College landslide. It was a real election and a real victory, but the man it carried into the White House was largely compounded of mythology.

Like all compelling personal mythologies, Reagan's was a synthesis of multiple emotional, intellectual, and cultural streams. It was partly self-made and partly imposed—by the circumstances of Reagan's birth, upbringing, and vocation, and by history. Partly, too, it was the product of the imagery, celebrity, hopes, and ideals 43,903,230 American voters projected onto him.

The vessel that received these projections and held so powerful a myth did not bear the hallmarks of exceptionalism. A talented radio sportscaster turned journeyman movie actor who converted from Roosevelt Democrat to Goldwater Republican, Reagan defeated a complacently incumbent Pat Brown in 1966 to become governor of California; survived a 1968 attempt by senior citizens, educators, and organized labor to recall him; and won a second gubernatorial term in 1970, albeit by a slimmer margin than before.

No matter. Despite courting impeachment in his second presidential term, the vessel that was Ronald Reagan held together, the myth endured, and Reagan became the standard bearer for the conservative movement and the Republican Party.

There was Reagan as tax cutter; deficit hawk; promoter of deregulation, traditional family values, and small government; and champion of free-market capitalism—all indelible images nevertheless belied by historical fact. And there was Reagan, victor in the Cold War, a hero an assassin's bullets could not kill, and savior of the United States and Grenada, too. All debatable.

The myth of Ronald Reagan far outshone and has long outlasted his eight years in the Oval Office. It became the gossamer framework on which the modern-day Republican Party transformed the Gipper's hopeful, if

1

gauzy, message of "morning in America" into the small-minded rancor of Donald Trump's MAGA.

Politically, the authors came of age when Reagan was elected president in 1980. As the senior author of this volume, I owe the reader a word or two about my background. I made a career as a DC tax attorney and served as an attorney-advisor with the Clinton administration in the U.S. Treasury's Office of Tax Legislative Counsel, where I worked on tax policy and legislative matters impacting municipal bonds and public infrastructure. I come forward now neither to praise nor to bury Ronald Reagan but to explain him—in the surprisingly objective non-partisan terms of contemporary mythology. The Western world is starved for myth, and perhaps this craving is part of the reason why Reagan's myth still burns so brightly and has, to the astonishment of some and the chagrin of even more, spawned a fringe political figure who wreaked so much political, institutional, and cultural havoc as the forty-fifth president of the United States.

For the Reagan "myth" is actually the most salient "fact" of two very momentous presidencies, Reagan's and Trump's—as it is of FDR and, for that matter, of Eisenhower, Kennedy, and then back to Theodore Roosevelt, Lincoln, Jackson, and George Washington himself. By understanding the transformative presidency of Ronald Reagan in the context of American history and of the American presidency, we can understand how a transformative president creates far more than policy by also shaping culture with the instrumental force of mythology. Reagan believed in the power of stories, often sprinkled with midwestern and patriotic values. Over his eight years in office, as the "Great Communicator," he was largely successful in shaping the soul of America to reflect his views and beliefs regarding the role of government. That American soul also created and embraced Donald John Trump, a politician and a man to whom Reagan, personally, would not have given the time of day.

The Reagan presidency was the springboard into our current political, economic, and cultural era. Excepting Franklin Delano Roosevelt, Ronald Wilson Reagan was the most consequential president of the last century. The two men were the matter and antimatter of American political-social policy. Where FDR offered the people a New Deal, with the federal government serving as the engine that moved the nation forward, Reagan blithely dismissed government as "the problem." As FDR created the mythology of benevolently efficient government, which culminated in LBJ's Great Society until it was strangled by the Texan's other obsession, the Vietnam War, so Reagan and his many acolytes countered with the elevation of the individual over society—great, small, or utterly indifferent.

A consequential aspect of this political springboard are Reagan's economic and tax policies, often referred to as Reaganomics, supply-side economics, or trickle-down economics. Call it what you will, the DNA of Reagan's economic policies lives on some forty years later. The fundamental framework and philosophy of Reaganomics—cut taxes for the wealthy, which will increase demand for goods and services, the benefits of which will "trickle down" to the lower rungs of the socioeconomic ladder and any associated tax cuts will pay for themselves through economic activity—remains the cornerstone of GOP policy. (Spoiler alert: It didn't and doesn't work.)

Four decades and counting, the societal cost of Reaganomics is historic economic inequality within the United States. Measured from 1979 to 2019, the cumulative growth in real income before transfers and taxes for the top 20 percent quintile of households was 114 percent, while cumulative growth in real income before transfers and taxes for all other households was no higher than 45 percent.

Moreover, within the political arena, the lingering Reagan legacy has rendered taboo the mere mention of tax increases. The phrase has been banished from even the most courageous elected officials, Republican and Democrat. Do you remember how voters treated Reagan's vice-president and heir, George Herbert Walker Bush in 1991 after he violated his "read my lips—no new taxes" pledge? Do you remember how voters treated Walter Mondale, who ran against Reagan in 1984, after he stated that he would "raise taxes" in his presidential nominee acceptance speech? Once an electorate accepts as axiomatic the proposition that "government is the problem," no rationale can justify adequately funding it. Hence, measured from 1981 to the day of this writing, the federal budget deficit has ballooned to more than $30 trillion.

This book examines the rise, reign, and enduring legacy of Ronald Reagan, which still drives politics, economic policy, and culture in a time when the American morning has entered the twilight of Trumpian eclipse. It has yet to emerge. Understanding the mythology at work, we believe, is a necessary step toward the hope of new dawn.

—Edwin G. Oswald

CHAPTER 1

Government Is the Problem

"...government is not the solution to our problem; government is the problem."
—From the First Inaugural Address
of Ronald Reagan, January 20, 1981

The biggest things often start from the smallest and most trivial. This is true of the universe, according to the Big Bang Theory, which pegs the origin of all that we know to the explosion of an infinitesimal point of undifferentiated matter and energy some 14 billion years ago. And it is true as well of the globe-engulfing coronavirus, Covid-19. Some believe it originated in a live-animal market in the Jianghan District of Wuhan, China, a virus vectored there in a scaly anteater, possibly, or maybe a horseshoe bat. Perhaps the virus animal host was sold to a customer in Jianghan's famous open-air wholesale "wet" market. Or perhaps, as *The New Yorker*'s Carolyn Kormann wrote, some "weary traveler" passing through the market "rubbed his eyes, or scratched his nose, or was anxiously, unconsciously biting his fingernails. One invisible blob of virus. One human face. And here we are, battling a global pandemic."[1] A growing number of scientists believe it was created in a Wuhan medical research laboratory and somehow leaked out.[2]

An angry, eloquent editorial published on March 30, 2020, in *The Boston Globe*[3] noted that, at the time, 745,000 people were infected globally, more than 140,000 of them in the United States, a number greater than that of any other nation. The editorial board asked us to remember that "the reach of the virus here is not attributable to an act of God or a foreign invasion, but a colossal failure of leadership." The editorial, titled "A president unfit for a pandemic," claimed that "much of the suffering and death coming was preventable," and it concluded: "The president has blood on his hands."

In the brief compass of an editorial opinion, the writers did their best to build their case against Donald J. Trump, a "president epically outmatched" by the pandemic. When the first U.S. case was announced in January 2020, he "downplayed the risk and insisted all was under control." He ignored all scientific advice, touted unproven "cures," and blithely spoke of "reopening" the country by Easter, envisioning "packed churches" at that "beautiful time." Observing that "Timing is everything in pandemic response," the editorial board cited Trump's "critical errors" over February and March, such as choosing not to collaborate with other countries' efforts to contain their outbreaks and study the disease, choosing to invest time in developing an (initially faulty) American-made test for the disease instead of adopting the World Health Organization's existing, proven, and readily available test—"a move that kneecapped the US coronavirus response and ... will cost thousands of American lives." The president refused to use his statutory authority to "mobilize rapidly to distribute needed gowns, masks, and ventilators to ill-equipped hospitals and healthcare workers." Instead, he left cities, states, and individual hospitals to bid competitively with each other for scarce supplies, the prices of which rose in what became a national, even global, auction.

"It is not too much for Americans to ask of their leaders that they be competent and informed when responding to a crisis of historic proportions," the *Globe* editorialists protested. "Instead, they have a White House marred by corruption and incompetence...."

The truth is that, in electing Donald Trump, Americans did not ask for a leader who was competent and informed. What they got was the very leader they voted for, the one who disavowed government, free trade, science, climate change, objective facts, and expertise alike, proclaiming in messianic fashion at the GOP convention, "I alone can fix it."[4]

Trump campaigned against what he and his supporters called the "Deep State"—that is, the 2.2 million career professionals who, in fact, *are* the federal government. A month after Trump took office, his then chief strategist, Steve Bannon, announced that every day would be a battle for "deconstruction of the administrative state"—another word for "Deep State," another word for 2.2 million career civil servants. Later, speaking in Warsaw on July 6, 2017, the president himself "warned of a danger invisible to some but familiar to the Poles: the steady creep of government bureaucracy that drains the vitality and wealth of the people."[5]

No one should have been surprised that, in the words of a February 26, 2020, *BuzzFeed* headline, "Trump's Biggest Supporters Think the Coronavirus Is a Deep State Plot." At a press conference that very evening, Trump claimed: "Because of all we've done, the risk to the American people remains very low.... The level that we've had in our country is very low and those people are getting very better." He went on to agree with the conspiracy theory articulated by far-right commentator "Rush Limbaugh

... that the deep state had created the coronavirus as a political weapon 'to bring down Trump.'" The president later tweeted, "Low Ratings Fake News MSDNC (Comcast) & @CNN are doing everything possible to make Caronavirus [*sic*] look as bad as possible, including panicking markets, if possible."[6]

On March 26, 2020, *The New York Times* reported: "Of the 75 senior positions at the Department of Homeland Security, 20 are either vacant or filled by acting officials, including [former lobbyist] Chad F. Wolf, the acting secretary who recently was unable to tell a Senate committee how many respirators and protective face masks were available in the United States." As of April 2020, approximately 80 percent of all senior government positions below the cabinet level had turned over since Trump took office, some 500 people having departed since the inauguration. "Now, current and former administration officials and disaster experts say the coronavirus has ... left parts of the federal government unprepared and ill equipped for what may be the largest public health crisis in a century."[7]

"I alone can fix it"?

By 2020, the United States government was a bereft and amputated thing, far more dysfunctional and even non-functional than Ronald Reagan had claimed it was in 1980. Confronted with the global Covid-19 pandemic beginning in early 2020, the federal government responded chiefly with inaction, denial, and deception, even to the point of suppressing the work of such agencies as the CDC and the U.S. Public Health Service and resolutely refusing to create a national strategy for controlling the spread of the virus. "Government is the problem," the mantra mythologized and enshrined during the Reagan administration, became manifest reality during the regime of Trump. By the time the 45th president left the White House on January 20, 2021, Covid-19 was the leading cause of death in America, with 3,049 Americans dying daily.[8]

* * *

As many saw it in 2015–2016, Donald Trump's candidacy was a joke or trivial at best. In fact, many believe that President Obama's roasting of Donald Trump—to his face—at the 2011 White House Correspondents Dinner so humiliated and enraged "the Donald" that he decided then and there to make a serious run for the Oval Office.[9]

At that dinner, President Obama mocked Trump's infamous efforts to fan the flames of the "birther conspiracy," the weird viral canard that Barack Obama was not born in the United States:

Donald Trump is here tonight. Now I know that he's taken some flak lately. But no one is happier—no one is prouder—to put this birth certificate matter to rest than The Donald. And that's because he can finally get back to focusing on the issues that matter: Like, did we fake the moon landing? What really happened in Roswell? And where are Biggie and Tupac? All kidding aside, obviously we all know about your credentials and breadth of experience. For example, ... no seriously, just recently, in an episode of *Celebrity Apprentice*, at the steakhouse, the men's cooking team did not impress the judges from Omaha Steaks. And there was a lot of blame to go around, but you, Mr. Trump, recognized that the real problem was a lack of leadership, and so ultimately you didn't blame Lil Jon or Meat Loaf, you fired Gary Busey. And these are the kinds of decisions that would keep me up at night. Well handled, sir. Well handled. Say what you will about Mr. Trump, he certainly would bring some change to the White House....[10]

Yes, just imagine the "star" of *Celebrity Apprentice*—a real estate developer whose best days seemed very much behind him, a huckster of everything from Trump Steaks and Trump Vodka to Trump University,[11] a man who somehow managed to go broke *in the casino business!*—just imagine this carnival barker, WWE wrestling promoter, and reality TV frontman—just imagine *him* running for the office of leader of the free world.

We didn't have to imagine. We just needed to review recent history. Go back to 1980, when another celebrity not only ran for the White House but also ended up occupying it for two terms, a span that transformed the GOP and the nation, a portion of which elevated the man to secular sainthood. In fact, the notion of Americans voting for "celebrity" candidates is not at all unusual, as America's recently elected officials have included the likes of Governor Arnold Schwarzenegger, Governor Jesse "The Body" Ventura, Representative Sonny Bono, and Senator Al Franken.

Yes, there were plenty of people who scoffed at a Ronald Reagan candidacy, Republicans as well as Democrats. They thought of him not as the two-term governor of California but as a glibly genial, eternally smiling entertainer, a Hollywood actor who rose but once above grade–B fare—in 1942's *King's Row*—although his place in the pop culture cinema pantheon was more firmly secured by *Bedtime for Bonzo* (1951), in which his costar was the eponymous chimpanzee.

In stark contrast to Trump, as we will recount in some of the chapters that follow, Ronald Reagan certainly had political bona fides, culminating in his California governorship. We also want to make sure that, while many saw both Reagan and Trump as primarily media celebrities, the manifested personality and character each brought did have starkly different features. Where Trump is mercurial, infantile, and profoundly narcissistic, Reagan possessed a stable character, a flawed but nevertheless real moral compass, and a version of patriotism that, while narrow and exclusionary, nevertheless demonstrated a love for country. Trump, unapologetically, seems never to have looked beyond his own self-interest.

Like Trump, who was for most of his life a Democrat (prior to 2012, he registered sporadically as a Republican in 1987, 2001, and 2009), Reagan hardly began life as a Republican. Indeed, his interest in politics began when he was an unabashed Democrat and a full-on FDR New Dealer, who was elected to the presidency of the Screen Actors Guild (SAG) seven times—twice in 1947, and again in 1948, 1949, 1950, 1951, and 1959. His liberal bent soon straightened, as he grew fervent in his anti-communism, even testifying as a friendly witness before the infamous House Un-American Activities Committee in 1947.

Numerous accounts exist of his growing interest in government and politics while he was still in Hollywood. However, given his level of income at that time, a central motive for his political aspirations was the effect that taking home $169,750 in pay had on his 1946 income taxes. The haul pushed him precariously close to the 91 percent marginal rate bracket, which, in the war-strapped late 1940s, kicked in at $200,000. Even though he had dodged that bullet by $30,250, he felt that the federal government had its big hand stuck in something that pissed him off: *his* pocket. So, he scrambled to do something about it, using his position as SAG president to promote what he called a "human depreciation allowance" for actors and athletes, whose years of earning power were inherently limited. In later years, including those as President, Reagan spoke of how his fellow actors deliberately restricted themselves to making four movies a year to avoid "creeping" into that punitive 91 percent bracket.[12]

Big things often start from the smallest and most trivial. Ronald Reagan mightily resented his personal tax bill. That resentment helped to propel him away from the Democratic to the Republican Party, a migration, as we will see, that was mentored by several strong personalities, most of them corporate and entrepreneurial figures. Among these was Lemuel Ricketts Boulware, VP of labor and community relations for General Electric, infamous for his union-busting policy of "take-it-or-leave-it" collective bargaining. In part, under Boulware's tutelage, longtime union president Reagan turned against unionism as a drag on business growth. Union demands drove up prices, Boulware argued. Both the government *and* the unions had their hands in American pockets. Boulware catalyzed Reagan's ultimate transformation from New Deal tax-and-spend liberal to Goldwater tax-cutting, entitlement-limiting conservative.

In 1954, with his Hollywood acting career rapidly waning, Reagan eagerly accepted Boulware's offer to host the *General Electric Theater,* a weekly television drama series, and to travel to GE plants and offices across the country to deliver motivational speeches to employees. Some of these were canned speeches written by GE messaging people, but most were written by Reagan himself. Company policy dictated that they be non-partisan, but most delivered an unmistakably conservative, free market, limited government message. When Reagan was fired by GE in 1962 (adopted son Michael Reagan believes the company was pressured by then attorney general Robert F. Kennedy[13]), he had a moment of panic. The job, after all, had been lucrative, and the Reagans were living large.

Yet Ronald Reagan was nothing if not congenitally optimistic. He lost his job, but also gone, he realized, were the shackles of GE's strict prohibition against employees engaging in politics. In 1961, Reagan recorded an LP for the American Medical Association, a celebrated argument against Medicare as "socialized medicine," and in 1964 he parlayed his GE speechifying experience into a series of speeches, which he both wrote and delivered, supporting emerging ultra-conservative icon Barry Goldwater. His 1964 televised Goldwater presidential campaign speech, "A Time for Choosing," gave him a strong injection of political credibility, and a group of conservative California Republicans responded by recruiting him to run for governor.

Reagan defeated the popular two-term Democrat Edmund G. "Pat" Brown by a margin of more than 57 percent. This victory shocked many Californians, including the uncomprehending Brown himself. This was a foreshadowing of Reagan's own unlikely rise to the presidency and, in the fulness of time, the even more unlikely election of Donald Trump.

*   *   *

Reagan's rise attracted the fuzzy stuff of myth as a piece of hard candy attracts the lint in one's pocket. It became bound up with legends of a small-town Illinois childhood and young manhood—shades of Honest Abe Lincoln—and an image of a working-man-everyman-American-man, who proved that the American Dream was real and attainable, provided that the gosh darn government didn't get in the way.

Yes, Ronald Reagan ran for the White House with two eventful terms as California governor under his belt. And no, Donald Trump had no such political credentials. But the fact is that, for both men, entertainment experience was a far greater political asset than political experience. Ronald Reagan made no secret of the fact that his performance in *King's Row,* which was indeed an admirable turn in a decent role, was his career favorite. But the more valuable lesson he had learned, beyond memorizing his lines and addressing the camera, was the power of simple, one-dimensional canned portrayals of simple, one-dimensional canned characters who exhibited simple, one-dimensional canned values. This—and not the nuanced "arty" work of such "method" actors as Monty Clift and Marlon Brando—was the stuff of myth for the masses. Trump found much the same in promoting WrestleMania or presiding over *The*

Apprentice. All of it was comfort food for the masses—the kind of thing Reagan's Hollywood excelled at churning out during his 1940s heyday.

It had to be simple, and it had to resonate.

Speaker of the House Tip O'Neill invited President-Elect Reagan to his office in 1980. Future Speaker of the House Jim Wright was there:

> Tip sat behind a large desk which, he explained to the president[-elect], had once belonged to Grover Cleveland. "I played him once in a movie," Reagan said. "No, Mr. President," Tip gently corrected, "you played Grover Cleveland Alexander, the baseball player."[14]

It was a small, trivial error that nevertheless implied a big truth about Ronald Reagan. Grover Cleveland? Grover Cleveland Alexander? What was the difference? To Ronald Reagan, apparently, it was a difference insufficient to have prompted him to recall whether he played the president (a Democrat, by the way) or the ball player. Both were figures out of American history—and all that mattered was that he, Ronald Reagan, had been hired to play at least one of them.

*   *   *

Playing somebody with the name Grover Cleveland was important enough to Reagan that Tip O'Neill's mention of the desk's previous owner rang a bell for him. It just proved to be the wrong bell. Legless Drake McHugh in *King's Row* was a meatier role than Grover Cleveland Alexander, of course, but even it could not top the role of *actual* president of the United States. And that new actual president got off to a resonant start by delivering an inaugural address built around a key line everybody old enough to have heard it remembers. Or thinks they remember.

Ronald Reagan assumed the presidency over a disgruntled America. The Nixon-Ford years had plunged the nation into a nasty and stubborn recession, to which the single term of Jimmy Carter added insult to injury. The Carter years were plagued by "stagflation"—a recessionary, flat economy to which the rotten cherry of inflation had been added on top. Since the economy was stagnant yet afflicted by inflation, economists had to coin a new word for it. Hence, *stagflation.*

In his inaugural address,[15] the incoming president began by thanking the outgoing president for his "gracious cooperation in the transition process" and extended to Carter his thanks "for all your help in maintaining the continuity which is the bulwark of our Republic." This was in the grand tradition of the peaceful transfer of power that had marked the American democracy since John Adams grudgingly—but peacefully and without protest—yielded the brand-new White House to Thomas Jefferson in 1801. Like Adams, Trump did not pay the new president the courtesy of attending his inauguration. Unlike Trump, however, the outgoing second U.S. president both acknowledged defeat and the legitimacy of the election that had defeated him, making Jefferson the third U.S. president. Trump, of course, never formally conceded defeat and did nothing but deny the legitimacy of the election that delivered him from office. On January 6, 2021, as a Joint Session of Congress convened to conduct the essentially ceremonial duty of counting state-certified electoral college ballots, Trump rallied thousands of supporters gathered in Washington to march on the Capitol. There, for only the second time in its history—the first had been during the British invasion of Washington during the War of 1812 on August 24, 1814—the seat of American government was sacked. Though it was spared the arson of 1814, the capital invasion was a full-scale insurrection, in which the constitutionally mandated counting of the ballots was interrupted, legislators sent into flight and (in the cases of Vice President Mike Pence and Speaker of the House Nancy Pelosi and others) even targeted for assassination. In addition, four insurrectionists died, five police officers who had served at the Capitol on January 6 died in the days and weeks after the riot and more than 140 police officers were injured.[16]

The truth is that the courtesy incoming President Reagan extended to outgoing President Jimmy Carter in 1981 could hardly be imagined in 2021. And yet, reading the words in which that 1981 courtesy was couched, we cannot help seeing them as superficially courteous at best and belittling and demeaning at worst. Reagan's emphasis was not on Carter's four years of stewardship but on the present "transition process," and the new president seemed to be thanking the old for at least not mucking up *that* part of the national machinery as well as managing to maintain the "continuity" from an obviously botched single term to the regime of the new sheriff who, by the grace of God, had at last arrived in town.

Having given Carter the back of his hand, rhetorically speaking, Reagan continued: "The business of our nation goes forward. These United States are confronted with an economic affliction of great proportions," which he characterized as "one of the worst sustained inflations in our national history." He went on to explain, "The economic ills we suffer have come upon us over several decades. They will not go away in days, weeks, or months, but they will go away."

The language he used here was that of a kindly physician assessing the "affliction" of a fearful patient. It's a bad illness, all right, but it *is* an illness, long in coming on and likely to hang on for a while, but by no means permanent. The economic ills will "go away because we, as Americans, have the capacity now, as we have in the past, to do whatever needs to be done to preserve this last and greatest bastion of freedom."

Like Grover Cleveland Alexander, the Hall of Fame pitcher he had played, Reagan was just winding up for the Big Pitch of the game—the line everybody remembers. Or thinks they do.

"In this present crisis, government is not the solution to our problem; government is the problem."

Is this how you remember it? If so, you either have a very good memory or have, for whatever reason, recently read the transcript of the speech. For, when this line is quoted, it is almost invariably minus the introductory clause, *In this present crisis*. All that is reproduced and all that is remembered is "Government is not the solution to our problem; government is the problem."

The omission of four words is a trivial thing, a little thing. Yet from trivial and little things very big things may get their start. A presidency, for example, a presidency shrouded and enshrined in myth.

As Ronald Reagan delivered the sentence, it was a diagnosis of a *present crisis*. These two words are both time sensitive. They do not speak of eternity but of an immediacy that implies a temporary situation. Attached to the independent clause that follows, the four words limit it severely. Government is "not the solution"—*in this present crisis*. Government "is the problem"—*in this present crisis*. Thus stated, the Big Pitch is not an oracular pronouncement, but a diagnosis of a temporary economic "affliction."

Take away the limiting clause, crumple it up, and forget about it. Do this, and you have created a pronouncement of mythic proportion. *Government is not the solution to our problem; government is the problem.* It is no longer an issue of the *present* crisis. Government is bad. Period. Government is always bad. Period. This is the Gospel, the *New* Testament, and, politically speaking, its recollection, minus the first four words, cast Ronald Reagan in his greatest role ever: Messiah.

But what of the nation welcoming deliverance on January 20, 1981? *Government is not the solution to our problem; government is the problem.* The truncated memory of a line in an inaugural address was destined to figure as a *reductio ad absurdum* packing the annihilating punch of a thermonuclear weapon. Beginning in 1981, it licensed the relentless dismantling of much that was great and benevolent in American government, namely, the constitutionally mandated mission to "promote the general welfare." Even worse, the *reductio ad absurdum* that ushered in the 40th presidency was reduced to even greater absurdity by the 45th president who both minimized and vulgarized Reagan's formulation to candidate Trump's proclamation at the 2016 GOP National Convention: "I alone can fix it." It did not destroy government but simply denied both the existence and the necessity of government. As a vision of America, it was the vision of Reagan both simplified and amplified by exponential orders of magnitude.

* * *

If President Reagan was ever bothered by the misquotation of the biggest line in his biggest script, and if the national act of collective selective memory that followed his inauguration and prevailed throughout the succeeding eight years and beyond caused him any disquiet, he never let on. He either thought the misquote too trivial and too small to correct, or he took no note of it, or he liked it, approved of it, and wanted to keep it. Certainly, he made ample use of it.

In the wake of this declaration, he and his fellow Republicans used it to drive and to justify what Trump adviser, federally indicted fraudster, and presidential pardon beneficiary Steve Bannon, thirty-six years later, called the "deconstruction of the administrative state." It's just that Ronald Reagan's superb speech writer, Ken Khachigian, used a more direct, far larger, and far more truthful word. What he and his boss were after was the deconstruction of *government*.

This was the founding myth of Reagan's reformation of America. It was a negative myth, which swept aside the model of government that his early political hero, Franklin Roosevelt, had raised to mythic proportions himself: government that *was* the solution, providing for the common defense, promoting the general welfare, and securing the blessings of liberty to ourselves and our posterity. FDR had offered the model of a government that could save a people suffering from a lapse in capitalism during the 1930s. It was the model of a government capable of winning a second world war on *two* fronts and then putting a broken, smoldering world back together better than ever through the likes of the Marshall Plan. It was the model of a government that could harness the atom, provide a social safety net with programs such as Social Security, build a nationwide network of superhighways, and send people to the moon—and bring them back, too. It was the model of a government that led the cure for polio and declared a war on cancer. It was the model of a government that dared to imagine a "Great Society."

The economic uncertainly Americans experienced during the 1970s and Carter's dour televised diagnosis of a national "malaise"[17] injected painful self-doubt into the body politic. Carter's mature, if politically ill-advised, introspection was replaced by Reagan's pointedly unnuanced expression of values, such as "America is a shining city upon a hill whose beacon light guides freedom-loving people everywhere" whereas the Soviet Union was the "Evil Empire." End of story.

Given the cultural and global forces at play in the late 1970s,

Americans grew increasingly frightened by ambiguity, self-examination, and nagging doubts about America's role in the world. In his own role of a lifetime, Ronald Reagan played the president who raised a myth that knocked down these creeping self-doubts and, along with them, the former twentieth-century models of a government that, in the name of promoting the general welfare, intervened liberally in the nation's life. In place of introspection and the welfare state, Reagan brought into being instead a new verity that passed for eternal: *Government is the problem.*

If government is the problem, how it operates and how it is funded are central. The Reagan presidency was the springboard into our current political, economic, and cultural era. A consequential aspect of this springboard is Reaganomics and the trickle-down mythology: cutting taxes for the wealthy increases demand for goods and services, the benefits of which inevitably trickle-down to the lower rungs of the socio-economic ladder as the associated tax cuts pay for themselves through increased revenue. Some four decades later, this mythology continues to drive historic economic inequality, an inequality that is the stuff revolutions are made on.

As a candidate, Reagan railed against deficit spending and preached that government must live within its means. As we will see in subsequent chapters, the tax cuts associated with the implementation of Reaganomics tripled the national debt during Reagan's two-term presidency, bringing it from approximately $950 billion to $2.86 trillion dollars.

He added more red ink to the national debt than that accumulated by the thirty-nine US presidents who had preceded him. Combined. He rode to office in 1980 complaining of an "out-of-control debt" as tall as "a stack of $1,000 bills 67 miles high." After eight years, he added another 125 more miles to that stack. Such is the power of Reagan's myth that the American political psyche does not hold him accountable for birthing the blithe acceptance of massive annual deficits. That same myth also papers over the hard fact that Reagan raised taxes eleven times.[18]

Ronald Reagan was often described as "the Teflon president," because nothing bad seemed to stick to him. Okay. So, he left a national debt requiring a 192-mile-high stack of greenbacks to pay. But just look at the Reagan Legacy!

What did we get for a national allegiance to contempt for government? Among other things, we got the dismantling of government, especially of the so-called administrative state, which consists of the cadre of professionals and experts with the kind of specialized knowledge to combat—oh, we don't know, but, say, a global pandemic the likes of which has not visited planet Earth since 1918–1919. We got a level of economic disparity that nullifies the American Dream for many of our fellow citizens, destroys national unity, and threatens to foment a revolution, not to affirm and protect truths that should be held as self-evident but that denies these truths and is thus a revolution of cynicism and nihilism.

What we got from the Reagan Legacy, four decades after it was created, is the America of Donald Trump, who has sold the soul of American democracy and stuck us all with the bill that is at least in part calculable in an increase in national debt of approximately $8 trillion over his four-year presidential term.

Candidate Trump claimed he would pay down the national debt in eight years. He would doubtless protest that, having been "cheated" out of another four years, the failure is not on him. In any case, we cannot say for certain at this point whether we still live in Trump's America, but it is certain that we still live in Reagan's America despite its four years under new, far more extreme and far less competent management.

Regarding Trump's unexpected rise to power, George Packer of the *Atlantic* wrote, "Trump came to power as the repudiation of the Republican establishment. But the conservative political class and the new leader soon reached an understanding. Whatever their differences on issues like trade and immigration, they shared a basic goal: to strip-mine public assets for the benefit of private interests." With respect to the role of the federal government under Trump, Packer noted "republican politicians and donors who wanted government to do as little as possible could live happily with a regime that barely knew how to govern at all...."[19]

Like the infamous Kristallnacht of Nazi Germany during November 9–10, 1938, the January 6, 2021, sack of the Capitol of the United States was a real event of actual shattered glass and shattered bodies, but it was also a profound metaphor. In 2018, a poll of American political scientists ranked Reagan ninth among the nation's chief executives, one notch above LBJ, one below Barack Obama, just seven short of Washington, and a mere eight degrees below Lincoln. Such is the power of mythology. The reality is that Reagan's war on "big government" and eight years of the Reagan presidency bequeathed to us the America of the president many of those same political scientists rank dead last among our chief executives, Donald John Trump. The 45th president did not merely deconstruct American government but, from 2017 to January 6, 2021, he vandalized it, much as that word's namesakes, the Vandals, sacked Rome in 455 and the modern-day vandals he himself summoned on January 6, 2021, sacked the Capitol.

CHAPTER 2

MAGA: Dumbing Down a Stolen Lie

"Reagan was fun to be around," former Speaker of the House Jim Wright wrote in 1996. "Reagan was an entertainer, a super salesman, an enjoyable companion with a ready sense of humor, but his grasp of issues, and of history, was superficial."[1] Wright's was a common view of the 40th president, held in one form or another by Reagan critics and supporters alike. What President George W. Bush once famously told Senator Joe Biden—"I don't do nuance"[2]—could just as easily have issued from the lips of Ronald Reagan. After all, he was dubbed the "Great Communicator," not the "Great Philosopher." It is the business of philosophers to "do nuance." The greater the philosopher, the deeper the thought and the finer the nuance. For great communicators, however, nuance is less a virtue than is the ability to entertain, to sell, to convey good humor, and to outline history and issues boldly, employing no finer point than that of the flattest Trumpian Sharpie.

It is, in fact, easy to dismiss much of what Reagan said in public as collections of so many comforting bromides, which, in truth, is the way we Americans tend to treat the speech of most politicians. Yet if we make a conscious effort to resist the easy kneejerk response and read Ronald Reagan's words—or those written for him by others, at his direction—carefully, as if he intended them to be more than merely anodyne, we realize they came from a deeper place, resonant with meaning for him and for those many who supported him. What he communicated often so well though often so glibly were the elements of a mythology that informed his life and career, including his presidency and the nation from which these emerged.

This chapter and the next look at Ronald Reagan's personal background, including his ancestry, childhood, youth, and early manhood in the way we believe he looked at them: as a personal origin myth. To one degree or another, most of us do something similar. It is part of looking for the meaning of one's existence. As the writer James Baldwin once penned, "history is not the past ... we carry our history with us, ... we are our history." Along with this impulse comes another common behavior, a tendency to valorize the past, to see it through a gauzy scrim or perhaps even a lens liberally slathered with Brylcreem. We call such a past "the good old days." So familiar is this impulse that it is easy to ascribe to it (and thereby dismiss) this passage from Reagan's Farewell Address of January 12, 1989[3]:

> An informed patriotism is what we want. And are we doing a good enough job teaching our children what America is and what she represents in the long history of the world?
>
> Those of us who are over 35 or so years of age grew up in a different America. We were taught, very directly, what it means to be an American, and we absorbed almost in the air a love of country and an appreciation of its institutions. If you didn't get these things from your family you got them from the neighborhood, from the father down the street who fought in Korea or the family who lost someone at Anzio. Or you could get a sense of patriotism from school. And if all else failed, you could get a sense of patriotism from the popular culture. The movies celebrated democratic values and implicitly reinforced the idea that America was special. TV was like that, too, through the mid–Sixties.
>
> But now we're about to enter the Nineties, and some things have changed. Younger parents aren't sure that an unambivalent appreciation of America is the right thing to teach modern children. And as for those who create the popular culture, well-grounded patriotism is no longer the style.

This is a wistful sigh for the good old days, to be sure, but the thought behind it is also much more fully developed. Reagan does not argue that the good old days of his youth were inherently and simply better. He quite precisely defines the respect in which they were better. For him, the era that ended in the mid–1960s was full of advocates for patriotism or, more precisely, teachers of "informed patriotism." American institutions, communities, and popular culture were primed to inculcate a patriotic orientation. The approaching 1990s, Reagan argued, did not deliberately set out to be somehow inferior to the previous generations. They just suffered from an attack of skepticism and "ambivalence" about whether teaching unalloyed patriotism was the right thing to do. The problem was not a dearth of patriots, but a dearth of advocates and teachers.

Reagan had a solution, and it was surprisingly nuanced. First, he defended the success of his two terms, the second of which he had won with a campaign message claiming to have brought back "morning in America." He proclaimed, "Our spirit is back."

So, whence the ambivalence?

> Our spirit is back, but we haven't reinstitutionalized it. We've got to do a better job of getting across that America is freedom—freedom of speech, freedom of

religion, freedom of enterprise—and freedom is special and rare. It's fragile; it needs protection.

His presidency, he implies, had vanquished the "malaise" of the Carter years and introduced in its place the feeling of morning in America. Nevertheless, this sentiment had not yet been instilled into American institutions. Accomplishing this will require doing a "better job of getting across" not patriotism, per se, but something else: *freedom.*

What is America? "America is freedom." This was the equation Ronald Reagan wanted to leave with the American people.

Freedom is not a synonym for *patriotism*. Indeed, the outgoing president performed a rhetorical sleight-of-hand by shifting terms, effectively narrowing the definition of patriotism from love of country to love of what the country *is*, namely freedom, freedom of speech, religion, and enterprise. Those who admire the "Great Communicator" in Reagan would identify this shift as part of the Reagan magic. Students of rhetoric would simply call it equivocation, shifting the meaning of a term in mid-argument.

When Thomas Jefferson drafted the preamble to the Declaration of Independence, he defined a set of "self-evident" truths, namely that "all men are created equal" and that they are "endowed by their creator with certain unalienable rights," including the right to "life, liberty, and the pursuit of happiness." Now, Reagan's Farewell Address certainly does not nullify Jefferson, but where Jefferson defines natural rights as God-given and thus "unalienable"—not just durable, but inborn and eternal—Reagan defines freedom as "special," "rare," and so "fragile" that it requires "protection." He does not say that freedom must be fought for, but, rather, protected. It is almost as if he were talking about some Easter egg elaborately painted and gilded, so that it is special and rare and, being a hollowed-out egg, fragile, requiring protection.

Against what must we protect our fragile freedom? By way of explanation, Reagan outlines another myth:

> The past few days when I've been at that window upstairs, I've thought a bit of the shining "city upon a hill." The phrase comes from John Winthrop, who wrote it to describe the America he imagined. … He journeyed here on what today we'd call a little wooden boat, and, like the other pilgrims, he was looking for a home that would be free.
>
> I've spoken of the shining city all my political life, but I don't know if I ever quite communicated what I saw when I said it. But in my mind, it was a tall proud city built on rocks stronger than oceans, wind-swept, God-blessed, and teeming with people of all kinds living in harmony and peace—a city with free ports that hummed with commerce and creativity, and if there had to be city walls, the walls had doors, and the doors were open to anyone with the will and the heart to get here.

This passage is rich with mythic meaning, and the "city on the hill" metaphor has been exploited by Republicans and Democrats alike. First, we need to know that John Winthrop was an English Puritan, who led the founding of the Massachusetts Bay Colony in 1628, the second major New England settlement, after Plymouth Colony, which had been planted in 1620. Like the earlier Plymouth settlers, he was a Puritan, but, strictly speaking, he was not what Reagan called him, a Pilgrim. This term is reserved for the founders of the Plymouth Colony. The Puritans were six-teenth- and seventeenth-century English Protestants who were intent on "purifying" the Church of England by purging it of Roman Catholic practices. Their claim was that Anglican Christianity was not sufficiently reformed. The Church of England was the state religion of England, and the ruling powers objected to the upstart Puritan reformers. The First English Civil War (1642–1646) would be fought between Puritan forces and Royalist forces, leading to the overthrow of King Charles I and—after the Second Civil War (1648)—his execution and the creation of a short-lived Puritan-dominated republic called the Commonwealth, which endured until 1660.

The English civil wars were revolutions, which some view as vio-lent struggles for religious freedom. But this is not what Ronald Reagan is talking about. The Puritans who founded the Plymouth and Massachu-setts Bay settlements did not fight King Charles I or anyone else to win religious freedom. They fled the king and the others who persecuted them, running away to America to set up their own colonies across the Atlantic. In this way they "protected" their "fragile" freedom, snatching away their precious Easter egg from clumsy and apostate Anglican hands.

Reagan identifies Winthrop and his fellow Puritans as immigrants, although they were not obliged, like other immigrants, to fit themselves into an existing nation. They instead created their own colonies with their own laws, which—and here is where Reagan's mythologizing becomes outright fiction—were at best only marginally tolerant of non–Puritans. Indeed, these colonies showed such limited tolerance that, in 1636, the rogue Puritan Roger Williams established the Providence Plantations (later the Colony of Rhode Island) as a haven of greater religious freedom.

In calling the Massachusetts Bay Colony a shining city on a hill, Win-throp was describing the settlement as an example of the only true and correct form of Protestant religion for all the world to see. His implica-tion? If the people of that outside world knew what was good for them, they would emulate the shining city. Given this historical backdrop, Win-throp and his fellow Puritans would have been appalled by the idea of their colony "teeming with people of all kinds living in harmony and peace," though the Bay Colony was more open to trade than the Plymouth Colony.

There were no walled cities at Plymouth or on the Bay, but neither were there "doors ... open to anyone with the will and the heart to get" to these places.

Ronald Reagan's policies on immigration were far more liberal than those of the Puritan leaders or, for that matter, those of Donald Trump and his GOP. Indeed, recall that shortly after being sworn-in, Trump signed an executive order on January 27, 2017, banning travel to the United States for ninety days from seven predominantly Muslim countries. In contrast, shortly after he assumed office, President Reagan issued a "Statement on United States Immigration and Refugee Policy," announcing his intention to continue the American tradition of welcoming immigrants and, especially, refugees from oppression. He also called for millions of undocumented "illegal immigrants" then living in the United States to be offered a path to legal status. On November 6, 1986, he signed into law the Immigration Reform and Control Act of 1986, which, among other provisions, granted what Reagan himself called "amnesty" to some three million immigrants who applied for legal status and paid any back taxes and fines.[4]

For President Reagan, immigration was a cornerstone of American identity, the American dream, and the mythology of America, as well as central to his own origin myth, and we will return to the subject shortly. At the moment, however, we are still left with the question of why the president considered freedom so special, rare, and fragile that it needed protection. Winthrop and his co-religionists fled their native land to protect their freedom from a "tyrant" king and his tyrannical state church. Eight years before his Farewell Address, in his first inaugural address, Reagan had sketched the contours of his version of tyranny. It was government itself.[5]

Years earlier, in "A Time for Choosing," telecast on October 27, 1964, in support of the presidential candidacy of Barry Goldwater, Reagan, who held no office at the time, declared: "We need true tax reform that will at least make a start toward restoring for our children the American dream that wealth is denied to no one, that each individual has the right to fly as high as his strength and ability will take him."[6] Vanquishing the tyranny of government was starkly simple. Just get government's hand out of our pockets, and we will enjoy the "American dream," each individual's freedom "to fly as high as his strength and ability will take him." This freedom must be protected against the pickpocketing tyrant that is Big Government. Tax *cutting* and shrinking the size of government at the expense of entitlements and other Big Government "welfare" programs is all the protection our fragile freedom demands.

*   *   *

Winthrop and the other Puritans were not wealthy people. Whatever their religious motivations for immigrating to America, they also sought a bit of mammon in the form of more financially prosperous lives. Perhaps this aspect of the Puritan story resonated most powerfully with Ronald Reagan, whose ancestral heritage was one of poverty.

Much of the history of Ireland is marked by English oppression. The 1801 Acts of Union were supposed to ameliorate this dreadful situation by giving Ireland parliamentary representation. However, 70 percent of Irish representatives were landowners or their sons. This left Ireland with what future British prime minister Benjamin Disraeli described in 1844 as "a starving population [of tenant farmers], an absentee [landowning] aristocracy, an alien established Protestant church, and in addition the weakest executive in the world."[7] The impoverished population was largely dependent on selling their potato crops, which were subject to periodic devastating blights. The blight that swept Ireland in 1845–1846 was exceedingly severe, bringing starvation and epidemic diseases born of poverty and privation. Estimates of famine-related deaths between 1845 and 1849 vary widely, but the toll was likely between 1 and 1.5 million.[8] By 1854, as many as 2 million Irish emigrated, many of them coming to America.[9]

Among these was Michael Regan (originally O'Regan), Ronald Reagan's great-grandfather, who emigrated from the Parish of Ballyporeen in County Tipperary. He did not immigrate directly to the United States, but first to England, an 1851 census record showing him living in Peckham, Surrey, where, at age twenty-one, he was working as a soap maker. That census also shows in Peckham a Tipperary-born Catherine Mulcahey, twenty-six, working as a gardener's laborer. The next year, the record of St. George's Roman Catholic Church, in the poor Southwark section of London, records the marriage, on October 31, of Michael Regan (spelled Reagan in the civil record) to Catherine Mulcahey.[10]

The couple left England aboard the *Joseph Gilchrist,* which sailed from Liverpool and arrived in New York City on November 28, 1857. At the time Michael was listed as twenty-seven years old and Catherine as thirty. With them were their three children, Thomas, John, and Margaret. The United States Census for 1860 shows a Michael Reigan, age twenty-five, living as a farmer in Carroll County, Illinois, with his thirty-year-old wife, Catherine. Their children were English-born Thomas (age seven), John (five), and Margaret (three) along with American-born one-year-old William. The household also included two additional "Reigans," Nicholas and John P., Michael's brothers. On March 6, 1866, Michael "Ragan" declared his intention for naturalization as a United States citizen, and by 1870 is shown as a registered voter in Fair Haven, Carroll County. He died shortly before

March 10, 1884, the date on which the county probate court issued a warrant to appraise his estate. No actual death record exists.[11]

So, there is no doubting Ronald Reagan's Irish ancestry or the fact that his desperately impoverished great-grandparents both fled the potato famine of Ireland.

In fact, there is a unique record of the president's *great*-great grandfather and his great-uncle, both named Thomas Reagan, as residents of Ballyporeen. The two signed the 140-foot-long "Morpeth Roll" in 1841, a document to which 160,000 Irish people signed their names as a thank you note to Lord Morpeth on his departure from Ireland, where he had been the English government's Chief Secretary to Ireland. In contrast to earlier Chief Secretaries, Morpeth had earnestly sought to better the lives of ordinary Irish folk under English rule, and the people were genuinely grateful. Within four years of Morpeth's departure, however, the famine swept Ireland like a great scythe.[12]

And Ronald Reagan may have been even more Irish. On November 12, 1980, days after he defeated Jimmy Carter, the *Daily Kent Stater*, newspaper of Kent State University, published an AP story headlined, startlingly enough, "Ronald Reagan is descendant of Irish high-king":

> Ronald Reagan's election climaxes a rags-to-eminence saga that began when his great-grandfather left a stone shanty in Ireland in the potato famine of the 1840's, British and Irish genealogists said Monday. Further back, they said, there is royal blood. Reagan is descended from Brian Boru, an 11th century high king of all Ireland and the Emerald Isle's first national hero, according to experts from Debrett's research organization of London and Hibernian Research based in Dublin.[13]

Born about 941, Brian Boru reigned from 1002 to 1014, meeting his death that year, in the April 23 Battle of Contarf (near what is today Dublin). Here he led the final defeat and expulsion of Viking invaders, achieving a great victory, only to be killed by Brodir, a Dane who was one of the commanders of Viking forces. (Brodir found Brian offering a prayer in his tent and treacherously cut him down.) Debrett's Peerage research traced Reagan's ancestry to Brian Boru's nephew, a Regan. "Although that was only an uncle of [the Reagan] ancestors, it does show royal blood," Harold Brooks-Baker, U.S. managing director of Debrett's, told the AP.[14]

It is hard to be more Irish than to be a relative of the king who freed Ireland from Viking occupation back in the early Middle Ages. And yet, a story published in the *Independent* in 2004 reported that "Reagan hushed up his Irish roots and even asked the Irish Ambassador to Washington to keep his Celtic heritage secret because he was terrified it would ruin his political career." Candidate Reagan did not merely "play down his

Irishness on his way to the White House, ... he gave the impression that his ancestry was rooted in England and he was a pedigree WASP."[15]

Sean Donlon, who was Irish ambassador to the United States from 1978 to 1984, called on candidate Reagan during a visit to California.

"I commented to him, given his name, 'You must be Irish, what part of Ireland do you come from?'"

"He said, 'No, no I am not Irish, I have an English background.' I said, 'With a name like Reagan, you have to be Irish.'"

"When I told Reagan coming up to the election in 1980 that his roots were definitely Irish not English, he asked if that information could be kept quiet until after the election. He was a political package and presented as a WASP."

"He was appealing to the right-wing element in the Republican party for support, The Democrats traditionally played more to the Irish side...."

"He didn't want to change his package at the last minute. We kept it quiet. When he became president he said, 'Now I will be happy to embrace my Irishness. I will come to the embassy on St Patrick's Day.'"[16]

*　　*　　*

Ronald Reagan would indeed learn to relish his Irish heritage, but only after he was safely ensconced in the White House. While he was running for his first term, however, he scornfully traded one myth for another. Or, more accurately, he suppressed a myth and elevated a fiction. The myth, of which the Irish-American experience is very much a part, is the very myth of America as the shining city on a hill. It is the myth behind the Statue of Liberty, which was titled by its sculptor, Frédéric Bartholdi, "Liberty Enlightening the World," a name that is far closer to "Shining City on a Hill" than the more pedestrian "Statue of Liberty." It is the myth expressed most movingly in "The New Colossus," the sonnet Emma Lazarus composed in 1883 to help raise money to build the pedestal for the statue. "Mother of Exiles," Lazarus calls the statue, and she has it speak with "silent lips" these words:

> "Give me your tired, your poor,
> Your huddled masses yearning to breathe free,
> The wretched refuse of your teeming shore.
> Send these, the homeless, tempest-tost to me,
> I lift my lamp beside the golden door!"[17]

It is, in fact, the reality-based myth in which Reagan *should* have recognized the story of his ancestors. Indeed, he seems to have done just that in his conception of America as place of welcome, which gave his Irish ancestors both succor and a life on farmland they themselves owned—an impossibility for people of their class in nineteenth-century Ireland itself.

For all his conservatism, it is the myth that moved him to sign into law an immigrant amnesty that would be unthinkable in Trump's GOP.

It is the myth that moved him to deliver the following message in the second-to-last speech he gave as president, on January 19, 1989, when he awarded Presidential Medals of Freedom to Mike Mansfield, former U.S. ambassador to Japan, and to George Shultz, former secretary of state. He quoted a "letter I received not long ago":

> A man wrote me and said: "You can go to live in France, but you cannot become a Frenchman. You can go to live in Germany or Turkey or Japan, but you cannot become a German, a Turk, or a Japanese. But anyone, from any corner of the Earth, can come to live in America and become an American."
>
> Yes, the torch of Lady Liberty symbolizes our freedom and represents our heritage, the compact with our parents, our grandparents, and our ancestors. It is that lady who gives us our great and special place in the world. For it's the great life force of each generation of new Americans that guarantees that America's triumph shall continue unsurpassed into the next century and beyond. Other countries may seek to compete with us. But in one vital area, as a beacon of freedom and opportunity that draws the people of the world, no country on Earth comes close.
>
> This, I believe, is one of the most important sources of America's greatness. We lead the world because, unique among nations, we draw our people—our strength—from every country and every corner of the world. And by doing so we continuously renew and enrich our nation. While other countries cling to the stale past, here in America we breathe life into dreams. We create the future, and the world follows us into tomorrow.[18]

And yet Reagan the politician ("a super salesman," Jim Wright called him, but "superficial"—at least when he needed to be) could kick that legitimate mythology under the sofa, take a seat on that very sofa, and smilingly protest, "No, no I am not Irish, I have an English background." Then, when pressed, could unapologetically explain that he didn't want to damage his political "package," not now, not while he was running for office.

* * *

The story of Ronald Reagan's childhood presented the candidate with a fertile field for campaign mythologizing. But it was also a field littered with stubborn rocks called facts. Illinois was, after all, the Prairie State, and prairie soil, though rich, is thickly sown with hard rocks, rooted stumps, and thickly clotted clay. The Reagan family into which the future president was born were no longer farmers, but Ronald knew all about John Deere, who had invented the "Grand Detour Plow," specially designed and patented to serve as the "plow that broke the plains." The village of Grand Detour, site of the John Deere House and Shop, was just six miles northeast of Dixon, the town in which young Reagan did most of his growing up. His imagination was like the Grand Detour Plow, busting through every painful rock and fierce clod in the soil of his young life and leaving behind the neat, smooth, clean, and fertile furrows of a picture-perfect American tale. It was a Horatio Alger idyll processed through Hollywood, in which ancestral memories of relentless famine compliantly yielded to visions of boundless opportunity.

"Idyll" may not sound like a typical Ronald Reagan word, but he himself used it when he characterized his childhood as "one of those rare Huck Finn-Tom Sawyer idylls."[19] He entered the world, February 6, 1911, in a bedroom overlooking Main Street, Tampico, Illinois, above the general store that employed his father. It was an especially difficult delivery, so perilous that the midwife had run out to fetch a doctor she knew had been fortuitously stranded in tiny Tampico by a blizzard. The physician advised Nelle Wilson Reagan not to have any more children after this one.[20]

The Reagans already had a boy, Neil, just past two at the time of his brother's birth, and Nelle followed the doctor's advice. Keeping the family at two children was, in any case, a financial necessity. The Reagans were poor.

Nelle has been described as "pietistic," "soft-voiced," "supportive," and "nurturing." John Edward "Jack" Reagan, however, struggled. A "dapper orphan who had been raised by an aunt," Jack was an alcoholic, "at once a drinker and a dreamer who, much like Willy Loman in *Death of a Salesman,* pursued the big sale or the unlikely deal with a shoeshine and a smile."[21]

Reagan biographer Lou Cannon wrote that Tampico "was too small for Jack Reagan" and called him a "dreamer." Yet his dreams were, in fact, remarkably small. He had been a store clerk most of his life but never a store owner. What he dreamed of was not becoming a second Marshall Field or Richard W. Sears, but the proprietor of a fancy shoe store—somewhere, anywhere. He had taken a course at the "American School of Proctipedics," from which he emerged (he believed) a great shoe salesman. But he never could raise the capital to buy a store in any of the towns to which the nearly nomadic family moved.

When he was three, Ronald's family moved to Chicago, where Jack worked at The Fair, a major department store. The job lasted no more than a year, and the Reagans moved on to Galesburg, Illinois, when Ronald was four. At seven, his family moved to Monmouth. At eight, it was back to Tampico, and, at nine, the boy found himself in Dixon. Dixon would become the closest thing Ronald Reagan had to a hometown, though even within its limited confines, the Reagans moved no fewer than five times.

Huck Finn made friends with both Tom Sawyer and Jim, the fugitive slave. Young Ronald Reagan, chronically rootless, made "few lasting friendships." In fact, after he left Dixon for Eureka College, in the town of Eureka, Illinois, about 90 miles south, he "never returned [to Dixon] for any length of time ... never again had any solid ties to any American community." Save his older brother, Neil, he had "no lifelong friends and no set of people to whom he had always been loyal."[22] Even the mature Reagan's second wife, Nancy, acknowledged what Lou Cannon called "her husband's inwardness, remarking that his childhood left him 'never feeling any roots anywhere and never having an old friend.'"[23]

Little wonder, then, that candidate Reagan had no compunction about suppressing public knowledge of his Irish roots so that he could preserve himself as what he and his handlers believed was a more acceptable political "package." No serious critic would ever pronounce Ronald Reagan a *great* actor, and yet it is clear that he was from childhood a *natural* actor, who had no trouble taking on and taking off one role after another. To him, playing these roles must have seemed more substantial than any deep conviction or core belief.

As an adult, Reagan cast his child self in the role of Huck Finn or Tom Sawyer. "We were poor," he admitted, "but we did not know we were poor," and he spoke blissfully of discovering butterflies and birds' nests, of exploring the woods and the waterways just beyond Dixon's city limits. He always professed himself an optimist, and, as Lou Cannon relates, even in the dark days of the mid–1970s, when the GOP wallowed in the Watergate scandal, "Reagan often began his political speeches with a story about two little boys, one a pessimist and the other an optimist, who were taken by their parents to a psychiatrist."

> The parents hoped to make the pessimist more cheerful and optimist more conscious of life's obstacles. So they lock the pessimistic child in a room with shiny new toys and the optimistic child in a room with a shovel and a pile of horse manure. When the parents return, the pessimistic child is crying, refusing to play with the toys because he fears they might break. The optimistic child is cheerfully shoveling through the manure. He tells his parents, "With this much manure around, I know there's a pony in here someplace."[24]

Was Reagan really an optimist or did he just play one onscreen, on the podium, and on TV? Did it really matter? Did it really matter to him? Did it really matter to those who voted for him or to his promoters?

Optimist though he was or portrayed, Ronald Reagan was by no means delusional or even, as some characterize him, naive. His own description of his childhood as a Tom Sawyer-Huck Finn idyll, Lou Cannon points out, was included in *Where's the Rest of Me?* a 1965 campaign autobiography written to support his successful bid for the California state house. The description immediately follows a description of his mother's nearly fatal bout with influenza and immediately precedes a depiction of numerous drownings of children in the canals near Tampico.[25]

No, Reagan's optimism seems in part a conscious desire to don rose-colored glasses, which is not uncommon in children raised in alcoholic families. In *Where's the Rest of Me?* he describes his alcoholic father, who bounced from one menial sales job to another, as "a sentimental Democrat who believed fervently in the rights of the working-man" and vigorously opposed religious and racial intolerance. Yet, elsewhere in that same book, he wrote of how, at age eleven, he came home "to find my father flat on his back on the front porch and no one there to lend a hand but me." He describes him as "drunk, dead to the world," his arms spread out as if in crucifixion, "his hair soaked with melting snow," as the eleven-year-old child labored to drag him inside and put him to bed.[26] It is a remarkable revelation—and one rarely, if ever, duplicated in any other utterance Reagan made out loud and in public.

But we are left to wonder if it is less revelation than self-aggrandizing fiction. The senior Reagan was a fully grown adult, dead drunk dead weight. Young Ronald was an undersized and underweight eleven-year-old with no indication that a later growth spurt would put him on course for topping six feet as an adult. Is it plausible that he, alone, could have dragged his father from the porch, inside the house, and then *upstairs* to the bedroom? Or is it more likely that this was a scene drawn less from life than from low-budget Hollywood—a scene that transformed the shame of having an alcoholic father into a depiction of a heroic young son?

If Ronald Reagan was capable of conveying something of the ugly reality of his father's alcoholism, he did not do so without counterbalancing that picture against a depiction of his own early gallantry and nobility of spirit. Still, the harshest outright judgment he leveled against Jack Reagan was to characterize him as cynical when he pointed out, in *Where's the Rest of Me?* that his "father's cynicism never made the slightest impression on" his mother. Much as Richard Nixon always spoke of his mother as a "saint," so Reagan described Nelle as deeply religious, a member of the Disciples of Christ (Christian Church) and imbued with a "sweetness" born of "the conviction everyone loved her just because she loved them."[27] Whether this latter description is of a saint or a simpleton depends largely on what the reader brings to it.

Perhaps the influence of his mother helps to explain how Ronald Reagan could bring himself to recall his childhood as positively as he did. Perhaps his mother's "sweetness" fueled his talent for mythologizing. He appears to have had a bond with her beyond what his brother Neil had. For one thing, whereas Neil was baptized in the Catholic Church of his father, Ronald was baptized as a Disciple, in the Church of his mother. Whatever else this connection may have produced, it occasioned Ronald Reagan's introduction to acting. Nelle taught adult women attending the "True Blue Class" in her church's Sunday school. Ronald was assigned to help clean up and, at the age of five, also began performing in the skits Nelle composed and directed for her class. Reagan dubbed her "the dean of dramatic recitals for the countryside," characterized her as "a frustrated actress," and even speculated that his "dramatic yen" was directly derived from his performances with his mother. Tellingly, several of Nelle's skits, in this era leading up to Prohibition, dealt with the evils of alcohol. One gave this line to a drunkard's daughter: "I love you, Daddy, except when you have that old bottle."[28]

Did young Ronald's involvement in Nelle's Sunday school plays create in his mind an association between his mother's religion and acting? All we know is what Lou Cannon, who knew Ronald Reagan more intimately than most people, said of him. He "adored his mother and accepted her teachings," including her conception of divine providence. "I was raised to believe that God has a plan for everyone and that seemingly random twists of fate are all a part of His plan."[29] This certainly reinforced his optimism, as he remarked that his mother had taught him that "even the most disheartening setbacks" were part of the divine plan.[30] By 1922, when he would have been eleven years old—the very age at which (he reports) he dragged his dead-drunk father off the snowy porch and into bed—he and his mother entertained patients at Dixon State Hospital, Nelle on banjo and Ronald delivering dramatic readings.[31]

We do not intend to dismiss religion as mythology or to elevate mythology to the stature of religion. But we would argue that the mechanisms of mythology and religion are related, and we do suggest that acting—playing roles—fed into the self-mythologizing that was central to Ronald Reagan's sense of self and his ability to communicate both a personal and a national mythology. The doctrine of divine providence, of an ordained destiny, both fed and was fed by the self-mythologizing habit created by the circumstances of Reagan's childhood and youth, the poles of influence created by his father and mother, and the religious precepts he imbibed from his mother. These all found their way to Reagan's vision of America as a shining city on a hill.

* * *

Nobody thinks of Ronald Reagan as a military man turned president—not like Washington or Grant or Eisenhower. But we know three things about his relationship with the military.

First, he grew up in a small-town culture that revered the military. Dixon, in which he lived from age nine to seventeen, erected an arch over

Main Street to honor those Americans who had died in the Great War—
World War I—the town was home to more than a few Civil War veterans, and young Ronald loved to play, alone and for hours, with a set of lead
Civil War soldiers. The military, as he saw it, was a source of heroes, and he
once remarked: "I'm a sucker for hero worship."[32]

Second, his military service during World War II was spent in Hollywood, *acting* in training films.

Third, as president, he presided over the biggest peacetime defense
buildup in American history. For this, some credit him with both restoring the morale of the U.S. military after the long debacle of Vietnam and
with winning the Cold War (in part, at least, by forcing the Soviet Union
to spend itself into the equivalent of bankruptcy). Others just as fervently
believe that his costly militarism was a continual threat to world peace.

There is a tangency, if not a confluence, between Reagan's relation to
the military and that of Donald Trump. Reagan did volunteer for military
service during World War II but was kept out of combat because of poor
eyesight. So, instead of fighting, he acted the part of fighting soldiers and
fliers in a series of training and propaganda films. Trump famously—or
infamously—won five draft deferments during the Vietnam War when his
father used his influence with a neighborhood physician to obtain a spurious diagnosis of bone spurs. Yet thirteen-year-old Trump's chronic "mis-
behavior—fighting, bullying, arguing with teachers" got him kicked out of
a Queens-based prep school, Kew-Forest, and prompted his father to pack
him off to New York Military Academy, which his fellow students called a
"reform school."[33]

In the case of Reagan, both streams of early influence—his mother's
religion and the heroic aura of the military—fed into his habit of hero worship and, perhaps, created in him a sense that he himself could become
heroic. Trump neither worshipped heroes nor saw himself as a hero. In
fact, when he canceled a scheduled visit to the Aisne-Marne American
Cemetery near Paris during a 2018 visit to commemorate the service of
American troops during World War I, *The Atlantic* reports: "In a conversation with senior staff members on the morning of the scheduled visit,
Trump said, 'Why should I go to that cemetery? It's filled with losers.'"
In another conversation on the same trip, "Trump referred to the more
than 1,800 marines who lost their lives at Belleau Wood as 'suckers' for
getting killed."[34] Nevertheless, Trump claimed that his experience at a
military-themed "reform school" gave him "more training militarily than
a lot of the guys that go into the military."[35] Reagan, legitimately in uniform, at least acted the role of hero. Draft-dodging Trump spit on heroism
and, lacking any shame, was not above exploiting a disobedient school-
child's contact with uniforms and drill as a major military qualification.

Donald Trump was so indifferent a student that he paid one "Joe Shapiro, a smart kid with a reputation for being a good test taker, to take his SATs for him," so that he could get into the University of Pennsylvania.[36] In contrast, young Reagan possessed natural gifts. He excelled in school. He was no genius, to be sure, but he found it easy to learn how to read, was facile with arithmetic calculation, and had a superb memory, which he used to memorize poetry, school assignments, and his mother's Sunday School dramatic scripts. Indeed, while Donald Trump freely boasted that he was "like, really smart" and called himself a "very stable genius,"[37] Ronald Reagan was routinely judged as less intelligent than he demonstrably was. As a youngster, he would never have been mistaken for a bookish child, but he loved to read, referring to the Dixon Public Library as his "house of magic."[38] In contrast, a 2020 opinion piece by Windsor Mann in *The Week* was titled "Trump's lethal aversion to reading" and begins "If you're reading this sentence, you've read more than the president has today" and cites Tony Schwartz, ghostwriter of *The Art of the Deal,* who speculated that "Trump has never read a single book in his adult life." According to Mann, when White House trade advisor Peter Navarro wrote a memo in January 2020 warning of "'full-blown coronavirus outbreak on U.S. soil,' Trump said he didn't see it because 'Peter sends a lot of memos,' none of which he reads."[39]

Reagan's childhood reading included the likes of tales of King Arthur and the Knights of the Round Table, Rover Boys adventures, *The Last of the Mohicans,* the Western novels of Zane Grey, and *The Count of Monte Cristo.* There was nothing unusual about this fare for a young reader, especially a boy. Nor was it unusual to enjoy Arthur Conan Doyle and Edgar Rice Burroughs—except that Ron Reagan dug deeper than most. *Sherlock Holmes* he read, but also Conan Doyle's less well-known *The White Company.* Burroughs's *Tarzan* books were on his list but so were the John Carter "Barsoom" stories set on the planet Mars.[40]

There were others, too. Horatio Alger tales, of course, but also Harold Bell Wright's *That Printer of Udell's: A Story of the Middle West,* in which the hero, Dick Falkner, works as a printer, earns a degree in night school, redeems a beautiful woman from prostitution, and generally blends Christian precepts with sound business to lift a downtrodden midwestern town onto its feet. Then he gets elected to Congress. As Reagan observed many years later, his boyhood "reading left an abiding belief in the triumph of good over evil" by "heroes who lived by standards of morality and fair play."

Of course, the book heroes and their triumphs were mostly fictional. No matter. As someone who excelled naturally at playing roles, young Ronald Reagan had little difficulty overcoming the reality of his severe nearsightedness and short stature—he was small for his age, a growth spurt closing in on his adult six feet not coming until well into his junior year in high school. The former impediment required him to wear glasses, the geeky look of which he hated, so he got along without them as well as he could whenever he could. To compensate for his other physical limitation—slight build, short stature—he asked that people use the nickname his father had given him when he was a newborn: Dutch. It is said that Jack thought the roly-poly infant looked like a fat, little Dutchman. This story of the nickname's origin may be true, but Reagan liked what he thought of as the masculine ring of name, which he found a big improvement over "Ronald." Whatever Reagan's motivation, the sobriquet stuck—and it seems that its ethnic implications, namely a Dutch or German heritage, did not in the least disturb this Irish-American.

Those familiar with the life of Richard Nixon will recall that young Nixon set his sights on playing football with the Whittier College team. The trouble was that he had no natural talent as an athlete. On the other hand, he had a seemingly infinite capacity to take punishment and suffer humiliation. So, he was allowed on the team but never rose above the status of tackling dummy. Dutch Reagan had a similar problem. His nearsightedness largely disqualified him for baseball and basketball, but he was a willing scrapper. So, that left football. Here, however, the problem was that, as a high school freshman, he weighed just 108 pounds. Every uniform hung off him. Nevertheless, he was so enthusiastic and optimistic that he not only won a place on the team but also was voted its captain.

Without question, however, Ronald Reagan excelled as a swimmer. And this opened up remarkable new vistas. He had a swimmer's body, he sprouted up to six feet by the end of his junior year, and, at Northside High School, he began passionately crushing on one Margaret Cleaver. Better known as "Mugs," she was the daughter of his Christian Church pastor, and her wit, sense of humor, and good looks made her tremendously popular. This left Dutch with the problem of how to stand out in a crowd of suitors. His solution was to audition for and win the male lead in *You and I,* a Philip Barry play the school drama club was staging. He well knew that the female lead had already been chosen. It was Mugs Cleaver.

He got the part, and he went on to edge out one Dick McNicol for the real-life role of Mugs' steady boyfriend. That victory was doubtless made sweeter by the fact that McNicol was the Northside quarterback.

Junior year ended in triumph. God's plan, perhaps, was working. Senior year, Dutch was elected student body president, and the motto that appears beneath his yearbook picture, a motto taken from "Life," a poem he himself had penned, went: "Life is just one grand sweet song, so start the music."

Senior year spanned 1927–1928, and it was during the summer of 1927 that Dutch turned his prowess as a swimmer to account. He applied for the position of lifeguard at Lowell Park, located on the Rock River, three miles north of downtown Dixon. Here, the water flowed swiftly, posing considerable danger to neophyte swimmers. But the woodsy seclusion and beauty of the park made the river challenge irresistible for many. Young Dutch had to persuade Edward and Ruth Graybill, who held the license as Lowell Park concessionaires, to hire him. Reagan was slender as a reed that summer, and the Graybills doubted he could rescue any struggling swimmer heavier than he. It helped, however, that Mrs. Graybill went to the same church as Dutch and his mother, and that Pastor Cleaver thought highly of him. But, in the end, it took the salesmanship of Jack Reagan to close the deal. He assured the Graybills that his son could do the job, and he backed up his endorsement by pointing out that Ron had taken the full lifesaving course at the YMCA.

Ronald Reagan began what would be the first of six summers as Lowell Park lifeguard. His starting pay was an impressive $15 a week. By his sixth and final summer, he was earning $20. During his second term in the White House, speaking at a Gridiron Club dinner in 1987, Reagan self-deprecatingly joked, "It's true hard work never killed anybody, but I figure, why take a chance."[41] Those six summers as a lifeguard may well have been the hardest work Reagan would ever do. His "shift" was twelve hours a day, seven days a week, until at least 10 p.m. (the park was flood-lit), and each day started early in the morning with Reagan having to fetch concession stand refreshments at the Graybills' house, stop at the icehouse to pick up a 300-pound block of ice, and transport everything down to the riverbank.

That was the unglamorous aspect of being a lifeguard. The drama—the heroism—came during his hours on patrol. He reported in *Where's the Rest of Me?* that, during his six seasons, that he rescued a total of 77 souls from death by drowning. A 1931 newspaper article, written in praise of Lifeguard Reagan, credited him with 71 saves (up to that point), noting that he had lost no one, despite often overseeing a thousand or more bathers without backup or assistance of any kind.[42] Detractors during Reagan's gubernatorial run and later challenged Reagan's figures. In fact, the local newspaper, *The Dixon Daily Telegraph,* reported most of the incidents, which tallied closely with what Reagan reported.

At his father's suggestion, Reagan himself cut notches in a log to commemorate each rescue. Yet he was quite charmingly modest about his achievement. He never bragged about any rescue, but he did complain, later in life, that nobody ever thought to thank him for saving their lives, adding that the only monetary reward ever tendered him was the $10 he received from a man after he presented him with the dental plate he had retrieved from the riverbed.

Reagan loved the role of lifeguard. He was vigilant, by all reports fearless, and he was effective. He did the job—a matter of life and death, for real—twelve hours a day, seven days a week. He was a hero, not in fiction but in fact. Surely, this gave some substance to his evolving self-mythology. Lifeguard was, perhaps, the only position Ronald Reagan held, governor and president not excepted, in which he was a genuine, selfless, courageous, and highly competent public servant, an everyday hero. This was the first culmination of his personal origin myth, and he treasured it lifelong.

We are not denigrating the achievement of the youthful Reagan. Saving the drowning is real and cannot be successfully simulated by B-level acting or even acting worthy of an Oscar. The youth of Donald Trump offered no such opportunity for real achievement and tangible, let alone lifesaving, service. We know from the 2020 tell-all by Mary L. Trump, Donald's niece, that he was raised in a notably loveless family, presided over by a father whose only standard of worth was measured in money made. The leading lesson of Fred Trump, Sr., was that success in business was measured by the pile of cash one accumulated at the expense of everyone else. Financial success was a zero-sum game in which your triumph required everyone else to lose. In pursuit of this zero-sum victory, lying was not only justified but also required.

Mary Trump explains that Fred Trump willingly depleted his coffers to finance his son Donald. A successful real estate developer, Fred was nevertheless a notably dull figure. He deliberately used his brash, flamboyant son as a front, the public face that enabled him to expand his real estate empire from Queens and Brooklyn to Manhattan and beyond. Mary argues that Fred deliberately created the "myth"—her term—of his son's invincible Midas touch. This mythology was ultimately "reinforced by the world at large," she writes, Yet Donald Trump remained "Fred's construct," even though he came to belong "to the banks and the media."[43]

As PhD psychologist Mary Trump sees it, the mythology clinging to her brother was a thin veneer. "He had a streak of superficial charm, even charisma, that sucked certain people in. When his ability to charm hit a wall, he deployed another 'business strategy': throwing tantrums during which he threatened to bankrupt or otherwise ruin anybody who failed to let him have what he wanted. Either way, he won."[44]

Ronald's Reagan's mythology of self ran much deeper; however, in politics, both he and Trump would appropriate the same political campaign doctrine formulated during the Nixon years, especially the "Southern Strategy" (which dramatically increased support among white southerners by appealing to racism against African Americans) and the notion of a "Silent Majority" (Nixon's unspecified fraction of Americans who do not publicly express their opinions). But whereas Reagan's identity was always linked to a genuinely American mythology imbibed in his early life experience, Trump simply lifted and leveraged the products of that mythology, including the notion of an American greatness somehow lost but recoverable by electing the "right" (white native-born American Christian) candidate who would favor the "right" (white native-born American Christian) people.

It was Ronald Reagan who ultimately translated his personal mythology into the slogan "Make America Great Again." In a broader public context, the slogan was based on the false premise that America was once great but that greatness had been somehow lost. Bluntly put, the slogan was a lie. Yet it was a lie born of personal belief and mythology. When Donald Trump purloined that lie, he simplified it to something he knew would appeal to those likely to support him. It was a secret code. It was an acronym that marked its user as an insider. It was MAGA.

MAGA was stolen property, lifted from the lived mythology of another person, Ronald Wilson Reagan. The elements of this personal mythology bore no emotional or truly formative relationship to Trump's lived experience. But such elements had touched and spoken to Ronald Reagan, even in childhood, of his place in God's plan. The implementation of this plan would not become manifest for many years, and yet, even when fully manifested, it never eclipsed the simple, straightforward satisfaction of "Dutch" Reagan's youthful real-life performance. Trump? He never made a connection sufficiently intimate to elicit a nickname from anyone.

CHAPTER 3

Crystal Radio

*What Ronald Reagan inherited from his childhood is an
astounding ability to turn away from any realty that is too
harsh and paint one that is softer and gentler to the eyes.*
                                            —Patti Davis, on her father[1]

In America, people don't ask who you are but what you do. Ronald
Reagan glimpsed his true vocation when he was just nine years old. On
November 2, 1920, KDKA, the nation's first commercial radio station,
debuted with a broadcast of returns from the Harding-Cox presidential
election. Sometime after this, Ronnie visited his aunt on her farm in Mor-
rison, Illinois. She owned what was still a novelty if not a rarity that year:
a crystal radio set. The boy was fascinated and immediately began imitat-
ing the announcer.

He reminisced about this event in his 1965 autobiography and for the
rest of his life. It was something of a sacred moment. His mother, a faithful congregant of the Disciples of Christ Church, taught him that God had
a plan for everyone, including him. The boy believed her, and the man
never had cause to doubt that belief. In retrospect, Reagan came to believe
that his providential destiny appeared full-blown in the crystal diode of
a primitive radio receiver on his aunt's Illinois farm. He put on the head-
phones, took communion from the airwaves, and echoed out of his child's
mouth the distant words of a KDKA announcer.

Born that day was more than a vocation. It was the germ of a sense of
destiny. For Reagan never doubted he would get what he wanted. It was of
a piece with what journalist John L. O'Sullivan had written about in 1845:
the "manifest destiny" of the United States. A career in radio emerged as
Reagan's personal manifest destiny—an individual dimension of the same
divine plan God had laid out for the United States itself.

*   *   *

Ronald Reagan put his name to two autobiographies, *Where's the Rest
of Me? The Ronald Reagan Story* (1965) and *Ronald Reagan: An American*

Life (1990). In that second one, he included what could be described as a nativity story. There is no manger, but what he briefly describes is not much more promising: "I was born February 6, 1911, in a flat above the local bank in Tampico, Illinois. According to family legend, when my father ran up the stairs and looked at his newborn son, he quipped: 'He looks like a fat little Dutchman. But who knows, he might grow up to be president some day.'"[2]

So, now we know. He was born in a humble flat in a humble town— yet above the local bank. Hmm. "He looks like a fat little Dutchman," his well-meaning alcoholic father proclaimed. Here, then, is the origin of the nickname Reagan himself favored: "I never thought 'Ronald' was rugged enough for a young red-blooded American boy and as soon as I could, I asked people to call me 'Dutch.' That was a nickname that grew out of my father's calling me 'the Dutchman' whenever he referred to me." Jack Reagan, his son tells us, appended to his "fat little Dutchman" quip an off-handed prediction: "But who knows, he might grow up to be president some day."[3]

It is an American destiny served up just as it should be, in a flat mid-western accent. If we look hard enough, however, we can find a tasty lit-tle kink in Reagan's destiny. "During my mother's pregnancy, my parents had decided to call me Donald. But after one of her sisters beat her to it and named her son Donald, I became Ronald."[4] But for his entrance having been upstaged by that of a cousin born and christened before him, the for-tieth and forty-fifth presidents would have shared a first name.

Looking back on his life, Ronald Reagan embraced an idea of destiny that was not just manifest, but divine. His father may have mused that his newborn might become president, but Ronald Reagan was convinced that his "dad ... was destined by God, I think, to be salesman."[5] This begins a description of his father that is a patronizing blend of filial piety and white-wash with a dash of wishful tenderness. In contrast to his earlier attempts to disguise the humble Irish immigrant origins of his patrimony (Chapter 2), Reagan in the autumn of his days celebrated his ancestors' potato fam-ine escape from County Tipperary to America—noting, however, that it was "by way of England." Jack Reagan, he wrote, was "endowed with the gift of blarney and the charm of the leprechaun. No one I ever met could tell a story better than he could." Reagan notes the "brevity" of his father's schooling but credits him with "street smarts." He calls him "restless" like "a lot of Americans whose roots were on the nineteenth-century frontier."[6] In truth, the Reagan immigrants settled in Carroll County, Illinois, in the northwestern part of the state, which was, by the mid-nineteenth century, at most the gateway to the frontier and, besides, his father was, if anything, more rooted to Ireland than to the United States. It is as if Reagan were remodeling his heritage into the product of *Anglicized* Irish immigrants who, somehow, were also good old American frontier folk driven by good old American frontier restlessness.

Interestingly, Reagan the autobiographer cast his father as a passionate believer "in the rights of the individual and the working man." Jack, he said, "was suspicious of established authority," which was personified by "the Republican"—yes, you heard that right, *Republican*—"politicians who ran the Illinois state government." Reagan did add that he considered the Illinois Republicans "as corrupt as Tammany Hall," referring to the nineteenth-century Democratic machine that ruled New York City.[7] So, he managed to picture his father as a son of the frontier who held above all the rights of the individual and distrusted government, which, though Republican, was as corrupt as the most corrupt Democrats. This reveals the extent of Reagan's pretzel-like gift for self-mythology.

Reagan tells us that his father "passed on to" him "the belief that all men and women, regardless of their color or religion, are created equal and that individuals determine their own destiny; that is, it's largely their own ambition and hard work that determine their fate in life."[8] Perhaps this mash-up of democratic equality and Ayn Rand orthodoxy reflects Jack's beliefs, but no one would ever single out President Reagan as a defender of civil rights. He also credits his father with having a "singular dream," which seems to have been a dream of remarkably modest and unimaginative proportions: "to own a shoe store," albeit "not an ordinary shoe shop, but the best, with the largest inventory in Illinois, outside Chicago."[9] This recollection does seem quite genuine, in large part because Reagan's own first "dream" was to become a radio sportscaster—as dreams go, likewise modest and unimaginative.

Reagan made it quite clear that he received from his mother something of greater value than his father could ever give him. Nelle Wilson Reagan taught her son "the value of prayer," which he understood to be "how to have dreams and believe I could make them come true." Theologians, doubtless, would dispute that this is indeed the "value" of prayer, but Reagan seems very much to have believed it. At the same time, he wrote, "While my father was filled with dreams of making something of himself, [my mother] had a drive to help my brother and me make something of ourselves."[10]

A nativity, a destiny, dreams (however mundane), prayer (however shallow its value), and drive. These were the ingredients of Reagan's private mythology of destiny. But no such mythology is complete without a miraculous brush with death.

> When I was a baby, we moved from the flat above the bank into a house facing a park in the center of Tampico that had a Civil War cannon flanked by a

pyramid of cannonballs. One of my first memories was of crossing the park with my brother on our way to an ice wagon that had pulled up to the depot. A pair of toddlers intent on plucking some refreshing shards of ice from the back of the wagon, we crawled over the tracks beneath a huge freight train that had just pulled in. We'd hardly made it when the train pulled out with a hissing burst of steam. Our mother, who had come out on the porch in time to see the escapade, met us in the middle of the park and inflicted the appropriate punishment.[11]

* * *

The Reagan family "moved a lot," Jack's search "for a better life," as Reagan described it, meant that his son "was forever the new kid in school." Over one four-year period, he attended four different schools. Reagan wrote that the family moved "wherever my father's ambition took him."[12] More likely, his uncontrollable drinking made it impossible for him to hold any one job for long.

Involuntarily mobile, the young Reagan learned to get along with new people. Perhaps he also learned how to be agreeably superficial. He seems not to have suffered greatly as long as he lived in small towns. When the prospect of a solid job selling shoes in the upscale Marshall Field department store lured Jack Reagan to Chicago, his son for the first and last time saw the family's life as bleak. Field's was on State Street in the Chicago Loop, but the family settled a good distance away, on the city's working-class South Side, in a "small flat near the University of Chicago that was lighted by a single gas jet brought to life with the deposit of a quarter in a slot down the hall."[13]

This vignette of squalor is amplified in Reagan's autobiography by the understated observation that "Jack's job didn't pay as well as he had hoped" (Dreamed? Prayed?) "and that meant Nelle had to make a soup bone last several days and be creative in other ways with her cooking." She would, for instance, send Reagan's brother to the butcher with a request for liver—not a popular meat back then—"to feed our family cat—which didn't exist. The liver became our Sunday dinner."[14]

In Chicago, Reagan fell ill with "a serious case of bronchial pneumonia." This is one of the few times he describes himself as seriously ill, languishing in a miserable apartment in a slum district of a "congested urban world of gaslit sidewalks." When he saw a fire engine one day "with a cloud of steam rising behind it," he decided "it was my intention in life to become a fireman." But, after less than two years in the Windy City, the family followed another job offer, this time from O.T. Johnson's department store in Galesburg, which, instead "of noisy streets and crowds of people, … consisted of meadows and caves, trees and streams, and the joys of small town life."[15]

The family was certainly no wealthier in Galesburg than it had been in Chicago, but Reagan felt he was in a kind of paradise. They rented first a bungalow and then a larger house, in the attic of which was a "huge collection of birds' eggs and butterflies" the previous tenant had left behind. "I escaped for hours at a time into the attic, marveling at the rich colors of the eggs and the intricate and fragile wings of the butterflies. The experience left me with a reverence for the handiwork of God that never left me."[16] (And yet it was President Ronald Reagan in 1981 who declared that trees produce more air pollution than cars.[17])

In Galesburg, Reagan entered first grade, became a precocious reader, discovered a love for books and stories, and discovered as well that he "had a pretty good memory. I could pick up something to read and memorize it fairly quickly." Yet even this gift, a gift that would allow him to absorb a great deal of information, a gift that would open worlds for him, and, not incidentally, a gift that would prove of great value to him as an actor, even this gift he interpreted in a remarkably shallow manner, calling it "a lucky trait that made schoolwork easier."[18]

World War I made an impression on young Reagan, who claimed that Jack, as a father of two, was "rejected for the army." This is untrue on its face. Per statute, "Married registrants with dependent spouse or dependent children under sixteen with sufficient family income if drafted" were put in class II, meaning that they were temporarily deferred, but available for military service. Most likely, Jack Reagan's family would not have been deemed to have sufficient family income to do without him, so he would almost certainly have been exempt from the draft. But in saying that he was "rejected," Reagan implies that his father volunteered for service and was turned down. This would not have been the case. Had he wanted to serve, he would have been accepted.[19] While young Reagan remembered being "filled with pride" whenever he heard "Over There" or even "thought of our doughboys crossing the Atlantic on a noble mission to save our friends in Europe," he notes that, at age seven, the "realization that some of those boys to whom I'd waved on the troop train later died on European soil made me an isolationist for a long time."[20]

During and after the war, Jack Reagan changed jobs, and the family moved more than once. Shortly after the Armistice, the Reagans even moved back to Tampico, so that Jack could work at the general store he had worked in when Ronnie was born. The store's owner, H.C. Pitney, had promised to help him buy an interest in a shoe store. Surprisingly enough after a year or so, Pitney opened a "swank shoe store called the Fashion Boot Shop," with (as he had promised) Jack as his partner. This necessitated a move to Dixon, Illinois. Dixon's population of 10,000 was more than ten time larger than Tampico. Reagan was nine in 1920 when the family arrived, and to him "it was heaven."[21]

In *An American Life,* he recalls Dixon as a bustling place, a "small universe where I learned standards and values that would guide me for the rest of my life." Relatively big as the town was, everyone knew everyone else, and, in church, people prayed alongside their neighbors. Residents helped one another, as he remembered it. "If a farmer lost his barn to a fire, his friends would pitch in and help him rebuild it." He grew up "observing how the love and common sense of purpose that unites families is one of the most powerful glues on earth." He "learned that hard work is an essential part of life ... and that America was a place that offered unlimited opportunity to those who did work hard. ... I have always wondered at this American marvel, the great energy of the human soul that drives people to better themselves and improve the fortune of their families and communities. Indeed, I know of no greater force on earth." This made "growing up in a small town ... a good foundation for anyone who decides to enter politics."[22]

Here is another aspect of Reagan's self-perceived self-mythology. He was in the position of Goldilocks. Tampico was too small, too constraining. Chicago, a bustling city of 2.2 million when the Reagans lived there, was congested and bleak. His recollection of the family's Southside apartment, where gaslight was available if you put a quarter in the slot, is the only hint of outright squalor that creeps into his autobiography. Unspoken is the other feature of Chicago: a diverse population, including many immigrants from eastern and southern Europe and, when the Reagans lived in the city, a modest but significant black population of some 40,000 persons, many of whom likely lived not far from the Reagans on the Southside. But racially and ethnically homogenous Dixon, as Reagan saw it, was large yet still rural. It was, as the Goldilocks tale puts it, "just right" and, therefore (in his perception), typically American.[23]

Although Dixon felt to him like a town in which everyone knew everyone else, he did not recognize that his family was considered poor. "...I didn't know that when I was growing up. And I never thought of our family as disadvantaged." Well, you can't blame a small child for being ignorant of inequality or for feeling no discontent with his family's lot in life. But the adult Reagan, writing in his post-presidential years, adds: "Only later did the government decide it had to tell people they were poor."[24] Here, Reagan seems to be saying that ignorance is indeed bliss, and damn the government to hell for letting people know where they stood economically. Poverty and economic inequality were unknown to a nine-year-old child. Why couldn't the mettlesome government resist revealing the reality of these things? Government-furnished facts are the problem. Nine-year-old-level ignorance, on the other hand, made a heaven of Dixon, Illinois.

The unawareness and social ignorance of early childhood played a significant role in Ronald Reagan's vision of American society. He recalled how his mother would stretch precious hamburger meat by mixing it with oatmeal and some gravy. "Oatmeal meat," she called it, and little Ronnie thought it was "the most wonderful thing" he'd ever eaten. "Of course, I didn't realize oatmeal meat was born of poverty." "Nowadays," Reagan observed of oatmeal meat, "I bet doctors would say it was healthy for us, too."[25] But, then, in the Republican Party Ronald Reagan prepared for Donald Trump, the medical profession was as useless as government.

*   *   *

Ronald Reagan recalled how Dixon straddled the Rock River, "a stretch of blue-green water flanked by wooded hills and limestone cliffs." It was his "playground during some of the happiest moments of [his] life. … In my hand-me-down overalls, I hiked the hills and cliffs above the river, tried (unsuccessfully) to trap muskrats at the river's edge, and played 'Cowboys and Indians' on the hillsides above the river. … I think my life was as sweet and idyllic as it could be, as close as I could imagine for a young boy to the world created by Mark Twain in *The Adventures of Tom Sawyer*."[26] This is especially telling, given that Reagan was in his late seventies when he provided this childhood narrative. Reagan's vision of Dixon as what America should be and once was is not a vision of America at all. It is a vision of childhood—and of childhood not as actually lived but as imagined in a beloved work of American fiction.

Yet without taking a breath from painting his idyll, Reagan mentions that the America in which he grew up was still riddled with "ugly tumors of racial bigotry … including [in] the corner of Illinois where we lived." He mentioned the segregated seating mandated in Dixon's sole movie theater, and he said that his mother and father "urged" him and his brother "to bring home our black playmates, to consider them equals, and to respect the religious views of our friends." Reagan, who, as a presidential candidate tried to deny his Irish lineage, believed that his father was an egalitarian because he "had learned what discrimination was like firsthand. He'd grown up in an era when some stores still had signs at their door saying, NO DOGS OR IRISHMEN ALLOWED." Jack Reagan told his family of how he was checking into a hotel during a shoe-selling trip when the clerk remarked, "You'll like it here, Mr. Reagan, we don't permit a Jew in the place." Jack, according to the story Jack himself told, looked at the clerk; picked up his suitcase; and told him, "I'm a Catholic. If it's come to the point where you won't take Jews, then some day you won't take *me* either."

With that, he left. Discovering this was the only hotel in town, he had to spend the night in his car—during a winter blizzard. Reagan added to this: "I think it may have led to his first heart attack."[27] In a slightly roundabout way, then, according to Ronald Reagan, racism caused bodily harm to his father. We are left to contemplate how slight an effect these early lessons about racism, bigotry, and injustice had on the mature Reagan's political life.

In the meantime, Mr. Pitney did make Jack Reagan part owner of his shoe store, and everyone who knew the Reagans assumed that he and his brother would go to work there after his father retired. Reagan tried but "found it boring; besides, those books I'd read about college life had given me my own ideas about the future." He admitted that the characters in those books were "from rich old Eastern families," and the Ivy League life was "pretty remote from the reality of my life as a towheaded kid in overalls from a poor family in rural Illinois." But reality was not what young Reagan wanted from his fiction, and he "read and reread" the stories of wealth, so that "I began to dream of myself on a college campus, wearing a college jersey, even as a star on the football team."[28]

Yet not all his heroes, he recalled, were college football stars. At age eleven, he read *That Printer of Udell's,* a 1903 novel by Harold Bell Wright, whose hero Reagan describes only as a "devout itinerant Christian." Dick Falkner is the child of a broken home, in which his father is a hapless alcoholic who leaves his mother starving. After his parents die, Dick Falkner goes to a midwestern town in the belief that "Christians won't let me starve." He is hired by a printer, who, in company with Falkner, decides to become a Christian. Falkner rapidly rises in the religious community because of his talent as a public speaker and his attitude of unrelenting optimism. The book ends with Falkner entering politics in Washington.[29]

That Printer of Udell's inspired Reagan to join his mother's church, the Disciples of Christ and, rejecting his father's Catholicism, to accept, at age twelve, baptism in that Church. At about this time, Nelle Reagan explained to him and to his brother why their father frequently left on unexpected trips. He had a "*sickness* he couldn't control." Reagan believed that his father "wasn't one of those alcoholics who went on a bender after he'd had a run of bad luck.... No, it was prosperity that Jack couldn't stand." When things were going well, he'd "let go" and get drunk.[30]

Reagan did not dwell on his father's infirmity. In fact, he was more disturbed by what he perceived at the time as his own ineptitude at sports, and the resulting "feelings of inferiority and lack of self-confidence" caused him "a lot of heartache."[31] Fortunately, while even silent movies were a novelty in 1920s Dixon and visits by vaudeville troupes were rare,

Nelle was a star performer in a group that staged dramatic readings from poems, plays, books, and even speeches. Looking back at how she "threw herself into a part," Reagan concluded that "performing ... was her first love." She coaxed the shy Reagan into following his older brother, Neil, in memorizing a reading and presenting it. "I'll never forget the response," he wrote. *"People laughed and applauded"* (the italics are Reagan's). "When I walked off the stage that night, my life had changed."[32]

*   *   *

The magnitude of the change was not immediately apparent, although Reagan did begin to appear regularly in amateur theatricals his mother wrote for presentation at church events. Far more dramatic was what happened when, finding that Nelle had left her glasses on the backseat of the family car, he slipped them on. Suddenly, at the age of thirteen or fourteen, he discovered for the first time what it was to see. He was "extremely nearsighted," and now, at last, he had an explanation for his poor showing in sports.

He was thrilled to be fitted for glasses, but they were thick, and even his friends started calling him "Four Eyes." This prompted him to seek a place in Dixon's brand-new boys band by way of boosting his sense of self-worth. That he played no instrument at all should have disqualified him. Instead, something in his newly confident manner, his stage presence, perhaps, landed him "out in front of the band as drum major." He "felt very special about it," becoming not just a member of the band but its leader, despite an absence of any musical talent or knowledge.[33]

He was chosen to lead, even though he had remarkably few close friends. The truth was, however, that Reagan might have been at the head of the band, but he was not the leader of the parade. That was the position of the marshal, who rode a horse and had a more impressive uniform. One day, the marshal unexpectedly led the parade down a cross street—something Reagan, so intent on his own role ahead of the others, failed to notice until the volume of the music diminished, and he was marching all alone. To his credit, he neither despaired nor panicked but broke into run, cut across backyards and vacant lots, and fell into step again. In retrospect, he didn't scold himself for being out of place and out of step but credited himself for marching "to a different drummer."[34]

*   *   *

The Reagans kept moving, even within Dixon. Their peripatetic lives meant that Ronnie had few close friends yet was very good at making acquaintances and getting along. He was also relieved that by the time he entered high school in 1924, the family had moved from the south to the north side of town. This meant that he would attend the Northside campus of Dixon High. His older brother, Neil, already attending high school, decided to remain at Southside, for which Reagan gave thanks. "Although he and I were close ... we had our share of fistfights and rivalries." Neil was outspoken, with a "self-confident personality that was a little like Jack's, which made him a natural leader, and.... I probably felt a little under his shadow. On my own at Northside, I knew I wouldn't have to be compared with him." Through the rearview mirror of a man who had been president of the United States for eight years, "leadership" was equated with being outspoken and self-confident, which made brother Neil and their alcoholic, semi-impoverished, nomadic shoe-salesman father "natural" leaders.[35]

Reagan, all five feet, three inches, and 108 pounds of him, went out for football. Unable to find pants small enough, the coach managed to dig up a sufficiently small "antique pair of football pants with thigh pads made out of bamboo." Thus equipped, Reagan struggled against the much bigger boys. He didn't make the team, but he was determined to try again as a sophomore. Come summer, he got a job in construction.

With the new school year, Reagan had grown sufficiently to make the football team and was even elected captain. He loved the game because it was "as fundamental as anything in life—a collision between two bodies, one determined to advance, the other determined to resist; one man against another man, blocking, tackling, breaking through the line." By his junior year, he made the varsity team; however, he warmed the bench until the coach, dissatisfied with the play of one of the team's regular guards, impulsively put Reagan in as right guard. "Once I got in, I never let the other guy get his position back. The first string job was mine for the rest of the season and during my senior year, when I'd grown even bigger, I was a starter from the beginning."[36]

* * *

The next summer, Reagan found a much better job as a lifeguard at the city's Lowell Park. As discussed in Chapter 2, it was a pivotal experience for him, and he worked at it for seven seasons. Along with football, swimming was his great love, though he wrote about finding "two other loves" while he was at Dixon High, the "first was named Margaret, and the other was named acting."[37]

Margaret Cleaver was the daughter of his church's new minister. Perhaps, he recalled, "it was love at first sight, I'm not sure." In any case, for nearly six years, he *was* sure Margaret was going to be his wife. Their romance nearly died aborning, however, when she confronted Ronnie about his father's drinking. Reagan had tried to keep Jack's alcoholism a secret, but somebody had gossiped to Margaret and delivered a lurid narrative of his bad behavior. Ronnie tried to explain it to her as his mother had to him: his father is "sick." But she was having none of it, and a "brokenhearted" Reagan believed he would lose her. To his mother, he confessed that if he lost Margaret, he would "probably disown" his father "and never speak to him again." Nelle Reagan asked him to be patient, and, in the end, Margaret told him she would rather accept Jack's drinking than break up.[38]

In the meantime, a new English teacher, B.J. Frazer, came to Dixon High, asked Reagan to read aloud some of his student essays, and then encouraged him to act in a play he was directing at the school. The mature Ronald Reagan seemed to make no absolute distinction between destiny and good luck. Either way, he was certain that Frazer had a life-transforming impact on him. Certainly, he seems to have been a remarkably imaginative and ambitious teacher, who "staged complete plays using scripts from recent Broadway hits." The prevailing pedagogical method of Reagan's day was brute memory. Frazer, in contrast, taught his student actors "that it was important to analyze [the] characters [they played] and think like them." He credits Frazer's direction with developing in him "a knack" for putting himself in someone else's shoes and for understanding why they think the way they do, even if they come from a different background than you do.[39]

His achievements in high school—being a lifeguard, playing football, acting, acquiring a girlfriend, and even gaining election as student body president—emboldened Reagan to set his sights on going to college—and doing so (he points out in his book) in an era when fewer than 7 percent of high school graduates went. His ambition was to go to Eureka College, which the son of the minister who had preceded Margaret's father had attended. Reagan confessed to hero worship of that young man, Garland Waggoner, and when Margaret announced that she was also going to attend Eureka (it was owned by the Disciples of Christ and was only some 110 miles southeast of Dixon), his mind was set "in concrete." He wrote in his autobiography: "I'd like to be able to recall that my burning desire to go to college was planted first and foremost in a drive to get an education. But at seventeen, I think I was probably more motivated by love for a pretty girl and a love for football."[40] (He knew he would have no trouble making the Eureka team.)

Humbling himself, Reagan managed to secure a "Needy Student Scholarship," which cut his tuition in half, and he was promised a job to defray the cost of room and board. The boyfriend of one of Margaret's sisters (she also attended the college) belonged to the TKE fraternity, which quickly accepted seventeen-year-old Reagan as a pledge. He loved the little school—enrollment, 250—all his life, insisting that if he had his choice of any college or university, he'd still take Eureka. Ronald Reagan was consistent in his attitude that nothing he experienced as an adult was better than the small-scale, small-town life he had lived as a child and young man.

Despite the 1929 stock market crash and the Depression that followed, Ronald Reagan played football, swam for the swim team, excelled in the debate club, and was a star in drama club productions. He worked as well as a reporter on the school newspaper, wrote for the yearbook, of which he was also editor, and served as president of the student council. An economics major, he seems to have barely squeezed academics into this schedule, managing to maintain no more than a C average. Reagan liked to tell a story, which has never quite withstood scholarly scrutiny, about how he rescued Eureka College from imminent Depression-era dissolution by leading a student strike to restore popular classes a straitened college administration had eliminated. His victory, as Reagan himself tells it, prompted the resignation of the college president. Clearly, government was the problem even then.

In the wider world beyond Eureka, the Depression closed in with a vengeance. Among its first casualties, Reagan wrote, was his father's "grandest dream." The Fashion Boot Shop went belly up when Mr. Pitney could no longer pay to support it. Reagan wrote that, with its demise, Jack's "only chance of ever owning his own store" died as well.[41] This was likely a reasonable assessment, yet, at forty-seven, Jack Reagan was not an old man, and to say that the Fashion Boot Shop, financed by a third party, was his last chance to own a business—ever—is a far cry from the Ronald Reagan who would relentlessly celebrate America as a fount of endless opportunity. As the very title of his autobiography proclaimed, his own abundantly successful life was "An American Life." Moreover, neither Jack nor Nelle Reagan simply gave up. Nelle found work as a dress shop seamstress, Jack hit the road in search of employment, and the couple sublet a portion of their house. When they could no longer pay the rent, they rented the upper floor of someone else's home. Jack got a job as a traveling shoe salesman but was quickly laid off—by mail, the letter arriving on Christmas Eve. Nelle borrowed $50 from Ronnie (he dipped into his lifeguard job savings) and swore him to keep it secret from his father. (He did.)[42]

Still, Jack did not quit. He found work as the shoe clerk/manager of a "grim, tiny hole-in-the-wall" store on the outskirts of Springfield, the Illinois state capital, some 200 miles due south of Dixon. When the Eureka football team played in Springfield, Reagan paid a call on him. The son's eyes filled with tears.

Beaten down by alcoholism and the Great Depression, Jack worked. Reagan, emulating his mother, prayed—"prayed a lot; in those days I prayed things would get better for our country, for our family, and for Dixon. I even prayed before football games." He recalled that the team's coach, Mac McKinzie, once asked the team if any of them prayed. Reagan, who "never faced a kickoff without a prayer," confessed in his autobiography to being afraid to reveal his own prayerful ways to his teammates. But then every one of them answered McKinzie's question with yes, and that was the "last time I was ever reluctant to admit I prayed."[43]

* * *

God, Reagan wrote, has a "plan with my name on it." Just as He sent B.J. Frazer, essentially his first acting teacher, to Dixon High exactly when Reagan enrolled there, so He now sent Professor Ellen Marie Johnson to Eureka to teach English and dramatics. She directed numerous student productions, Reagan became fully hooked on acting, and, when he was a junior, thanks to her, he was a member of the Eureka troupe that competed in a national collegiate one-act play contest held at Northwestern University in Evanston, just north of Chicago. "For college actors, the competition was comparable to the Super Bowl," Reagan wrote.[44] Eureka, enrollment 250, found itself competing against Yale, Princeton, and the like. Who could fail to see God's hand in *that* miracle?

Eureka presented Edna St. Vincent Millay's *Aria da Capo*. A precocious antiwar comedy-fantasy written in 1919 by the young poet and future Pulitzer Prize winner, it was by any measure the most intellectually sophisticated material for which Reagan the actor would ever be cast. In recalling it, however, Reagan wrote simply that he "played a shepherd strangled before the final curtain," adding, "Death scenes are always pleasant for an actor and I tried to play it to the hilt." In fact, he played one of the play's two shepherds who, starting out as friends, end up killing one another. No matter. Reagan did recall well enough that Eureka placed second in the competition and he was one of just three actors singled out for an individual award. Both were extraordinary achievements, and while God did not personally congratulate him, the head of Northwestern's Speech Department summoned Reagan to his office to ask if I he had ever thought about making a career as an actor.

"Well, no."

"Well, you should."[45]

Ronald Reagan was thrilled but, as he had been afraid to admit that he prayed, so he now believed that "Hollywood and Broadway were at least as remote from Dixon as the moon was in 1932. If I *had* told anyone I was setting out to be a movie star, they'd have carted me off to an institution."[46]

He did not abandon his dream, but he did scale it back. Both Hollywood and Broadway were indeed remote from Dixon, but Chicago lay a tad over 100 miles to the east, and, as it was the hub of the nation's railroads, so it was the nexus of the early radio broadcast industry. Even as a callow college senior, Reagan had an insightful grasp of the significance of radio. It was "magic," he believed. "It was theater of the mind." Yet Reagan's ambition did not leap to becoming an actor on radio. Instead, he recognized that the medium had created a whole new profession, the sports announcer: "Broadcasting play-by-play reports of football games, people like Graham McNamee and Ted Husing had become as famous as some Hollywood stars and often they were more famous than the athletes they reported on."[47]

After graduating in June 1932, Reagan went back to Dixon, hoping to get a summer job at a resort hotel that served Lowell Park. The Depression had sharply curtailed summer vacationing, however, and he came up empty. He did know someone he described as a Kansas City businessman who had told him to reach out when he graduated and he would make some calls on his behalf. Reagan was reluctant to tell him that he wanted to break into the world of entertainment, but the man pressed him, and, apologetically, Ronnie blurted out what sounded like the confession of a crime: "I have to tell you, way down deep inside, what I'd really like to be is a radio sports announcer."[48] The man took him seriously, explained that he had no contacts in radio but suggested that he start knocking on doors, tell each prospect that he was a believer in the new industry and would take any job that would break him into broadcasting.

Reagan followed his advice. Parting with Margaret Cleaver, who went off to take a scarce teaching job, he set off for Chicago, where he found rejection behind every door. Discouraged, he hitchhiked back to Dixon (in the rain, of course), and confided in—of all people—his father. One radio program director who had rejected him did offer advice: get experience in "the sticks" and then try the big city. Jack thought this was a good idea and loaned his son the family car to drive to the Tri-Cities—Moline and Rock Island, Illinois; and Davenport, Iowa, clustered on either side of the Mississippi River. In Davenport, he met with Peter MacArthur, a former vaudevillian who was now program director for WOC. The station was owned by Colonel B.J. Palmer, founder of the Palmer School of Chiropractic—WOC stood for "World of Chiropractic"—and it broadcast from the Palmer Chiropractic campus.

Heeding the advice to take any job, Reagan told MacArthur he was looking to be an announcer. MacArthur listened to his pitch and then told him they did have a job, but it had been filled just the day before.

"Where ye been?" he asked.

Dejected, Reagan left MacArthur's office and headed toward the elevator, loudly asking himself, "How the hell can you get to be a sports announcer if you can't get a job at a radio station?"

MacArthur came after him.

"Hold on, you big bastard. What was that you said about *sports* announcing?"

Reagan told him that that was what he wanted to do.

"De ye know anything about football?"

"I played football for eight years in high school and college...."

"Could ye tell me about a football game and make me see it as if I was home listening to the radio?"

"Yes.... I'm sure I could," [he] replied with the bravado of youth.

"Come with me."

MacArthur asked him to get on the mic while he listened in another room. "Describe an imaginary football game to me and make me see it."[49]

He crushed the audition, and the job was his: $10 per game plus transportation expenses. It was a dream come true. He loved sports but had no illusions about playing professionally. He loved acting but thought Broadway and Hollywood were in a different universe from the one he inhabited. But he also loved radio—and had, ever since he was nine years old, listening to his aunt's crystal set. Well, now he was being paid to consummate at least two of his loves.

CHAPTER 4

Holiday

"Theater of the mind," Ronald Reagan called radio. When Peter Mac-Arthur auditioned him at WOC, he asked Reagan to broadcast an imaginary game and to do it so that he could *see* it. Reagan took up the challenge but then realized that he was faced with certain problems: "First, nothing had been said about how long my imaginary game should go—and if it was to last any length of time, I would need names of players.... Second, my dream game should get to some kind of climax to permit a little excitement to creep in." His solution was to recall a game Eureka had played that fall against Western State University. It had gone down to the wire in the fourth quarter, with Eureka trailing six to nothing. Eureka was on its own 35-yard line. Everyone was expecting a pass. Instead, the team went for broke—a 65-yard dash for the touchdown and victory. With this plot summary in mind, Reagan called the game from a mixture memory—how it was—and myth—how he wanted it to be. Beginning with a "chill wind blowing in through the end of the stadium and the long blue shadows ... settling over the field," he spun out the running battle that culminated in a dropkick over the goal post followed by "We return you now to our main studio."[1]

Of course, he got the job. And, right now, that's all he wanted. We are left to wonder if he appreciated the magnitude and import of what he had accomplished. In that "theater of the mind," he had recreated reality and then trumped it—yes, *trumped it*—with something far more powerful. It was a mythic reality, which is a super reality, a reality that could be mobilized, weaponized, if need be, to accomplish a purpose. It wasn't lying, exactly. It was amplification, broadcasting for deep penetration.

To be sure, Reagan lacked experience as a broadcaster, but then broadcast radio was still so new that very few of his peers had much more experience than he. What he did possess was the combination of a resonant "radio voice" and an extraordinary imagination, one that was already adept at mythologizing and magnifying experience. He announced football games with such skill, relish, and artful embellishment that listeners

really did feel they were present. Moreover, he made an important discovery. Given the script of a commercial to read on air, he learned always
to memorize the opening line. Many who worked with Reagan in radio
and movies noted his remarkable ability to quickly memorize material.
He discovered that if he did this, everything else he read from the script
would emerge as if spontaneously, from his heart. It sounded utterly natural, even though it was a combination of memory and reading.

After two years at WOC, he moved up to another Palmer-owned station, WHO in Des Moines, Iowa's capital. It was not only a high-wattage,
clear-channel station, but also an NBC affiliate, which meant it was
national. In the middle of the Great Depression, Ronald Reagan was suddenly earning an enviable salary recreating for a large radio audience Big
Ten football games and Chicago Cubs baseball games.

But what of his dreams of being an actor on Broadway or in the movies? Had he lost that ambition?

The truth was that Ronald Reagan didn't need ambition—not when
he had the manifest destiny of God's plan on his side. Besides, being a
professional radio sportscaster *was* his dream. It was a bigger dream than
owning a high-class shoe store. It was, in fact, the "American Dream"—or
at least a piece of it—just as it has always been defined by Thomas Jefferson's felicitous phrase, *the pursuit of happiness.* For Ronald Reagan at age
twenty-five, that pursuit looked to be over and won. He was happy. By all
accounts, he felt fulfilled by a career as a radio sportscaster.

Young Reagan's six grueling seasons as a lifeguard proved that he
could work hard, but his work ethic did not encompass any of the boundless dreams so often found in youth. The gibe "he's got a face for radio" was
originally applied to anyone in radio who lacked the good looks to make
the transition to film. But Reagan, who had a voice for radio, also clearly
had a face for film. He was just over six feet tall, broad-shouldered, with
an enviable head of hair and Irish-blue eyes, as well as a most disarming
midwestern syncopation in his rhythmic vocal delivery. Maybe Homer
himself possessed some ancient Greek equivalent of Reagan's manner of
speech. Reagan had the imagination, the sense of what people wanted to
hear and needed to hear, and he possessed the voice, rhythm, and accent to
deliver it with nothing less than intense believability.

Right now, what sports-minded radio listeners needed to believe
was that they were not sitting at a bar or in their home's parlor listening
to a radio but were at the game, seeing it with their own eyes, hearing it
with their own ears. Was this enough for Ronald Reagan? He had already
enjoyed acting as an avocation. He was a quick study, with an amazing
ability to learn lines, and he could spit back those lines with an easy conviction. His lifeguard's body was toned and attractive, and his face was

easy to look at. When would a new and more expansive vision of his providential destiny dawn on him?

He began at Davenport's WOC in 1932, broadcasting under those call letters for two years until he transferred to the Palmer NBC affiliate WHO in Des Moines. He was quickly gaining professional traction for his vivid recreations of Chicago Cubs baseball as well as Big Ten football games. His friend and biographer Lou Cannon wrote that Reagan dreamed "of an acting career" even as he continued to enjoy life as a radio sportscaster. If he was indeed dreaming, his dreams must not have been terribly compelling. He hardly risked anything on a bid to get into the movies. On the contrary, he carefully hedged his bet. Cannon wrote that Reagan deliberately "came up with a plan that would allow him to test the waters in Hollywood without cutting his ties to WHO."[2]

In 1937, five full years after he broke into radio sports announcing, WHO sent him to Southern California to cover Cubs spring training there. With his cross-country trip paid for by WHO, he made time for a side trip to an LA-based agent's office. He wanted to throw his hat into the Hollywood ring, though he was by no means sure where to aim it. Through another stroke of good luck that only added to his sense of living God's plan, he arrived in Hollywood and at this particular agency precisely at the moment when the signed-up star for a forthcoming Warner Bros. film had been killed in a car accident. Tough luck for him but a jackpot—or perhaps a godsend—for Ronald Reagan. Whatever else he saw in Reagan, the agent could not miss the fact that the newcomer not only resembled the departed leading man but also was, in actual real life, just what the role called for. *Love Is on the Air* was all about a radio broadcaster who falls afoul of a corrupt mayor and ends up being demoted to host of a kiddie show. What indeed were the odds that a hopeful actor, already a broadcast veteran with a Northwestern University second-place acting award in his hip pocket, not only looked like the dead man who had been signed up for a role in a picture about to start shooting but also possessed literal working knowledge of the role?

Reagan tested for the part and got it—plus a seven-year, $200-a-week contract. This was the top starting salary for a contract player! He wasn't the male equivalent of Esther Victoria Blodgett in *A Star Is Born*. But he was Ronald Reagan in *A Journeyman Is Born*. This was the start of a twenty-year career as what he good-naturedly called himself, "the Errol Flynn of the B's."

Even as he was easing his way into films and out of radio, Reagan began developing another career. On March 18, 1935, he had enrolled in a series of home-study Army Extension Courses. After he completed fourteen of the courses, he enlisted in the Army Reserve on April 29, 1937, as a private, assigned to Troop B, 322nd Cavalry at Des Moines. In short order, on May 25, 1937, he was jumped to second lieutenant in the Officers Reserve Corps of the Cavalry. When he moved to Hollywood, he was assigned to the 323rd Cavalry on June 18, 1937.[3] None of this, however, interfered with his fledgling film career.

His debut in *Love Is on the Air* failed to snag him the lead in a far more important 1938 George Cukor film—that went to Cary Grant, playing opposite Katharine Hepburn—but the title of that near miss, *Holiday*, aptly describes the spirit in which Reagan began a prolific screen career that would run to 53 films. For Reagan, Hollywood was a dream, albeit of definitely limited dimensions. Tinsel Town needed journeyman players even more than it needed a stable of genuine movie stars. Reagan fared much better than the legions of young hopefuls who ended up in the discard pile along the Boulevard of Broken Dreams. He was a success—though not a runaway success. He was positioned to earn a handsome, though hardly spectacular, living and even to build a solid, though not towering, fan base. He had succeeded where his father had failed. He owned the equivalent of Illinois' biggest, fanciest, most dazzling shoe store—outside of Chicago.

For a long time, probably the full two decades of his Hollywood run, this was enough. For Ronald Reagan, acting was a holiday that paid. But it was also much more. If not always fully consciously but certainly subliminally, Reagan came to understand precisely what Hollywood was: a mythology factory, turning American dreams into a business. And that was just fine with him. On the spectrum of movie acting, Reagan was between movie star and shoe store proprietor, yet always leaning a tad closer to the shoe store. Still, the mythic aspect of his new trade came naturally to him, and acting—as he understood it, more craft than art—came easily to him. And, for a child whose father was never a good provider, a steady income was pretty much all that he desired.

His breakthrough film, *Knute Rockne—All American* (1940), was a hearty distillation of mythmaking. It elevated to pop-culture Olympus the figure of Notre Dame's legendary football coach, played by Pat O'Brien, who made sure that his new pal and fellow Irishman Ronald Reagan copped the small but prominent role of George Gipp, a rising football star cut down by virulent viral pneumonia. It was a touching role, and, brief though it was, Reagan made the most of it, delivering his one big line memorably. "Someday, when things are tough," he gasps out to Rockne from his deathbed, "maybe you can ask the boys to go in there and win just once for the Gipper." Years later, in presidential politics, Reagan embraced "the Gipper" as a nickname. Reporters gobbled it up.

In fact, Reagan talked less about playing the Gipper than he reminisced about *King's Row* (1942), the film he believed (with arguable justification) featured his best acting. After suffering an accident working on the railroad, poor Drake McHugh awakens from anesthesia to discover that his legs have been amputated by a sadistic surgeon. "Where's the rest of me?" is the chilling line he delivers, and he even resurrected it as the title of the 1965 autobiography he coauthored to further his 1966 gubernatorial campaign. But for sheer political legend-making, McHugh couldn't hold a candle to the Gipper, a fragment of myth Reagan and the press snatched right off the Hollywood assembly line.

* * *

Donald Trump was born thirty-five years after Ronald Reagan and far from Hollywood, in the affluent but not especially stylish Jamaica Estates neighborhood of Queens, at the time the whitest of the five New York City boroughs. Unlike Reagan, he seems never to have thought of anything other than following in the footsteps of his father, Fred, to make a career as a real estate developer. It turned out, however, that his talent lay less in real estate *per se* than in the branding that often went along with it. Officially a real estate developer, he was, in fact, a brand developer, and his brand was success as defined by the flaunting of gaudy wealth and playboy celebrity. In this, the early Trumpian mythologizing was of a very different stripe from that of Ronald Reagan. Where Reagan was a Horatio Alger character with a dash of Western rancher, Trump was, well, Donald Trump with a pinch of Hugh Hefner.

In 1987, Tony Schwartz ghostwrote Trump's *The Art of the Deal,* which developed and refined Trump's more mature brand as a dealmaker of mythic—as in Olympian Zeus—proportions. Again, it would seem a far cry from Reagan, yet in an early review of *The Art of the Deal,* Christopher Lehmann-Haupt, writing for the *New York Times,* proclaimed, "He makes me believe in the American Dream again." In fact, it was doubtless Schwartz's writing that rekindled Lehmann-Haupt's dying vision of the American Dream. The reality of Trump's real estate career and business career was marked by far more bad or downright disastrous deals than by profitable ones. Calling himself the "King of Debt," he borrowed extravagantly and was multiply bankrupted in the infamous collapse of his Atlantic City gambling empire.

No matter. When myth meets reality, myth generally prevails. The titular if not the actual author of *The Art of the Deal* was recruited in 2004 by British-born reality TV producer Mark Burnett to be the hub around which his latest confection *The Apprentice* would spin. In this show, Burnett, through Trump, fused the fiction of an invulnerable dealmaker brand with the national mythology of the American Dream in a show featuring aspiring young businesspeople competing with one another to execute tasks Trump (putatively) set for them. "Mr. Trump" then summoned the contestants to "the Board Room" where he passed judgment upon them, whittling down the field of contestants one by one (always with the iconic curse, "You're fired!") until, at the end of the season, just one was left standing.

The Apprentice, which ran from 2004 to 2017, was a so-called reality show that was, in fact, a blend of carefully scripted fiction and American popular mythology, mixing Horatio Alger this time with Gordon Gecko. The show's success, however, was quantifiable in very real cash. While many of Trump's other ventures stalled, crashed, and burned, the TV show not only kept him aloft but made him a fortune—and positioned him in America's popular consciousness for his winning presidential run.

*   *   *

Playing uniquely American heroes, incarnations of and variations on the American Dream, was indispensable to winning the presidency for both Trump and Reagan. Now, when Ronald Reagan ran for president, he did so at the end of the long era in which overseas military service was virtually a prerequisite for office. As a U.S. Army Cavalry reservist, Second Lieutenant Reagan was called to active duty on April 19, 1942, a few months after Pearl Harbor. Thanks to his severe nearsightedness, however, he was classified for limited service, which barred him from serving overseas. It was far from glamorous work and hardly the stuff of mythology. He was assigned first as liaison officer of the Port and Transportation Office of the San Francisco Port of Embarkation at Fort Mason, California. The U.S. Army Air Forces requested that he apply for a transfer from the Cavalry to the AAF on May 15, 1942. After the transfer was approved on June 9, 1942, he was reassigned to AAF Public Relations and subsequently to the 1st Motion Picture Unit in Culver City, California. Reagan was promoted to First Lieutenant on January 14, 1943, and was sent to the Provisional Task Force Show Unit of *This Is the Army,* a musical comedy morale-booster film adaption of an Irving Berlin Broadway show. It was a major production, and Reagan shared topline billing with Joan Leslie and leading song-and-dance man George Murphy.

Murphy, nine years Reagan's senior, was a big-budget movie star, with whom Reagan developed a cordial relationship. Indeed, Reagan later dubbed him "John the Baptist" because he was an inspiration and even model for his own entry into politics, pioneering the notion that an actor could and even should enter the political arena. In 1944, Murphy succeeded Jimmy Cagney as president of the powerful Screen Actors Guild (SAG), serving until 1946. In 1947, Reagan would succeed Murphy's successor,

Robert Montgomery, in that office, serving until 1952 and returning for one year in 1959. Murphy retired from acting in 1952 and joined the leadership of the California Republican Party, having already directed planning for the entertainment at the upcoming Eisenhower-Nixon inauguration. (Reagan at this time was still a Democrat.) In 1964, Murphy defeated Democrat Pierre Salinger for the U.S. Senate. The late JFK's former press secretary, Salinger had been appointed by Lyndon Johnson to serve the remainder of Democrat Clair Engle's senatorial term, Engle having died in office, from cancer.

In a demonstration of bipartisanship almost impossible to imagine today, the defeated Salinger resigned his seat two days early, so that Democratic governor Pat Brown could appoint Republican Murphy to serve out the last forty-eight hours of his term, thereby enabling California to retain a senior Senate seat. Salinger and Brown put their state ahead of their party. As for Murphy, while he was certainly a precedent-setting model for Reagan, he was hardly an exemplar of conservatism. He voted in favor of the Voting Rights Act of 1965, voted for the confirmation of Associate Justice Thurgood Marshall, and voted for the Civil Rights Act of 1968. In 1966, he was also a supporter of U.S. Representative Howard "Bo" Calloway, who was running for governor of Georgia—the first GOP candidate for that office since Reconstruction. Although Calloway outpolled segregationist opponent Democrat Lester Maddox, he received a plurality and not a majority, which, by Georgia law, threw the election to the state legislature. The Democratic super majority in that body overrode the popular vote and made Maddox governor. Thus, Murphy was, de facto, no proponent of the so-called Southern Strategy, which was on the cusp of emerging. In the 1968 Nixon presidential campaign, the Southern Strategy empowered the GOP conservative wing to support white supremacy in the South as a means of converting southern Democrats (especially the Dixiecrat wing of that party) to vote for Republican candidates who generally continued to stand against civil rights policies and legislation. Richard Nixon and then Ronald Reagan became early beneficiaries of the strategy. For what shall it profit a man, if he shall gain the whole world, and lose his own soul? Clearly, he wins the presidency.

After Reagan had finished his work on *This Is the Army,* he returned to the 1st Motion Picture Unit and, on July 22, 1943, was promoted to captain. He was sent to temporary duty in New York City in January 1944 to participate in the opening of the sixth War Loan Drive, returning to California in November, where he was assigned to the 18th AAF Base Unit in Culver City. Reagan was separated from active duty on December 9, the war having ended in September.

Ronald Reagan's war was fought on a soundstage, and his first and second marriages were created there as well. He met Jane Wyman during the filming of *Brother Rat* (1938) and married her on January 26, 1940. The studio promoted them as Hollywood's "ideal couple." The thing is, Wyman's film career soared during the war years as Reagan's was interrupted and curtailed. To be sure, he made plenty of movies during the war. Working out of the Hal Roach Studios at 8822 Washington Boulevard in Culver City, the 1st Motion Picture Unit and the 18th Army Air Forces Base Unit, in which Captain Reagan served as Personnel Officer, Post Adjutant, and Executive Officer, churned out more than 400 training films for the Army Air Forces. Reagan appeared in or narrated many of them. He also starred in a number of theatrically released propaganda and morale-boosting films. Arguably, the likes of *For God and Country*, *This Is the Army*, *Target Tokyo* (all 1943), *The Fight for the Sky*, *The Stilwell Road*, and *Wings for This Man* (all 1945), among others, served to associate his image and voice with the heroic aspects of the war, but training shorts with titles like *Recognition of the Japanese Zero Fighter* and *Cadet Classification* and the like did nothing for his career, either in film or, later, in politics.

Reagan did complete *King's Row* in 1942, before his military service claimed most of his time. He justifiably regarded it as the height of his acting career. His postwar films fell at the B-picture end of the spectrum, however. *Bedtime for Bonzo* was a 1951 box office success, but it was hardly made of the same stuff as *King's Row*. Reagan played a psychology professor who sets out to resolve the old nature-versus-nurture debate by endeavoring to teach morals to Bonzo, a chimp. "If you can stomach all this," the *Washington Post* reviewer opined, "you'll find some giggles in this farce" but "Ronald Reagan, as the naive professor of things mental, must have felt like the world's sappiest straight man playing this silly role, and the others [in the movie] aren't much better off."[4] Later, in 1980, when Reagan was emerging as the GOP presidential frontrunner, *Bedtime for Bonzo* came back to nibble at the margins of the candidate's well-crafted mythology. The dominator of late-night TV, Johnny Carson's *The Tonight Show* was produced by Fred de Cordova, who had directed Reagan in *Bedtime*! Carson had high time with this, and the Democrats displayed advertising posters from the film at their August convention. Soon, Bonzo film posters began appearing on t-shirts, belts, belt buckles, suspenders, baseball caps, and an array of novelty items. Bonzo became the easy basis of many political cartoons, *People* magazine ran a two-page spread on the chimp (long deceased by this time), even as entrepreneurs produced Bonzo sleeping bags and a line of children's clothing. There was talk of a syndicated Bonzo comic strip featuring "Bonzo as a wisdom-dispensing 'elder stateschimp,' a kind of cross between Henry Kissinger and Will Rogers."[5]

Just as well for both Kissinger and Reagan, the comic strip never materialized (though both the popular "Calvin and Hobbes" and "Bloom County" strips featured Bonzo references[6]), but one wonders if Reagan himself appreciated the irony in the fact that the film's screenwriters, Ted Berman and Rafe Blau, originally wanted Cary Grant to play Gonzo's professorial mentor. "We were not that happy that Reagan got the part," Blau told an interviewer in 1980. "He was never a leading man type." Berkman explained, "We were hoping to get Cary Grant. It would have been a more suave, elegant comedy. But then we probably wouldn't have been here—or Cary Grant would be president."[7] Reagan surely must have recalled that Grant, not himself, was tapped for *Holiday,* the big 1938 Columbia Pictures film he coveted as a quick route to leading-man status.

* * *

Reagan continued in the U.S. Army Reserves until his commission automatically expired on April 1, 1953. It had been an honorable service and, in truth, the military found the best use to which Reagan's gifts could have been put in the war effort. Moreover, for a rising film actor, it was a genuine patriotic sacrifice and far more than any service Donald Trump ever rendered his country.

Trump came of age during the Vietnam War, and his father, developer and landlord Fred C. Trump, reportedly prevailed upon one of his commercial tenants, podiatrist Dr. Larry Braunstein, to diagnose his son with bone spurs in his heels to secure a medical exemption from the draft. According to Elysa Braunstein, the late doctor's daughter, obliging the senior Trump by delivering the desired diagnosis secured her father "access to Fred Trump. If there was anything wrong in the building [in which Braunstein had his office], my dad would call and [Fred] Trump would take care of it immediately. That was the small favor he got." A 2018 *New York Times* story reports that Elysa Bernstein "said the implication from her father was that Mr. Trump did not have a disqualifying foot ailment. 'But did he examine him? I don't know,' she said." Donald Trump himself told the *Times* in 2016 that "a doctor provided 'a very strong letter' about the bone spurs in his heels, which he then presented to draft officials."[8] Before the House Oversight Committee, Trump's former lawyer, factotum, and "fixer" Michael Cohen testified that "Mr. Trump claimed (his medical deferment) was because of a bone spur, but when I asked for medical records, he gave me none and said there was no surgery." Cohen told the committee that Trump "finished the conversation with the following comment: 'You think I'm stupid, I wasn't going to Vietnam.'" The medical excuse was just one of five draft deferments Donald Trump received during the Vietnam War, the other four being student deferments that many college kids received.[9]

Like Reagan, Trump was the beneficiary of some very good luck. (Or was it all part of God's plan?) It was Trump's good fortune to have escaped military service in an enduringly unpopular war and to run for president at a time when the electorate no longer deemed military service a pre-requisite to candidacy. And yet candidate Donald Trump was not will-ing to forgo some claim to a military record. He denounced Senator John McCain, a decorated naval aviator who had spent years in a Hanoi POW camp, as no "war hero. He's a war hero because he was captured. I like peo-ple that weren't captured." Shortly after this, he told Michael D'Antonio, who interviewed him for what was then his forthcoming *Never Enough: Donald Trump and the Pursuit of Success*, that he "always felt that he was in the military" because he had attended New York Military Academy, a military-themed prep school. Trump's authoritarian father, despairing of his inability to discipline his son, had sent him there in the hope of bring-ing him to heel. Trump told D'Antonio that the school gave him "more training militarily than a lot of the guys that go into the military."[10] If this seems quite a stretch, those with long memories may remember that, in a 1997 interview with radio shock jock Howard Stern, Trump laid claim to having been a "brave soldier." On what basis? For avoiding STDs during his bachelor years in the late '90s, he explained. "It's amazing, I can't even believe it. I've been so lucky in terms of that whole world, it is a dangerous world out there. It's like Vietnam, sort of. It is my personal Vietnam. I feel like a great and very brave soldier."[11]

Trump, of course, was not the first modern presidential candidate who sought to inflate a thin military record. LBJ proudly wore a minia-ture battle ribbon version of the Silver Star he was awarded in 1942 for evidencing "coolness" on a B-26 flight that was "intercepted by eight hos-tile fighters." A lieutenant commander in the U.S. Navy, the future presi-dent was part of a three-man survey crew assigned to find under-reported problems facing U.S. forces in the Pacific. He volunteered to fly with a B-26 crew on a hazardous bombing mission. Surviving crew members later revealed that the plane developed mechanical trouble before reaching its target and never had come under fire. No other crew member was deco-rated. The award was "the outcome of a deal with Gen MacArthur, under which Johnson was honoured in return for a pledge 'that he would lobby the president, FDR, to provide greater resources for the southwest Pacific theatre.'"[12] To his credit, Reagan never sought to inflate or exploit his mil-itary service, but he unquestionably relished his presidential role as com-mander in chief, and he was not above creating an opportunistic mini-war.

On October 23, 1983, over two hundred U.S. Marines were killed in their sleep when a truck loaded with 25,000 pounds of TNT was driven into the headquarters of the U.S. and French contingent of the Multinational

Force (MNF) stationed in Beirut, Lebanon, during the Lebanese Civil War of 1975–1992. This disaster brought a firestorm of criticism upon Reagan and military planners. It also prompted him to withdraw American forces from Lebanon, a move that brought accusations, even from his own party, of executing a cut-and-run policy. Again, to his credit, when a commission led by retired admiral Robert L.J. Long produced in 1984 a highly critical report on the Beirut truck bombing, President Reagan responded, "If there is to be blame, it properly rests here in this office and with this President. I accept responsibility for the bad as well as the good."[13]

Yet just two days after the bombing, Reagan authorized the invasion of the West Indies island nation of Grenada. Cuban troops had been sent to the diminutive country (at the time populated by some 110,000 souls) at the request of the recently installed anti–American dictatorship there. Reagan decided to "liberate" Grenada and, in so doing, to rescue the approximately 1,000 U.S. citizens there, mainly students at a local medical school. Dubbed Operation Urgent Fury, the invasion force consisted of a naval battle group (one landing ship, one aircraft carrier, three destroyers, two frigates, and an ammunition ship) with two Marine amphibious units, two army Ranger battalions, a brigade of the 82nd Airborne Division, and special ops units. Supported from the air by 27 F-14A Tomcats, U.S. troop strength was 7,300 men.

They landed on a Grenada beach on October 25, 1983, entirely unopposed. Advancing inland, the invaders encountered about 2,500 members of the People's Revolutionary Army, 600 Guatemalan regulars, and 800 Cuban military construction personnel. These forces were rapidly neutralized; the airport was seized; and the government radio station, Radio Free Grenada, was destroyed. The U.S. nationals were rescued and evacuated, and Grenada was declared to be totally under U.S. military control by October 28. American losses were eighteen U.S. service members killed. Grenadian forces lost twenty-five killed, and the Cubans forty-five. (Also present were 49 Soviet troops, 16 East German troops, 14 Bulgarian troops, and even three or four from Libya.)

Whatever its motivation, Operation Urgent Fury, successful though it was, was also marred by embarrassing snafus, the most serious of which was a major failure of communications due to the lack of interoperable radios used by different elements of forces. The legality of the invasion was questioned, and the UN General Assembly adopted on November 2, 1983, by a 108 to 9 vote, Resolution 38/7, which "deeply deplores the armed intervention in Grenada, which constitutes a flagrant violation of international law and of the independence, sovereignty and territorial integrity of that State." President Reagan commented that the resolution "didn't upset my breakfast at all."[14]

*   *   *

Although Captain Ronald Reagan had been recommended for promotion to major on February 2, 1945, the recommendation was disapproved, almost certainly because he had no combat experience. This does not mean that Reagan escaped World War II unscathed. On balance, his acting career was sidelined, never to recover. Worse, his declining star was counterpointed to the rising star of his wife Jane Wyman. Although her husband was never far away, he was in active service and not regularly at home. For her part, Wyman was now playing in one big film after another. *The Lost Weekend* won an Academy Award as did its star, Ray Milland, as the alcoholic would-be writer Don Burnham. While Wyman, playing Burnham's long-suffering sweetheart, was not nominated for an Oscar, she did receive much critical acclaim. It was from this high that she went into her next film, *The Yearling*, which demanded her undivided concentration. Reagan knew when he was unwanted and holed up, alone, in the couple's Lake Arrowhead cottage.

Still, Reagan managed to eke out the last ounces of optimism left in him. He despaired of his acting career but believed his marriage to Jane Wyman was still strong. God, however, seemed to smile less and less upon him. The usually robust Reagan suddenly fell ill with viral pneumonia. It could hardly have escaped him that this was the very disease that killed the hale and hearty young George Gipp. An actor committed to her art in a way that the more facile Reagan never was or could have been, Wyman worked herself to exhaustion even after she became pregnant. While the ailing Reagan had to be transported to Cedars of Lebanon Hospital (today Cedars-Sinai Hospital) by ambulance and quickly became so critically ill that "my next of kin were being notified that the hospital might be my last address," Wyman was likewise brought by ambulance to the hospital. Her baby was about to be born prematurely, but the early labor ended in a miscarriage. Reagan, semi-conscious, semi-delirious, had no idea that this had happened. He may well have been aware, however, that his wife, as usual, was absent. He recounted in *Where's the Rest of Me?* that one night his fever "reached a new high."

> Finally I decided I'd be more comfortable not breathing. I don't know what time of night it was when I told the nurse I was too tired to breathe anymore. I wish I knew who she was—God bless her. There in the dark she leaned over me, coaxing me to take a breath. "Now let it out," she'd say. "Come on now, breathe in once more."
>
> This went on, over and over, with her arguing me into another breath when all I wanted was to rest and stop making the effort. Wherever she is and whether she remembers our midnight contest or not, I don't suppose I'll ever know. But the memory is vivid to me.[15]

With a career in collapse, he himself balanced precariously on the knife edge between life and death, and his own wife once again unavailable to him, Reagan remembered most powerfully the woman who saved his life, in the dark night, the woman who would not let him go, even as he was succumbing both to a viral infection and his own strange inability to fight, fight, fight for himself. Like George Gipp, he would have slipped away, were it not for this strong and tender woman.

It was at a very low ebb—career fading away, weak from illness, learning that the child he and Jane had expected was now dead—that the failing marriage finally failed. "Our marriage produced two wonderful children, Maureen and Michael," Reagan wrote in *An American Life*, his later autobiography, "but it didn't work out, and in 1948 we were divorced."[16] This terse sentence contains the only mention of Jane Wyman in that entire second autobiography.

The multiple blows of 1948 were the first bumps in Ronald Reagan's providential pathway. Four profoundly depressed years would grind by before he met another actress, Nancy Davis, who did what Jane Wyman did not. She gave up her career to serve his. They married in 1952, and the Reagan optimism reemerged. Yet the movies and the movie audiences had passed him by during the war years, and they were not coming back. Nancy Davis, whose ambitious nature stood in contrast to Reagan's resigned passivity, now took over. If his own drive to succeed no longer came from him, Nancy was willing to dole out to her husband ambition by the fistful from her own ample reserves. Under her influence, with her encouragement, and in almost grudging response to her relentless prodding, Reagan battled Warner's for coveted roles. He lost the battles, and, with that, left the studio that had made him but that was no longer much interested in him.

CHAPTER 5

"A Near Hopeless Hemophiliac Liberal"

Jane Wyman and Ronald Reagan were Hollywood actors and would never have encountered one another, let alone married, were it not for their living and working in Hollywood making pictures. They met on the set of *Brother Rat* (1938), in which they co-starred, and which proved sufficiently successful to spawn a sequel, *Brother Rat and a Baby* (1940). Between these two productions, they became engaged and, on January 26, 1940, married at Wee Kirk o' the Heather, erected between 1929 and 1930 on the grounds of Forest Lawn Cemetery in Glendale, California, on the pattern of a seventeenth-century village church at Glencairn, Scotland. The copy is known today as the Chapel of the Stars, not so much for the Reagan-Wyman wedding as for the funeral services of the likes of Jean Harlow, Carole Lombard, Clark Gable, and others. (In 1940, another Wee Kirk o' the Heather was built in Las Vegas, not to bury people but to marry them in a hurry.)

Reagan's 1940 marriage was his first and Wyman's third. The putative cause for their divorce, filed for in 1948 and finalized in 1949, was Wyman's having fallen in love with actor Lew Ayres, her costar in *Johnny Belinda* (1948). She played a deaf-mute rape victim in that movie, which catapulted her from the B-picture berth she shared with Reagan to the A-star pantheon of Oscar-winning actors. It was indeed a bravura performance, in which she did not utter a single line. The affair with Ayres proved short-lived, and Wyman herself, who went on to a fourth marriage—to Hollywood composer and bandleader Frederick Karger—may have given a more compelling reason for her break with Reagan than the Ayres affair: "Some women just aren't the marrying kind—or anyway, not the permanent marrying kind, and I'm one of them."[1] Indeed, the marriage to Karger lasted just two years (1952–1954), after which she never remarried.

It is also true that Reagan's deep involvement in the Screen Actors Guild (SAG) became a consuming passion for him. He was elected its president in November 1947 and served to November 1952, returning in November 1959 and serving through June 12, 1960. Wyman reportedly felt both neglected and bored, and she did explicitly cite Reagan's preoccupation with his union duties as the cause of his neglect. The death of their second daughter, Christine, who died on June 26, 1947, after having been born prematurely, likely added to the stress on their union. Finally, Reagan was likely envious of his wife's Oscar-worthy success in *Johnny Belinda,* which left him in the B-player dust.

Ironically, perhaps, Wyman herself casually remarked that the dissolution of the marriage was related to political differences. She was a lifelong registered Republican, he a Democrat.[2] In fact, well before he met Wyman, Reagan was becoming increasingly interested in politics as a committed Democrat and an avid New Dealer, for whom Franklin Delano Roosevelt was "a true hero."[3] Certainly, he must have recognized in FDR a master of personal mythology, whose commanding presence was pulling the nation through (if not quite out of) the Great Depression and would lead the United States—and its allies—to victory in World War II. He did this, of course, while making everyone forget that polio[4] had deprived him of the use of his legs. (In his only movie role that even approached Wyman's *Johnny Belinda* performance in quality, as double-amputee Drake McHugh in *King's Row* [1942], Reagan delivered his most memorable line: "Where's the rest of me?")

Long after the bitterness of the divorce had left them both, Jane Wyman, who almost never spoke publicly about Reagan—"It's bad taste to talk about ex-husbands and ex-wives. Also, I don't know a damn thing about politics"—observed that her ex had always been "more interested in politics than anything else."[5] Without question, during the Depression, World War II, and its immediate aftermath, Ronald Reagan not only became increasingly attracted to politics but also really did believe that government could solve all the nation's problems. He also shared the working man's distrust of big business. Later, after transferring allegiance to the GOP, Reagan mocked his earlier self as "a near hopeless hemophiliac liberal."[6]

Reagan's inexorable transition to the GOP began after he recoiled from a political naivete that had unwittingly involved him in organizations with distinct Communist affiliations while he served as Screen Actors Guild (SAG) president (1947–1952 and 1959–1960). As it turned out, had it not been for Communism, Reagan would likely never have met his next wife. As he recounts in his first autobiography, *Where's the Rest of Me?* (1965), the powerful director Mervyn Le Roy phoned him one afternoon. The actor's first impulse was a thrill of great expectation. With his postwar career seriously slumping, there flashed before him the sudden prospect that this director was "paging me for one of the many fine pictures he did so well." It soon became apparent, however, that he "was calling in behalf of a young lady under contract to MGM, who was working on his picture. (It should happen to me.) It seems that this young hopeful, Nancy Davis by name, was very much distressed because her name kept showing up on the rosters of Communist front organizations, affixed to petitions of the same coloration, and her mail frequently included notices of meetings she had no desire to attend, and accounts of these meetings as covered by the *Daily Worker*. Mervyn wanted me to call the young lady and have a talk with her about this problem." Telling "Mervyn" that he'd "take care of it," Reagan "made the switch from Ronald Reagan, actor, regretfully to Ronald Reagan, SAG president." He stopped at the Guild office and "did a little quick checking." Discovering "nothing detrimental to her," he called "Mervyn and told him ... to assure the young lady she had nothing to worry about." But Le Roy called back. "It seems the young lady was not satisfied with the secondhand report: please, wouldn't I call her and take her to lunch or dinner, and quiet her fears?" Reagan mused: "I don't know why it took all of this to get me to call an unknown girl. She surely couldn't be repulsive and on the contract list at MGM."[7]

On November 15, 1949, Reagan made a call inviting Nancy Davis to dinner. Expecting a "fan magazine version of a starlet," he was surprised to see a "small, slender lady with dark hair and a wide-spaced pair of hazel eyes that looked right at you and made you look back." En route to the restaurant, Reagan suggested that the most expeditious way to purge her name from "those 'bleeding hearts' lists" was to ask the MGM publicity department for a new name. "'But Nancy Davis is my name,'" she replied. Deeply steeped in Hollywood, Reagan assumed she was using a name the studio had supplied. The dinner meeting quickly extended into a date—attending Sophie Tucker's opening night at Ciro's—and the two stayed out until three in the morning.

Ronald Reagan avidly pursued the issue of her name and quickly discovered she had been confused with another actress of the same name. At the same time, however, his pursuit of her was desultory. It was off and on, and she was only one of several women Reagan dated. Yet there was enough there to make for good reading in the gossip columns. One account played up a man-bites-dog angle, calling the budding Reagan-Davis relationship "the romance of a couple who have no vices."[8] It took three years before marriage was on the table. "The truth is, I did everything wrong, dating her off and on, continuing to volunteer for every Guild trip to New York—in short, doing everything which could have lost her if Someone up there hadn't been looking after me."[9] The "truth" was that Reagan was dating other women, but the myth he himself projected in his first autobiography was the familiar theme of divine providence.

If God had a plan for him, He had chosen the right instrument in Nancy Davis. Whereas Jane Wyman saw her husband's attraction to politics as a distraction from her even as she overtook him on the silver screen, Davis gladly sacrificed her own embryonic acting career not only to encourage Reagan's political aspirations but—often—to supply the ambition he himself lacked to achieve them.

So, three years after their first dinner together, Ron and Nancy discussed marriage in a booth at Chasen's Beverly Hills restaurant. It was right there and then that they decided to take the plunge and, on March 4, 1952, were wed at the Little Brown Church, in the San Fernando Valley, putting the ceremony at arm's length from the Hollywood press. Leading man William Holden and his actress-wife Ardis Ankerson (stage name Brenda Marshall) were the only guests. Nancy was almost certainly pregnant with Patricia Ann Reagan (alias Patti Davis), who was born less than eight months after the ceremony.[10]

*   *   *

"At the end of World War II, I was a New Dealer to the core," Ronald Reagan wrote in his second autobiography, published in 1990. He confessed to believing "government could solve all our postwar problems just as it had ended the Depression and won the war. I didn't trust big business. I thought government, not private companies, should own our big public utilities; if there wasn't enough housing to shelter the American people, I thought government should build it; if we needed better medical care, the answer was socialized medicine." When his brother, Neil—already having defected to the GOP—"complained about the growth of government[,] claimed Washington was trying to take over everything in the American economy from the railroads to the corner store, and said we couldn't trust our wartime ally, Russia, any longer," Reagan shot back that he "was just spouting Republican propaganda."[11]

As Reagan described himself, he was not just a Democrat, but a leftist liberal activist. "What troubled me most was what I saw as the rise of fascism in our country, the very thing we had fought to obliterate. Scores of new veterans' groups had sprouted up around the country and were trying to peddle some of the same venom of fascist bigotry that we had just defeated in the war." If anything, Reagan's stance sounds quite admirable, but he himself denigrated the cause and, even more, denigrated himself. "In Hollywood, as I've often said, if you don't sing or dance, you end up as an after-dinner speaker. And almost before I knew it, I was speaking out against the rise of neofascism in America. I joined just about any organization I could find that guaranteed to save the world, like the United World Federalists and American Veterans Committee, which got me with their slogan: 'A Citizen First, a Veteran Afterward.' I really wanted a better world and I think I thought what I was saying would help bring it about."[12] He later admitted that, during the first months after the war, when he was decrying the rise of "neofascism" in the United States, he was "a favorite of the Hollywood Communists," even calling himself "their boy."[13]

With all this self-loathing, Reagan here falls on his sword, owning up not merely to naivete but depicting himself as something of a needy stick figure with no mind of his own. He mentions that his pastor persuaded him that his speech about neofascism "would be even better if you also mentioned that if Communism ever looked like a threat, you'd be just as opposed to it as you are to fascism." Although Reagan responded that he "hadn't given much thought to the threat of Communism," he believed the pastor's suggestion would improve the speech, so he decided to include it. He thus added what he called his "new line" at the conclusion of his speech—as if he were touching up a shooting script: "I've talked about the continuing threat of fascism in the postwar world, but there's another 'ism,' Communism, and if I ever find evidence that Communism represents a threat to all that we believe in and stand for, I'll speak out just as harshly against Communism as I have fascism."

Instead of being greeted by the applause his straight antifascism "script" had always elicited, he "walked off the stage—to a dead silence."

> A few days later, I received a letter from a woman who said she'd been in the audience that night. "I have been disturbed for quite some time," she said, "suspecting there is something sinister happening in that organization that I don't like." Then she added: "I'm sure you noticed the reaction to your last paragraph when you mentioned Communism. I hope you recognize what that means. I think the group is becoming a front for Communists. I just wanted you to know that that settled it for me. I resigned from the organization the next day." Thanks to my minister and that lady, I began to wake up to the real world and what was going on in my own business, the motion picture industry.[14]

With that, an anti–Communist was born and a liberal Democrat at least began to die—albeit very slowly.

The early postwar period saw sometimes violent struggles between members of rival unions involved in the multifarious aspects of movie production. Under Reagan, SAG endeavored to act as a neutral party in resolving some of the disputes. Reagan does not detail this process in either his early or late memoir, but he notes that SAG brought an end to the war ("we beat 'em") in February 1947. In his 1990 memoir he recalled:

> Later, several members of the Communist Party in Hollywood who had been involved in the attempted takeover went public and described in intimate

detail how Moscow was trying to take over the picture business. The California Senate Fact-Finding Committee on Un-American Activities, after a lengthy inquiry, confirmed that the strike was part of a Soviet effort to gain control over Hollywood and the content of its films. Although the principal leader of the strike told Congress that he had never been a Communist, investigators produced evidence that they said proved he was a secret member of the party, and a year later, national leaders of his union concluded he had "willfully and knowingly associated with groups subservient to the Communist Party."[15]

Reagan, who had made numerous government-commissioned propaganda movies during the war, concluded that "Joseph Stalin had set out to make Hollywood an instrument of propaganda for his program of Soviet expansionism aimed at communizing the world." At first—and for "a long while"—Reagan wrote, "I believed the best way to beat the Communists was through the forces of liberal democracy, which had just defeated Hitler's brand of totalitarianism: liberal Democrats believed it is up to the people to decide what is best for them, not—as the Communists, Nazis, and other fascists believed—the few determining what is good for the rest of us." This seems to prove Reagan's early belief in the efficacy of "liberal democracy," which had already "defeated Hitler's brand of totalitarianism." But he went on to foreshadow his later discovery "that a lot of 'liberals' just couldn't accept the notion that Moscow had bad intentions or wanted to take over Hollywood and many other American industries through subversion, or that Stalin was a murderous gangster. To them, fighting totalitarianism was 'witch hunting' and 'red baiting.'"[16]

At this point, it would seem, Ronald Reagan was still "the near hopeless hemophiliac liberal" he chided himself for being through the postwar years.[17] Yet, in his 1990 memoir, he recalls a knock on his door "during the strike" (which would put the knock in 1947).[18] "I peeked through a little hole in the door and saw two men holding up the credentials of FBI agents." He invited them in, asking what he "could possibly know that the FBI didn't know already. One of them answered, 'Anybody that the Communists hate as much as they do you must know something that can help us.'" An FBI informant had reported that his "name had come up during a meeting of the American Communist Party in downtown Los Angeles" and that, during the meeting, "one of the Party members had said: 'What the hell are we going to do about that son-of-a-bitching bastard Reagan?'"[19]

The fact is that Ronald Reagan had extensive contact with at least five organizations accused of being "Communist fronts."[20] He joined the leftist American Veterans Committee (AVC), some of whose membership were indeed Communist Party members. He was a member of the World Federalists, advocates of one-world government. He signed a petition circulated by the Committee for a Democratic Far Eastern Policy, which demanded that the United States abandon support for Chiang Kai-shek. He was also active in the Hollywood Independent Citizens Committee of the Arts, Sciences and Professions (HICCASP). It was his attendance at a July 10, 1946, meeting of HICCASP that brought him to the attention of the FBI, which interviewed him on April 10, 1947, in connection with its investigation of the organization. Indeed, in September 1985, the *San Jose Mercury News* revealed that Reagan had been formally recruited by the FBI as an informant, codenamed T-10. Both he and Jane Wyman, to whom he was still married in 1947–1948, provided the FBI with the names of actors they believed were Communist sympathizers.[21] Apparently, Reagan was to some degree torn by the way the FBI was using not just him but, by virtue of his SAG presidency, SAG itself. He complained to one FBI agent: "Do they"—by which he meant HUAC, the House Un-American Activities Committee—"expect us [i.e., SAG] to constitute ourselves as a little FBI of our own and determine just who is a Commie and who isn't?"[22] This last statement suggests why Reagan did not go too far to the right at this time. As much as he resented what he called Stalin's efforts to hijack Hollywood for propaganda purposes—and Reagan did feel a sense of responsibility in the knowledge that some 80 percent of the films the world saw came from Hollywood—he also resented the efforts of the FBI and Congress to hijack or at least commandeer Hollywood.

Reagan's role as SAG president during a difficult time for the film industry did turn him against Communism. To be sure, however, he was no Joe McCarthy red baiter. For instance, he did not believe that the Communist Party should be outlawed in the United States. In 1947, Reagan told the hard right-wing and highly influential Hollywood gossip columnist Hedda Hopper, "You can't blame a man for aligning himself with an institution he thinks is humanitarian; but you can blame him if he deliberately remains with it after he knows it's fallen into the hands of the Reds." He told her that he was a liberal, who believed that "[o]ur highest aim should be the cultivation of the individual, for therein lies the dignity of man. Tyranny is tyranny, and whether it comes from right, left, or center, it's evil."[23] Still, before 1947 was out, he voluntarily appeared before HUAC's infamous hearings on Communism in Hollywood. He was a so-called friendly witness, but he did not roll over before the Congressmen, who (he told his friend and biographer Lou Cannon) were "a pretty venal bunch." The answer to Communist inroads into Hollywood and American life, he asserted, was simply "to make democracy work."[24]

Reagan remained through the 1940s and 1950s a Democrat and a reasonably liberal one. He joined Americans for Democratic Action (ADA) in 1947. It was an organization tailormade to his evolving beliefs.

It welcomed people like him, pro–New Deal, anti–Communist liberals who supported President Harry Truman's centrist policies. Reagan organized an ADA chapter in Southern California and was named to the organization's national board of directors.[25] He enthusiastically supported Truman's reelection in 1948 to a four-year term in his own right, having dinner with him in L.A. and standing by him as he spoke at a rally. He helped to found and accepted the chairmanship of the Labor League of Hollywood Voters, which embraced the twin purposes of fighting Communism and reelecting Truman. The Democratic Party approached Reagan twice to run for Congress, in 1946 and in 1952.[26] While he demurred both times, in the latter year he did join many other fellow Democrats in voting for a newly minted Republican, Dwight D. Eisenhower, for president. At the same time, he took a public stand against a pair of California Republican congressional candidates because they belittled Hollywood's efforts to rid the film industry of Communist influence.[27]

Throughout his first stint as president of the Screen Actors Guild, from 1947 to November 1952, Reagan walked a thin line between preserving the liberal independence of SAG and fending off Communist influence. From the left, this brought charges of "naming names" to add to the growing blacklist of "Reds" and "Fellow Travelers" that ruined many careers. He denied this lifelong, but his SAG role and his credibility with the FBI did facilitate his ability to clear the name of young Nancy Davis.

*   *   *

One of the minor myths surrounding the rise of Ronald Reagan as a political conservative is that Nancy was the catalyst of change. This does not seem likely, but marriage to her did of necessity bring Reagan into the orbit of her stepfather, Dr. Loyal Davis, who was a renowned brain surgeon and almost equally renowned supporter of conservative candidates and causes. The nexus of Dr. Davis's conservative philosophy was the specter of "socialized medicine," which became for Reagan an early calling card into conservative politics. Whatever political discussions Dr. Davis may have had with his son-in-law, he did usher him into a new circle of acquaintances outside of Hollywood, the core of American conservatism, among whom was Senator Barry Goldwater, who lived in the same Phoenix, Arizona, neighborhood as Dr. Davis.[28]

Although Reagan's star was fading, he remained prominent and popular in the movie industry as a defender of Hollywood, arguing against the developing stereotype that it was infested with effete, elitist Communists. He freely presented himself as Exhibit A to project the image of an industry made up of normal, moral Americans, hard-working and churchgoing, employed in an industry that was a monument to capitalist free enterprise. On the speaking circuit, SAG President Reagan spoke out against "political censorship" of the movie industry, arguing that it was an assault against a great democratic institution that never sought anything remotely resembling a government handout. To this, he added criticism of what he called the "insidious" federal tax policies targeting Hollywood. No industry, he claimed, "has been picked for such discriminatory taxes as have the individuals" in the movie business. "If they"—meaning the U.S. government—"can get away with it there, it is aimed at your pocketbook and you are next."[29] Thus, in presenting a liberal Democratic defense of his industry, Ronald Reagan entered the realm of conservatism via the twin backdoors of government interference in free enterprise and tax policy.

He could hardly avoid talking about taxes on Hollywood. The film industry, like Reagan himself, was oozing into a slump by the early 1950s as television, its development no longer hobbled by the priorities of war, increasingly drew eyeballs away from the big silver screen to the little glass one. This came at a time when the Supreme Court had decided (in *United States v. Paramount Pictures, Inc.*, 334 U.S. 131 [1948]) that the big Hollywood studios, whose ownership of major theater chains was a masterpiece of vertical integration, were in violation of the hoary Sherman Antitrust Act. Suddenly, the studios were compelled to divest themselves of America's movie houses. Even worse, President Truman—for whom Reagan had campaigned in 1948!—proposed in 1950 legislation closing a raft of tax loopholes, including those that both filmmakers and actors relied on to reduce their formidable income tax burden.[30]

By 1952, when Democrat Reagan cast his presidential ballot for Republican Dwight David Eisenhower, he had reached two conclusions. First, the government had an "adversarial relationship with its own business community"[31] and, second, the government was picking *his* pocket. In 1958, Reagan came before Congress as a spokesman for the movie industry and presented testimony arguing for the reduction of federal income taxes, with emphasis on what he characterized as "confiscatory" rates at the topmost brackets. His angle was that these rates were hobbling the film industry because they took away any incentive the most successful actors and writers had to make more than a film or two a year. Getting paid for, say, three films in any one year would put them in a 91 percent tax bracket. Now, when the most marketable names in Hollywood limited their productivity, Reagan argued, everyone employed in the film industry suffered—not just rank and file actors but grips, camera operators, and on down the line. In a preview of what would become a cornerstone of supply-side Reaganomics, he made the counterintuitive case to Congress that lowering tax rates would stimulate business and investment thereby increasing the revenue available for taxation. Reducing tax rates would actually increase the inflow of income tax money into the federal coffers.[32]

* * *

Testifying before Congress in 1958, Ronald Reagan complained that the progressive income tax system was hardly democratic and could "be defended [only] by endorsing the principles of the Socialism we are sworn to oppose." Four years earlier, in the privacy of his own home, Reagan's emphasis on tax policy focused more sharply—and bitterly—on his own case. His son Michael recalled that, about 1954, his father grumbled to him, "I don't get to keep very much of the money I earn."[33]

In his 1934 *I, Candidate for Governor: And How I Got Licked,* the novelist and socialist Upton Sinclair wrote a most concise and elegant analysis of self-interest: "It is difficult to get a man to understand something, when his salary depends on his not understanding it." Raised by beleaguered working-class parents perpetually struggling to make ends meet in a similarly beleaguered small-town Illinois, Ronald Reagan was primed to become the hemophiliac liberal Democrat he retrospectively mocked himself for having been. As one of the have-not (or have-not-enough) American majority, he experienced economic injustice very personally. Only when he stepped foot on the threshold (and it was only the threshold) of the doorway to the have-plenty elite minority did an entirely new view of economic injustice become equally personal. It was no longer the wealthy who were picking his pocket. Now it was a government verging on socialism, and there was much more in his pocket to pick.

What transformed Ronald Reagan from bleeding heart Democrat to free-market Republican? Self-interest—self-interest pursued from the perspective having wealth and wanting to keep it and even to make more of it. For Reagan, this was a new perspective, and, self-interested though it was, it struck him as a revelation damn near divine. The year 1954 brought him to an inflection point. And the bend in his trajectory would come courtesy of the General Electric Company.

CHAPTER 6

General Electric Theater

The early postwar years were good to America. Sure, there was the "Soviet menace," the Korean War, and the early proliferation of nuclear and even thermonuclear weapons. But the generation that had marched off to war returned victorious, launched a Baby Boom, and ignited an explosion of demand for consumer goods, which created a tide of unprecedented prosperity for a great many Americans.

After a hardscrabble start, Ronald Reagan's life looked like one lucky break after another, culminating in a motion picture career that seemed to fall into his lap. By 1952, this was all bogging down. World War II had done a lot of young Americans a lot of good, providing the GI Bill, which gave many young men a college education, a loan to buy a home, and generally provided seed opportunity to launch a better life. For Reagan, however, the war was an interruption in a movie career that, while never spectacular, was the best job he'd had since being the hometown lifeguard. It wasn't that Reagan had to go to Europe or the Pacific to fight a long war. His long war was fought right there in Hollywood, as his filmmaking switched from features to military training and propaganda reels. After the war, it was as if that switch were frozen, and he could never get off the rusty rails of a lonely siding overgrown with tall grass and weeds.

He got divorced and remarried. His new wife, the former Nancy Davis, was pregnant in 1952. Reagan's agent since 1938, Lew Wasserman, virtual inventor of the Hollywood star system and czar of MCA (Music Corporation of America), the most powerful Hollywood talent agency of the decade, could not reverse his client's decline. Reagan was running low on box office appeal and running short on money. Lew approached him—not with the major film role he so desperately needed, but with a request for a waiver that Reagan, as president of the Screen Actors Guild (SAG), had the unique power to grant. Under Wasserman, MCA had spawned a production company—Revue Productions—which was looking to produce fodder for the upstart medium that was threatening the Hollywood feature film industry: television. All that stood in Wasserman's way was an ironclad SAG rule barring actors from retaining agents who produced movies, including filmed TV entertainment. Through Revue, behemoth talent agency MCA was looking to become a behemoth television entertainment producer.

What would induce Reagan to give Lew Wasserman the waiver he needed? Wasserman had plenty of ways of putting money in Reagan's pocket. And, Lord knows, Reagan needed money. But it was not such a quid pro quo he proposed. He and Jules Stein, who had founded MCA and first hired Wasserman, had just come up with the concept of "reuse fees," which would pay actors who appeared in a filmed television show "residuals," a kind of royalty each time the show was rerun. And TV shows were rerun. A lot—potentially season after season, year after year. Right now, only Revue Productions offered the residual. But, Reagan knew, every other production company would have to follow suit to remain competitive in the market for talent. He ensured that his friend and agent got the waiver.[1]

Arguably, granting the waiver was a selfless act performed in service to actors. Not that many in Hollywood saw it that way. Reagan stepped down as SAG president on November 9, 1952, but continued to serve as a member of the SAG Board of Directors. In that capacity, he agreed to extend MCA's waiver permanently. This was a tricky proposition because, at this point, SAG was applying its ban on television producers agenting actors. With MCA now permanently exempted from the ban, however, the company enjoyed a huge competitive advantage. Frankly, the whole thing stunk—and, as MCA found ways to make Reagan a rich man, the obvious conflict of interest tainted Reagan for years to come. At the same time, one cannot help wondering if the lack of any truly damaging professional or legal consequences gave Reagan a feeling of invincibility, giving him the coat of Teflon he wore in what some have called a Teflon presidency.

Lew Wasserman was a committed Democrat, who supported John F. Kennedy's 1960 run against Richard Nixon. After JFK's election, his brother, Attorney General Robert F. Kennedy, opened an exhaustive investigation of MCA expansion, which was surely fueled by the permanent extension of the waiver to MCA. Reagan was subpoenaed to testify before a grand jury, giving, in all, some 6,000 pages of transcribed testimony. In the end, however, no evidence of criminality—neither racketeering nor bribery—was found. For his own part, Reagan protested that he had done nothing wrong. On the contrary, he believed that the Kennedy brothers had gone after him in retaliation for Reagan's support of Nixon in 1960.

Perhaps that was even the case. Perhaps Ronald Reagan was the victim of retribution he said he was. Yet Reagan was always reluctant, perhaps even evasive, when it came to answering questions about his wealth, which was estimated to be greater than $4 million in the late 1980s. His finances were never subjected to particular scrutiny when he ran for president, both in 1980 and 1984, and no one—other than the Kennedy DOJ—seemed interested in querying the extent of his financial ties to MCA. In his 1987 *Dark Victory: Ronald Reagan, MCA, and the Mob,* writer Dan E. Moldea portrayed Reagan as extensively networked within a mysterious web encompassing both MCA and organized crime. As was true of many powerful Hollywood figures, Reagan did have links to one Sidney Korshak, a Chicago lawyer whose clients included various mob figures and who was openly known as the Mob's man in L.A.[2] There is no question that the sweetheart deal SAG President Reagan made with his friend and agent brought a lot of money his way, even as his movie career rapidly deflated. Yet the deal and its consequences savored far more of Hollywood movie industry cronyism than of quid-pro-quo bribery or a Mafia fix. That Reagan himself thought the deal was unsavory does not mean it was criminal. More likely it should be slotted in the vast category of behavior that is "awful but lawful."

* * *

Still, the Kennedy DOJ publicly concluded that the decisions made by SAG while under Reagan's leadership constituted "the central fact of MCA's whole rise to power." Just how powerful did MCA become? Industry trade papers called it "the Octopus," and when comic Jerry Lewis was asked about the role of MCA in Hollywood show business, he answered in three monosyllables: "They own it." During the 1950s alone, MCA's Revue Productions "supplied the television networks with some forty hours of programming, including such top-rated shows as *Wagon Train, Alfred Hitchcock Presents, The Jack Benny Show, Ozzie and Harriet, Dragnet, This Is Your Life,* and *Leave It to Beaver.*" (Early in the 1960s, MCA acquired Universal Studios, and Revue became Universal Television, which produced the likes of *Marcus Welby, M.D.; Columbo: McMillan and Wife; Kojak; The SIx-Million-Dollar Man; The Rockford Files: The Incredible Hulk; Magnum, P.I.;* and *Miami Vice* in addition to blockbuster theatrical movies such as three Oscar-winning classics: *The Sting, The Deer Hunter,* and *Out of Africa.*)[3]

One of MCA's earliest and most profitable television shows was *General Electric Theater,* a dramatic anthology that premiered in February 1953 without a host. Just a month earlier—soon after the waiver had been awarded—MCA threw Reagan a nice fat life preserver in the form of a contract for a Western and a $75,000 signing fee for renewing his master contract with Universal Pictures. By this time, Reagan had been sufficiently desperate to book himself a two-week gig as a Las Vegas comic (yes, a stand-up comic) in a casino-hotel called the Last Frontier. The versatile Reagan was an unlikely hit, but he hated working a club, and neither he nor Nancy had a taste for gambling. Reagan turned down several new club dates, hoping that more opportunity would come through via MCA.[4]

And it did. Moreover, MCA came through before the money ran out. MCA decided that what the already well-received *GE Theater* needed to make it an even bigger hit was an affable host. Taft Schreiber, Wasserman's righthand man, called Reagan with an offer to host the General Electric show for $125,000 a year—paid directly by GE. Reagan jumped on it, and he immediately proved to be a natural in the "role." Soon, GE showed its gratitude by bumping him up to $150,000 per annum, roughly the equivalent of $1.6 million in 2023 money. The company also outfitted his Pacific Palisades home with every appliance GE made, transforming the residence into a permanent GE promotional set. Reagan and his family appeared in frequent commercials, demonstrating the gadgets simply by living with them.

In addition to hosting *GE Theater*, Reagan did some narrative voice-over work and occasionally acted in an episode of the series. In theatrical terms, it was a TV gig far more creditable than most. *GE Theater* was a showcase for some excellent, even standout, drama that put Reagan (at long last) in company with bona-fide A-listers, including Broderick Crawford, a young Tony Curtis, an even younger Michael Landon, Bob Cummings, Jimmy Stewart, Burgess Meredith, Teresa Wright, Richard Boone, Sir Cedric Hardwicke, Ward Bond, June Havoc, Alan Ladd, Cornel Wilde, Myrna Loy, Jack Benny, Bette Davis, Anne Baxter, and Barbara Stanwyck.[5] Beyond question, the show was a hit, grabbing ownership of the primo Sunday night Nielsen ratings. For GE, it was a splendid platform from which its many consumer products could be hawked. Besides, the company's familiar slogan, "Progress Is Our Most Important Product," sounded all the more persuasive spoken through Ronald Reagan's lips. By 1959, more than twenty-five million Americans every Sunday tuned in to *General Electric Theater*. In each of its eight years on the air, it was the most-watched program in its time slot and one of the most popular shows of television's "Golden Age."[6]

Reagan's dimming star had been rekindled. Already a known quantity, he now had a prominent place on a hit show, which made him a welcome Sunday evening visitor in American living rooms. *General Electric* had shrewdly included in the Reagan contract an agreement that the star would serve as a "GE goodwill ambassador," periodically touring company plants to deliver motivational speeches to rank-and-file workers as well as to top executives.

The studio work was no sweat, but the road show among the far-flung outposts of the General Electric industrial empire was truly grinding. Under GE chairman Ralph Cordiner, the company's manufacturing operations were distributed across the nation—139 plants in thirty-nine states.[7] Moreover, the work was also even more time-consuming than it needed to be. Reagan was phobic about flying, so he traveled by car or train whenever possible, always in the company of a corporate PR "handler."

> The hours were long, frequently from dawn to after midnight. In one five-day tour of New England in late 1954, he "addressed five Good Neighbor fund meetings; made four TV and four radio appearances; attended 12 receptions, luncheons, and dinners; addressed five miscellaneous groups; toured five departments at the River Works, West Lynn, Bridgeport, and Plainville; and got writer's cramp from signing well over 1000 autographs."[8]

The speeches were always a hit, and GE asked for more and more. By the start of 1956, Reagan was delivering as many as thirteen speeches—a day—not just to employees but also to local community organizations. His record day came in 1957, in Lynchburg, Virginia, when he delivered eighteen speeches—or maybe it was twenty-five (he really couldn't remember).[9]

The thing is, he liked it. His handler struggled to keep up, finding his stamina incredible. GE scripted some of his early speeches, but in many places the PR department asked only that he do a meet-and-greet, saying a few words of his choice and then taking questions. Soon, however, it became clear that Reagan had a natural talent as an improvisational speaker. He did far more than the company asked of him. Grueling? Yes. But, for Reagan, remarkably satisfying. More and more, GE made use of the "goodwill ambassador" aspect of his duties, sending him out to speak at Rotary luncheons and chamber of commerce events. Before 1957 was out, GE did not even have to solicit appearances for their star. The requests poured in, and the PR department had to schedule "Ambassador" Reagan farther and farther in advance. He was doing well for GE, to be sure, but he was also building a proto-political political reputation.

Subject matter had to be cleared by the culturally and politically conservative company. Reagan was happy to oblige. As president of SAG, he had honed what he called his "basic Hollywood speech," which consisted of two principal themes: the battle against Communist influence not just in Hollywood but throughout the nation and an increasingly acidic critique of federal tax discrimination against the film industry. He discovered that the latter issue was accepted by his audiences as a broader criticism of federal income tax rates and policy. In fact, audience members often approached him to give him an earful. They let him know that *his* industry wasn't being picked on. Taxes were killing us all!

As his subject matter broadened out from Hollywood, so the scope of his complaints spread from unfair taxation to criticism of government overreach, intrusive legislation, arrogant attitude, and stifling overregulation of business and industry. Reagan recognized that, given a chance, people found they had much to complain about. Most strident among their complaints was the sense that government was making deep inroads into *their* liberty and *their* lives.

*   *   *

Reagan had already voted for Ike Eisenhower in 1952, but even after hitching his wagon to the GE star in 1954, he persisted in calling himself a liberal Democrat as well as a strong union supporter. The income tax burden that came with his burgeoning financial success disturbed him deeply and personally, yet he nevertheless found himself having genial though "fierce" debates with the GE executives who worked most closely with him. Both the executives and Reagan seemed to enjoy their sparring, yet, when pushed, Reagan inevitably took an Alamo-like stand when it came to defending the New Deal and the Democratic Party. His assigned handler went so far as to call Reagan "the least malleable man I ever met."[10]

Ronald Reagan's opting to vote for Eisenhower over Adlai Stevenson while still identifying as a Democrat was not all that unusual, let alone aberrant, in the 1950s. Eisenhower was a Republican because the Republicans had asked him to run. As a career U.S. Army officer, he had done what virtually all U.S. military men did. He eschewed political allegiance and, in fact, did not even vote. As a soldier, his allegiance was to the nation, not a party. In voting for Ike in 1952, people of both parties were voting for a man they liked. And they really did "like Ike." Who wouldn't? It was generally felt that he had done more than any other individual to win the war in Europe. The more thoughtful among the electorate attributed his success as much to his diplomatic and political skills as to his military acumen. He had held together a highly contentious alliance. It was a brilliant achievement. Moreover, he was part of the movement that was determined to make the United States the dominant force in the postwar world. Besides, he had the spectacular political gift of possessing benign yet winning smile.

So, voting for Ike was not, for Ronald Reagan, so much a rebellion against the Democratic Party as it was the embrace of a great man. Still, non-malleable as he might have seemed, the cumulative feedback from his GE audiences and the cumulative effect of his debates with GE executives were having an impact on him. He listened. He thought. He did some reading on his own. More and more, he wrote his own speeches—or large parts of them—working out in that writing his own evolving position. Yet behind this evolution there was always a personal motive, the consciousness (as he saw it) that the American government was discouraging *him*—and, yes, people like him—from making more money. The high end of the marginal tax brackets seemed, in a word, extortionate.

> Those GE tours became almost a postgraduate course in political science for me. I was seeing how government really operated and affected people in America, not how it was taught in school. From hundreds of people in every part of the country, I heard complaints about how the ever-expanding federal government was encroaching on liberties we'd always taken for granted. I heard it so often that after a while I became convinced that some of our fundamental freedoms were in jeopardy because of the emergence of a permanent government never envisioned by the framers of the Constitution: a federal bureaucracy that was becoming so powerful it was able to set policy and thwart the desires not only of ordinary citizens, but their elected representatives in Congress.[11]

Reagan claimed that he never felt pressured by GE to take any particular political stance. "Although GE gave me a platform, it left it up to me to decide what to say. As a liberal in my younger days I'd had an inherent suspicion of big business and couldn't believe there wouldn't come a day when the company would begin trying to write my speeches for me. Never once did that happen."[12]

As Reagan himself portrayed it, his conversion to Republican conservatism came from the voice of the people. An avid reader lifelong, he nevertheless denied that he was influenced in his political transformation by any books in particular. But he did read some classic conservative literature, including Whittaker Chambers' *Witness*. Published in 1952, this autobiography of the Communist spy turned informer (mainly against Alger Hiss) is considered a Cold War classic. It impressed Reagan so deeply that, in 1984, he not only awarded Chambers, posthumously, the Presidential Medal of Freedom, he also frequently recited passages of the man's autobiography from memory.[13]

Reagan also had in his library Henry Hazlitt's 1946 *Economics in One Lesson*, a foundational book in modern free-market capitalism. He read conservative periodicals, including *Human Events* (which "helped me stop being a liberal Democrat"), *The Freeman*, and any number of *Reader's Digest* articles on conservativism and conservative economic theory. While there is no reason to disbelieve Reagan's assurance that GE never pressured him toward the GOP, it is also true that he was drawn to the conservative culture of the corporate giant, particularly as manifested in GE's vice president of employee and community relations, Lemuel R. Boulware. He befriended Reagan and freely nurtured the younger man's budding conservatism, going so far as to give him the gift of a charter subscription to William F. Buckley Jr.'s *National Review,* founded in 1955. He remained a subscriber throughout his life, writing to Buckley in 1962, "I'd be lost without *National Review*."[14]

* * *

By 1957, his third year working for GE, the volume of speeches he delivered to civic and corporate audiences overtook his factory tours. Subject matter had morphed from his "Hollywood speech"—government interference in the movie business—to the universal threat of government. In June 1957, he gave a commencement address at his alma mater, Eureka College. After an oratorically kitsch recital of American history, from the American Revolution through the world wars, he turned to the "cold war."

> This cold war between great sovereign nations isn't really a new struggle at all. It is the oldest struggle of human kind, as old as man himself. This is a simple struggle between those of us who believe that man has the dignity and sacred right and the ability to choose and shape his own destiny and those who do not so believe. This irreconcilable conflict is between those who believe in the sanctity of individual freedom and those who believe in the supremacy of the state.
>
> In a phase of this struggle not widely known, some of us came toe to toe with this enemy, this evil force in our own community in Hollywood, and make no mistake about it, this is an evil force. Don't be deceived because you are not hearing the sound of gunfire, because even so you are fighting for your lives. And you're fighting against the best organized and the most capable enemy of freedom and of right and decency that has ever been abroad in the world. Some years ago, back in the thirties, a man who was apparently just a technician came to Hollywood to take a job in our industry, an industry whose commerce is in tinsel and colored lights and make-believe. He went to work in the studios, and there were few to know he came to our town on direct orders from the Kremlin. When he quietly left our town a few years later the cells had been formed and planted in virtually all of our organizations, our guilds and unions. The framework for the Communist front organizations had been established.

Reagan spoke of the eruption of violence "under the guise of a jurisdictional strike involving a dispute between two unions." It was, he said, "war come to Hollywood. Suddenly there were 5,000 tin-hatted, club-carrying pickets outside the studio gates. We saw some of our people caught by these hired henchmen; we saw them open car doors and put their arms across them and break them until they hung straight down the side of the car, and then these tin-hatted men would send our people on into the studio. We saw our so-called glamour girls, who certainly had to be conscious of what a scar on the face or a broken nose could mean careerwise going through those picket lines day after day without complaint. Nor did they falter when they found the bus which they used for transportation to and from work in flames from a bomb that had been thrown into it just before their arrival. ... We won our fight in Hollywood, cleared them out after seven long months in which even homes were broken, months in which many of us carried arms that were granted us by the police, and in which policemen lived in our homes, guarding our children at night...."

Reagan warned the Class of 1957 that many Americans have made themselves "fair game for those people, well-meaning though they may be, who believe that the answer to the world's ills is more government and more restraint and more regimentation." Suddenly we find that we are a group of second-class citizens subject to discriminatory taxation, government interference and harassment....

> Now today as you prepare to leave your Alma Mater, you go into a world in which, due to our carelessness and apathy, a great many of our freedoms have been lost. It isn't that an outside enemy has taken them. It's just that there is something inherent in government which makes it, when it isn't controlled, continue to grow. So today for every seven of us sitting here in this lovely outdoor theater, there is one public servant, and 31 cents of every dollar earned in America goes in taxes. To support the multitudinous and gigantic functions of government, taxation is levied which tends to dry up the very sources of contributions and donations to colleges like Eureka. So in this time of prosperity we find these church schools, these small independent colleges and even the larger universities, hard put to maintain themselves and to continue doing the job they have done so unselfishly and well for all these years. Observe the contrast between these small church colleges and our government, because, as I have said before, these have always given far more than was ever given to them in return.
>
> Class of 1957, it will be part of the terms of the will for you to take stock in the days to come, because we enjoy a form of government in which mistakes can be rectified. The dictator can never admit he was wrong, but we are blessed with a form of government where we can call a halt, and say, "Back up. Let's take another look."[15]

It is possible to see in this 1957 commencement address Ronald Reagan's personal graduation from Democratic liberalism to Republican conservatism, although he himself identified his Rubicon as the election of 1960, the year Kennedy ran against Nixon for the White House. "One day I came home and said to Nancy, 'You know, something just dawned on me: All these things I've been saying about government in my speeches (I wasn't just making speeches—I was preaching a sermon), all these things I've been criticizing about government getting too big, well, it just dawned on me that every four years when an election comes along, I go out and support the people who are responsible for the things I'm criticizing.'"[16]

In his second autobiography, Reagan explained that as a liberal Democrat, he "was naturally opposed to Richard Nixon." In 1950, he supported

"Congresswoman Helen Gahagan Douglas, the wife of an actor-friend of mine, Melvyn Douglas" in her unsuccessful Senate contest against a Red-baiting Nixon, who called her "pink, pink down to her underwear." In fact, in those days, Reagan wrote, "I worked on the campaigns of just about any Democrat who was willing to accept my help."

> In 1948, I campaigned for Hubert Humphrey and for Harry Truman, and to this day, I think Truman was an outstanding president, with one exception. He had a common sense that helped him get to the root of problems; he stood up to the bureaucrats, and when he had a tough decision to make, he made it. And he wasn't a tax-and-spend Democrat; during the past sixty years, there have been only eight scattered years when the federal budget was in balance and four of those years were under Truman. Looking back, I think he and I were in tune on a lot of things about government and I think if he had lived longer he might have come over to the other side like I did. In my view, the only thing that kept Harry Truman from real greatness was his decision not to completely back General Douglas MacArthur and win the Korean War.[17]

He wrote that he "also greatly admired the man who followed Truman into the White House, Dwight Eisenhower" and "joined several other Democrats in sending a telegram to Ike urging him to run for president as a Democrat." When Eisenhower chose to run as a Republican, "I decided: If I considered him the best man for the job as a Democrat, he still ought to be my choice. So I campaigned and voted for Ike—my first for a Republican." In 1960, GE's Cordiner counseled Reagan, "I think you might be wrong about Nixon." Reagan unselfconsciously confessed in his autobiography: "I was such a fan of Ralph Cordiner by then that I decided to reevaluate some of the things that the liberals (including me) had been saying about Nixon."[18]

Reagan told Nixon he was going to register as a Republican. Nixon surprised him by asking that he remain a Democrat but campaign for him. This, he believed, would carry more weight. Catching wind of this turn of events, Joseph Kennedy Sr., a man who had made a large part of his fortune in Hollywood, tried to win Reagan over, asking him to vote for his son. Reagan turned him down. "Although I agreed at Nixon's request not to register as a Republican, I was really no longer a Democrat by 1960. ... I had completed the process of self-conversion."[19]

Self-conversion! There it was again: autobiography as mythology, this time with a change of party affiliation raised to the level of a quasi-religious experience. As the Puritans would have put it, Ronald Wilson Reagan had *suffered a conversion.* Moreover, it had the mystical overlay of secrecy. So, for the second time in his life, the New Deal Democrat voted for a Republican. Converted, he would nevertheless remain registered as a Democrat for two more years.

CHAPTER 7

A Speech Is Born

In his 1990 memoir, *An American Life,* Ronald Reagan wrote that by the early 1960s, "GE was receiving more speaking invitations for me from around the country than I could handle." In his 1965 memoir, *Where's the Rest of Me?* Reagan was both franker and, it seems, more conflicted. The GE speaking tours "were murderously difficult. I could lose ten pounds in three weeks and eat anything I wanted. The schedules were dovetailed on a split-second basis, and the demand on energy so great when you had to meet the fourteenth group with the same zip you'd shown ten hours earlier that I didn't really sleep until a trip was over." After thus griping, Reagan added: *"But I enjoyed every whizzing minute of it."*[1]

The italics were Reagan's. And the self-reflection he offered to accompany this masochistic declaration is revealing: "It was one of the most rewarding experiences of my life. There was an understandable glow at being welcomed so warmly, but in addition it was wonderful to encounter the honest affection most people had for the familiar faces of Hollywood." Reagan was feeling the love, and it felt good, even as his acting career grew dimmer and dimmer. He continued: "No barnstorming politician ever met the people on quite such a common footing. Sometimes I had an awesome, shivering feeling that America was making a personal appearance for me, and it made me the biggest fan in the world."[2]

One hardly knows what to say. Ronald Reagan got everything he wanted. He wanted to be a radio sports broadcaster, and he became one; he had a notion to become a successful Hollywood actor, and so it came to pass—when he traveled to L.A. on assignment as a sportscaster. Both achievements, as they occurred, seemed to him the culmination of everything he could have wished for. But then World War II intervened. He worked hard as an actor, but in the service of Army and then the Army Air Corps. He served his country honorably, but it interrupted his career. It proved to be a stumble from which he could not recover. Fortunately, television—which came as a scourge to so many in the film business—proved a godsend to the affable B-lister. His gig on *General Electric Theater* led him to the speaking circuit. In GE plants, he was well-received, and in community speaking engagements on behalf of the company, he was received with even more enthusiasm.

General Electric had hired Reagan in no small part because his increasingly conservative Republican identification (though he was still a registered Democrat) was precisely the orientation GE wanted to inculcate into its workforce and broadcast to the American community. Lou Cannon, the journalist turned Reagan biographer, has sometimes been accused of crossing the line from biographer to hagiographer. In fact, while Cannon clearly admired his subject, he was most often very clear-sighted about him. He explained that, by the late 1950s, Reagan's speeches on the road for GE began "to have an edge." The early speeches "blended a patriotic theme with a defense of Hollywood," which was under attack by rightwing politicians and many in the public as a hotbed of communism, atheism, and immorality. Reagan's early GE speeches portrayed Hollywood as a vessel of American values, a town where "the crime rate was low and the divorce rate 10 percent below the national average" (no thanks to the union of Ronald Reagan and Jane Wyman). But, Cannon observes, the drift of his GE speechmaking "became more specifically antigovernment over time, with titles such as 'Encroaching Control' and 'Our Eroding Freedoms.'"[3]

In 1959, Reagan crossed another line when he turned his criticism against the showpiece of the FDR-era New Deal, the Tennessee Valley Authority. Reagan claimed in his GE speeches that "the annual interest on the TVA deal is five times as great as the flood damage it prevents."[4]

Now, GE had learned to cut their traveling speechmaker a considerable length of slack. Relentlessly colloquial, he had an apparently unshakable habit of referring to refrigerators, including those made by GE, as "Frigidaires." True, many people in 1950s America called their fridge a Frigidaire, regardless of its manufacturer. But to do so on General Electric's dime was a bridge too far. Still, the colloquial tic drew no more than mild reproof. Even his ongoing role as host of *General Electric Theater* had its share of landmines. For example, when GE censors vetoed a script about a fogbound airliner suffering from instrument failure—GE had an avionics division that made many aircraft instruments—Reagan strenuously objected, only to back down and retract his objections, remarking that GE was "naturally sensitive" on the subject.[5]

But the TVA did $50 million (about $510 million in 2022 dollars) in business with GE each year. Reagan was scheduled to speak at a convention in Los Angeles when he received a phone call from his GE PR handler letting him know that (in Reagan's words) a "government bureaucrat was on the warpath" over what he had said about the cost of the TVA. The PR man "made pretty plain that I was to be fired," Reagan wrote in his 1965 memoir.[6]

Three days before the convention, Reagan was told that Ralph J. Cordiner, GE's CEO and Chairman of the Board, had been put on notice by the "bureaucrat": fire Reagan or lose the TVA business. Reagan called Cordiner.

"Mr. Cordiner, I understand you have a problem that has to do with me."

"Well, I'm sorry you found that out," Cordiner replied, "It's my problem, I've told them we don't tell an employee what he can or can't say, and we're not going to start."[7]

Reagan "tried to tell him how much I admired his stand, but that I wouldn't want to think that someday they might have to lay off a few thousand men in a turbine plant because he had defended my right to speak."

According to Reagan, Cordiner didn't take the bait. So, Reagan offered: "What would you say if I said I could make my speech just as effectively without mentioning TVA?"

"Well, it would make my job easier."

Done.[8]

Reagan was consistent throughout the years that he was selflessly motivated in this capitulation. He didn't want GE employees to be laid off. This may well have been the case. Or it may have been an instance of going along to get along. Even more likely, it was a bit of both. In any event, it did win him another lucrative four years or so on the GE payroll. He continued to host *General Electric Theater*, and he continued to stump for the company. As he became increasingly identified as a spokesman for the Republican right, Reagan came to believe he was being painted as a right-wing extremist. In his 1965 memoir, he wrote that the Committee on Political Education of the AFL-CIO "tagged me as a strident voice of rightwing extremism ... and issued bulletins long on name-calling and short on truth." In St. Paul, Minnesota, he wrote, the Teachers Federation passed a resolution protesting a Reagan speech scheduled to be delivered at the city's Central High School because he was a "controversial personality."[9]

The resolution failed, but—in what in retrospect looks like a foreshadowing of Donald Trump's perpetual plaint of victimhood—Reagan did not give up on seeing himself as a victim of Democratic liberal sniping. He was convinced that his public support for Nixon persuaded GE that he was a liability in the new era of JFK. In both his 1965 and 1990 memoirs, he claimed that no sooner did Ralph Cordiner retire as chairman and CEO of General Electric than the new management ushered him toward the exit. In fact, as Lew Cannon points out, Cordiner stayed with GE through December 1963. The real issue was not a changing of the guard but Reagan's stubborn insistence that he be permitted to continue his conservative political speeches with GE footing the bill. GE responded by asking that he discontinue the political speeches and (as Reagan put it) "become a pitch-man for General Electric products."[10] It is hard to blame GE for not already considering Reagan their pitchman for the simple reason that he had been for some seven years precisely that—and that he lived in a house fully out-fitted by GE with every futuristic appliance GE manufactured. Pitchman? Reagan and his household *were* the pitch.

He told GE that he had developed a political following among the people and that he intended to keep making political speeches—on his own dime, if necessary. As he put in his 1990 memoir, when "They insisted and when I resisted, they canceled" both his role on *General Electric Theater* and his PR duties.

It was at least a little more complicated than he made out. There is no denying that *General Electric Theater* had been a smash hit for seven seasons and that Reagan had a lot to do with its success. But in season eight, the show found itself occupying a time slot opposite *Bonanza,* a network Western juggernaut, and fell to second place. Probably even more import-ant in GE's decision to cancel both the show and the company's affiliation with Reagan was the fact that the MCA-SAG scandal (the sweetheart deal SAG president Reagan gave MCA founder and longtime crony Lew Was-serman; see Chapter 6) had resulted in an indictment of MCA and SAG as co-conspirators. The prospect of employing in a high-profile PR role a potential felon appealed neither to the GE board nor to the GE investors.

* * *

In 1961, while he was still hosting *General Electric Theater,* Reagan accepted an assignment from the American Medical Association to make an LP recording. No, he was not starting a singing career or reprising his most memorable movies lines: "Win one for the Gipper," "Where's the rest of me?" The AMA wanted him to record a warning that legislation intro-ducing Medicare would, well, spell the end of freedom in America. The leading message of the record was that if those who listened to his voice failed to write their representatives and senators letters protesting passage of the legislation, "we will awake to find that we have socialism. And if you don't do this, and if I don't do it, one of these days, you and I are going to spend our sunset years telling our children, and our children's children, what it once was like in America when men were free."[11] Before the new decade was out, Reagan would speak out his opposition to the Food Stamp Program (today known as SNAP), moves to raise the federal minimum wage, and legislation to create the Peace Corps.

On May 2, 1962, Ronald Reagan testified before the MCA-SAG anti-trust grand jury. Dan E. Moldea, author of *Dark Victory: Ronald Reagan, MCA and the Mob* (New York: Penguin, 1987), published a feature story in *The Washington Post* (March 15, 1987) presenting one of the often over-looked talents that served Ronald Reagan long before either the presidency or the onset of Alzheimer's disease near the end of his life. One could call it a talent for selective memory, although a more accurate description would be a talent for selective failure of memory. Presidential historians Sidney K. Milkis and Michael Nelson observed, "Coolidge raised inactivity to an art." Or, as the inimitable Will Rogers said of "Silent Cal": "He don't say much, but when he does say somethin,' he don't say much."[12] Reagan, who wrote in his 1990 memoir that he "always thought of Coolidge as one of our most underrated presidents,"[13] may fairly be remembered by many as a chief executive who raised vague recollection to an art and, though he was called the Great Communicator and certainly could be eloquent ("Mr. Gorbachev, tear down this wall!"), he more often didn't say much, even when he said somethin'.

Questioned before a federal grand jury about the SAG-MCA scandal, he replied, "I don't want to appear as though I am trying to be deliberately vague, but, as I say, I would like you to realize in my history of holding an office with the guild, my memory is like a kaleidoscope of meetings...." Federal antitrust lawyer John Fricano asked Reagan about the relationship between MCA and SAG, approaching the topic indirectly: "Which company, whether a member of the Alliance [of Television Film Producers] or not, was the first to capitulate with respect to repayment for reruns [payment of residuals to actors]?" Reagan answered, "There you have me. I wouldn't know where we cracked that and if you tell me I'll have to take your word for it."

"Well, you were president of Screen Actors Guild in 1952, were you not?"

"Yes."

"This was a very important matter, which Screen Actors Guild was taking up and it was the most important point of the guild?" Reagan insisted on asking *Fricano* to tell him when the Guild took this up. "July 1952," came the reply.

"Well," Reagan responded, "maybe the fact that I married in March of 1952 and went on a honeymoon had something to do with my being a little bit hazy."

Fricano would not let him go. "I'm glad you raised that point. If we might digress, who is your wife?"

"Nancy Davis."

"Was she a member of the board of directors of SAG in 1952?"

"Yes."

"Do you recall any other unusual or momentous events in 1952 with respect to SAG's relations with one or more TV film production companies?"

"Well, now what kind of events?"

"In 1952 when you were president of the Screen Actors Guild, did not the Screen Actors Guild grant to MCA what is known in the trade as a blanket or unlimited waiver to produce TV films?"

"Oh, we have granted—I didn't know when it exactly started, we granted an extended waiver to MCA to be engaged in production as we had done with other people."

After sparring with Reagan over this, Fricano asked: "Can you tell this grand jury why Screen Actors Guild gave to MCA a blanket or unlimited waiver?"

"Well, my own reasoning and one of the reasons perhaps why this doesn't loom so importantly to me is I personally never saw any particular harm in it. I was one who subscribed to the belief, and those were times of great distress in the picture business, I was for anyone that could give employment. I saw no harm in this happening…."

"Do you recall whether or not you participated in the negotiations held by MCA and SAG with respect to the blanket waiver in July of 1952?"

"No, I think I have already told you I don't recall that. I don't recall. There were times when I wasn't involved on a committee. Whether that is one of them or not I wouldn't recall. I must tell you that I always told [the executive secretary] in the guild that I realized I felt a little self-conscious sometimes about that, lest there might ever be a misunderstanding because of the fact that I had been so long with MCA [as a client of agent Wasserman], and sometimes I kind of ran for cover and was very happy to duck a committee duty in these matters."

"Did you participate in any negotiations in 1954 on SAG's behalf with respect to a waiver to MCA … ?"

"I don't honestly recall. You know something? You keep saying [1954] in the summer. I think maybe one of the reasons I don't recall was because I feel that in the summer [of 1954] I was up in Glacier Park making a cowboy picture … so it's very possible there were some things going on that I would not participate in but I have no recollection of this particularly."

"I would like to know, sir, if you can tell the grand jury why in June 1954 the blanket waiver to MCA was extended and the negotiations which SAG held with MCA were private negotiations, whereas 24 days later, negotiations were held for other talent agencies who had also requested waivers and the waivers of those agencies were limited waivers?"

"I wouldn't be able to tell you."

"Were you aware of the fact?"

"I will say one thing. I don't know what you are getting at with the question and I am certainly in no position to infer that I want to tell you what to do or not. I can only say this. I have tried to make plain why my memory could be so hazy on a great many things … [but] in all my years with the Screen Actors Guild I have never known of or participated in anything, nor has the guild, that ever in any way was based on anything but what we honestly believed was for the best interests of the actor….”

"Were you aware, sir, that in 1954 negotiations did take place between MCA and Screen Actors Guild with respect to the waiver which had been entered in 1952?”

"No," Reagan angrily said. “It’s like saying what I was doing on October 25, the night of the murder.”

"I don’t care what you were doing October 25.”

"I mean you pick a year that is going back eight years and you say, ‘Where were you?’ I have tried to picture what hassle the guild was in at that time.”

"Take your time and think about it. I don’t expect an immediate answer.”

"I don’t know. The guild….”

"Do you recall now, sir, whether or not you were aware in 1954 of the renegotiations of the letter of agreement of 1952 between Screen Actors Guild and MCA?”

"All I can say, usually these negotiations and things of that kind seemed to fall in the even years. So I would have to say probably 1954, yes, this would be. To tell you of my own memory, in my mind I can tell you whether we did nor not, I can’t. Serving with Screen Actors Guild long years of negotiating on meetings for a long time, just retaining things that happened, the lawyers’ reports and then so forth, and then you find yourself in a battle like we had with the communists or with the strikes.”[14]

Reagan’s (mostly) easy-going evasion during his grand jury testimony in May 1962 was remarkably successful in that he suffered no legal blowback from the scandal, although he was convinced that his career had been irreparably damaged.[15]

* * *

In November 1962, Ronald Reagan officially changed his party registration from Democratic to Republican. By 1964, Reagan realized he needed a job. He believed that “appearing on the General Electric Theater for so long probably hadn’t endeared me to the people who owned the movie theaters of America,” but he managed to get a role in *The Killers*. Directed by tough-guy action specialist Don Siegel (today best remembered for the 1956 *Invasion of the Body Snatchers* and five iconic Clint Eastwood movies, including Reagan’s 1971 favorite, *Dirty Harry*[16]), *The Killers* was a remake of a 1946 Burt Lancaster film based on Ernest Hemingway’s 1927 short story of the same name.

"I had seen the original picture and hadn't liked it very much because everybody in the script was a villain and there was no one to root for." Reagan had never played a villain in any film, and when Universal asked him "to play a gangster ... my instinct was to say no. But I'm afraid they took advantage of an actor's ego. ... It was a challenge no actor could resist." It is equally true that no actor, out of work, can refuse a paycheck. In his 1990 memoir, Reagan (who had been billed fourth, after Lee Marvin, Angie Dickinson, and John Cassavetes) insisted that a "lot of people who went to see *The Killers* ... kept waiting for me to turn out to be a good guy in the end and dispatch the villains in the last reel, because that's how they had always seen me before. But I didn't, and for whatever reason, the picture didn't ring many bells at the box office."[17]

Reagan admitted that his "movie career was coming to a close"— *The Killers* was his last movie, so, yeah—but he was "still receiving lots of offers to act as a guest star in television shows."[18] Among these offers was a steadier TV gig, as host of *Death Valley Days*, a rather low-budget but quite popular syndicated (non-network) Western anthology show, which had first aired in 1952, having started out in radio in 1930. The sponsor back then was 20 Mule Team Borax, makers of the Boraxo line of heavy-duty Borax-based hand soaps and detergents. The same sponsor carried the show into television and stuck with it. Reagan replaced Stanley Andrews, who, as "The Old Ranger," had hosted the TV show since its 1952 small-screen inception. Reagan began production in 1964 and was on the air with the show from 1965 to 1966.

Although Reagan also occasionally acted in the series, his main job, filming the host material, was not in the least time-consuming. Reagan would "drive down to the studio from our ranch, spend an hour or so taping an introduction for the next show, then drive home.... The job left me plenty of time for speeches and Republican activities."[19]

Among these activities was serving as California co-chair of the 1964 presidential campaign of Arizona senator Barry Goldwater. He was eager to do it—"I didn't hesitate a moment."[20] Reagan's second wife, Nancy Davis, had been born Anne Frances Robbins in New York, the only child of farmer-turned-car salesman Kenneth Seymour Robbins and Edith Prescott Luckett, a beautiful but minor actress whose godmother was none other than silent film superstar Alla Nazimova. When Anne was just seven in 1928, Robbins and Luckett divorced, and Luckett remarried the following year, upgrading from farmer/car salesman to prominent Chicago neurosurgeon, Dr. Loyal Edward Davis. After a distinguished career—he "reigned supreme as chief of surgery at Northwestern University medical school in Chicago"[21]—Davis retired and moved with his family to Phoenix, Arizona. Among his friends was Barry Goldwater, with whom he shared an intense Republican conservatism.[22] Reagan met "Barry" at the Davis home in Phoenix early in his marriage to Nancy and was impressed by Goldwater's 1960 book, *The Conscience of a Conservative*. It "contained a lot of the same points I'd been making in my speeches," Reagan wrote, "and I strongly believed the country needed him."[23]

Reagan was opposed to virtually all the "Great Society" social programs Lyndon Johnson had built upon the legacy of the slain John F. Kennedy. In his 1990 memoir, he dismissed the "so-called 'Great Society'" as an effort to "make most of the tax-and-spend Democrats of the past seem miserly be comparison. I thought we sorely needed Goldwater to reverse the trend. I said I'd do anything I could to get him elected."[24] Reagan argued that LBJ was taking the nation on the road to socialism. In the summer of 1964, he spoke to some eight hundred GOP donors at the Coconut Grove nightclub at the Ambassador Hotel in Los Angeles:

> I gave basically the same talk I'd been giving for years, altering it slightly so that it became a campaign speech for Barry. I recounted the relentless expansion of the federal government, the proliferation of government bureaucrats who were taking control of American business, and criticized liberal Democrats for taking the country down the road to socialism. As usual, I included some examples of Americans whose business or personal lives had been tormented by bureaucrats and cited examples of government waste, including one federal job training program that was costing taxpayers about seventy percent more for each trainee than it would have cost to send them to Harvard. I said America was at a crossroads: We had the choice of either continuing on this path or fighting to reclaim the liberties being taken from us. It was a speech, I suppose, that, with variations, I'd given hundreds of times before.[25]

This recycled speech was an inflection point in the political career of Ronald Reagan. "After dinner, five or six people from the audience came up and asked if I would join them for a few minutes at their table." By this time of the evening, the nightclub was nearly deserted. Reagan didn't know it, but the half-dozen individuals gathered at the table were among the largest GOP donors in the state. They asked Reagan if he would repeat the speech on national TV—if they could raise the money to air it. "Sure," Reagan answered, "if you think it would do any good."[26] Showbiz-savvy, Reagan suggested that the speech be taped before a live audience.

What became known as the "A Time for Choosing" speech was shot before a packed NBC studio audience and aired on October 27, 1964, approaching the eve of the election.

But the broadcast almost didn't happen. "A few days before the speech was scheduled to go on the air, I got a telephone call from Barry Goldwater. He sounded uneasy and a little uncomfortable. Some of his advisors, Barry said, wanted him to use the airtime that had been purchased for my speech to rebroadcast a videotape of a meeting he'd had at Gettysburg with Ike Eisenhower. He said they were afraid my speech, coming so close to the eve of the election, might backfire on him because of references in it to problems with the Social Security system."[27]

Reagan responded that he made his support for Social Security clear in the speech but conceded that he did argue for "improvements." He pointed out that "Americans had been deceived regarding the security of their money that was deducted from their paychecks to pay for Social Security benefits. For years we'd all been told that we were contributing to an old-age insurance fund that was being set aside for our retirement years, but, in fact, there was no 'fund' at all; it had become a compulsory payroll tax producing revenues Congress could—and did—use for any purpose it wanted...." He told Goldwater that he had been making the speech "all over the state for quite a while and I have to tell you, it's been very well received, including whatever remarks I've made about Social Security."[28]

Goldwater admitted he had not yet heard the speech. He said he would listen to a recording when he was in the campaign's hotel suite during a stop in Cleveland. After hearing it, he turned to his staff. "What the hell's wrong with that?" he asked. He next called Reagan and told him to go ahead with it.

Suddenly, Reagan got cold feet. "Who was I to tell a presidential candidate what he should or shouldn't do in his campaign? ... I thought for a while of calling the group who had purchased the airtime and asking them to withdraw my speech. ... But then I thought back on some of the other times I'd given that speech—it had always gotten a good response—and decided, after some lost sleep, not to ask them to withdraw it."[29]

Reagan himself never called it "A Time for Choosing." To him, then and for the rest of his life, it was simply "The Speech," and it distilled much of what he thought most important in 1964[30]:

> Thank you. Thank you very much. Thank you and good evening. The sponsor has been identified, but unlike most television programs, the performer hasn't been provided with a script. As a matter of fact, I have been permitted to choose my own words and discuss my own ideas regarding the choice that we face in the next few weeks.
>
> I have spent most of my life as a Democrat. I recently have seen fit to follow another course. I believe that the issues confronting us cross party lines. Now, one side in this campaign has been telling us that the issues of this election are the maintenance of peace and prosperity. The line has been used, "We've never had it so good."
>
> But I have an uncomfortable feeling that this prosperity isn't something on which we can base our hopes for the future. No nation in history has ever survived a tax burden that reached a third of its national income. Today, 37 cents out of every dollar earned in this country is the tax collector's share, and yet

our government continues to spend 17 million dollars a day more than the government takes in. We haven't balanced our budget 28 out of the last 34 years....

In what would always be a hallmark of Reagan's thought, the economic argument was based not on modern double-entry accounting but on ancient single-entry bookkeeping. It was all about spending to the exclusion of what value that spending purchased. It was all about the numbers—but the only numbers he delivered were the outlays.

When Reagan turned to the Vietnam War, his argument combined an appeal to emotion and wholly unproven assumptions:

> As for the peace that we would preserve, I wonder who among us would like to approach the wife or mother whose husband or son has died in South Vietnam and ask them if they think this is a peace that should be maintained indefinitely. Do they mean peace, or do they mean we just want to be left in peace? There can be no real peace while one American is dying some place in the world for the rest of us. We're at war with the most dangerous enemy that has ever faced mankind in his long climb from the swamp to the stars, and it's been said if we lose that war, and in so doing lose this way of freedom of ours, history will record with the greatest astonishment that those who had the most to lose did the least to prevent its happening. Well I think it's time we ask ourselves if we still know the freedoms that were intended for us by the Founding Fathers.

The result was a string of non-sequiturs delivered with utter confidence and conviction. It was followed by an anecdote twisted effortlessly into appearing as an illustration of self-government versus government by an "elite in a far-distant capitol," completely passing over the fact that this so-called elite was sent to the "capitol" through the will of the people.

> Not too long ago, two friends of mine were talking to a Cuban refugee, a businessman who had escaped from Castro, and in the midst of his story one of my friends turned to the other and said, "We don't know how lucky we are." And the Cuban stopped and said, "How lucky you are? I had someplace to escape to." And in that sentence he told us the entire story. If we lose freedom here, there's no place to escape to. This is the last stand on earth.
>
> And this idea that government is beholden to the people, that it has no other source of power except the sovereign people, is still the newest and the most unique idea in all the long history of man's relation to man.
>
> This is the issue of this election: Whether we believe in our capacity for self-government or whether we abandon the American revolution and confess that a little intellectual elite in a far-distant capitol can plan our lives for us better than we can plan them ourselves.

Next came an attempt to erase the unpopular political meaning of "left" and "right":

> You and I are told increasingly we have to choose between a left or right. Well

I'd like to suggest there is no such thing as a left or right. There's only an up or down—[up:] man's old-aged [age-old] dream, the ultimate in individual freedom consistent with law and order, or down to the ant heap of totalitarianism. And regardless of their sincerity, their humanitarian motives, those who would trade our freedom for security have embarked on this downward course.

The rest of the speech equated government with socialism—not, of course, as an attempt to better the lives of people, but as a means of control. Indeed, "A Time for Choosing" is an exercise in reductive argument. It reduces the objective of government to one thing, oppressive control, and it reduces oppression to controlling the economy:

> [The Founding Fathers] knew governments don't control things. A government can't control the economy without controlling people. And they knew when a government sets out to do that, it must use force and coercion to achieve its purpose.

This is certainly an arguable theory, but what follows next is a breathtaking and even fatuous assertion: "They also knew, those Founding Fathers, that outside of its legitimate functions, government does nothing as well or as economically as the private sector of the economy."

From here, Reagan talked about the "government's involvement in the farm economy over the last 30 years," arguing that "Every responsible farmer and farm organization has repeatedly asked the government to free the farm economy." Yet it was the farmers themselves who clamored for government subsidies. Reagan's own director of the Office of Management and Budget, David Stockman, spoke of a "Hayseed Coalition" of agricultural interests that fostered the crony capitalism of massive federal agricultural subsidies spawned by wartime demand in World War I but continued indefinitely ever since.[31] To be sure, a more careful speaker than Reagan could find plenty of instances of government waste or of administrative error. Instead, Reagan painted with the broadest possible brush, obliterating the fact that government does often act in response to perceived need as expressed by the people. As the Preamble to the Constitution stipulates, one of the purposes of government is "to promote the general welfare."

But, never mind. Ronald Reagan argued in 1964 that government is inevitably and unavoidably incompetent as well as often corrupt, and it always draws the same "socialist" conclusion: "We have so many people who can't see a fat man standing beside a thin one without coming to the conclusion the fat man got that way by taking advantage of the thin one. So they're going to solve all the problems of human misery through government and government planning."

Reagan turns on a veritable firehose of figures to prove that LBJ's "War on Poverty" has somehow increased poverty. In fact, he purports to demonstrate that government simply cannot intervene without making things worse. The proof? "Not too long ago, a judge called me here in Los Angeles. He told me of a young woman who'd come before him for a divorce. She had six children, was pregnant with her seventh. Under his questioning, she revealed her husband was a laborer earning 250 dollars a month. She wanted a divorce to get an 80 dollar raise. She's eligible for 330 dollars a month in the Aid to Dependent Children Program. She got the idea from two women in her neighborhood who'd already done that very thing." Who was this judge? Why did she call him? What was the date? Where were you on the night of the murder?

> Yet anytime you and I question the schemes of the do-gooders, we're denounced as being against their humanitarian goals. They say we're always "against" things—we're never "for" anything.
>
> Well, the trouble with our liberal friends is not that they're ignorant; it's just that they know so much that isn't so.

*   *   *

It's just that they know so much that isn't so. Such glib sophistries were the stuff of Ronald Reagan's earliest success with the electorate. With these, he began to garner a reputation as the Great Communicator. And from this unmeaning barb—"It's just that they know so much that isn't so"—he goes on to tackle Social Security, the "third rail" of politics. He makes an argument that Republicans have used ever since. "Now, we're for a provision that destitution should not follow unemployment by reason of old age, and to that end we've accepted Social Security as a step toward meeting the problem." Well, that's a relief. But he goes on to explain that if you get yourself insurance on the private market, you will do better than you do through Social Security; therefore, Social Security payroll taxes should be voluntary contributions. If we lived in an era before the advent of civilization and society, this would be a valid argument. But the idea of Social Security is that everyone participates in order to fund the program so that everyone can benefit.

From Social Security, "The Speech" moved on to foreign aid:

> I think we're for an international organization, where the nations of the world can seek peace. But I think we're against subordinating American interests to an organization that has become so structurally unsound that today you can muster a two-thirds vote on the floor of the General Assembly among nations that represent less than 10 percent of the world's population. I think we're against the hypocrisy of assailing our allies because here and there they cling to a colony, while we engage in a conspiracy of silence and never open our

mouths about the millions of people enslaved in the Soviet colonies in the satellite nations.

I think we're for aiding our allies by sharing of our material blessings with those nations which share in our fundamental beliefs, but we're against doling out money government to government, creating bureaucracy, if not socialism, all over the world. We set out to help 19 countries. We're helping 107. We've spent 146 billion dollars. With that money, we bought a 2 million dollar yacht for Haile Selassie. We bought dress suits for Greek undertakers, extra wives for Kenya[n] government officials. We bought a thousand TV sets for a place where they have no electricity. In the last six years, 52 nations have bought 7 billion dollars worth of our gold, and all 52 are receiving foreign aid from this country.

Once again, how are we funding bureaucracy and socialism and where? $146 billion of foreign aid went where? And over what time period? Is any of this foreign aid related to Vietnam or addressing the growing cold war with the Soviets (i.e., the evil empire)? You stumped us, Ron. What happened to those TV sets?

Where Reagan and Goldwater were most closely aligned was in their foundational avoidance of criticizing America or, for that matter, the United States government. They certainly criticized aspects and leaders of the U.S. government—What political candidate does not? If I tell you things are just fine as they are, why would you vote for me?—but their message was that American government was fixable. The target at which both aimed was generic Big Government, an affliction that attached to any number of nations. In this, they both differed from their future political spawn, Donald Trump, who took aim more specifically at the government of the United States, including when he was that government's chief executive. Included among such infamous moments was the July 2018 Helsinki summit, at which Trump, standing with Putin, publicly rebuked the U.S. intelligence community's assessment that Russia had interfered in the 2016 presidential election, saying he didn't "see any reason why Russia would be responsible."[32] It was as if Trump could never believe he had been elected president. His public condemnations are always delivered from the perspective of a mere bystander.

As for Reagan, his aim always went wider than Big Government. The reason for this was made clear in an aphorism from "The Speech": "No government ever voluntarily reduces itself in size." Accept this as true, then you must agree that all government is doomed to be or become Big Government. Thus, Reagan, like Goldwater, was inherently suspect of government itself. This is the significance of the phrase Reagan used earlier in his address, when he spoke of "the sovereign people." It is no accident that the so-called sovereign citizen movement came into being as the Republican party began turning the wheel harder and harder to the right. The idea that people are naturally "sovereign citizens," answerable to no law except certain aspects of common law and subject to no government statutes or proceedings to which they do not explicitly consent developed out of an eccentric 1950s tax-protest movement (aimed mainly against payment of federal income taxes). Now, Ronald Reagan was never a member of any tax protester group, but he groused about the higher income tax bracket that came with his increasing success in Hollywood. This claim of personal victimhood expanded into a generalized political talking point, even as early as his days as chief of SAG. It was one of a tight constellation of causes that propelled him into politics—an effort to stop government from picking his personal pocket.

Donald Trump would attack taxes for what were doubtless many of the same personal reasons as Reagan did, but he carried them further, and his actions were gleeful in the vandalization of government. Certainly, Reagan was no vandal, but the two presidents were far more aligned in their efforts to arouse fear of what Reagan called the bureaucracy and Trump called the Deep State. "So governments' programs," Reagan said in "The Speech," "once launched, never disappear. Actually, a government bureau is the nearest thing to eternal life we'll ever see on this earth." He went on to point out that "federal employees number two and a half million; and federal, state, and local, one out of six of the nation's work force employed by government. These proliferating bureaus with their thousands of regulations have cost us many of our constitutional safeguards. How many of us realize that today federal agents can invade a man's property without a warrant? They can impose a fine without a formal hearing, let alone a trial by jury? And they can seize and sell his property at auction to enforce the payment of that fine. In Chico County, Arkansas, James Wier over-planted his rice allotment. The government obtained a 17,000 dollar judgment. And a U.S. marshal sold his 960-acre farm at auction. The government said it was necessary as a warning to others to make the system work."

Both Reagan and Trump eagerly painted all federal employees as either agents of tyranny or loafers on the government dole or both. Moreover, Reagan extended this vision to state and local governments. Neither man acknowledged nor understood that the unelected agents of the government are in fact, for most Americans most of the time, the government. When you call 911, it is not a Congressman, a Senator, or the President who responds to save your life and protect your property. It is a public servant, an unelected member of the "bureaucracy" or the "Deep State."

Having painted in "The Speech" this extreme picture, Reagan refocused on "socialism," conflating it with Marxism, Leninism, and Stalinism but then arguing that "it doesn't require expropriation or confiscation of private property or business to impose socialism on a people. What does it mean whether you hold the deed to the, or the title to your business or property if the government holds the power of life and death over that business or property? And such machinery already exists. The government can find some charge to bring against any concern it chooses to prosecute. Every businessman has his own tale of harassment. Somewhere a perversion has taken place. Our natural, unalienable rights are now considered to be a dispensation of government, *and freedom has never been so fragile*, so close to slipping from our grasp as it is at this moment." Reagan appears oblivious of the Constitution here, insisting that the government's power is absolute and unconditional, as if the ballot didn't exist and as if the judiciary was not a coequal branch.

Reagan was well aware of the elephant in the room: the possibly unhinged "personality" of Barry Goldwater. Concerning the Vietnam War, Goldwater seemed to align himself with USAF general Curtis LeMay, who had commanded the unit that dropped two atomic bombs on Japan in World War II. His solution to Vietnam? "Tell them [the North Vietnamese] that they've got to draw in their horns and stop their aggression, or we're going to bomb them back into the Stone Age." Goldwater, himself an Air Force general who remained in the USAF Reserve, observed, "I could have ended the war in a month. I could have made North Vietnam like a mud puddle." How would he have done this? Make available to the military a supply of "small conventional nuclear weapons," which would not require presidential authority to use. Reagan was more aligned with LeMay and Goldwater than not, but he sought to avoid actually mentioning the nuclear arsenal by reducing the threat of annihilation and mutually assured destruction to a non sequitur quip: "It's silly to talk about how many years we will have to spend in the jungles of Vietnam when we could pave the whole country and put parking stripes on it and still be home for Christmas."[33]

The fact was that Goldwater's personality *was* very much at issue, not just for his willingness to use atomic weapons but for his reductive, myopic, and non-empathetic justification for voting against the Civil Rights Act of 1964: "I voted against the Civil Rights Act and I'd probably vote against it again. No one has the right to tell me who I have the right to rent a room to."[34] Reagan refused to acknowledge the validity of the personality issue, however, claiming only that the Democrats brought it up because they were "unwilling to debate these issues. They want to make you and I believe that this is a contest between two men—that we're to choose just between two personalities." Yet Reagan went out of his way to personally endorse Goldwater's *personality*: "I've never known a man in my life I believed so incapable of doing a dishonest or dishonorable thing," and he listed a number of philanthropic deeds, including running his business on a profit-sharing plan, "putting in health and medical insurance for all his employees," taking "50 percent of the profits before taxes [to] set up a retirement program, a pension plan for all his employees," sending "monthly checks for life to an employee who was ill and couldn't work," and so on. None of this, however, explains opposition to the Great Society.

Reagan closed this part of his speech by calling Goldwater "a man who said to his 19-year-old son, 'There is no foundation like the rock of honesty and fairness, and when you begin to build your life on that rock, with the cement of the faith in God that you have, then you have a real start.' This is not a man who could carelessly send other people's sons to war. And that is the issue of this campaign that makes all the other problems I've discussed academic, unless we realize we're in a war that must be won." Those who do not accept this proposition "would trade our freedom for the soup kitchen of the welfare state." He summed up: "Now let's set the record straight. There's no argument over the choice between peace and war, but there's only one guaranteed way you can have peace—and you can have it in the next second—surrender." This is the liberal policy, a "policy of … appeasement." Khrushchev, Reagan told his audience, hears "voices pleading for 'peace at any price' or 'better Red than dead,' or as one commentator put it, he'd rather 'live on his knees than die on his feet.' And therein lies the road to war, because those voices don't speak for the rest of us. … You and I know and do not believe that life is so dear and peace so sweet as to be purchased at the price of chains and slavery. … should Moses have told the children of Israel to live in slavery under the pharaohs? Should Christ have refused the cross? Should the patriots at Concord Bridge have thrown down their guns and refused to fire the shot heard 'round the world'? … Well, it's a simple answer after all. … You and I have the courage to say to our enemies, 'There is a price we will not pay.' … this is the meaning in the phrase of Barry Goldwater's 'peace through strength.' … You and I have a rendezvous with destiny." Perhaps Reagan's audience recalled the origin of this line. It was from Franklin D. Roosevelt's 1936 acceptance of the Democratic Party's nomination as their candidate for reelection to the presidency. Reagan concluded:

> We'll preserve for our children this, the last best hope of man on earth, or we'll sentence them to take the last step into a thousand years of darkness.
> We will keep in mind and remember that Barry Goldwater has faith in us. He has faith that you and I have the ability and the dignity and the right to make our own decisions and determine our own destiny.

*   *   *

"A Time for Choosing" failed in its assigned mission. The following month, Barry Goldwater was defeated by Lyndon Johnson in a landslide, 43,129,040 to 27,175,754 (486 electoral votes to 52). But The Speech was the rocket fuel that launched the political career of Ronald Wilson Reagan.

CHAPTER 8

California Dreaming

Ronald Reagan's "A Time for Choosing" did nothing to stop the LBJ landslide in 1964. With considerable justification, Reagan blamed this failure on the refusal of a "lot of liberal Republicans ... to support Goldwater against Johnson. The split was especially deep in California, where moderate and conservative factions of the party had already been feuding for years." In his 1990 memoir, he was blasé about Goldwater's dismal showing: "After the election, I went back to doing what I'd been doing before it—speaking on national issues and doing my job on 'Death Valley Days.'"[1] He had good reason not to care too much. For if "The Speech" failed to excite support for Goldwater, it put Reagan on the GOP radar.

Holmes P. Tuttle (1905–1989) was born in an Oklahoma town named for his father. But while the Tuttles were prominent, they were not wealthy, and, at seventeen, young Tuttle moved to Oklahoma City, where he found work in a Ford automobile parts facility. After three years working in car parts, the young man hopped onto a westward-bound freight train, intent on seeking his fortune in Los Angeles. Railroad cops ejected him and a traveling buddy, but he managed to persuade a well-heeled dowager, whose chauffeur had broken his leg, to put them behind the wheel and drive her to Los Angeles.

In LA, Tuttle found a job as parts manager at a Ford dealership, and he worked his way up from there. In 1945, with the end of World War II producing a boom in demand for cars, Tuttle was able to open Holmes Tuttle Ford. He hit a speed bump in the late 1940s, when he ventured into distributing English Fords—imported British-made Fords—and lost badly. This forever confirmed his allegiance to the bedrock of his developing conservative philosophy, Made in America. Later offered an opportunity to distribute the newly available Volkswagen nationally, he flat-out refused, reasoning that "if our returning GIs wouldn't buy a car built by our allies, then they certainly won't buy a car built in Germany." Before long, Tuttle had opened fourteen Ford dealerships in California and Arizona.[2]

Tuttle was among the Southern California businessmen Reagan had met at the Coconut Grove dinner, where he had delivered an early version of "A Time for Choosing." It had been Tuttle's idea to buy TV airtime for it. Now, in the aftermath of the election, he called Reagan and invited himself "and several friends" to "drop by" the Reagans' Pacific Palisades home. "After I heard what they said," Reagan recalled in 1990, "I almost laughed them out of the house. I can't remember my exact words, but I said, in effect: 'You're out of your mind.' Tuttle and the other members of his group said they wanted me to run for governor in 1966, when Pat Brown, the liberal Democrat who had beat Nixon for reelection in 1962, was expected to run for a third term."[3] Reagan wrote in *An American Life* that he had "no interest ... whatsoever" in running for office, having concluded from his "research ... on the operations of government" that the "last thing I wanted was to become a part of it." He preferred making speeches about it, protesting to Tuttle and his associates, "I'm an actor, not a politician, I'm in show business."[4]

If Reagan was recalling things accurately and in good faith, his was a remarkably honest and insightful response. What he said about the counterargument Tuttle and company offered is even more revealing: "they claimed the party was in such shambles following the 1964 election that its survival as a force in California was in doubt and, mentioning my speech for Goldwater, they said they thought I might be the only Republican around who had a chance of beating Brown and bringing the party back together." Then Reagan revealed that he had no illusions: "Nothing was said, incidentally, about whether I would make a good governor or not. They just said I was the only one who could bring the party together."[5]

At this point, Reagan gave them a flat no. Running "was out of the question," he still wanted to help his party and promised that if they could find somebody they thought would make a good governor, he would "campaign for him as hard as I can, the way I campaigned for Barry." Given the magnitude of the landslide under which LBJ buried Barry, it must not have sounded like much of an offer. Reagan himself seems to have understood this, remarking in his 1990 memoir, "I hoped I'd put the idea to rest."[6]

He had not. They "kept coming back," followed by the Federated Republican Women's Club. Reagan protested that he was "happy in show business," and Nancy was "flabbergasted" by the very idea. "We loved our life as it was and didn't want it to change. We had our children, our friends in Hollywood, our home, our ranch, our privacy; we had a good income and all the opportunities I ever wanted to speak about the issues that concerned me. I was approaching an age when some of the men I knew were already starting to think about retirement. ... I had a good job and a good life and, at fifty-four, the last thing I wanted to do was start a new career."[7]

Under what he portrayed (accurately, it would seem) as relentless pressure from Tuttle and others, Reagan sought counsel from Loyal Davis, who reinforced his reluctance, telling him he "would be crazy to run for office; he said there was no way a man could go into politics without sacrificing his honesty and honor, because no matter how well intentioned he was, a politician was inevitably forced by the realities of political life to compromise." Reagan replied "that he didn't need any convincing, he wasn't going to run."[8]

Tuttle the salesman wouldn't take no for an answer. Soon, Reagan recalls, both he and Nancy were plagued by insomnia. The "constant emphasis that I was the only guy around who could beat Brown and heal the split in the party put a lot of weight on our shoulders." In his 1990 memoir, he portrays both himself and Nancy as racked with guilt: "*If they're right and things get worse for the party and we could have done something about it, will we ever be able to sleep at night again?*"[9]

Apparently seeking little more than a good night's sleep, Reagan wrote that he "finally decided to make an offer to the people who wanted me to run for governor: 'Even though I think you're wrong about my being the only Republican who might be able to beat Brown, if you fellows will arrange it for me to go on the road and accept some of the speaking invitations I'm getting from groups around the state, then I'll go out and speak to them and come back in six months, on the last day of 1965, and tell you whether you're right or whether you should be looking for somebody else to run for governor.' His belief, he said, was that in six months, *he* would be able to find a candidate."[10]

*   *   *

Maybe this really was the way Reagan remembered it in 1990. It seems more likely that, in his memoir, he was playing the classic role of the reluctant candidate—a part that is at least as old as George Washington, who loved Mount Vernon even more that Reagan loved Pacific Palisades.

It is true that the failed Goldwater candidacy was highly divisive for the GOP. Reagan biographer Lou Cannon calls the situation in 1964 "self-consuming fratricide." He notes that Reagan was less interested in the defeat of Goldwater than in the victory of his good friend, fellow actor George Murphy. In the 1964 general election, Murphy defeated Democrat Pierre Salinger for a seat in the California senate. Cannon believes Reagan took away two very interesting lessons from this victory. Number one, a "former actor with a conservative message could win in California," and, number two, Murphy's ticket-splitting victory indicated that Californians rejected Goldwater, not the GOP. In his memoir, Reagan portrayed himself as a political novice, but in an article he wrote for the December 1, 1964, issue of *National Review*, he revealed himself as a canny politician, political strategist, and, more to the point, a salesman with his foot firmly in the door: "All of the landslide majority did not vote against the conservative philosophy, they voted against a false image our Liberal opponents successfully mounted. Indeed, it was a double false image. Not only did they portray us as advancing a kind of radical departure from the status quo, but they took for themselves a costume of comfortable conservatism." Listen, and you can hear a pre-echo of Donald Trump's infinitely well-worn trope of projection: casting upon your opponents that which they throw upon you. "I would remind you that extremism in defense of liberty is no vice. And let me remind you also that moderation in the pursuit of justice is no virtue," Goldwater had declared in the speech Karl Hess (his speechwriter) had written for him to accompany his acceptance of his party's nomination. Yet, according to Reagan, it is the Liberals who "portray us as advancing a kind of radical departure from the status quo." In fact, Reagan doubles down on the projection, claiming that it is the Democrats who have clothed themselves in "a costume of comfortable conservatism." Without a touch of shame, he tells fellow Republicans that it is "Time now for the soft sell to prove our radicalism was an optical illusion." Some would call this clever, others shockingly cynical. But then Reagan finds the note that would carry the GOP on the shoulders of a dubious populism directly into the eventual presidency of Donald John Trump: "We represent the forgotten American—that simple soul who goes to work, bucks for a raise, takes out insurance, pays for his kids' schooling, contributes to his church and charity and knows that there just *'ain't no such thing as a free lunch.'*"[11]

"Reagan," Cannon wrote, "had sounded like a prospective candidate in the *National Review* article, written a few days after the Goldwater defeat. I believe he had already decided to seek public office, in no small part because he knew he could better Goldwater's showing." In fact, Reagan shared this very conviction with Holmes Tuttle, who believed Goldwater had made a foolish political error by choosing the extremely conservative William Miller as his running mate instead of the moderate governor of Pennsylvania William Scranton. If Reagan played hard to get when Tuttle pushed him to become governor, it may have been because he already had his sights set on what his pal George Murphy had aimed at and hit: national office. Cannon quotes a letter from Maureen Reagan to her father, in which she observed that he "could" be governor. Reagan wrote back, "Well, if we're talking about what I could do, Mermie, I *could* be president." Shortly after this epistolary exchange, Maureen visited her father and urged him to run for governor. "Gesturing to Nancy with a smile, Reagan said, 'Oh, my God, they're closing in all over.'"[12]

By this time, his observation was not hyperbole. Tuttle, first and last a salesman, always was closing. Many assume that Reagan's early rise was financed by Wall Street and its equivalent. In fact, the money behind it belonged to men like Holmes P. Tuttle, self-made men, whose realization of the American Dream was earned entrepreneurially rather than inherited or conferred by involvement with some corporate behemoth. Early on, the only establishment millionaires associated with Reagan were A.C. (Cy) Rubel, chairman of the board of Union Oil Company, and Leonard Firestone, president of the eponymous rubber company. The others included MCA executive Taft Schreiber, who became an intimate of Reagan during Reagan's long association with MCA; Henry Salvatori, a wildcat oil driller, who founded Western Geophysical and did mortal combat against communists and big oil; investment banker Leland Kaiser; Edward Mills, VP at Holmes Tuttle Enterprises; Arch Monson, Jr., an executive of Autocall Company; and Jaquelin Hume, president of Basic Vegetable Products. Together with Tuttle, these were organized as "The Friends of Ronald Reagan," and Tuttle recruited Spencer-Roberts, Southern California political strategy consultants, to help their "friend."

Stuart Spencer and Bill Roberts gravitated toward managing moderate Republican campaigns, including that of Nelson Rockefeller in the 1964 presidential primary. Spencer-Roberts, therefore, did not jump at the chance to manage the Reagan campaign. In 1968, Roberts told Lou Cannon in an interview that they "had heard that Reagan was a real right-winger and we thought that a right-wing kind of candidacy would not be a successful one." Roberts also told Cannon that Reagan had a reputation of being "difficult to work with." When Reagan met with the two consultants in Cave de Roy, a tony LA key club, his trademark geniality won them over. They found him "candid … easy to talk with, and a good listener," according to Roberts. Spencer's reaction was even more to the point: he was "not a nut," and he had "a moral center … always important in a candidate."[13]

For his part, Reagan was glad he had won over Spencer-Roberts because he believed they knew how to manage a winning campaign. They had made no attempt to hide their moderate leanings, but Reagan was less interested in striking an ideological harmony with the pair than he was in being led over the finish line by two competent political operatives. He demanded no ideological litmus tests. He was a political pragmatist, meaning that he would work with whomever had the best chance of making him a winner.

Having met with Spencer-Roberts, Reagan now took the initiative. He called Tuttle and told him he was ready to run. Soon after, at his third meeting with Spencer and Roberts at the Reagan home, he popped the question: "Well, what about it? Are you going to do it? You've been asking me questions for three meetings now." Roberts spoke for the partnership: they were ready to manage the campaign.[14]

In his own account of the campaign, Reagan put the responsibility for hiring Spencer-Roberts totally upon Holmes Tuttle, and he said that the consultants' role was largely just "look[ing] over my speaking invitations and pick[ing] out ones they thought would get me around the state, ... exclude[ing] Republican functions; the idea was to avoid partisan events and speak to ordinary Californians."[15] He also maintained the fiction that he was really trying to speak to the people's discontent, not to advance his own political future but to find someone else—someone more qualified— to run for governor. A long-time supporting actor turning down a chance to be a star? Did anybody bet on that?

Reagan recalled beginning his campaign—or was it really and truly a fact-finding tour?—on July 1, 1965, driving "up and down the length and breadth of California for six months.... I'd give a speech, then get in my car and drive to the next one, meeting the members of organizations like the Rotary Club, Chamber of Commerce, and United Way. The speeches had pretty much the same flavor that my speeches had had since the later years on the General Electric plant tours...." Reagan reported that, "after the speeches, I'd hear a lot of the same things from members of the audience that I'd heard for years on the GE tours: People were tired of wasteful government programs and welfare chiselers; and they were angry about the constant spiral of taxes and government regulations, arrogant bureaucrats, and public officials who thought all of mankind's problems could be solved by throwing the taxpayers' dollars at them." He claimed that, after each speech, people would urge him to run for governor. "I'd laugh and give my standard response: 'I'm an actor, not a politician,' then ask them to suggest someone who was really qualified to be governor. But all I heard were voices of more people chiming in to urge me to run against Brown."[16] This may be true. It may be what Reagan heard. Yet, in the context of future history, it all sounds a lot like the line Donald Trump uses as a substitute for evidence: "People are saying...."

The people drafted me. That was the gist of the account Reagan gave in his 1990 memoir. It was a familiar American myth, founded on George Washington, the American Cincinnatus, the servant leader, who only with reluctance answered the country's call to serve. He even dishes up a scene with Nancy, which reads as if it had been lifted from one of the B-movie scripts Reagan so easily committed to memory: "After about three months of this, I returned home one night and said to Nancy, 'This isn't working out the way I thought it would. You know, these guys may be right. All these people are telling me after my speeches that I ought to run for governor; this may end up putting us in an awful spot.'" The couple suffered more sleepless nights: "How do you say no to all these people?" ... [Nancy,] "I don't think we can run away from it." On January 4, 1966, Ronald Reagan broadcast his intention to seek the GOP nomination for governor.[17]

*   *   *

In the primary, Ronald Reagan's principal adversary was George Christopher, a Republican moderate and former mayor of San Francisco, who pushed all of the Gipper's buttons. Christopher "tried simultaneously to portray me as a right-wing extremist and attack me because I'd admitted having been in Communist front groups—without mentioning that I'd resigned and declared war on them as soon as I'd realized what they were," Reagan recalled in 1990. He was especially bitter about what happened at a convention of black Republicans. Reagan spoke to the group, "followed by Christopher, who got up and implied during his speech that I was a racial bigot." That was when Candidate Reagan lost it. "I fumed about it for a moment or two, stood up, and said (some people there say I shouted) to Christopher that he was wrong, that I'd never been a bigot and I deeply resented his attack on my integrity. Then I walked off the stage and drove home, leaving a startled audience behind me."[18]

Fortunately for Reagan, two members of his campaign team followed him home, knocked on the door, and persuaded him to return to the convention. "I got back on the platform and tried to explain how I had been raised and why I took such offense at Christopher's remarks. I think they understood why I had exploded in response to the attack on my integrity. But it was the last time I stalked off a stage during a political debate."[19]

Reagan not only survived that day but also won the primary and found himself facing incumbent two-term Democratic governor Edmund G. (Pat) Brown. Brown was dismissive of Reagan's candidacy. He misjudged the staying power of "The Speech," and though he was a veteran politician, he could not appreciate the mojo of the image Reagan had, both deliberately and incidentally, crafted over the years. Brown and the Democratic establishment saw only the Boraxo-hawking host of *Death Valley Days* and the befuddled star of *Bedtime for Bonzo* wedded to a rightwing extremist presidential candidate who had been utterly crushed by LBJ.

Indeed, many believe that Brown and his equally tone-deaf consultants had deliberately maneuvered during the GOP primaries to encourage what they saw as Reagan's strawman candidacy. They were delighted when he won the primary, believing it would be a California replay of the 1964 downfall of Goldwater.

Their delight did not last long. In the general election, candidate Reagan defused every bomb Brown hurled at him. In response to accusations that he lacked political experience, he claimed this would allow him to govern with fresh eyes and an open mind—a prospect many voters found as appealing in 1966 as they would in the presidential race of 2016. Asked what kind of governor he would be, he responded, "I don't know, I've never played a governor."[20] It proved to be a brilliant retort. Where his opponent saw it only as confirmation of Reagan's vulnerability, voters interpreted it as supreme self-confidence. Ronald Reagan carried 53 of 58 California counties.

*   *   *

After a hardscrabble childhood, everything seemed to come easily to Ronald Reagan. This impression was amplified by the very rhythms of his speech and his generally affable public persona. Because he had been a journeyman actor, never an A-lister, it was easy to assume that he was lazy. In fact, Reagan had a powerful work ethic. For nearly eight years, he gave General Electric more than their money's worth, beating across the country to carry the GE standard and to inculcate the politely conservative values mega-corporations like GE favor. Although he himself, writing in 1990, sought to portray his campaign for governor as nothing more or less than a humble response to the people's call, he campaigned hard. And when it came time to be sworn in as governor, he did not wait for the public ceremony but took the oath of office at 12:10 in the morning of January 2, 1967, lest Pat Brown name partisan judges at the eleventh hour.

It was a surprising level of efficiency that would characterize his first term. Yes, he was an actor, not a politician. His political career drew heavily on his acting experience, including his understanding the value of an able supporting cast. He had his campaign supporters, including Spencer-Roberts, Holmes Tuttle, and the rest of the "Friends of Ronald Reagan." He had his money and business connections. And far from turning his back on Hollywood in some misguided effort to distance himself from his deeply entrenched identity as an actor, he welcomed the enthusiastic support lavished on him by the likes of Walt Disney, Bob Hope, John Wayne, Jimmy Stewart, Dinah Shore, Jack Benny, George Burns, and James Cagney. Nor did he seek to distance himself from MCA, source of scandal though it had been. Company cofounder Taft B. Schreiber remained a valuable confidante and friend.

Taft Schreiber did not, however, serve as one of Governor Reagan's key staffers, a gubernatorial version of what would be President Reagan's "Kitchen Cabinet." The gubernatorial version included Lyn Nofziger, a journalist and GOP political consultant who served as press secretary to the Reagan gubernatorial campaign and then, for two years, as the governor's Director of Communications. He would later work on Reagan's two presidential campaigns and served in the Reagan White House for about a year as Assistant to the President for Political Affairs.

Thomas C. Reed, an organizer during the campaign, became senior aide to Governor Reagan. California rancher and lawyer William P. Clark, Jr., became Governor Reagan's Executive Secretary and was subsequently appointed by Reagan as judge in the Superior Court of California, Associate Justice of the California Court of Appeal, and then as Associate Justice of the California State Supreme Court. (Interestingly, Clark had never graduated from Stanford University, but scored high enough on entrance exams to gain admittance to Loyola Law School, which he likewise left without a degree, preferring to devote his time to managing his ranch. Nevertheless, he took and passed—on a second attempt—the California bar examination.)

Edwin (Ed) Meese III developed a special relationship with the governor. A lawyer who maintained a private practice even as he served as a prosecutor in the Alameda County DA's office, he drew the attention of an influential California state senator, Donald Grunsky, who recommended him to the new governor. Reagan appointed him to his legal staff and soon named him Legal Affairs Secretary and, later, Executive Assistant (1967–1968) and Chief of Staff (1969–1974). He was never an overtly partisan Reaganite, but he was early on known as a kind of Reagan whisperer, who developed a unique rapport with his boss. Lou Cannon called him "Reagan's geographer"[21] because he was able to guide him over difficult political terrain. Meese did not merely explain complex ideas to the governor but did so in a language and style of expression that, observers noted, mirrored if not outright mimicked Reagan himself.

Rounding out the gubernatorial Kitchen Cabinet were three others. William French Smith II was a white-shoe Harvard Law School lawyer who became Reagan's attorney and was nominated by the governor in 1968 to serve on the University of California Board of Regents. Thomas Reed, a mechanical engineer and former U.S. Air Force officer (specializing in thermonuclear weapons physics), was an organizer in the Reagan gubernatorial campaign and, during the first term, worked with Philip Battaglia, a young man with a remarkable talent for organization, to set up the nuts and bolts of administration operations.

Lyn Nofziger commented that the Reagan gubernatorial campaign "materialized out of thin air"—that is, without a political machine behind it. The campaign was "run by hired people who then walked away and left it; therefore, when he was elected, the big question was, 'My God, what do we do now?'"[22] This was hyperbole. Not everyone walked away. The transition from campaign to administration sat heavily on the shoulders of Reed and Battaglia.

Phil Battaglia was a rising star, who took his degree from the University of Southern California Law School at the remarkable age of twenty while working as a law clerk in the LA firm of Flint & MacKay, which he subsequently joined. He was not a politico by nature, but Holmes Tuttle saw in him a talented organizer, and he and Reed made an effective team, helping to get the new administration on its feet. Now it could *run*.

*   *   *

Arguably, Reagan entered politics because he resented the fact that his financial success pushed him into a higher tax bracket, which meant that he kept less of the money he was making. With a personal passion driving him, he campaigned as a tax cutter and vowed to reduce the size of government. Once in office, however, he mostly raised taxes but did freeze government hiring. Even this gesture toward controlling the expansion of Big Government was mitigated by a 9 percent increase in government spending, he reached across the aisle to Democratic Assembly speaker Jess Unruh to enact tax increases that both raised rates and balanced the budget. The state sales tax was raised from 3 percent to 5 percent. The highest state income tax bracket rose from 7 percent to 10 percent. Taxes on banks, corporate profits, and inheritance were increased very modestly, but liquor taxes jumped from $1.50 to $2.00 per gallon, and cigarette taxes soared from three to ten cents per pack.[23] Significantly, Reagan cut property taxes. Thus, despite his campaign promises, Reagan did not cut taxes—except for property taxes, which are the most regressive of taxes to cut, as the reductions benefit solely those wealthy enough to own property (skew Republican) while excluding less affluent renters (skew Democratic). Of the property owners, those who benefited most from the Reagan tax cuts were those who owned the most and most expensive properties (skew Republican even more). His ultimate—and quite nuanced—objective was to arrest the expansion of government while raising the budget of government as well creating enough new tax revenue to balance the budget.

While he was governor, Reagan's conservatism was less about tax cuts than curbing Big Government. This was his main lever in balancing the budget. Yet while raising most taxes, Reagan protected property ownership, the asset most closely associated with the affluent.

When Reagan entered office, Big Government, reckless suspending (deficit spending), and burdensome taxes were the principal target issues of conservative politicians. Very soon, another issue emerged, and California found itself in the thick of it. Abortion was rapidly becoming a new source of liberal/conservative division. Yet it is telling that Reagan did not have a knee-jerk response to the issue.

The year he took office as governor, 1967, the abortion debate targeted California, where the California Medical Association and the California Bar Association joined the American Medical Association, the American

Bar Association, and the American Academy of Pediatrics in support of legislation to shield physicians from criminal prosecution if they performed abortions under strict hospital controls. The California legislature introduced the Therapeutic Abortion Act, which provided such protection. While the Catholic Church opposed the law, the Catholic laity were divided on it. Reagan was in a quandary and sought advice from his physician father-in-law, Loyal Davis (he favored the law), and Los Angeles archbishop Cardinal James McIntyre (he opposed it). Reagan synthesized the two positions, announcing that he would support abortions to protect the health of the mother but would veto the current legislation because it also permitted abortion in the case of birth defects. The legislature was quick to respond by dropping the birth defect provision, the legislation was passed, and Reagan signed it into law.

It was, quite arguably, a positively pragmatic decision. Moreover, Reagan and many others who supported the California legislation, which became a model for numerous states, believed it would reduce the number of abortions performed in California while at the same time making it medically safer. In reality, while California recorded 5,018 abortions in 1968, the year the law went into effect, numbers shot up throughout the 1970s, when about 100,000 abortions were performed annually in California. With legal sanctions removed, the burgeoning women's movement found that women not only had the right to control their own bodies, including the role of their bodies in reproduction, but now were free to claim that right.

In 1976, the year after his second term as governor ended, Ronald Reagan retreated from his support for abortion rights. With Republican conservatism looking to garner support among increasingly powerful anti-abortion groups, Reagan, eyeing national office, made a remarkable "admission." While campaigning for the GOP nomination for president, he announced that he would support a constitutional amendment "overthrowing" *Roe v. Wade* (410 U.S. 113 [1973]), which liberalized the basis for abortion, effectively legalizing abortion on demand. How did he account for this radical change of position? He said that in 1967, as governor, he had made a "mistake," explaining that "If I had it to do all over again I would have more restrictions than I agreed to. … I placed too much faith in those who were entrusted with insuring that the patient met the terms of the bill," those terms being (primarily) protecting the health of the mother.[24]

While Reagan's stance on taxes and abortion would change when he entered national politics, his early actions on these issues in California, coming very soon after he assumed office, were enabled in part by the organizational skills of his staff, especially Reed and Battaglia. Yes, he was lucky to have them.

That luck ran out—suddenly—on August 25, 1967, when nine of Reagan's aides descended upon their boss demanding that Phil Battaglia be fired for gross misconduct. Battaglia was a sexually active gay man, who had affairs with members of Reagan's junior staff. At the time, this was not a Republican versus Democratic issue. Famously, in 1964, President Lyndon Johnson dismissed his top aide, Walter Jenkins, when he was arrested for solicitation in a YMCA men's room. Valuable as Battaglia was, Reagan and his advisors deemed him urgently expendable, and he resigned on August 28, 1967, announcing his decision to return to the private practice of law.[25] William P. Clark replaced him.

*   *   *

Ed Meese was legal affairs secretary from 1967 to 1968 and executive assistant and chief of staff to Governor Reagan from 1969 to 1974. He earned praise, including from some Democrats, even though he reinforced many of Reagan's more reactionary expressions of conservatism. At various times in the 1960s, going back to the governorship of Reagan's Democratic predecessor, Pat Brown, the Berkeley campus of the University of California erupted in protests against the Vietnam War. During Reagan's watch, a "People's Park" created by political activists near the university, became the epicenter of frequent demonstrations and rallies. On May 15, 1969, during an police operation to clear out People's Park, an officer fatally shot a student, James Rector, who was guilty of nothing more than walking to class. The law enforcement efforts to end the "occupation" of People's Park on that "Bloody Thursday" also resulted in injury to hundreds, many of them bystanders. Contrary to the expressed will of the Berkeley City Council, Reagan took Meese's advice to declare a state of emergency throughout the entire city. As a result, the state's National Guard was rushed in, and helmeted M14-toting Guardsmen occupied People's Park for two weeks. Predictably, conservatives were gratified by Reagan's show of strength, while liberals were outraged by the introduction of military force on top of police overreaction and brutality. While the decision to which Meese moved Reagan was subject to interpretation, one thing was certain. It branded Ronald Reagan as a hardline law-and-order conservative, and, in the public mind, for better or worse, wedded him to what was seen as the Goldwater ethos.

Meese and Reagan were clearly fond of one another, but Nancy Reagan, to whom husband Ron frequently turned for advice, never trusted Meese. Still, she was unable to pry him away from the governor. (She would have better luck during his presidency.) Nancy Reagan was far more amiably disposed toward Michael Deaver, whom Meese had recruited. Deaver had the double distinction of having been a "barroom piano player" and a graduate from San Jose State with a degree in political science. He and a business partner ran an LA-based advertising agency. Meese thought Deaver was especially valuable because he was "sensitive to Reagan's moods" and (along with his wife, Carolyn) was well-liked by Nancy. Indeed, in *Nancy Reagan: The Unauthorized Biography* (1991), Kitty Kelley wrote that other Reagan staffers took to calling Deaver "Nancy's Nancy" and (somewhat more puzzling) "Lord of the Chamber Pot."[26] Perhaps Meese thought that some of her affection for Deaver would rub off on him. That never happened.[27]

*   *   *

"Happy wife, happy life" goes the shamelessly sexist cliché. Ronald Reagan was not a political junkie. "He forgot the names of people he had met a dozen times and displayed an absolute disinterest in the mechanics of politics, but he thrived on political performances," according to Lou Cannon in an article for *Politico*. Nancy, however, did not care for those performances, "despite her adoration of her husband," and when "the Reagans went to Sacramento in 1967 after his election as governor, she made little effort to conceal her distaste for politics and politicians." However, if there was one thing she had even less appetite for, it was Sacramento: "She possessed a Southern Californian's strong dislike of Sacramento, then suffering through a dank winter, and refused to live in the old governor's mansion, a Victorian relic on a one-way truck route through town. With a frankness that offended the government community, Nancy Reagan complained that the mansion was a firetrap and unsafe for their eight-year-old son."[28]

Sacramentans, however, happened to love the large, quirky Victorian Gothic governor's residence, which had been built by local merchant Albert Gallatin in 1877 and purchased by the state in 1903 for $32,500. Residents of the state capital didn't much appreciate their First Lady's disparagement of it. Her husband, however, had no qualms about renting a Tudor-style house in a more residential neighborhood. He did not ask California to foot the bill, but Holmes Tuttle and the "Friends of Ronald Reagan" paid $150,000 for it and leased it to the Reagans for $1,500 a month. In the meantime, the governor who advocated for small government and froze hiring immediately upon taking office authorized design and construction of a new governor's residence, which the cultural journalist and Sacramento native Joan Didion wrote about in 1977, calling it "an altogether curious structure, this one-story one-million-four dream house of Ronald and Nancy Reagan's," which she compared, aesthetically, to "supermarkets and housing projects and Coca-Cola bottling plants." She noted that Reagan's successor, Governor Jerry Brown, refused to live in it, denouncing it as a "Taj Mahal," while others called it a "white elephant," a "resort," and a "monument to the colossal ego of our former governor." Didion, however, wrote that it "is not exactly any of these things" but "simply and rather astonishingly an enlarged version of a very common kind of California tract house," which she compared to the "lobby area in a Ramada Inn." The Reagans never, in fact, lived there, as the house was completed at the very end of the governor's second and final term.[29]

It wasn't all Nancy's fault. Ronald Reagan was an active and very consequential governor, yet, even as he served in that office, his ambitions were national in scope. Very soon after embarking on his first term, he and his kitchen cabinet sensed the possibility of a 1968 presidential run. The Republican Party was still painfully torn between its moderate and conservative wings. George Romney (father of Mitt) and Nelson Rockefeller were the moderates, and Richard Nixon was emerging as the more conservative-leaning possibility. Among Reagan's advisers, Reed and Nofziger rejected the two moderates in favor of Nixon—at least on the basis of ideology. But they doubted that Nixon, a candidate congenitally unlikable, appearing uncomfortable in his own skin, could win. Reagan was affable, confident, and conservative. There seemed to be a gap waiting for him to enter.

Reagan was not so sure. Phil Battaglia's homosexual "escapades" (the contemporary word for his affairs) left behind a whiff of scandal, which some in his circle believed would be difficult to overcome, even though Battaglia had hurriedly and quietly left the gubernatorial staff. Amid a growing "Stop Nixon" wave—the 1960s equivalent of the "Never Trump" movement—Reagan became increasingly willing to explore the possibility of entering the primary race as a compromise candidate between Rockefeller and Nixon. But he proceeded cautiously, awaiting the results of the 1968 GOP convention. His only path was if neither Nixon nor Rockefeller received a first-ballot majority. By August 1968, however, the GOP convention took place in Miami Beach and gave Nixon 692 delegate votes, 25 more than he needed to secure the nomination on a first ballot. Rockefeller was a distant second, and Reagan, whose name had been put in contention, was a remote third. When the ballots were actually cast, Nixon emerged with 1,238 votes, Rockefeller with 93, and Reagan trailed dismally at just 2.

Ronald Reagan pulled in his horns—which he had never really extended very far in the first place—and returned to governing California. The prospect of being subject to a recall vote had been a landmine in California gubernatorial politics since the late nineteenth century. No recall attempt, however, had ever succeeded in getting the required number of signatures to carry it from petition to popular referendum. By August 1968, a coalition of senior citizens, educators, and union members—which *The New York Times* characterized as "political amateurs"—had gathered 456,000 signatures on a recall petition, which fell far short of the 780,414 registered voter signatures (12 percent of the last election vote total) required for holding a recall ballot. "I've had faith in the people of California," Reagan commented, "and that faith is vindicated."[30] Thus, Reagan joined a long list of elected California state officials who survived recall attempts. He ran for reelection in 1970, defeating Democrat Jesse M. Unruh—with whom he had worked cordially during his first term—by a nearly 3 percent margin. It was not a landslide, but a solid majority nevertheless.

During his second term, Reagan zealously championed the application of capital punishment, which was legal in California but faced court challenges, the most serious of which was the February 1972 decision of the Supreme Court of California in *People v. Anderson* (6 Cal. 3d 628), which invalidated all California death sentences issued prior to 1972 on the grounds that capital punishment was contrary to the state's constitution. Reagan successfully pushed for a constitutional amendment, resulting in the passage of Proposition 17 (November 7, 1972) and the reinstatement of capital punishment. Despite his hawkish stance on the death penalty, only one execution took place—in 1967, during the governor's first term—while another death sentence was stayed that year by Reagan himself.[31]

The governor faced a more nuanced dilemma in 1971, after the state supreme court decided in *Serrano v. Priest* (18 Cal.3d 728) that the state must take steps to bring equity between wealthy and poor districts in school spending. Working with a Democratic legislative majority, Reagan had no choice but to compromise. His strategy was to keep the costs of equalization down. This meant limiting school spending overall while providing more money for poorer school districts to bring them to parity. At the same time, he was determined to make further cuts in property taxes for homeowners. Reagan knew what he was trying to accomplish and worked with the Democratic speaker, Bob Moretti, to strike a compromise that would give both the Republican and Democratic bases things they wanted. Reagan secured support from Republicans, business groups, and the school lobby as well as moderate Democrats. In the end, he negotiated a package of cuts, grants, and assistance that gave funds to poorer districts while enabling a *reduction* in school tax rates. "Special assistance" was specifically earmarked for inner-city districts, which were heavily Democratic. As for homeowners, who skewed Republican, Reagan pushed through a hike on the property tax exemption, while also giving renters (a Democratic-leaning group) an income tax credit. Businesses received a sweetener in the form of a property tax cut on inventories, while local governments received funding to develop open spaces. This appealed to environmentalists, who, in the 1970s, were to be found in both political parties. Once again, Reagan found it necessary to increase some key taxes. Sales tax went up a point, corporate income taxes were raised even more significantly.[32] Reagan also brought in federal funding. As a sop to voters, the legislation he endorsed barred local governments and school districts from raising taxes without the approval of voters.

In the end, Governor Reagan crafted a deal that earned praise from both parties. Nevertheless, he never softened his rhetoric concerning government spending, even as his actions were indeed mostly moderate. By 1973, he was inclined to judge his administration a success, and this gave him the confidence to turn to an issue that, he believed, would attract national attention, branding him as a hardline tax and spending cutter.

He put Proposition 1, a constitutional amendment "limiting the taxing and spending powers of the state, cities, counties, and other government agencies," on the November 1973 ballot, with Michael Deaver assigned to run the campaign in support of adoption. The language and terms were set in stone, leaving no possibility of negotiation. Reagan wanted a straight up or down vote. He got it, and it was down. Fifty-four percent of California voters said no.[33]

The great irony in the failure of Proposition 1, which Reagan clearly hoped would be his legacy signature as a tax cutter, is that, on balance, this governor "gave Californians the biggest tax hike in their history—and got away with it."[34] In this collision of mythology (Reagan cuts taxes) and historical reality (Reagan increases taxes), the governorship of Ronald Reagan set the stage for what many would deem a "Teflon" presidency.

Chapter 9

From Dog Whistle to Dogma

*My father's greatest fault was his stubbornness about facing
up to unpleasant realities, particularly concerning America.
It was difficult for him to grapple with national shames—
slavery, the treatment of Native Americans and Vietnam.*
—Ron Reagan Jr. on his father[1]

On October 26, 1971, a day after the United Nations voted to expel
Taiwan and recognize the People's Republic of China, the governor of California, Ronald Reagan, put in a call to President Richard Nixon.

"Last night, I tell you, to watch that thing on television as I did"—
Reagan was alluding to the response of the Tanzanian delegation, who did
a tribal victory dance in the General Assembly chamber—"to see those
monkeys from those African countries—damn them, they're still uncomfortable wearing shoes!"

Nixon laughed.[2]

Reagan makes Nixon laugh! That might have been a worthy headline,
but the real takeaway after the National Archives released this recording in
2019 could be something more like *Was Ronald Reagan a racist?* Some say
it's a legitimate question, inasmuch as there are other recordings in which
President Nixon gleefully shared Reagan's remark with others, embellishing his retelling with his own opinion that the African delegates were
"cannibals."[3]

In truth, offensive as it is, Reagan's slur is the least consequential evidence of a racism that often reveals itself in the candid utterances of aging
white men.

Now, Reagan always denied that he was a racist. He often recounted
how he was ashamed that his hometown of Dixon, Illinois, exhibited "ugly
tumors of racial bigotry" but how grateful he was when his mother and
father "urged" him and his brother "to bring home our black playmates,
to consider them equals, and to respect the religious views of our friends"
(Chapter 3). He treasured and frequently trotted out a story his traveling

shoe salesman father told about how he was checking into a hotel during one trip and was offended when the clerk told him that he would like the hotel because "we don't permit a Jew in the place." The senior Reagan stormed out without checking in and spent a winter night curled up in his car, but not before telling the clerk: "I'm a Catholic. If it's come to the point where you won't take Jews, then some day you won't take *me* either" (Chapter 3).

In his 1990 *An American Life,* Reagan claimed that "the myth about myself that has always bothered me most is that I am a bigot who somehow surreptitiously condones racial prejudice." He sought to counter this "myth" by noting that he had appointed "more blacks to important positions in the California government than all the previous governors combined," a deed that "managed to dispel that image when I was in Sacramento" but unaccountably failed to do so "when I became president."[4]

Governor Ronald Reagan presented himself as a new kind of politician, apparently owing allegiance to no party, projecting all the mythologically freighted confidence of a lifeguard-turned-actor, a kind of bland, blank star on whom his fans could project themselves. Yet when he decided to leave the Democratic Party (or, as he liked to say, when the Democratic Party left him), he did not become an independent or emulate Teddy Roosevelt by helping to found a new party. No, he joined the Grand *Old* Party. Eventually, that party backed him in the way political parties do: with endorsements, a platform, and money. But the GOP had something else to offer Reagan. It was nothing less than the catalyst essential to the man's conversion from governor to president. Neither a new formula nor a secret one, it had, in 1968, already worked wonders for Richard Nixon. It was called the Southern Strategy.

Nixon, who called the Tanzanian UN delegation "cannibals," did not invent the Southern Strategy, which was, in fact, far from novel. It may be traced to the so-called Corrupt Bargain that settled the disputed election of 1876. The defeat of Donald Trump by Joe Biden in 2020 occasioned a bogus but nevertheless powerful election dispute. It was certainly not the first disputed election, however. Two decades earlier the result of the race between Republican George W. Bush and Democrat Al Gore came down to a dispute over a few hundred popular votes in Florida and was resolved, in effect, by a majority-conservative Supreme Court. Before this, the 1876 contest between Republican Rutherford B. Hayes and Democrat Samuel Tilden was the most famous example of a disputed election, one that, like the elections of 2020 and 2000, was deeply tainted. In 1876, the taint was the startlingly undemocratic bargain struck between the two political parties.

On election night that year, Hayes, a Union general in the Civil War and now governor of Ohio, went to bed believing he had lost to Tilden, the Democratic governor of New York. But dawn brought a different story—and an election dispute that would go on for four months amid charges of voter fraud, intimidation, and even the murder of black voters in the South; manipulation of ballots by partisan election judges; the threat of lawsuits; and a recount of votes in contested states. Sound familiar?

Stories seeming to bear out the dubious assertion that history repeats itself are often in themselves fascinating, but the resolution of the 1876 contest was an ordeal that may fairly be called a *coup d'état*. It was an election bought and paid for with cash, influence, intimidation, and the rights of African Americans. In the immediate aftermath of the election, dissatisfied Democrats in several Southern states did what dissatisfied Republicans in numerous states would do in 2020. They fielded alternate electors to rival those certified by the state legislatures. Some states went so far as to send to Congress *two* sets of Electoral College returns, one for Tilden, the other for Hayes.

The fact is that the popular vote tally gave Tilden a 250,000-ballot lead over Hayes. This did not discourage Republican operative Daniel Edgar Sickles. A one-legged former Civil War general, Sickles nearly lost the Battle of Gettysburg for the Union—singlehandedly. By 1876, however, the public knew him best as the man who had, years earlier, shot and killed his wife's lover in Lafayette Park, virtually on the doorstep of the White House. The victim, by the way, happened to be Philip Barton Key II, a man of smooth wit and incredibly good looks who had the added distinction of being the son of Francis Scott Key, writer of the verses that became our national anthem.

Sickles had a way of doing the impossible. He never denied murdering Key, but—for the first time in American judicial history—gained acquittal with a plea of temporary insanity. In 1876, he pulled out another rabbit, managing to persuade his fellow Republican party leaders to attempt the impossible as well. Do not concede defeat, he counseled. Look for a way to reverse the result of the election. Sound familiar?

Sickles argued that the fate of their candidate could be determined by contesting electoral votes in Oregon, Louisiana, South Carolina, and Florida. If these disputed electoral votes could be delivered to Hayes, he would win. The resulting battle raged wildly and with no end in sight before the looming March 4 inauguration date. There was talk of authorizing the current Secretary of State to serve as interim chief executive. Many in the South were talking about secession and were already setting up rival governments. (What! *Again?*)

Just two days before the inauguration deadline, Congress authorized a bipartisan Electoral Commission while legislators negotiated a behind-the-scenes deal to decide the issue. In essence, the deal was this: the Democratic South would give the election to Republican Hayes in return for the president-elect's pledge to bring full home rule to the Southern states and an immediate end to the military-enforced post–Civil War Reconstruction governments. If this meant that the rights of the newly enfranchised African American citizens were menaced or destroyed, so be it. The Republican Party, the Party of the Great Emancipator, would prevail—even at the cost of everything Lincoln had stood for. The Southern legislators agreed to a commission composed of eight Republicans and seven Democrats, who voted straight down party lines to rule in favor of Hayes. As for the country, it held together—after a fashion; for the rift between North and South was wide, and the gulf between white and black Americans both deepened and widened. As for Hayes, he bore throughout his single term the mocking title of "His Fraudulency." But never mind. The Southern Strategy was conceived. It would be born following a ninety-three-year gestation, in 1968.

Between the end of Reconstruction in 1877 and passage of the Civil Rights Act in 1964, the South was an overwhelmingly Democratic stronghold—the "Solid South"—but after LBJ succeeded in gaining passage of the Civil Rights Act of 1964, southern support for the Democratic Party melted, dissolved, and vaporized. Various Republican candidates exploited the racism of many white southerners to gain their support, but it was a GOP strategist named Kevin Phillips who laid out the approach as a full-blown strategy, explaining both bluntly and cynically to James Boyd of *The New York Times* in 1970 that the "more Negroes who register as Democrats in the South, the sooner the Negrophobe whites will quit the Democrats and become Republicans. That's where the votes are."[5]

Barry Goldwater, the horse Reagan backed and subsequently rode into national political prominence, exploited the precursor of this strategy in his failed 1964 GOP presidential bid. Four years later, in 1968, Richard Nixon used it to great success, gaining important victories in what had suddenly become southern swing states. Voters there responded to passage of the Civil Rights Act of 1964 and the Voting Rights Act of 1965 as well Great Society legislation passed during Lyndon Johnson's administration by voting Republican.

The corrupt bargain of 1876 had not transformed the South into a Republican stronghold. The South got what it wanted—the end of Reconstruction, the restoration of home rule, and what looked to be the perpetual quasi-enslavement of the region's black population. Yet the "Solid South" remained solidly Democratic until the rise of the Southern Strategy, first with Nixon and then with Reagan. LBJ's breach of the Corrupt Bargain split the Democratic Party as the South broke away with a political halfway house dubbed the Dixiecrats and then, finally, found a new home in the GOP.

Of course, an American president is elected president of the United States, not president of the South. Goldwater made no apology for his opposition to the Civil Rights Act and all aspects of the Great Society. He thus fashioned himself into a presidential candidate who combined a willingness to use nuclear weapons with a policy that seemed to many Americans frankly racist. The combination was a bridge too far for the vast majority of the American electorate.

No. What Nixon and Reagan realized is that, when it came to racial politics, you could not say the quiet part too loudly. A keystone tactic in the execution of the Southern Strategy was the use of what is today called "dog whistle politics," which employs suggestive "coded" language to transmit a racist message without venturing beyond the pale of social propriety by speaking "in the clear," as Goldwater did. Robert L. Coate, the Northern California chair of the California Democratic Party, stated, "Reagan handles racism in such a manner that racists understand exactly what he is saying, without his having to spell it out for them"[6]

Some of Reagan's positions are truly shocking. Like Goldwater, he opposed the Civil Rights Act of 1964 and even agreed with him that its passage had been a mistake. He also, however, had objections to the Voting Rights Act of 1965—legislation Goldwater supported without reservation. It was in the general election of 1964 that Reagan—in a radio ad for Goldwater—first referred to America's inner cities as "jungles." As noted by Jeremy D. Mayer in *Reagan and Race*, in a racially charged era of black riots and in a time when a racial slur tagged blacks as "jungle bunnies," the word struck some as a direct appeal to white racism."[7] He blew that dog whistle again during the 1966 gubernatorial campaign, when he told Californians, "Our city streets are jungle paths after dark," reiterating that the "jungle is closing in on this little patch we have been civilizing for a long time."[7] Later that year, he declared, "If an individual wants to discriminate against Negroes and others in selling their house, it is his right to do so."[8] Although harshly expressed, the elevation of individual rights (in this case, property rights) over civil rights was typical of many Republican conservatives. The point those others and Reagan missed is that, in a democracy, any "*individual* right" ends wherever that right denies an "individual right" to another. When "property rights" mean (as it does in this case) the right to sell or refrain from selling your property to a buyer on account of race, that is a collision between property rights and human rights. In a democracy, human rights must prevail. There may well be ambivalence in this principle, but there is no ambiguity. Governor Reagan either *could* not or *would* not see that the Fourteenth Amendment's

guarantee of "equal protection of the laws" sometimes requires "infringe-
ment on individual rights" to prevent any given individual from infring-
ing the rights of others. Holding property rights as sovereign and absolute
violates the Constitution, which is first and last a *social* compact.

It is evident that Ronald Reagan, a man not without empathy, was
troubled by at least an undercurrent of cognitive dissonance. Recall March
6, 1966, when he stormed out of the National Negro Republican Assembly in Santa Monica, mentioned in Chapter 8. A delegate to the assembly asked Reagan how he could hope to win votes from black Republicans
after opposing the Civil Rights Act of 1964. Reagan responded with his
usual platitudinous denunciation of racial bigotry. His primary opponent,
George Christopher, piped in, telling the audience that *he* would have
voted for the law, adding that Goldwater's opposition to the Civil Rights
Act "did more harm than anything to the Republican Party" and "still
plagues" the party. Christopher concluded with a warning: "unless we cast
out this image [of racism]. We're going to suffer defeat."

Reagan should have just let it go. Instead, he jumped up to claim a
point of personal privilege, shouting that he resented "the implication that
there is any bigotry in my nature." Not in my opposition to the Civil Rights
Act, mind you, but *in my nature*. "Don't anyone ever imply I lack integrity," he threatened. "I will not stand silent and let anyone imply that—in
this or any other group."[9]

This said, he abruptly left. Some reporters said there were tears in his
eyes. One reported hearing Reagan mutter, "I'll get that S.O.B.," referring
to Christopher.[10] Clearly, a raw nerve had been plucked. Somewhere within
him, Ronald Reagan knew he was on the wrong side of the Civil Rights
issue. The fact that embracing this *wrong* side was precisely the corrupt
bargain necessary to win elections—by gaining an edge among white voters—enraged Ronald Reagan.

Reagan's anger was not simple defensiveness. It came from the same
deep place that his self-mythologizing self-image came from: childhood.
He spoke and wrote fondly of Dixon, Illinois, yet he also acknowledged
that it was marred by the racial prejudice of its time. There was a black
population there, but was largely an underclass. Hotels were segregated.
Barbershops were segregated. No blacks were admitted as members of the
local golf club. In contrast to the South, the segregation was de facto and
not de jure, but it was real, and his father Jack deplored it. He proudly
recalled how his father would not let him attend the showing in the local
movie house of a rereleased version of D.W. Griffith's epic *Birth of a Nation*
because Jack Reagan assessed it (correctly) as a racist glorification of the
Ku Klux Klan. When young Ronnie, who already loved film and really
wanted to see this one, protested that the Klan portrayed was the historical

Klan, which really did protect people from violence, his father reportedly responded: "The Klan's the Klan, and a sheet's a sheet, and any man who wears one over his head is a bum."[11] In a letter to a friend, Reagan pointed out with pride that he had just completed shooting a movie [1951's *Storm Warning* with Ginger Rogers and Doris Day!] in which he played a police chief who did mortal battle with KKK. It would have made his father proud, he commented.[12]

Ronald Reagan sincerely believed he was not a racist. His proof was not in his actions, his words, or his policies. Rather, it was in his highly mythologized upbringing. His father and mother taught him that prejudice was wrong, and, in fact, set an example that was racially progressive for their time and place. Therefore, Reagan reasoned, he, as their child, could not possibly be a bigot. To call him one was to question the very values his parents had instilled in him, and that ignited an explosion of angry cognitive dissonance. As political scientist Jeremy D. Mayer put it, Reagan's enlightened upbringing had a paradoxical effect on him. It did not produce a racially progressive adult, candidate, or politician, but instead created a "man easily offended by the idea that he was burdened with racial prejudice." Worse, Mayer argued, "it also produced a man with an unusual willingness to express public disdain or anger at black people, particularly black women." Mayer cited Reagan's shouting match with a black female protestor outside of the 1968 Miami GOP convention—a verbal melee played out in front of reporters. Back in 1969, as governor, he sought to ban leftist black activist Angela Davis from the entire University of California system. Campaigning for president in 1980, when he ventured into the South Bronx for an impromptu streetcorner town hall, he lost his temper at a heckler, shouting back in highly visible and audible rage before rolling TV news cameras, "I can't do a damn thing for you if I don't get elected!"[13]

* * *

Ronald Reagan's outburst at the National Negro Republican Assembly in 1966 could have lost him the GOP gubernatorial nomination. And maybe it should have. But neither it nor subsequent displays of rageful contempt did not interfere with his political rise. This speaks volumes about what Republican voters wanted from their candidates. Yet Reagan—perhaps unlike Donald Trump—was not merely pandering to voters. "His faith that he lacked racial prejudice" was real, and it "allowed him to take positions widely perceived as antiblack without any hesitation. A more introspective or ambivalent white politician might have retreated in the face of nearly unified black anger at his policy positions and campaign tactics."[14]

When Reagan made his first tentative presidential primary bid, against Nixon in 1968, the Nixon campaign was worried. An internal

Nixon campaign memo noted that Reagan had successfully tapped into the "ideological fervor of the Right and emotional distress of those who fear or resent the Negro, and who expect Reagan somehow to keep him 'in his place' or at least to echo their own anger and frustration." The Nixon people saw Reagan as hijacking Southern support that should be the property of *their* candidate. Moreover, Reagan appeared to Nixon strategists as the only GOP candidate who could neutralize the third-party appeal of outright segregationist candidate Alabama governor George C. Wallace.[15]

The fears of Nixon strategists proved unfounded in 1968, as Nixon swept the nomination and then went on to a landslide in the general election. Reagan's 1976 primary bid against Gerald Ford likewise proved unsuccessful, even as he blasted the "welfare state" and used the fiction of the "welfare queen" to typify it, creating an enduring racist meme of welfare fraud, such as a woman who putatively used multiple false names to amass government money to buy a big house and a Cadillac, as well as to accrue some $150,000 in tax-free income.[16]

Regarding Reagan's 1976 campaign, Frank Rich, in *New York Magazine*, wrote "his appeal has to do not with competence at governing but with the emotion he invokes." Rich went on, "Reagan lets people get out their anger and frustration, the feeling of being misunderstood and mishandled by those that run the government, their impatience with taxes and with the poor and weak, their impulse to deal with the world's troublemakers and punch them in the nose."[17] Like so many of Reagan's anecdotes, his welfare queen story had many inaccuracies. As noted by Daniel S. Lucks, in *Reconsidering Reagan: Racism, Republicans, and the Road to Trump*, the forty-seven-year-old black Chicago woman named Linda Taylor was indicted for using four aliases, not eighty. The amount of her alleged welfare fraud was not $150,000 as Reagan claimed but $8,000.[18]

Finally, as the *New York Times*' Jon Nordheimer observed of the 1976 campaign, Reagan, in Florida, "hammered away at the welfare and law-and-order issues in the state, long attractive to Southern conservatives." Campaigning in Fort Lauderdale, Reagan declared to a rally that "working people were outraged when they waited in lines at grocery store check-out counters while a 'strapping young buck' ahead of them purchased T-bone steaks with food stamps." As Nordheimer pointed out, Reagan used the grocery line story before in states like New Hampshire, but "he never used the expression 'young buck' which to whites in the South, generally denotes a large black man."[19]

Was it Reagan's position on race that caused his failures in 1968 and 1976? Perhaps, but perhaps the GOP was simply more comfortable with establishment politicians like Nixon and Ford. Yet while the fears of Nixon strategists did not play out in 1968, their insight was prescient, nonetheless. The conservative wing of the GOP shared the racial attitude of Ronald Reagan (an attitude that was certainly not that of his racially progressive parents) but they stopped short of the segregationist rhetoric of George Wallace. Reagan learned to tie the likes of the Civil Rights Act of 1964, the Voting Rights Act of 1965, Equal Housing legislation, and the Great Society not to racial progressivism or the Fourteenth Amendment, but to government overreach and encroachment on individual liberties. In this way, he never attacked blacks directly. He attacked the legislation and policies intended to promote equality, at the perceived expense of the white majority. He did not, for example, oppose the Voting Rights Act by overtly stirring up white fear and resentment of blacks. Instead, he opposed it (to the extent that he did) as an assault on traditional American values, which prized local control by local governments over the intrusive domineering of the federal government. This was true in how elections were conducted, primary and secondary education matters, and, welfare policy among other traditionally local matters. For Reagan, federalism provided cover for what might be perceived as a racist appeal.

Was Ronald Wilson Reagan a racist?

Without question, Reagan deplored the federal government even as he often valorized local government. For him, this was a foundational article of conservative faith. Yet it was hardly a coincidence that local governments often opposed Washington on matters of racial policy and legislation, especially equal rights. It is not hyperbole but fact that both Reagan and George Wallace favored a constitutional amendment to put an end to busing as a means of racially integrating public schools. It is fact, not hyperbole, that Reagan, like Wallace, spoke favorably of the apartheid governments of Rhodesia and South Africa. In the wake of Reagan's refusal to sanction the apartheid government of South Africa by vetoing a 1986 bill imposing sanctions, Archbishop Desmond Tutu, a Nobel Peace Prize winner, declared the president "a racist, pure and simple."[20] Indeed, when Reagan made his primary bid against Gerald Ford, Ford's pollster concluded that Reagan supporters were practically indistinguishable from Wallace supporters. The 1976 Reagan primary campaign mailed some 100,000 brochures to identified supporters of George Wallace.[21]

* * *

If at first you don't succeed....

The history of the GOP is littered with the names of "perennial" failed presidential candidates. Harold Stassen ran in every GOP primary between 1944 and 1992, except for 1956 and 1972. Andy Martin ran in 1988, 2000, 2012, and 2016. Alan Keyes ran three times, 1996, 2000, and 2008. Jack Fellure has appeared in every presidential campaign since 1988. By 1980, Ronald Reagan was verging on membership in this unenviable association of perennials. Every unsuccessful repeat candidate risks being perceived as irrelevant, but Reagan had another strike against him. By 1980, he was long in the tooth. At sixty-nine, he would be, if elected, the oldest president to that date. Many saw him as a B-actor who turned to politics only after his film career faded—overlooking his having become a popular and highly consequential big-state governor, who would surely have been elected to a third term, had he chosen to run.

But old as he was, Reagan had good reason to see 1980 as his year at last, and, to the surprise of many, he was positioned as the frontrunner from the get-go of the GOP primary season. As the weeks and months passed, the nomination increasingly seemed his to lose. And mostly, he took a very different approach to this campaign. In contrast to 1968 and 1976, he avoided talk about civil rights, affirmative action, busing, and other race-related issues. Instead, he turned to taxes, defense policy, and economic recovery and revitalization. When he turned to the evils of big government, however, dog's ears were not required to hear the dog whistle. On August 3, 1980, Reagan kicked off his primary campaign with a speech at the Neshoba County Fair just outside of Philadelphia, Mississippi. It was a locale with a history. On June 21, 1964, the remains of James Chaney, Andrew Goodman, and Michael Schwerner, three Civil Rights activists working for the Freedom Summer campaign to register black Mississippi voters, were found in a shallow grave on Olen L. Burrage's Old Jolly Farm, a few miles southwest of Philadelphia. They had been shot and killed by members of the Ku Klux Klan, and the murders and trial three years later made Philadelphia a kind of Ground Zero for the modern Civil Rights movement.

Ronald Reagan—son of a man who roundly denounced the Klan as "bums"—made no mention of the three martyrs to the cause of Civil Rights or the Klansmen who killed them. Instead, he proclaimed to an enthusiastic all-white audience of some fifteen thousand, "I believe in states' rights." He could have said "I believe in local government." But, as he must have known very well, "states' rights" was a heavily loaded phrase and the loudest of all possible dog whistles. It expressed a doctrine holding (among other things) that the federal government had no authority or right to "dictate" how a state government handled such issues as racial discrimination and segregation. Ronald Reagan was the first presidential nominee to ever address this fair, which was notoriously associated with segregationist sentiment.

Reagan's own pollster had urged his client not to begin his campaign at the Neshoba fair. When he repeated his counsel once too often, Reagan hurled a folder at him.[22] It was a recapitulation of his response to accusations of racism during the 1966 gubernatorial primary—outrage at the very idea that he was a racist, let alone one celebrating states' rights at the scene of one of the nation's most shameful racist atrocities. Yet, after winning the nomination, Reagan did back off, and even arranged for the leader of the NAACP to have a prominent primetime speaking slot at the GOP convention. At one point in the general election campaign, Reagan even tried to turn the tables on Carter by linking him to the KKK. He criticized Carter for "opening his campaign down in the city that gave birth to and is the parent body of the Ku Klux Klan." Reagan subsequently apologized for the remark.[23] For his part, Jimmy Carter, the Democratic incumbent, was very worried about the tepid support he was getting from the black community. His own most prominent black supporter, Andrew Young, tried to turn up the heat with a warning to "blacks that if Reagan gets elected it would be 'okay to kill niggers.'" Carter did not comment on Young's offensive epithet, but he did underscore that Reagan supported white rule in Africa.[24] It was all to no avail. GOP voters heard from Ronald Reagan precisely what they wanted to hear on the subject of race—no more but certainly no less. Reagan won by a landslide, and when he campaigned for reelection in 1984, he repeated his strategy of avoiding overt mention of racial issues. It was also apparent to him and to his advisors that he really had no need for the black vote. Certainly, he never tried to court it.

* * *

Ronald Reagan could point with pride to signing into law in November 1983 the bill that created Martin Luther King Day. He had been pressured by the far right to veto it, and he had been pressured by the same forces to release the FBI's salacious J. Edgar Hoover–era files on King. Instead, he celebrated the bill by signing it. Reagan may well have sincerely believed that King deserved the honor of a holiday, but he also understood that signing a bill that would take nothing away from white America would buy some credibility with the black community while costing him little or nothing even among frank racists. The fact was that black voters, racial policy, and black lives occupied little space in President Reagan's mind and even less on his agenda.

He had already sent the necessary messages to the electorate. When it came to a choice between "individual" rights and black civil rights, he made his judgment in favor of individual rights. When it came to federal government versus state and local government, he came down heavily on the side of state and local, even where federal civil rights legislation had the protection of the Constitution's supremacy clause. Certainly, he had moderated his stance on racial policy from the 1960s, but he left only a vacuum where the stance had been. The words were never retracted or replaced. The fact is that Reagan's opposition to both the Civil Rights Act and the Voting Rights Act echo loudest in his legacy on race, and as Jeremy Mayor concluded, "More than any other political figure, Reagan was responsible for the defeat of the forces of civil rights within the Republican Party. In 1964–1965, Republicans were more positive toward civil rights for blacks than was the average Democrat. By the time of the Reagan revolution, while most Republicans, unlike Reagan, accepted the broad achievements and worth of the civil rights movement, the civil rights wing of the Republican Party was largely dead."[25]

*   *   *

They say that once a thing is dead, it doesn't get any deader. The exception to this otherwise universal truism may well be the "civil rights wing of the Republican Party." Donald Trump's 2016 capture of the GOP was made far easier than it might otherwise have been thanks to the deader-than-ever deadness of black civil rights in that party.

Now, just like Ronald Reagan, Donald Trump was for most of his life a Democrat. He did register as a Republican in 1987, was a member of the Independence Party in 1999, a Democrat in 2001, Republican in 2009, unaffiliated with any party in 2011, and then registered as a Republican in 2012. In his campaigning and during his presidency, Trump notably made scant reference to Reagan. Yet he emulated Reagan's focus on federal court appointments. Reagan appointed hundreds of federal judges—virtually all conservatives whose attitude toward black civil rights ranged from indifferent to hostile. The Reagan–era Supreme Court pruned back much of the legacy of the long-lived liberal Earl Warren court. Trump appointments, of course, utterly transformed the Supreme Court, giving the rightwing fringe a six to three supermajority.

Trump's landlord father, Fred, had a reputation for discriminating against black rental applicants and tenants. He was also implicated (by some) in involvement with the Ku Klux Klan.[26] For the most part, Donald Trump did not have a reputation as a racist—until the aftermath of a brutal event in Central Park on April 19, 1989. That night, a young white woman was assaulted, gang raped, and nearly beaten to death while jogging in an off-the-beaten-path area of the park. After five youths (four African American, one Hispanic) were convicted, Trump placed full-page advertisements in four New York City newspapers demanding that New York State reinstate the death penalty expressly to punish them. "I want to hate these murderers and I always will," Trump wrote in the ad, even though the victim had not been killed. "Bring back the death penalty and bring back our police!"[27] Long after all five had been incontrovertibly exonerated by DNA and other evidence and their convictions overturned, Trump continued to assert their guilt.[28]

In 2011, Trump first expressed doubt that then–President Barack Obama had been born in the United States. This gave rise to a so-called Birther Movement, based on a conspiracy theory concerning the origin of the president. Only in September 2016, when he was the GOP candidate for president, did Trump grudgingly concede that Obama "was born in the United States. Period."[29] Still, during the campaign Trump, unlike Nixon and Reagan, was more than a dog whistler. If Nixon and Reagan made the GOP safe for racists and racism, Donald Trump transformed their dog whistle into a Trump bullhorn, which he directed against an array of minorities, not just blacks. From the earliest days of his campaign, he reserved some of his most dehumanizing language for use against immigrants. In his campaign announcement at Trump Tower on June 16, 2015, Trump effectively classified the mass of Mexican immigrants as criminals: "When Mexico sends its people, they're not sending their best. ... They're sending people that have lots of problems, and they're bringing those problems with us. They're bringing drugs. They're bringing crime. They're rapists. And some, I assume, are good people."[30] Days before the 2018 midterm election, President Trump added to the lies and bombast that defined his presidency when he characterized individuals crossing the border to seek asylum as violent criminals bent on wreaking havoc on the United States. "Some people call it an 'invasion,'" he said. "It's like an invasion. They have violently overrun the Mexican border."[31]

As for that other territory Trump considered foreign, America's inner cities, he declared in the third presidential debate with Hillary Clinton that "Our inner cities are a disaster. You get shot walking to the store. They have no education, they have no jobs. I will do more for African Americans and Latinos than [Hillary Clinton] can ever do in ten lifetimes. All she has done is talk to the African Americans and the Latinos." Earlier, in the first presidential debate, Trump described black urban America as a hellscape: "We have a situation where we have our inner cities, African Americans, Hispanics are living in hell because it's so dangerous. You walk down the street, you get shot." His answer to this was simple: more aggressive policing. "Right now, our police ... are afraid to do anything." As commentator Victoria M. Massie suggests, Trump uses "inner city" as code for American cultural failings, not neighborhoods.[32]

Reagan, unlike Trump, was a man who possessed qualities we

welcome in our national leaders, namely empathy and shame. Neverthe-less, Reagan plowed the field in which Trump and his acolytes planted a poisonous crop. For both the fortieth and forty-fifth presidents, the fer-tilizer was the same. A brand of racial politics normalized by a language of indirection, misdirection, and redirection to individual rights, state's rights, and a promise to Make America Great Again.

Chapter 10

Taxes, Big Government, and Middle-Class Despair

"Reagan the Tax Cutter." No Reagan myth is more pervasive, persuasive, invasive, and, in the face of countervailing facts, evasive.

This is not to deny that restructuring the U.S. tax system was likely the most significant political and policy accomplishment of the Reagan administration. Though restructuring is not synonymous with tax cutting, Ronald Reagan remains the GOP's patron saint of lower taxes and its conjoined twin, smaller government. Federal spending incontrovertibly increased under Reagan,[1] and Reagan raised taxes in 1982, 1983, 1984, 1986 and 1987.[2]

Yet the myth burns on.

Reagan's watershed tax bill, the Economic Recovery Tax Act (ERTA), signed into law in August 1981, was the biggest tax cut in American history. ERTA cut federal revenues by 2.9 percent of GDP, according to the Committee for a Responsible Federal Budget. That makes ERTA the biggest tax cut since the introduction of the income tax in 1913, surpassing the significant post–World War II cuts passed in 1945 (2.7 percent of GDP) and 1948 (1.9 percent of GDP).[3] By contrast, the often-cited "Kennedy tax cuts" (signed into law by LBJ), trimmed tax receipts by 0.2 percent of GDP.[4] Among other changes, ERTA reduced the top individual tax bracket from 70 percent to 50 percent. Later, Reagan went on to cut the top tax bracket from 50 percent to 28 percent. His low-tax framework has proved remarkably durable for the past forty years. The politics of post–ERTA taxation have changed the paradigm of U.S. tax policy and made any potential restoration of higher marginal tax rates to pre–Reagan heights difficult, as in third-rail difficult. For the majority of the body politic, Reagan has made any mention of tax increases toxic, much like proposing cuts to Social Security.

The enactment of ERTA and subsequent tax legislation was a cornerstone of the so-called Reagan Revolution, which included the GOP's warm embrace of "supply-side" or "trickle down" economics. By whichever name, this theory holds that tax cuts weighted toward the wealthy will be used to create jobs and generate economic growth of such magnitude that government revenues will remain stable or even grow and ... wait for it ... *the tax cut will pay for itself!* On the presidential campaign trail in 2011, former Minnesota Governor Tim Pawlenty stated, "When Ronald Reagan cut taxes in a significant way, revenues actually increased by almost 100% during his eight years as president."[5] David Stockman, Reagan's first head of the Office of Management and Budget (OMB) and the administration's point person for the ERTA tax cuts, later confessed that "supply-side economics was merely a cover for the trickle-down approach to economic policy—what an older and less elegant generation called the horse-and-sparrow theory: If you feed the horse enough oats, some will pass through to the road for the sparrows."[6] Look to the left and to the right of you. Both of those people are the sparrows Ronald Reagan and his supporters never talked much about.

While you're contemplating your fellow citizens, please pause to think for more than a fleeting moment about this supply-side, trickle-down economic theory popularly known as "Reaganomics." It goes like this: If taxes are cut, which voters love, it will create jobs and increase economic growth so significantly that the tax cut will pay for itself. Who knew that cutting taxes of a modern western democracy could be both easy and free? If valid, why didn't Presidents Johnson, Nixon, Ford, and Carter adopt supply-side economics and institute the associated tax cuts? The voters would have loved it—and them!

Epistemology is a complex branch of philosophy that looks in vain for reliable ways to tell truth from fiction. Well, here's one way that never fails. "If something sounds too good to be true, it is."

Despite GOP claims of tax magic, multiple studies have shown that tax cuts don't pay for themselves. As set forth in a study by the Committee for a Responsible Federal Budget regarding tax cuts and revenue generation, the federal government collects only a certain percentage of funds from any additional economic activity generated by tax cuts. For example, assuming a current effective marginal rate of about 20 percent, the government would collect twenty cents on each additional dollar generated. Accordingly, every one-dollar tax cut would need to produce at least five dollars of additional economic activity to be self-financing. While a well-designed tax cut can promote economic growth, the committee's analysis shows that the amount of additional revenue will never be close to the size of the tax cut. At most—under the best circumstances—the additional economic activity will offset 25 percent of the cost of the initial tax cut. The Committee for Responsible Government is not alone in reaching these conclusions. Studies by the Congressional Budget Office, the Joint Committee on Taxation, the Tax Policy Center and the University of Pennsylvania Wharton School have come to similar conclusions.[7]

The passage of ERTA was a masterfully orchestrated political maneuver by the Great Communicator and a significant legislative victory. A veteran TV performer, Reagan had charisma, a compelling message, and an American public ready for change, especially coming from a familiar face with a familiar voice. Reagan sold ERTA to the American public on a primetime televised address on February 5, 1981. Speaker Tip O'Neill, Jr., a Massachusetts Democrat, commented in *The New York Times* that President Reagan's televised speech on taxes had touched off "a telephone blitz like this nation has never seen." It was accompanied by a "nationwide advertising blitz," O'Neill added, which had "a devastating effect" on the Democrats.[8]

Following on the heels of ERTA's success, Reagan enjoyed a second triumph by achieving bipartisan agreement on federal tax reform. In October 1986, he signed into law the Tax Reform Act of 1986. Among other things, the new law had just two tax brackets and lowered the top tax rate for individuals from 50 percent to 28 percent. In his signing statement, Reagan once again asserted the relationship between tax cuts and job creation. "When I sign this bill into law," he said, "America will have the lowest marginal tax rates and the most modern tax code among major industrialized nations, one that encourages risk-taking, innovation, and that old American spirit of enterprise. We'll be refueling the American growth economy with the kind of incentives that helped record new businesses and nearly 11.7 million jobs in just 46 months."[9]

The mantra that high tax rates discourage entrepreneurship and risk taking while low tax rates create jobs and fuel faster economic growth has been gospel for the GOP during the past forty years. Just turn on any political talk show, and you will hear a psalm sung from the Book of Reagan: "I'm not for raising taxes on the American people. I believe that, right now, if we want to get the economy going again and start creating jobs, we ought to be thinking about providing tax relief to American families and small businesses to get our economy going again" former Republican Speaker of the House John Boehner told Neil Cavuto of Fox News.[10] Fast forward to the next GOP Speaker of the House Paul Ryan: "So, when you are raising these top tax rates, you're raising taxes on these job creators where more than half of Americans get their jobs from in this country." In his interview with Chris Wallace, Ryan went on to add that "if you tax job creators more, you get less job creation. If you tax investment more, you get less investment"[11] In more recent years, the Republicans have changed their rhetoric describing proposed Democratic tax increases. During the

Reagan years, the GOP labeled these as a form of "class warfare." The current label is simply "socialism," a throwback to Reagan's own early rhetoric opposing Medicare and Medicaid. A recent example of this rhetorical shift in today's GOP can be found in Florida Senator Rick Scott's *Rescue America—11 Point Plan*, which refers to the "militant left" and its intent to replace America's Judeo-Christian ethic with "socialism," a foreign combatant that threatens to wipe out prosperity and freedom.[12]

To be clear, we are not saying that tax relief is never justified, nor are we arguing that none of the Reagan tax cuts were needed in 1981. The point we are making is that, for the past four decades, the GOPs prescription for *any* economic ill—real or perceived—has been tax cuts. This popular policy deployed by Reagan in firehose fashion during the 1980s remains the GOP's magic elixir, even though the economic challenges facing the U.S. today are starkly different from those posed by Mr. Carter's economy. For one, the U.S. population was growing in the 1980s, in contrast to the contracting population today. The Baby Boomers, who hit their peak earning years during the Reagan administration are now retiring. It is expected that 10,000 people will turn sixty-five every day through 2029.[13] The state of the world economy, globalization, crumbling U.S. infrastructure, the climate crisis, and the continued rise of China as a global power are vastly different from the circumstances Reagan and the nation faced in 1981. Moreover, years of Republican tax cuts have exacerbated the growing income and wealth gap within the U.S. and hollowed out the middle class.[14]

So, what do you call the GOP's long-lasting addiction to tax cuts? Zombie Reaganism? Zombie Economics (rhymes with Voodoo Economics) is not a healthy economic strategy. It remains, however, a stupendous political strategy. After all, what voter doesn't want a tax cut? Who's gonna punch Santa Claus in his white-bearded kisser?

Importantly, the tax cut mythology is fused with an expression of concern over the sin of big government and big federal spending. Criticizing federal spending is nothing more or less than GOP dogma. It is well documented that the GOP's worry over federal spending and the budget deficit is acute only when there is a Democrat in the White House. Nevertheless, the party ritual of expressing concern for the size of the budget deficit is sacrosanct. The combination of tax cuts and federal spending during the George W. Bush and Donald Trump administrations added trillions to the deficit with no pushback from Republicans in Congress, including former Speaker Paul Ryan, who reflexively holds himself out as a deficit hawk.[15] As with advocacy for tax cuts, the GOPs deficit dogma in opposition to big government, the deep state, federal spending and programs is also part of Reagan's enduring myth. The patron saint of tax cuts is likewise the patron saint of small government.

When running for president, Reagan attributed America's economic decline to the federal government's inability to control spending. Announcing his presidential bid in November 1979, Reagan asserted, "The people have not created this disaster in our economy; the federal government has. It has overspent, overestimated, and over-regulated. It has failed to deliver services within the revenues it should be allowed to raise from taxes." Then came Reagan's now legendary one-two rhetorical flourish, in which he stated "The key to restoring the health of the economy lies in cutting taxes. At the same time, we need to get the waste out of federal spending."[16] Candidate Reagan often railed against government "waste, fraud, and abuse." In his first speech as president before a joint session of Congress, he highlighted this concern: "Now, let me say a word here about the general problem of waste and fraud in the Federal Government. One government estimate indicated that fraud alone may account for anywhere from 1 to 10 percent—as much as $25 billion of Federal expenditures for social programs. If the tax dollars that are wasted or mismanaged are added to this fraud total, the staggering dimensions of this problem begin to emerge."[17]

Candidate Reagan's economic platform was infamously characterized by then presidential candidate George Herbert Walker Bush, who ran against Reagan for the Republican nomination by attacking in particular what he called "voodoo economics," by which he meant the very idea that cutting taxes would decrease the deficit and debt by magically increasing the revenue flows into the federal coffers.

Illinois Representative John Anderson, an erstwhile Republican running as an independent candidate for President in 1980, asked just the right question: "How is it possible to raise defense spending, cut income taxes and balance the budget, all at the same time?"

Candidate Reagan never responded. Thanks to a halo of mythology and a deftly staged projection of self-assurance, not responding was Reagan's best option. What mythology couldn't do for him, the optics of bluff confidence could.

Voodoo economics, tax cut mythology, whatever you call it, the operative principle was *step through the looking glass*. That is, if a budget deficit arises, that surely means more tax cuts are required. As Reagan said in his 1985 State of the Union address in defense of his economic program, "the best way to reduce deficits is through economic growth. More businesses will be started, more investments made, more jobs created, and more people will be on payrolls. The best way to reduce spending is to reduce the need for spending by increasing prosperity."[18] On the other hand, this mythology dictates that in a time of strong economic growth, raising taxes will hurt the economy and cause a recession. To sum it up, if government is the problem and big government (supported by tax revenues) means less freedom, then lower tax rates mean more freedom. Put even more simply: Taxes bad. Tax cuts good. (Context be damned.)

In the GOP voodoo economics sales literature, you won't find a word in favor of government, let alone big government, and you certainly won't see anything about the proven fact that most Americans actually like big government. They want clean water and air, airplanes that don't fall out of the sky, food that is not contaminated, military effectiveness, and federal law enforcement to protect against terrorism. Oh, and they also love those adorable twins of big government, Social Security and Medicaid. Somehow, the purveyors of the tax myth never get around to connecting the dots between taxes and all the features of (big) government people clamor for. Remember when geriatric Republicans loudly protested "health care reform" with shouts of "Keep your goddam government hands off my Medicare"?

Still, if you like tax cuts (and who doesn't?) but also happen to like what big government delivers (and who doesn't?), the GOP has an app for that. Behind the curtain, the Republican politicians simply heat up the USA Credit Card, borrowing money through deficit spending and thereby mortgaging our future—the very credit transaction the new president condemned in his January 20, 1981, inaugural address: "For decades we have piled deficit upon deficit, mortgaging our future and our children's future for the temporary convenience of the present."[19] Millions of the faithful heard this that frigid January morning and clutched their pearls accordingly.

Now, you will never see a Republican actually flash that USA Credit Card, especially not when he or she is busy promoting tax cuts. But Ronald Reagan was not shy about running up a very large debt on the USA credit card. It's so blatant a paradox that it hardly seems shocking: the man who rode to the U.S. presidency on a team of snow-white I'm-mad-as-hell jeremiads against federal deficits managed to run up the largest peacetime budget deficits in pre–Trump U.S. history. God bless the patron saint of small government within the GOP.

Walt Rostow, U.S. National Security Advisor under Presidents Kennedy and Johnson, a history professor, and all-around public intellectual, characterized Reagan as a "good-time Charlie"—in short, convivial and shallow. Rostow summed up the Gipper's perspective on budget deficits and looming unpaid bills: "Nothing bad's going to happen on my watch. Screw the future." Rostow added: "That's been the dark side of this guy."[20] Indeed, it was a very good time for the well to do as the top marginal individual income tax rate was 70 percent at the beginning of Reagan's first term and 28 percent at the end of his second term.

Reaganomics ushered in an era of blithely irresponsible fiscal policy. After 1981, annual budget deficits became endemic as Reagan put America on a path to habitually spending more than it collects. Once a society and political class become accustomed to living at the expense of future generations, it is nearly impossible to change course. If anything, the last forty years, during which the U.S. has run up a tab of more than $34 trillion in federal debt—during a time of relative peace and prosperity—gives little hope for reversing the trend.

We, by the way, are not against deficit spending, at least not as a matter of principle. Deficit spending is often appropriate in making investments, such as education expenditures, infrastructure, the environment, and similar expenditures. Certainly, it is appropriate and even essential in a time of war. But let's face the cold facts here, there is nothing "conservative" about passing tax cuts primarily for the wealthy and financing them through deficit spending. That is the very opposite of conservative. Nor, by the way, is it conservative to ignore objective economic data, analysis and basic math which prove that tax cuts don't pay for themselves. In polite circles, that is called being a fabulist. In less polite circles, it is called being stupid. And in clinical circles, it is called crazy.

David Stockman stated that Reagan told him that significant cuts to large and expensive government programs, such as Social Security and Medicaid were off limits for purposes of reducing federal spending.[21] In Reagan's eight-year presidency, the two most significant entitlement programs from which the greatest number of citizens receive federal benefits, Social Security and Medicare, were not substantially altered. As Stockman wrote in *The Triumph of Politics*, "He [Reagan] leaned to the right, there was no doubt about that. Yet his conservative vision was only a vision. He has a sense of ultimate values and a feel for long term directions, but he had no blueprint for radical governance. He had no concrete program to dislocate and traumatize the here and now of American Society."[22] Reagan biographer Lou Cannon in his book, *President Reagan: The Role of a Lifetime*, concluded that Reagan never asked Americans to sacrifice for the welfare of the country.[23]

Stockman and Cannon may have meant to convey that Ronald Reagan was essentially a nice guy, but what their comments imply is that despite his finely honed rhetoric against government spending and the peril of budget deficits, he never offered the American people an alternative plan for how the federal government should function given the tax cuts he was proposing. Both the size of the federal government and the size of the federal workforce increased during Reagan's time in office.[24] In fact, by the end of his presidency, Reagan's toothless message to fight against federal spending was a call for a balanced budget amendment and a line-item veto, neither of which was ever at his disposal.

In short, although Reagan was masterful in convincing America that the federal government was bloated and must be scaled back, he was also well aware that Americans liked big government. After all, when he was a gung-ho FDR Democrat during the Depression and World War II, *he* liked big government. When his alcoholic father couldn't get work, that big government kept a roof over the family's heads. All this being the case, it is further reasonable to assume that Reagan appreciated that taking a strong hand in deploying draconian cuts in federal programs equal to the tax cuts enacted would be hugely unpopular. Hence, many of the budget and spending cuts he trumpeted never materialized. He didn't want them to. His Republican successors also expressed concern about the size of the federal deficit, but none of them, not George H.W. Bush, George W. Bush, or Donald J. Trump—the last two of whom enacted significant tax cuts—implemented any significant cuts in federal spending. Quite the contrary.

The budget deficits accumulated during Reagan's eight years in office exceeded the cumulative deficits of the thirty-nine U.S. presidents who preceded him.[25] Despite his campaign promises to balance the budget and restrain federal spending, it was Reagan who presided over the executive

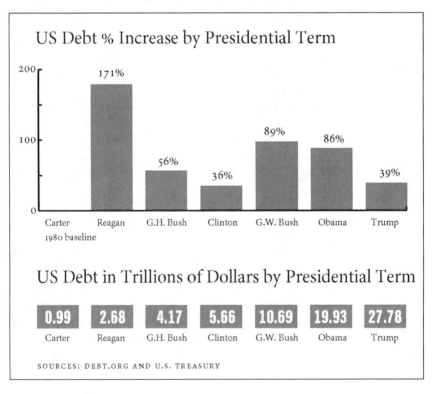

US Debt % Increase by Presidential Term

Carter 1980 baseline	Reagan 171%	G.H. Bush 56%	Clinton 36%	G.W. Bush 89%	Obama 86%	Trump 39%

US Debt in Trillions of Dollars by Presidential Term

Carter	Reagan	G.H. Bush	Clinton	G.W. Bush	Obama	Trump
0.99	2.68	4.17	5.66	10.69	19.93	27.78

SOURCES: DEBT.ORG AND U.S. TREASURY

branch as the gulf between revenues and expenditures widened to an average of 3 percent of GDP.[26]

Government spending grew annually during Reagan's presidency. That USA Credit Card? To provide some perspective, the federal debt at the end of 1990 was $3.20 trillion. By the end of 2020, it was $27.74 trillion.[27] As of this writing, the federal debt is in excess of $30 trillion, and the daily interest cost is in excess of $900 million![28] By 2031, interest payments on America's debt are predicted to surpass all expenditures other than Medicaid and Social Security.[29]

*   *   *

In 1991 candidate Bill Clinton accurately summed up the reckless tax cuts and spending of the 1980s, when he had begun his own presidential campaign. "The Reagan-Bush years," he said, "have exalted private gain over private obligation, special interest over the common good, wealth and fame over work and family. The 1980s ushered in a Gilded Age of greed and selfishness, of irresponsibility, and of neglect."[30] Unfortunately, Clinton did not significantly change the economic trajectory Reagan had established for the country, nor did he attempt to educate the public about the GOP mythology of big government ills and the party's delusional model of enacting supply-side tax cuts without thought to future consequences. In fact, in a shocking concession to the Republican right, Clinton declared in his 1996 State of the Union address that "the era of big government is over," drawing wild applause—from the GOP side![31]

In 1913, when it was introduced, the *progressive* structure of the U.S. income tax was overwhelmingly popular. In contrast to regressive taxes, which burden the wealthy, the middling, and the poor equally, a progressive income tax pegs taxes to incomes, which are sorted into different tax brackets. Generally, taxpayers pay a "marginal tax rate" on each dollar of income within a given tax bracket. The effective or average tax rate is the total amount of tax divided by the total amount of income. A progressive tax system is intended to shift the tax burden onto those with a greater ability to pay. Thus, those with higher incomes are taxed at higher rates. Importantly, a tax system with a high marginal rate does not mean that you pay the top tax rate on all income earned. It means you pay an effective tax rate based on your average marginal tax rate after deductions and other adjustments. We need to be wary of a common talking point for those on the political right. They describe a proposal to raise *marginal tax rates* as applying to "all income" instead of applying only to the income above a certain dollar threshold. It's in the name. Marginal tax rates apply to the margin of income above the threshold stipulated in the tax law current at the time. For example, a proposal to raise tax rates to 50 percent for incomes above $1 million is often falsely construed as taxing all income at 50 percent, instead of just the earnings above $1 million. If more Americans were in such a 50 percent marginal bracket, the country would be a happier place.

The top marginal individual income tax rate was over 90 percent under FDR and Eisenhower. Obviously, the income of very few Americans was taxed at this rate, and nobody, not even the wealthiest, was taxed 90 percent on 100 percent of their income. From 1941 through 1980, the number of tax brackets ranged from 32 to 15. During this same time span, the top marginal individual income tax rate ranged from 91 percent down to 70 percent. Over the period from 1932 to 1980, the top federal tax rate in the United States averaged 81 percent.[32]

Few approached the top rate, and no one had to pay 81 percent on 100 percent of their income. But without doubt, before Reagan, high-income individuals paid more in income taxes than they do today. That is the point of a progressive income tax. The rich can afford to pay more than the working class. They will still be richer, but American society and its economy will be better off. Wealth grows better in a healthy social and economic climate than in one that struggles.

Set forth below is a chart showing the lowest and highest marginal individual tax rates from 1913 through 2018.

The chart is a helpful illustration of the collapse of progressivity in

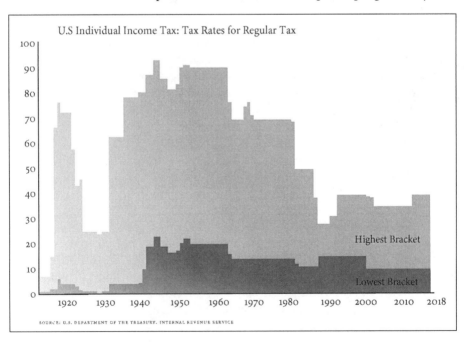

U.S Individual Income Tax: Tax Rates for Regular Tax

SOURCE: U.S. DEPARTMENT OF THE TREASURY. INTERNAL REVENUE SERVICE

the U.S. tax code beginning with Reagan's first term in 1981. In the 1930s, marginal individual income tax rates were increased significantly for upper-income taxpayers as were the number of marginal tax brackets. The highly progressive nature of the U.S. tax code remained relatively consistent for over four decades with upper-income marginal tax rates ranging from 63 percent to 92 percent. As you will observe from the chart, with the enactment of Reagan's signature tax-cutting bill, the Economic Recovery Tax Act, the U.S. tax system became far less progressive and more like a flat tax that actually becomes regressive at the top end of the income spectrum. Contrary to GOP dogma touting tax fairness and the need to flatten federal tax rates, it is neither fair nor right that the wealthiest Americans have a lower effective tax rate than the working class or middle class. This chart helps illustrate a primary goal of this book—to make citizens aware of how the internal revenue code has been manipulated by the GOP for over forty years to serve the interests of the wealthy and cause undue economic hardship to the majority of Americans.

Although Reagan was president half a lifetime ago, as a matter of U.S. tax policy, we still live in Reagan's America, which favors low taxes for the wealthy. This policy has contributed to America's wealth gap, which blew apart in the early 1980s under Reagan and continues to widen with a velocity that puts the Big Bang to shame. The cruel truth is that when there are fewer tax brackets, a flatter tax, and lower top marginal tax rates, the wealth gap grows. On the other hand, when there are more tax brackets, higher top brackets, and a higher top tax, the wealth gap decreases.[33] As discussed in Chapter 11, there is scant evidence that lower marginal tax rates for the wealthy give rise to greater GDP or employment. In fact, there is data to the contrary.

A recent Congressional Budget Office analysis examining the current state of Americans' wealth and the concentration of wealth provides the following. Measured over a period from 1989 to 2019, the share of total wealth held by families in the top ten percentile of income increased from 63 percent in 1989 to 72 percent in 2019, and the share of total wealth held by families in the top 1 percentile of income increased from 27 percent to 34 percent. By stark comparison, the share of total wealth held by families in the bottom half of the income distribution spectrum declined over that same period from 4 percent to 2 percent.[34]

According to a recent Pew Research poll, approximately 61 percent of Americans say there is too much economic inequality in the country today. When Americans who say reducing economic inequality should be a top priority for the federal government are asked why they believe that, 87 percent say inequality limits people's opportunities. A similar share (86 percent) says a major reason why reducing inequality

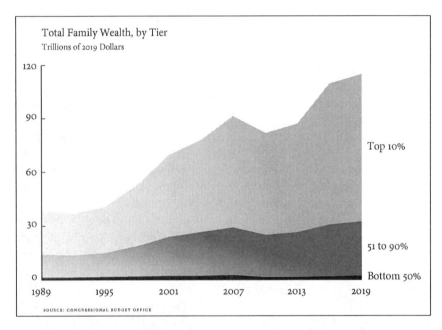

Total Family Wealth, by Tier
Trillions of 2019 Dollars

Top 10%

51 to 90%

Bottom 50%

SOURCE: CONGRESSIONAL BUDGET OFFICE

should be a priority is that inequality gives the wealthy too much political influence and access.[35]

In other words, it is anti-democratic. But it is also bad for business. The Great Depression of the 1930s had numerous causes. Often
cited is overproduction. Another way to look at overproduction is under-
consumption. Producers cannot make money if too few people can afford
to buy what they produce. Overproduction happens when too few con-
sumers can afford to consume what you are producing. The very wealthiest
among us are not immune from the effects of income inequality.

One of the most comprehensive studies to date on tax cuts for the
rich reveals that the cuts never pay for themselves, always fail to stimulate long-term growth, and do not lead to sustained business investments. A London School of Economics report by David Hope and Julian
Limberg examined five decades of tax cuts in eighteen wealthy nations
and found they consistently benefited the wealthy but had no meaningful effect on unemployment or economic growth.[36] The economist
Thomas Piketty, in *Capital in the Twenty-First Century*, has come to the
same conclusion: "the reduction of top marginal income tax rates and
the rise of top incomes do not seem to have stimulated productivity (contrary to the prediction of supply-side theory) or at any rate did not stimulate productivity enough to the statistically detectable at the macro
level."[37]

As established in a Rand Corporation analysis of income inequality, for the period after World War II, all levels of income and the economy had generally similar growth rates. Then, starting around 1975, incomes for the bottom 90 percent of individuals grew more slowly than the economy as a whole as incomes for the top 10 percent grew faster. In 1975, the share of income for the bottom 90 percent of individuals was 67 percent, the top 9 percent of individuals was 25 percent, and the top 1 percent was 9 percent. In 2018, the share of income for the bottom 90 percent of individuals was 50 percent, the top 9 percent of individuals was 28 percent, and the top 1 percent was 22 percent.[38]

The difference between 1975 and 2018, in terms of the share of income taken home by the bottom 90 percent, is 17 percentage points—or $2.5 trillion in a single year. Over 43 years, this difference amounts to $47 trillion.[39] This disparity in income is dramatic—exponential—and it is what happens when incomes at the bottom grow over four decades at a rate that's about 20 percent of GDP, and top incomes grow at 300 percent of GDP.

Piketty argues that potential solutions to the growing economic divide in America would include a top federal individual marginal tax rate of approximately 80 percent on incomes over $500,000 or $1 million a year, which would not reduce the growth of the U.S. economy and would distribute the fruits of economic growth more widely.[40] Historically, in terms of U.S. tax policy, a marginal individual income tax rate of 70 percent (or higher) for high wage earners was widely accepted for decades.

CHAPTER 11

Pure Tax Magic

JFK once said, "the great enemy of truth is very often not the lie—deliberate, contrived and dishonest—but the myth—persistent, persuasive and unrealistic.... We subject all facts to a prefabricated set of interpretations. We enjoy the comfort of opinion without the discomfort of thought."[1] Let's further examine the components of the tax myth and see how they hold up.

- The tax system has a powerful effect on economic growth and employment.
- Reagan's 1981 tax cut unleashed the American economy and led to an abundance of growth.
- Tax cuts pay for themselves through increased economic growth.

The myth was perfectly captured in something Senator Rand Paul (R-KY) said in an interview with Sean Hannity on Fox News, April 7, 2015: "The last president we had was Ronald Reagan that said we're going to dramatically cut tax rates. And guess what? More revenue came in, but tens of millions of jobs were created."[2]

Rand Paul's words, breathtakingly devoid of any factual basis, are emblematic of the enduring mythology of Reagan's tax policies: cutting taxes leads to additional tax revenue and significant job creation. Pure tax magic! This is not unusual, as extravagant claims are made for any proposed tax cut. Let's examine some of the comments made in support of what is at this writing the GOP's most recent tax cut bill, Trump's Tax Cuts and Jobs Act of 2017. In support of the bill, Arthur Laffer said, "If you cut that [corporate] tax rate to 15 percent, it will pay for itself many times over. ... So this will bring in probably a $1.5 trillion net by itself."[3] As the tax plan was being negotiated, Treasury Secretary Steven Mnuchin told the *Wall Street Journal* that Trump's tax cuts will pay for themselves: "Not only will this tax plan pay for itself, but it will pay down debt." Mnuchin further expressed confidence that the tax law would boost economic growth to a sustainable point without adding onto the nation's then $23 trillion debt. "We've tracked the numbers and we're right on track," he said.[4]

Then, of course, there is former House Speaker Paul Ryan, a Reagan disciple and Ayn Rand theologian. During the passage of Trump's tax cut Speaker Ryan employed the typical GOP talking points regarding any tax cut bill: "It's about faster growth and upward mobility. It's about a strong economy that makes all of us stronger and healthier," Ryan said on the House floor. "Those are the effects; those are the benefits of tax reform."[5] But then Ryan paused and dug deep, channeling his inner Reagan: "stagnation is a breeding ground for a class-based society where elites predetermine the outcome of our lives. Just hand over more freedom to the unelected bureaucrats and they'll figure it out. Hand over your hard-earned dollars to the IRS and it will all be OK. There's the scam right there … the hardworking family in America has got to jump through all the hoops that the IRS can muster."[6] Ryan's statement bashing the IRS is a bit curious, given that he was formerly chairman of the House Ways & Means Committee, which writes the tax laws, and so he was fully aware that the IRS does not write them. Finally, there are the statements of candidate Trump regarding taxes. In a 2016 tweet, he claimed, "I know our complex tax laws better than anyone who has ever run for president and am the only one who can fix them."[7]

Without much effort, one can observe Republicans frequently speaking about the fact that the tax code is "broken" and that they are committed to fixing our nation's broken tax code. In addition, you will further observe the use of such talking points as their wanting a "flatter, fairer, and simpler system." We have news for you: the laws regarding the taxation of income are by their nature complex. Yes, the Internal Revenue Code is complex, as is the Bankruptcy Code and, for that matter, much of federal law. This raises the question: If a system is complex, is it broken? A car, smartphone, and laptop computer are complex. So what? Trash 'em? The works in a traditional Swiss watch are incredibly complex. Give away your Rolex? A jet airliner is complex. Must we forego air travel for that reason?

The game here, and it is a game, is that in spite of earnest-sounding talking points highlighting the need for a "flatter, fairer and simpler" tax system, this really means a less progressive tax system, with fewer tax brackets and lower taxes on and for the wealthy. Simply said, a "flatter" tax rate increases the likelihood that Bob the investment banker and Ed the landscaper will pay the same tax rate. That is not only unfair but also widens a wealth gap that makes the nation less just. Without justice, there can be no peace—for anyone, rich, poor, or in between.

But what about job creation?

According to the Department of Labor, there were 90.9 million jobs at the start of Reagan's presidency—and 106.9 million at the end, for a total increase of 16 million jobs in eight years.[8] The Clinton administration, which raised income tax rates, generated over 23 million jobs over eight years.[9]

Let's examine the facts hiding behind the myth regarding the revenue side.

While nominal tax revenues grew from $517 billion in 1980 to $909 billion in 1988, revenues as a percentage of gross domestic product (GDP), dropped from 19.1 percent in 1980 to a low of 17.3 percent in 1984, before rebounding slightly to 18.2 percent in 1988.[10] In examining revenue over Reagan's eight years, when measured in 2010 dollars, revenues were $1.2 trillion in 1980 and $1.5 trillion in 1988, a mere increase of 25 percent.[11] A Treasury Department study on the impact of tax bills since 1940, first released in 2006 and later updated, found that Reagan's 1981 tax cut reduced revenues by $208 billion in their first four years.[12]

Under Reagan, the "share" of taxes paid by the top 1 percent went from 17.9 percent in 1981 to 25.2 percent in 1989, for an increase of 41 percent, according to IRS data. However, the income share of the top 1 percent increased from 8.3 percent in 1981 to 14.2 percent in 1989—a gain of 71 percent.[13]

To expose the Philosopher-Stone-perpetual-motion-machine magical thinking that tax cuts pay for themselves, Bruce Bartlett, the former Treasury Department official who helped craft the 1981 tax cut, reproduced and analyzed in a 2011 article for *Tax Notes* the Reagan administration and Congressional Budget Office scores of Reagan's tax plan. Contrary to the myth, both CBO and Treasury predicted—in 1981!—that revenue would fall as a result of Reagan's tax cut. Even so, both projections of just how far it would fall were underestimated because the 1981–1982 recession turned out to be deeper than expected and inflation fell more rapidly than expected. The steep decline in revenues is a major reason why Reagan increased taxes in 1982.[14]

Senator Rand Paul does not so much fall into the trap of asserting that the Reagan tax cuts paid for themselves as he jumps into it with both feet. The fact is that Ronald Reagan himself never claimed that the cuts were self-funding. In 2006, the U.S. Treasury officially confirmed that the tax cuts reduced revenue. Moreover, Reagan repeatedly raised taxes during his term as president, in large part to make up for revenue sacrificed to his original tax cut. Facts are stubborn things.

Reagan's tax cuts did have a positive effect on the economy. Nevertheless, Republicans continue to blithely overstate the impact of the 1981 tax cuts as well as the economic prosperity of the Reagan years. Aggregate real gross domestic product growth was 37.2 percent in the 1970s vs. 35.9 percent in the 1980s.[15] (Note: 37.2 is greater than 35.9.) As others have pointed out, there were many factors that led economic growth in the early 1980s. There was the sharp reduction in interest rates by the Federal Reserve. The federal funds rate fell from about 19 percent in July 1981 to about 9 percent in November 1982, thereby easing the credit strain that many Americans felt at the time. Moreover, Reagan's defense spending program stimulated the economy through increased federal spending on goods and services.

Today, Republicans steeped in this tax mythology extol the virtues of lowering marginal tax rates, citing as their model Reagan's Tax Reform Act of 1986, which lowered the top individual income tax rate to just 28 percent from 50 percent. What followed, they say, was an economic boom. The problem is that no significant evidence exists to show a boost in economic growth from the 1986 Tax Reform Act. Efforts by economists to find *any* growth effect from the 1986 Tax Act have failed to turn up much of anything. The most thorough analysis, by economists Alan Auerbach and Joel Slemrod, found only a shifting of income due to tax reform. There were no growth effects. "The aggregate values of labor supply and saving apparently responded very little," they concluded.[16]

In *A Brief History of Equality*, Thomas Piketty assembled data that directly supports the theory that a rise in progressive taxation does not discourage economic innovation or productivity. The notion that higher federal tax rates have no recognizable effect on economic growth in the long run is supported by an analysis undertaken by the Congressional Research Service.[17]

During the span examined in the CRS analysis, labor activity from 1966 thru 2012, the top individual marginal income tax rate on labor income ranged from a high of more than 70 percent to a low of close to 40 percent. As noted in the chart below, the top marginal income tax rate on labor income trended downward during this period and later fluctuated in a narrow range. Nevertheless, the hours of work remained steady or declined over this time span.

The report acknowledges the ongoing policy debate regarding whether to increase tax rates to reduce the federal budget deficit or further lower tax rates to broaden the tax base. In that light, the report provides the following:

- A review of statistical evidence suggests that labor supply, and savings and investment, are relatively insensitive to tax rates.
- Small business taxes are often emphasized as being important to economic growth, but the evidence suggests a modest and uncertain effect on entrepreneurship.

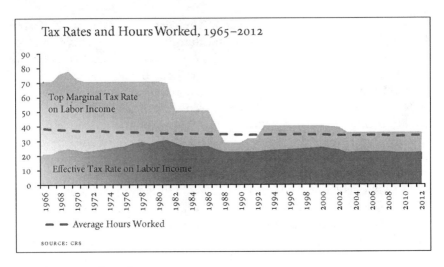

Tax Rates and Hours Worked, 1965–2012

Top Marginal Tax Rate on Labor Income

Effective Tax Rate on Labor Income

— — Average Hours Worked

SOURCE: CRS

But wait, there is more....

In further exploring the relationship of tax rates to economic activity, the CRS analysis examined GDP activity over a sixty-year span (1950–2010) and divides it into three shorter time periods, 1950–1970, 1971–1986 and 1987–2010, which correspond to periods of relatively high, moderate, and low income tax rates on labor. As set forth below, GDP was greater during periods of higher marginal individual income tax rates on labor.

Average Top Tax Rates on the Growth Rate of Real GDP and Real Net Fixed Investment, by Time Period, 1950–2010				
	Average Top Marginal Income Tax Rate on Labor Income	Average Top Marginal Tax Rate on Capital Gains Income	Rate of Growth inReal GDP	Rate of Growth in Real Net Fixed Investment
1950–1970	84.8%	25.6%	3.86%	0.93%
1971–1986	51.8%	30.2%	2.94%	0.32%
1987–2010	36.4%	23.0%	2.85%	0.23%

SOURCE: CRS

The CRS further analyzes the most recent time segment from above and divides it into three shorter periods, 1987–1992, 1993–2002 and 2003–2007, which correspond to periods of relativity low, high and moderate income taxes on labor.

Once again, the long-standing GOP dogma regarding "job killing taxes" and high tax rates discouraging innovation and entrepreneurship rings hollow when compared to economic data. As the CRS report concludes, "Again, the data do not appear to support a clear relationship

Average Top Income Tax Rate on the Growth Rate
of Real GDP, 1987–2007

	Average Top Marginal Income Tax Rate	Rate of Growth in Real GDP
1987–1992	33.3%	2.31%
1993–2002	39.5%	3.68%
2003–2007	35.0%	2.79%

SOURCE: CRS

between lower taxes and higher economic growth; if anything, they suggest the opposite...."

Despite clear and objective evidence to the contrary, the notion of any tax increase is portrayed by the GOP as an economic disaster, creeping socialism, and wealth redistribution by those under the tax mythology spell. As stated earlier, if government is the problem and big government (supported by those evil tax revenues!) means less freedom, then lower tax rates must mean more freedom.

* * *

In his convention speech accepting the 1988 Republican nomination, George H.W. Bush sought to reassure the Reagan faithful that he would preserve the Reagan tax cuts. In that speech, Bush predicted that Democratic legislators would push him to raise taxes. In response to his own prediction, he pledged to the frothed-up convention crowd in New Orleans, "read my lips ... no new taxes."[18]

Few presidential hopefuls have had more reason to regret a promise than Poppy Bush. Pledge or no pledge, he agreed to tax increases as part of budget negotiations in 1990. For believers in the tax myth, this broken promise became the main reason Bush was defeated for reelection by Bill Clinton. In fact, 1990 was the last time a Republican president supported an income tax increase. Such a view, however, ignores the fact that Bush was confronted in his reelection efforts in 1992 by a populist challenger to his center, third party candidate Ross Perot, and was also challenged in 1992 to his right by Pat Buchanan, well-known political pundit and former assistant and special consultant to Presidents Nixon, Ford, and Reagan. A candidate who appealed to the white working class, Buchanan wrote in 2017 that "Donald Trump is ... a direct descendant and rightful heir to Ronald Reagan."[19]

After the reelection defeat of George H.W. Bush, political theater and the GOP message machine would be significantly impacted by the rise of a congressman from Georgia. The sunny optimism of Reagan's "shining city on a hill" was replaced with the vile pugilism of Newton Leroy Gingrich.

Rahm Emanuel, a former Congressman and President Obama's Chief of Staff, called Newt Gingrich "the beginning of the modern new Republican Party, which was manifested in Donald Trump."[20]

George W. Bush, who defeated Al Gore in the controversial 2000 election, believed, unlike his father, in voodoo economics. He took over the presidency from Bill Clinton at a time of peace and prosperity and, more importantly, inherited an annual balanced federal budget. Well, if it ain't broke, break it.

Bush made tax cuts the centerpiece of his 2000 presidential bid and, upon taking office, made tax cuts his first legislative priority. He promoted a $1.6 trillion tax cut, the most ambitious tax cut since Reagan. Ultimately, the total tax cut in 2001 came to $1.35 trillion, and the top individual rate was reduced from 39.6 percent to 35 percent. Echoing the Gipper's tax cutting message in his signing statement, W noted that "Tax relief expands individual freedom."[21] What he failed to add to that sentence was a final clause: "and reduces collective, social freedom." For when taxes are collected and invested in public goods, such as education, healthcare, clean energy, research, and infrastructure they increase the efficiency and productivity of a society.

Bush signed into law a second tax cut bill in May 2003, approximately two months after the U.S. invasion of Iraq, which was an increasingly high-ticket item. Among other changes, Bush's 2003 tax cut accelerated the gradual rate reduction and increase in tax credits enacted in his 2001 tax cut. In signing the 2003 cut, Bush became the first (and so far only) U.S. president to enact a tax cut during in a time of war. Not surprisingly, the budget deficit expanded significantly under Bush, as it did under Reagan. During the eight years of his presidency, annual government outlays as a share of GDP grew from 17.7 percent to 24.4 percent.[22]

Contrary to mythology, despite enacting the largest tax cuts since the heady days of the Reagan era, real GDP growth during the eight years of the Bush administration averaged only 1.8 percent, and job creation averaged 95,000 private sector jobs per month, measured from February 2001 to January 2009, the least of any president since 1970.[23] In January 2009, *The Wall Street Journal* Staff published an article titled "Bush on Jobs: The Worst Track Record on Record" and noted that the Bush administration created about three million jobs (net) over its eight years, a fraction of the 23 million jobs created under President Bill Clinton.[24] Under Bush, who was a supply-sider like Reagan, income inequality continued to worsen and was accelerated by the new tax cuts, which disproportionally benefited higher-income taxpayers. A steep economic decline brought on by the sub-prime mortgage crisis occurred in the summer and fall of 2008, as the Bush presidency neared its end. The housing sector plunged, financial markets verged on meltdown, job losses mounted. George W. Bush began his presidency in 2001 with a budget surplus. Two weeks before President Obama's first inauguration, the CBO projected a 2009 budget deficit of well over $1 trillion.[25]

Donald J. Trump did not hesitate to take up the cleaver from Ronald Reagan and George W. Bush. His Tax Cuts and Jobs Act of 2017 was passed with only Republican votes and was the signature legislative achievement of the Trump administration. In selling the tax cuts, Trump stated that "our focus is on helping the folks who work in the mailrooms and the machine shops of America.... The plumbers, the carpenters, the cops, the teachers, the truck drivers, the pipe-fitters, the people that like me best."[26] Despite Trump's rhetoric and his support among the white working class, more than 60 percent of the tax cuts went to people in the top 20 percent of the income ladder, according to the nonpartisan Tax Policy Center.[27]

The Trump tax cuts failed to produce a permanent boost in economic growth, despite promises from Republican supporters. The Joint Committee on Taxation reported that Trump's Tax Act would marginally increase the size of the economy and boost job creation. As with prior tax cuts, the Congressional Budget Office increased the estimated national debt addition for the 2018–2027 period by $1.6 trillion, assuming the individual tax cut elements expire as scheduled after 2025.[28] The federal debt accumulated during Trump's time increased from $19.9 trillion to $27.78 trillion.[29] While running for president, Trump pledged to balance the budget and then pay off the entire national debt. He boasted to the *Washington Post*'s Bob Woodward, "I think I could do it fairly quickly.... I would say over a period of eight years."[30] Finally, annualized GDP growth under Trump was 1.6 percent, the worst since Herbert Hoover.[31] Brother, can you spare a dime?

*   *   *

In the span between Republicans Reagan and Trump, there were two Democratic Presidents, Bill Clinton and Barack Obama, both of whom raised income taxes. Let's examine how that worked out for the economy.

In 1993, Bill Clinton increased the marginal top individual tax rate from 31 percent to 39.6 percent. Not a single Republican member of Congress voted in support of the tax increase.

- Representative Newt Gingrich (R-GA) declared on February 2, 1993: "We have all too many people in the Democratic administration who are talking about bigger Government, bigger bureaucracy, more programs, and higher taxes. I believe that that will in fact kill the current recovery and put us back in a recession. It might take 1½ or 2 years, but it will happen."[32]

- Representative Jim Ramstad (R-MN), March 17, 1993: "These new taxes will stifle economic growth, destroy jobs, reduce revenues, and increase the deficit. Economists across the ideological spectrum are convinced that the Clinton tax increases will lead to widespread job loss."[33]
- Representative Christopher Cox (R-CA), May 27, 1993: "This is really the Dr. Kevorkian plan for our economy. It will kill jobs, kill businesses, and yes, kill even the higher tax revenues that these suicidal tax increasers hope to gain."[34]

Contrary to the myth that any tax increase will kill jobs and put the economy into a recession, the 1990s were the most prosperous decade in recent memory. The 37.3 percent aggregate real GDP growth in the 1990s exceeded that of the 1980s of 35.9 percent.[35] Nevertheless, almost thirty years later, believers in the tax myth continue to make the same statements today about any tax increase.

The tax myth was tested again in 2013, after President Barack Obama allowed some of the Bush tax cuts to expire, raising the top marginal individual income tax rate to 39.6 percent from 35 percent. The economy continued to grow afterward, and the stock market surged. The Dow Jones index was 7,949 on the day of Obama's inauguration in 2008. The Dow increased 11,783 points to 19,732 during his presidency, a 148 percent increase over eight years.[36] Economic growth during the Obama administration measured as the change in real GDP, averaged 2.0 percent from the second quarter of 2009 to the fourth quarter of 2016.[37] Note, real GDP during President George W. Bush's second term was only 0.5 percent.[38] Under Obama, U.S. corporate profits reached their highest level in history, both in terms of dollars and GDP percent.[39] Obama presided over the third longest economic expansion among the thirty-three expansions tracked since record-keeping began in 1857 and the longest continuous stretch of private sector job creation since records began in 1939.[40] A 148 percent increase in the Dow Jones index over Obama's eight years in the White House? So much for "Democrat socialism."

*   *   *

Growth in capital wealth has been outpacing economic growth, and thus wages, since the 1980s and contributing to an income gap which, in turn, contributes to an increasingly widening wealth gap. The wealth gaps between the bottom 80 percent and top 20 percent, between the bottom 99 percent and top 1 percent, between the 0.9 percent and 0.1 percent, and between the 0.99 percent and 0.01 percent are all yawning chasms.[41] While the cause is not singular, extremes of inequality are bad for democracy and, in the long term, create social, political, and economic unrest.

For decades, the GOP message machine has been dialed into the power of tax cuts, the threat of big government, and the freeloading of the welfare state. Republicans facilitate income inequality through enacting tax cuts. The resulting growth in inequality fuels anger and distrust among working-class voters. Although never accepting responsibility for the income and wealth gaps, the GOP exploits the discontent these gaps generate. Without any plan or intent to ameliorate the economic plight of its working-class supporters, the GOP has ginned up culture wars, grievance, race and identity politics to win elections. Despite Trump's bleat of "America First" and "Drain the swamp"—both mantras substituting for a genuine pro-worker message—during his one-term presidency, Trump moved in lockstep with the GOP orthodoxy founded in the 1980s. He cut taxes for the wealthy, cut regulation, and packed the courts with conservatives.

Over time, this wealth disparity and the gaps in social standing and political influence associated with it create a power gap between the so-called educated elites and others. Deprived of economic, social, and political equality, people legitimately begin to distrust government institutions and grow alienated from them. In addition, the downward socioeconomic spiral has resulted in a surge of depression and addiction among middle-aged working-class whites. As documented by Anne Case and Angus Deaton in *Deaths of Despair*, many white working-class Americans in their forties and fifties are dying of suicide, alcoholism, and drug abuse. In contrast to their counterparts in other wealthy countries, death rates in this group have been rising in America.

To understand how income inequality leads to wealth inequality over time, consider the ominous trends in the chart below from a recent analysis by the Congressional Budget Office.[42] This chart displays the growth rate of income for each quintile of the income distribution from 1979 to 2019.

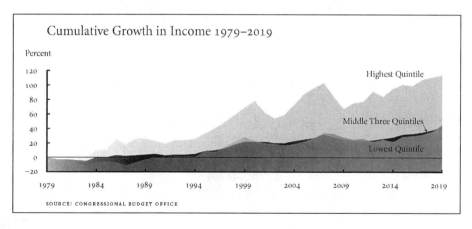

Cumulative Growth in Income 1979–2019

Percent

Highest Quintile

Middle Three Quintiles

Lowest Quintile

SOURCE: CONGRESSIONAL BUDGET OFFICE

Over the forty-one-year period, cumulative growth in real income before transfers and taxes for the quintile groupings was as follows:

- The highest quintile increased 114 percent (an average growth rate of 1.9 percent).
- The middle three quintiles grew by 43 percent (an average rate of 0.9 percent).
- The bottom quintile grew by 45 percent (an average rate of 0.9 percent).

In short, the cumulative growth in income for the highest income quintile over the past four decades has more than doubled when compared to those in the lower economic rungs.

Although the preceding table is helpful for highlighting income-growth disparity over this time span, the economic disparity becomes far more jarring when examining specific income data of the top quintile including the percentiles that make up the top 1 percent.

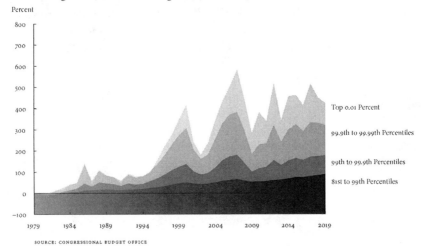

Cumulative Growth in Income Before Transfers and Taxes Among Households in the Highest Quintile, 1979 to 2019

SOURCE: CONGRESSIONAL BUDGET OFFICE

Over the forty-one-year period, cumulative growth in real income before transfers and taxes the for the top 1 percent (broken into percentiles) is as follows:

- 89 percent among households in the 81st to 99th percentiles, or an average annual rate of 1.6 percent, from $131,000 to $247,300.
- 178 percent among households in the 99th to 99.9th percentiles, or an average annual growth rate of 2.6 percent, from $423,400 to $1.2 million.

- 321 percent among households in the 99.9th to 99.99th percentiles, or an average annual growth rate of 3.7 percent, from $1.4 million to $5.7 million.
- 424 percent among households in the 0.01 percent of the distribution, or an average annual growth rate of 4.2 percent, from $8.2 million to $43 million.

Indisputably, the wealth and income gaps continue to widen apace. Emmanuel Saez at the University of California, Berkeley, has recently found that income inequality in the United States has reached a level last seen in the "Roaring" 1920s. To turn a phrase on its head, when Mitt Romney talked about "takers" during his 2012 presidential run, he could have been referring to the top 1 percent of wage earners, who have absorbed a growing portion of the national income at the expense of lower- and middle-class workers.

As the wealth gaps widen, economic displacement becomes the rocket fuel for social unrest. Today, we observe an American version of "dynastic oligarchy," as wealth is passed down through generations of the wealthy without adequate estate and capital gains taxes. This transfer of multigenerational wealth has been accelerated since 1980 by the GOP's war on another tax, the estate tax, which was reframed by Frank Lutz, Republican pollster and wordsmith extraordinaire, as the "Death Tax." Like progressive income taxes, the estate tax leaves a bad taste in the Republican mouth. Estate taxes had a top rate of between 70 and 80 percent from the 1930s to the 1980s.

As Thomas Piketty explains, U.S. income inequality increased sharply during the 1920s, peaking around the time of the 1929 Wall Street crash with more than 50 percent of the national income going to the top 10 percent.[43] According to Piketty, income inequality fell to its lowest in the U.S. between 1950 and 1980, when the top 10 percent of the income strata claimed 30 to 35 percent of U.S. national income.[44] Since 1980, income inequality has rapidly escalated in the U.S. The upper 10 percent's share of national income increased from 30–35 percent in the 1970s to 40–50 percent in the 2000s.[45] The bulk of the growth of inequality came from the top 1 percent, whose share of national income rose from 9 percent in the 1970s to about 20 percent from 2000 to 2010.[46] If you examine the total growth of the U.S. economy from 1977 to 2007, Piketty points out, you will note that 75 percent of the growth went to the richest 10 percent.[47] Moreover, the richest 1 percent absorbed nearly 60 percent of the total increase of U.S. national income over this thirty-year period.[48] In contrast, for the bottom 90 percent of the income strata, the rate of income growth was less than 0.5 percent per year.[49]

*   *   *

There is no doubt that the increase in inequality within the U.S. has contributed to the nation's current instability. Stagnation of the purchasing power of the lower and middle class in the U.S. has made it more likely that such households take on significant debt to keep up with the rising consumption norms of society and, therefore, are more vulnerable to economic shocks and setbacks. As Piketty observes regarding the United States, "it's hard to imagine an economy and society that can continue functioning indefinitely with such extreme divergence between social groups."[50] No doubt, some level of inequality is built into capitalism. It is inherent to the system. The question is, what level of inequality is acceptable? And when does inequality start doing more harm than good? In the United States, is it even possible to have a public discussion about that today? How much longer do we want to live in Reagan's America?

The payment of taxes is essential to the functioning of a society. Taxes make it possible for any society to take collective action. The question is, how can citizens in a democracy determine how taxes are collected and allocated? Should taxes be increased to make investment in infrastructure, healthcare, education, social programs, and employment, or should taxes be decreased to permit the free market to undertake these inherently governmental activities in the name of so-called efficiency?

A progressive tax policy plays a role in mitigating economic inequality. Moreover, given economic displacement caused by globalization, free trade, and changes in energy policy, a progressive tax is indispensable for making sure that everyone benefits from these policies in lieu of stoking fear or debunking science. In many ways, the lack of progressivity in the current tax code and the growing federal budget deficit have put America's policy makers in a terrible bind, as there is little latitude to adopt forward looking policies given the fragile economic status of the majority of Americans. Based on recent polling data, 40 percent of Americans would struggle to come up with $400 for an unexpected expense.[51]

As Piketty writes, the significant decrease in the progressivity of the income tax in the United States in 1980 likely explains much of the significant increase in the very highest incomes. Between the two world wars, all developed countries introduced high tax rates. When a government taxes a certain level of income or inheritance at a high rate, the primary goal is not to raise revenue but to diminish income, large estates, and prevent the rise of oligarchs.[52] Hence, the progressive tax is a method of reducing inequality. The United States was the first country to impose an income tax rate above 70 percent.

Contrary to the views of many, the economy of the United States has not grown any more rapidly since 1980 than comparable higher-tax European counties such as Germany, France, Denmark, or Sweden. In other words, a reduction of top marginal income tax rates and the shifting of national income to the top tier have not stimulated economic productivity.[53]

Sound ethics, morality, and the rule of law make a society fair and just. Given human nature, with status, money and power, an individual's ability to influence the law and government policy increases. One of the dangers for a democracy is money and power creating "special interests," which use the law to amass wealth over time at the expense of the greater good. As Piketty observes, the history of progressive taxation over the course of the twentieth century suggests that the drift toward oligarchy in the U.S. is real and, he adds, this gives little reason for optimism about where the U.S. is headed. Moreover, it was World War II, not suffrage, that gave rise to progressive taxation.[54] In the United States today, it is arguable that we are at a tipping point in terms of inequality of income and wealth. This may be the real message of the violent events of January 6, 2021, at the U.S. Capitol.

The unequal distribution of assets and wealth within a population does not just create powerful special interests. It also creates demagogues, who offer a cure only if we follow them. Trump is such a demagogue. You might recall him telling the crowd at the Republican convention in 2016 that he will be the "voice" for frustrated Americans who have been let down by government and the "elites" who run it. Trump went on to say that "nobody knows the system better than me, which is why I alone can fix it." If the scales of economic and social justice cannot be balanced through the appropriate policy making, they find a way to balance themselves often through tragic and violent means.

If America is at an inflection point, we should look back to the words spoken by Alexander Hamilton at the Constitutional Convention in 1787. "Real liberty," he said, "is neither found in despotism or the extremes of democracy, but in moderate governments."[55] Hamilton's words are not a liberal call to redistribute wealth. Rather, they are a message to conservatives, moderates, liberals, and independents who want to continue to enjoy the pursuit of economic wealth in a free society. A 401(k), stocks and bonds, a bank account, college savings, and a business are only as secure as the country itself, and we all have an interest in maintaining an economic and political balance. As JFK said, "if a free society cannot help the many who are poor, it cannot save the few who are rich."[56]

Or look back further, to the words of Jean-Jacques Rousseau, a Genevan philosopher who wrote of the function of the "Social Contract":

Do you want the state to be solid? Then make the wealth-spread as small as you can; don't allow rich men or beggars. These two conditions are naturally inseparable: any state that has very wealthy citizens will also have beggars, and vice versa. And they are equally fatal to the common good: one produces supporters of tyranny, the other produces tyrants. It is always between them that public liberty is put on sale: one buys, the other sells.[57]

In today's America, we have the significant challenge of convincing the richest elite to give up some of their wealth and power for the greater good—a "good" that, by definition, includes them. To see this requires seeing through the mythology. How much longer can we endure living in Reagan's America? At the very least, the spectacle of January 6, 2021, tells us that we cannot endure it for much longer. Not all revolutions are good. Most, in fact, produce at least as much harm as good. Most fail to improve life. The American Revolution, flawed though it was, was the most successful revolution in the history of the world. The Reagan Revolution? It has failed to serve the majority of us. Reversing the economic policies of that revolution is the existential challenge of our time.

CHAPTER 12

American Lazarus

Ronald Reagan was a popular governor and could have sailed to a third term, had he chosen to do so. Contrary to the mythology created by both the Republican Party and Reagan himself, the governor's economic policy included more significant tax increases than tax cuts. Californians not only swallowed these but also the tax-cutting, small-government aura surrounding Reagan was so thick that it proved essentially impenetrable. His self-promoted tax-cutting persona largely survived the reality of his governing.

But Governor Reagan's two early attempts to capture the GOP presidential nomination yielded no joy. He turned in a dismal third-place performance in 1968. In 1976, with the GOP reeling from the meltdown of the Nixon presidency and the subsequent reign of the affable but veto-happy Gerald Ford, the only unelected president in American history, Reagan saw what certainly loomed as a golden opportunity. Yet his party circled the wagons around Ford, leaving Reagan once again the odd man out. Even Barry Goldwater turned his back on his most effective cheerleader of 1964 and endorsed Ford.

As many saw it, the final nail had been driven into the Reagan coffin. And yet the most astute political observers of the time understood that Reagan's loss of the nomination to Gerald Ford was more a failure of the GOP imagination than it was of Ronald Reagan or his campaign manager John Sears. For even in defeat, Reagan made serious hay with a concession speech that decisively catapulted him out of the domestic arena and onto the world stage. It was a brilliant performance, in which he managed to be gracious to Ford and supportive of the Republican platform even as his eyes were firmly fixed on 1980. He was determined to direct the gaze of the party faithful toward that year as well. Consider the opening of the speech. He explained that he was addressing "fellow Republicans here [in the convention hall] but [also] those who are watching from a distance—all those millions of Democrats and Independents who I know are looking for a cause around which to rally and which I believe we can give them."

In the very next breath, he addressed Ford directly: "Mr. President, before you arrived tonight, these wonderful people, here, when we came in, gave Nancy and myself a welcome."[1]

Reagan conceded the 1976 nomination but claimed everything beyond it. Unspoken was the message that it was not the people but the convention that had just nominated Ford, and those "people" included more than the GOP faithful. Implicit in this statement was the assertion that none of them was committed to Jerry Ford. In fact, *these* people were "looking for a cause"—and a candidate—"around which to rally." Back in 1964, Ronald Reagan had delivered "A Time for Choosing" ostensibly in support of Barry Goldwater but more immediately to transform himself into a national political figure. Now he endorsed the candidacy of Gerald Ford as a means of presenting himself, the loser, as the far better candidate.

He went on to reference Ford's acceptance speech, a journeyman effort if there ever was one, and easily one-upped it. He digressed to mention "an assignment" given him, as former governor and longtime Hollywood star, just the other day:

> Someone asked me to write a letter for a time capsule that is going to be opened in Los Angeles a hundred years from now, on our Tricentennial. It sounded like an easy assignment. They suggested I write something about the problems and issues of the day.
>
> And I set out to do so, riding down the coast in an automobile, looking at the blue Pacific out on one side and the Santa Ynez Mountains on the other, and I couldn't help but wonder if it was going to be that beautiful a hundred years from now as it was on that summer day.
>
> And then as I tried to write—let your own minds turn to that task. You're going to write for people a hundred years from now who know all about us. We know nothing about them. We don't know what kind of a world they'll be living in.[2]

This not the usual convention boilerplate claptrap. It is, first and foremost, a stunning turn—by the *defeated* candidate—to autobiography. It reveals *Governor* Reagan, a man important enough to represent the present Los Angeles to the future America, as a visionary. Now, Gerald Ford was greeted by many in the nation as "avuncular"—that adjective was attached to Ford as if it had been part of his name—and a benign uncle was most welcome after the bitter pill of Nixonian chicanery. But nobody anywhere, and least of all in that convention hall, ever described Ford as a visionary. He himself, after having been sworn in as vice-president in December 1973 (Nixon appointed him after the elected VP, Spiro T. Agnew, entered a plea of *nolo contendere* on corruption charges and resigned from office), apologetically and rather hilariously managed public expectations by remarking, "I am a Ford, not a Lincoln."[3] In his convention speech, however,

Ronald Reagan actually did approach Lincoln in eloquence by not only contemplating the future but also inviting his audience to look at that future *with him*.

Of what did that future, the future toward which Reagan directed his audience, consist? Reagan said that he "thought to myself, 'If I write of the problems, they'll be the domestic problems of which the President [Ford] spoke here tonight,' the challenges confronting us: the erosion of freedom that has taken place under Democrat rule in this country; the invasion of private rights; the controls and restrictions on the vitality of the great free economy that we enjoy. These are our challenges that we must meet." He continued:

> And then again there is that challenge of which he spoke that we live in a world in which the great powers have poised and aimed at each other horrible missiles of destruction, nuclear weapons that can in a matter of minutes arrive at each other's country and destroy virtually the civilized world we live in.
> And suddenly it dawned on me: Those who would read this letter a hundred years from now will know whether those missiles were fired. They will know whether we met our challenge.[4]

The future Ronald Reagan saw—and, even more important, invited the millions beyond the confines of the convention hall to see—was the future that candidate Gerald Ford (were he to be elected) would at least partially create. In other words, it would be a future with the same problems, unchanged if not made worse, as those that threatened America and the rest of the world now, in 1976. As if this weren't sufficiently undermining of candidate Gerald R. Ford, Reagan twisted the knife of his soothsaying vision:

> Whether they [the Americans a hundred years hence] have the freedoms that we have known up until now will depend on what we do here. Will they look back with appreciation and say, "Thank God for those people in 1976 who headed off that loss of freedom? Who kept us now a hundred years later free? Who kept our world from nuclear destruction?"
> And if we failed they probably won't get to read the letter at all because it spoke of individual freedom and they won't be allowed to talk of that or read of it.
> This is our challenge and this is why, here in this hall tonight, better than we've ever done before, we've got to quit talking to each other and about each other and go out and communicate to the world that, we may be fewer in numbers than we've ever been, but we carry the message they're waiting for.

Bear in mind, the words Reagan's audience heard before this passage could not be unheard. Will the future look back at this 1976 nominating convention and give thanks for their Lord and Savior Uncle Jerry Ford? Not likely. He was the lesser man in the nominating contest. Reagan nevertheless counseled what sounds a lot less like the rally cry of freedom than a call to grin and bear it. "We must go forth from here united, determined," he said. *Must?* Yes, because we are saddled with a Ford when what we need is a Lincoln or, at least, a Reagan, and what we're going to end up with is a Jimmy Carter.[5]

Reagan closed with: "what a great general said a few years ago is true: 'There is no substitute for victory.'"[6] The great general, of course, was Douglas MacArthur, who addressed Congress on his retirement from the army because President Harry S. Truman had not allowed him to escalate the Korean War into World War III. In the general election of 1976, the substitute for victory was very clear. The GOP National Convention had just nominated him as the party's candidate for president.

* * *

Fortune shined on Ronald Reagan when Gerald Ford was defeated by Democrat Jimmy Carter. Reagan was determined not to let 1980 and his third shot at the presidency slip out of his grasp. Governor Reagan was approaching the end of his second term when the great television anchorman Walter Cronkite invited him to deliver commentaries from the conservative point of view twice weekly on his *CBS Evening News*. On two other nights each week newsman Eric Sevareid would deliver the liberal viewpoint. Cronkite's television newscast was far and away the most widely watched in the nation, and Reagan was sorely tempted. What stopped him from accepting the invitation, however, was the prospect of relinquishing control over each and every broadcast. A short time later, however, an old friend—actor Efrem Zimbalist, Jr., star of *77 Sunset Strip* and *The FBI*, two hit TV series—talked to Reagan about some radio work he was doing. His producer, Harry O'Connor, wanted to create a series of brief daily conservative commentaries. Reagan liked the idea, but before saying yes consulted Peter Hannaford, a professional publicist. Hannaford powwowed with O'Connor and then took the concept to Michael Deaver, at the time Reagan's gubernatorial PR advisor. An arrangement was struck, and Hannaford fit the radio broadcasts into a larger publicity plan intended to keep Reagan's name and viewpoint top of mind after he left the governor's mansion. The daily radio commentaries would be bolstered by newspaper columns and live speaking engagements.

A master of his trade, Harry O'Connor wanted his client to be excited about the radio broadcasts, so, for the debut recording session, he gathered a group of the governor's Hollywood friends to greet him and cheer him on. Besides Zimbalist, there were Jack (*Dragnet*) Webb and Art (*People Are Funny*) Linkletter. Each program opened with a tease for the topic, followed by "I'll be right back" and a commercial break. The commentary came next, ending always with "This is Ronald Reagan. Thanks for listening."

The commentaries, which were written by Reagan himself, were popular, and the series spanned 1975 to 1979. The broadcast of January 27, 1978, began, "It's nightfall in a strange town a long way from home. I'm watching the lights come on from my hotel room window on the 35th floor." He took a beat. "I'll be right back."[7]

Reagan came of age in the era of FDR's "Fireside Chats," intimate radio broadcasts that brought the president into the parlors of homes across the nation. In the "Looking Out the Window" script and those for his other broadcasts, Reagan spoke directly to his audience while carefully establishing his presence. The intimacy of this particular broadcast is uncanny. We are with him in that lonely hotel room. It is not an overtly political broadcast but a vision of an anxious American people. He tells his listeners that this is but one stop on "the mashed potato circuit," and as he looks "down on a busy city at rush hour," he sees the road below as "twin ribbons of sparkling red and white. Tail lights on the cars moving away from my vantage point provide the red and the headlights of those coming toward me the white. It's logical to assume all or most are homeward bound at the end of a day's work." He imagines the emotions of the occupants of all those vehicles:

> … I wonder about the people in those cars, who they are, what they do, what they are thinking about as they head for the warmth of home…. Some of our social planners refer to them as "the masses" which only proves they <u>don't</u> know them. I've been privileged to meet people all over this land in the special kind of way you meet them when you are campaigning. They are not "the masses," or as the elitists would have it—"the common man." They are very uncommon … individuals….
>
> Someone very wise once wrote that if we were all told one day that the end was coming; that we were living our last day, every road, every street & all the telephone lines would be jammed with people trying to reach someone to whom we wanted simply to say, "I love you."
>
> But doesn't it seem kind of foolish to wait for such a final day and take the chance of not getting there *in time? And speaking of time* I'll have to stop now. OPERATOR I'D LIKE TO MAKE A PHONE CALL—LONG DISTANCE.
>
> This is Ronald Reagan. Thanks for listening.[8]

This is the work of a master mythologist, who absorbed the lessons of Hollywood. The broadcast is a spot recorded in a studio, but we are with Reagan in the lonely intimacy of his hotel room, with him during his campaign, the campaign we are made to feel that he is running not for himself but for us, his intimate friends, who he knows too well to call "the masses." He knows what we want, which is, like him, to go home after a day's work, home to those who love us, depend on us, and give our lives whatever meaning they have. We are united with him by certain needs and wants and values. He proves this by ending the broadcast with a long-distance call home. For he is sacrificing valuable time with *his* family to campaign for the well-being of *ours*.

The Reagan vision is uncontaminated by ideology. It is instead suffused with a mythology that insinuates him into *our* lives, which are made to seem quintessentially *American* lives. One nation, indivisible, under Ronald Reagan.

*   *   *

Come 1980, Reagan had a formidable primary opponent in George H.W. Bush, who dared to attack him where he was weakest, namely his grasp of economic reality. Saddled with what many still call the "Nixon-Ford recession" and caught in an "energy crisis" triggered in part by the machinations of OPEC, the Carter administration compiled a dismal economic record. Voters might have forgiven some of this were it not for President Carter's bad habit of leveling with them about both the economy and the energy crisis, especially since the "leveling" often sounded like lecturing. Carter's soft-spoken drawl and easy-going manner had played well with voters, but it seemed that fewer people wanted this style to carry over after the inauguration. Carter was widely blasted for appearing on television in a cardigan sweater rather than a presidential suit and tie to give a depressing lecture on energy conservation in which he asked the American people to turn down their thermostats at home—just as he had done in the White House.

While it was reasonable advice, nobody wanted to hear it. Moreover, offering a cardigan and a lowered thermostat seemed like a weak substitute for bolder action on the economy, the state of the energy markets, and the Arabs who controlled so much of the oil supply. Anxious to break with the corrupt imperial presidency of Richard Nixon, Carter simply came off as prosaic, weak, and perhaps too small for the presidency. In truth, his problems were more than a matter of image. The Carter–era Congress had a two-thirds Democratic majority in both houses, yet Carter was rarely able to move his legislative agenda along. It was a failure of presidential leadership.

Once Reagan and his campaign had triumphed over Bush in the primaries, they showed no mercy to Jimmy Carter. The Reagan team had correctly identified the economy as a top voter concern. Reagan could make a case for having managed California's economy well, but he made no attempt to reconcile his mostly mythological reputation as a tax cutter with the many times he raised California taxes. He elided this truth to sell voters in the general election on large tax cuts, on reducing the government's spendthrift "waste, fraud and abuse," and on the perverse rhetoric of supply-side/trickle-down economics. It was the most elaborate and brazen myth of Reagan's political life thus far and, on the face of it, the most improbable. How on earth could *cutting* taxes on the wealthiest, while significantly increasing defense spending *increase* federal tax revenues by stimulating business, while also producing gains for the wealthiest that "trickled down" to the middle class and below?

Unlike Winston Churchill, Jimmy Carter did not offer the American people blood, toil, tears, and sweat. He promised what Americans regarded as much worse: self-discipline and self-denial in the form of turning down the thermostat, obeying a 55-mph speed limit on Interstate and federal highways, and buttoning up a cardigan. This was hardly a match for the Reagan riffs on deregulating industry, reducing the size of government, and slashing entitlements while cutting taxes on business and the wealthy to create a trickle-down of cash to everybody else while also rebuilding the military and using as much energy and oil as you want in a free America ... *damn it!*

The most memorable moment of the Reagan/Carter campaign came on the evening of October 28, 1980, during the second televised presidential debate of that cycle. Carter quite incisively pushed Reagan toward the infamous Third Rail of Politics, threatening Social Security and Medicare. He challenged his opponent squarely, seriously, and substantively:

> These constant suggestions that the basic Social Security System should be changed does call for concern and consternation among the aged of our country. It is obvious that we should have a commitment to them, that Social Security benefits should not be taxed and that there would be no peremptory change in the standards by which Social Security payments are made to retired people.... Governor Reagan, as a matter of fact, began his political career campaigning around this nation against Medicare. Now, we have an opportunity to move toward national health insurance, with an emphasis on the prevention of disease, an emphasis on out-patient care, not in-patient care; an emphasis on hospital cost containment to hold down the cost of hospital care for those who are ill, an emphasis on catastrophic health insurance, so that if a family is threatened with being wiped out economically because of a very high medical bill, then the insurance would help pay for it. These are the kinds of elements of a national health insurance, important to the American people. Governor Reagan, again, typically is against such a proposal.

A powerful indictment—and substantive, to boot. How was Reagan going to get out of this hammerlock?

Debate moderator Howard K. Smith turned to Reagan. "Governor?"

"There you go again," Reagan responded with adroitly dismissive affability.

Nobody remembers what Reagan said next. That four-word come-back, without a whiff of substance and totally void of meaning, neverthe-less defused the impact of everything Carter had said. Indeed, if we go on to examine the rest of Reagan's response, it is Reagan who reveals his own position as weak:

> When I opposed Medicare, there was another piece of legislation meeting the same problem before the Congress. I happened to favor the other piece of leg-islation and thought that it would be better for the senior citizens and provide better care than the one that was finally passed. I was not opposing the prin-ciple of providing care for them. I was opposing one piece of legislation versus another.[9]

In 1961, Reagan recorded an entire LP, *Ronald Reagan Speaks Out Against Socialized Medicine*, in an effort to block not only Medicare but also every other form of government support for private medicine. Reagan's record on Medicare was, in fact, an actual *record*, playable on any pho-nograph![10] No matter, his Hollywood-honed persona trumped substance and trounced Carter, making *him* look mean-spirited.

Ronald Reagan annihilated Jimmy Carter at the polls in 1980, win-ning 43,903,230 popular votes for 489 electoral votes to Carter's 35,481,115 and 49 electoral votes. It is difficult to argue that Jimmy Carter's perfor-mance in his first term merited election to a second, but that he was so severely beaten by a candidate who purveyed a pasteboard, even cartoon-ish, incarnation of the American Dream certainly smells like the stuff of tragedy. Fortunately for the thirty-ninth president, America, and the world, Jimmy Carter went on to a post-presidential career of extraordinary philanthropy, diplomacy, and public service that is more than a sufficiently ample legacy to earn him the title of a good man and a great American. Not since William Howard Taft, a thoroughly mediocre one-term presi-dent, went on from the White House to serve as the tenth Chief Justice of the United States has a former president so distinguished himself in post-presidential public life.

The American Dream Reagan peddled was born mainly in the Ameri-can pocketbook. It was a perversion built not on equality in America but on prosperity for the few and trickle-down crumbs for the masses. Years later, Donald Trump, whose value he himself seems to have measured solely by the enormous wealth to which he laid dubious claim, would offer much the same vision. As Thomas Piketty wrote in his *Capital in the Twenty-First Century*, the United States has reached the outer edge of what might be sus-tainable in terms of wealth disparity. Trickle-down assertions to the con-trary, four decades and counting of income disparity have transformed the American Dream from a pasteboard cutout to a zombie's corpse.

* * *

Ronald Reagan was first and last a lucky man. He emerged whole from a childhood that would have damaged many others. His earliest ambition was to be a lifeguard. He became a lifeguard, and very good one at that. He wanted to be a radio sportscaster. He became one. He had a somewhat attenuated ambition to become a Hollywood actor. He parlayed a baseball broadcasting assignment covering spring training on the West Coast into an all-expenses-paid trip to a talent agency in Los Angeles. He then left broadcasting for acting. The quasi-political post as president of the Screen Actors Guild served him as the basis for a political career, beginning with a successful campaign for California governor. Supporters came to him, willing to mold him into a presidential candidate. He lost his first two White House bids, defeated twice for the nomination, but his third try pitted him against a hard-luck president. Carter inherited a miserable economy, was caught in the jaws of an energy crisis, and then, on November 4, 1979, became a victim of the Iranian Revolution against longtime U.S. ally Mohammad Reza Shah Pahlavi, the Shah of Iran. At the beginning of that year, the Shah fled into exile. In October 1979, terminally ill with cancer, he was granted permission by President Carter to come to the United States for medical treatment. Enraged by this gesture, some 500 Iranians, presumably at the behest of the Ayatollah Khomeini, stormed the U.S. Embassy in Tehran on November 4. They took ninety hostages, including sixty-five U.S. nationals.

During November 19–20, the Iranian insurgents released all the non–American hostages in addition to thirteen American women and all black Americans. Fifty-two hostages remained captive. In return for their release, the captors demanded that President Carter send the Shah back to Iran to face revolutionary justice. When Carter refused to yield to this demand, the Shah, hoping to end the crisis, voluntarily left the United States in early December. This did not prompt the Iranians to release their captives. President Carter authorized an elite army Delta Force unit to attempt a rescue on April 24, 1980. The operation was plagued by a combination of mechanical and human errors and had to be aborted. It was not until November 1980 that the Iranian parliament proposed definitive terms for the release of the hostages. President Carter pledged that the United States would not "interfere" in Iranian affairs, he agreed to release the Iranian financial assets he had frozen in the United States, he agreed to lift U.S. economic sanctions against Iran, and he promised to return whatever American property the Shah possessed. An agreement was signed early in January 1981, but the Ayatollah Khomeini withheld his approval and the release of the hostages until January 20, the day Jimmy Carter left office and Ronald Reagan was inaugurated.

The Ayatollah aimed to humiliate Carter while elevating the incoming Reagan. Bad luck for Carter; a windfall for Reagan. In contrast to Donald Trump, who is congenitally unable to commit a selfless act or, indeed, even to glance beyond his own self-interest, the incoming president performed a deed of moving grace. He sent Carter as his special envoy to greet the returning hostages at a U.S. base in West Germany. This shifted the spotlight from him and onto the defeated ex-president, but it was no great sacrifice for Reagan. After all, he had other fish to fry on inauguration night. The release of the Iran hostages on inauguration day was a species of auspicious and propitious augury that preceded what *The New York Times* described as "an evening of shiny black limousines and nostalgic swing bands, of glittery Hollywood celebrities and wealthy Western oil men. The aura of big money was everywhere—expensive gowns by James Galanos, Bill Blass and Oscar de la Renta, unprecedented $100 tickets to dance to the music of Count Basie and other big bands." Los Angeles businessman Lloyd Hand proclaimed it "the introduction of an era of hope and promise."[11] Carter? He was on his way to Germany, a party of one eager to welcome the hostages home.

The Reagan inaugural celebration was mythic in opulence and cost, and the message of Reagan's inaugural speech was of liberation—from the American government itself. Barely two months later, a young man involved in his own solipsistic liberation myth, one manufactured in Reagan's old stomping ground, Hollywood, finally acted out his destiny. Elections? Governments? Who needed them? This man had a gun.[12]

At twenty-five, John Warnock Hinckley, Jr., was, to put it bluntly, an American loser. The drifter son of a wealthy Denver oil engineer, Hinckley had become obsessed with eighteen-year-old screen actress Jodie Foster, who had created a sensation playing a teenage prostitute in *Taxi Driver*, a 1976 Martin Scorsese masterpiece dealing in part with political assassination. Hinckley, who lived in Hollywood during the late 1970s, later reported that he had seen the movie at least fifteen times. Clearly, he saw himself as an apt avatar of protagonist Travis Bickle, played by Robert De Niro, who aims to save the Jodie Foster character, kills her pimp, and then attempts the assassination of a presidential candidate.

After fifteen rounds of this movie, Hinckley brought into real life his obsession with Foster, stalking her across the country and then enrolling in a writing course at Yale just because he had read in *People* that she was a Yale student. By late 1980, he was writing to her—constantly. He managed to get through to her by phone on two occasions and professed his love. She rebuffed him.

Well, Hinckley was a nobody, and he knew it. What better way to transform himself into a somebody—a national figure, no less—than by following the path of Travis Bickle? At first, he stalked Jimmy Carter, getting within a foot of the president at a public event. Hinckley was looking for a Hollywood ending but was stymied in October 1980 when he was arrested at Nashville International Airport for possession of an illegal firearm. Not coincidentally, Carter was making a campaign stop in Nashville, but the local cops did not see any connection, they did not alert the Secret Service, and Hinckley received nothing more than a fine. Alarmed, his well-to-do parents sent to him a psychiatrist. Whatever treatment he received didn't make much of a dent, because the young man quickly turned from Carter to Reagan.

In early March 1981, weeks after Reagan's inauguration, Hinckley wrote some more letters to Jodie Foster, who turned them over to one of Yale's deans, who, in turn, passed them on to the Yale University police. They were unable to locate Hinckley, who had traveled to Washington, and on March 30, 1981, stationed himself at the entrance to the Washington Hilton, where the new commander-in-chief was delivering a speech. As Reagan exited the venue, Hinckley stepped forward from the small crowd gathered outside the hotel and squeezed off six .22-caliber specially prepared explosive "Devastator" rounds. Although he fired from close range, he was not a professional assassin and not even a very disciplined shooter. Those bullets that found marks hit Secret Service agent Timothy J. McCarthy (who seems to have deliberately screened the president), Washington police officer Thomas Delahanty, and White House press secretary James S. Brady.

Ronald Reagan was a lucky man. Secret Service Special Agent in Charge Jerry Parr grabbed Reagan's shoulders, spun him around, and dove with him into the open doorway of the presidential limousine—apparently clear of any bullet's path. When Reagan complained of pain, telling Parr that being shoved into the limo had broken a rib, the agent ran his hands up and down the president's torso, feeling for a wound. When Reagan began coughing up blood, Parr ordered the limousine to proceed not to the White House but to George Washington University Hospital.

When they arrived, Reagan waved off a gurney and insisted on walking into the hospital under his own power. Optics were key. Once inside, his knees buckled and Parr caught him. ER physicians found a gunshot wound to the chest. As it turned out, one of Hinckley's rounds had ricocheted off the open car door and penetrated Reagan's chest. Fortunately, however, the explosive Devastator, its velocity reduced by the ricochet, lodged in the president's lung and failed to detonate.

Reagan was rushed into surgery. Wife Nancy arrived just before he was wheeled into the OR. The critically injured chief executive grabbed the opportunity to play the affable hero. His next words could not have been more artfully scripted.

"Honey, I forgot to duck."

Then, as he lay on the surgical table just before going under anesthesia, he looked up at his surgeons and said, "I hope you are all Republicans." It was the best B-picture line he had uttered since "Win one for the Gipper" in 1940's *Knute Rockne, All American.*

Unknown to Reagan, the event created chaos, assiduously concealed by publicity flacks as cabinet members argued over the order of presidential succession in the absence of Vice President George H.W. Bush, who was in midflight aboard Air Force Two. Everyone conspired to hide the truly serious nature of emergency surgery to remove a bullet, an explosive bullet, from the lung of a man just sixteen days shy of his seventieth birthday. Although photographs of Reagan sitting up in bed were quickly disseminated to the media, and Reagan accelerated his departure from the hospital, he did not convene a Cabinet meeting until almost a month after the shooting.

*   *   *

Being shot in the lung took a toll on Ronald Reagan. His physician later commented that the president was not fully recovered until October. But from the get go, Reagan took pains to avoid looking weak, impaired, or otherwise diminished.

"I was determined that, when I left the hospital, I was going to walk out," he wrote in his 1990 memoir, "and I did." The day after leaving the hospital, he wrote in his diary: "The first full day at home. I'm not jumping any fences and the routine is still one of blood tests, X-rays, bottles dripping into my arms but I'm home. With the let-up on antibiotics, I'm beginning to have an appetite and food tastes good for the first time." In his memoir, he made sure to note that he "did take an afternoon nap during the first three or four weeks after I came home from the hospital, but, despite reports to the contrary, that was the first and only time I'd needed one since I was a child."[13]

Ronald Reagan was a lucky man. The assassination was an appalling act. Metropolitan police officer Thomas Delahanty recovered from his gunshot wound but suffered permanent nerve damage to his left arm, which forced his early retirement from the police force. Secret Service Agent Timothy McCarthy, who did his duty by taking a bullet for the president, fully recovered. But James Brady, the presidential press secretary, shot in the head, survived but was left with brain damage that severely slurred his speech and partial paralysis that confined him to a wheelchair for the rest of his life. As for Reagan, as a *Washington Post* headline put it on April 2, 1981, "Shooting Gives Reagan Boost in Popularity." A Post-ABC poll conducted three days after the assassination attempt saw an eleven-point surge in his popularity, with 73 percent of poll respondents saying they approved of Reagan's performance as president and just 16 percent expressing disapproval, with 11 percent expressing no opinion.[14]

With the assassination attempt, life handed Ronald Reagan a strange gift in the form of the archetypal "Hero's Journey" Joseph Campbell writes of in *The Hero with a Thousand Faces*. It is the core of personal mythology. The journey's culmination is the point at which the hero grabs his piece of immortality. Ronald Reagan compiled an average overall approval rating of 52.8 percent during his two terms as American president. That post-shooting high of 73 percent was a full twenty-point bonus in the days and weeks immediately following the president's brush with death. Reagan and his team took full advantage of this boost, on August 4, 1981, pushing through Congress (even with a Democratic majority in the House) the administration's first signature tax cut, the Economic Recovery Tax Act of 1981, better known as the Kemp-Roth Tax Cut.

That legislation had come close to passing during the Carter administration, but that president successfully argued that the cuts would dramatically increase the federal deficit and was able to stop passage. Under Reagan, the cuts were signed into law on August 13. They were the largest tax cuts in American history and became the cornerstone of the so-called Reagan Revolution. The highest marginal tax rate plummeted from 70 percent to 50 percent, while the lowest rate declined more modestly from 14 percent to 11 percent. While Reagan supporters would later claim that the economic recovery during Reagan's presidency was due to the steep tax cuts, Reagan critics pointed out that the federal deficit materially worsened. Those faithful to the gospel of supply-side economics predicted that tax cuts would actually increase tax revenues. They did no such thing, however, and in September 1982, the Tax Equity and Fiscal Responsibility Act of 1982 (TEFRA) was passed to counter the impact of tax cuts on the deficit. TEFRA is widely viewed as the largest single tax *increase* since the end of World War II.

*   *   *

Ronald Reagan, like virtually every other Republican politician, preached a balanced budget. Yet he took the federal budget deficit from $70 billion to $175 billion. His successor, George H.W. Bush, took it to $300 billion. Bill Clinton, the Democrat who defeated Bush's bid for a second term, left office after eight years with the budget deficit at zero (indeed, there was a modest surplus). George W. Bush managed to take the deficit from zero to $1.2 trillion dollars, a figure Democrat Barack Obama cut in half to $600 billion. Donald John Trump, the political spawn of Ronald Wilson Reagan, left office with a $2.3 trillion deficit projected for 2021—though in 2020, amid a massive bipartisan response to the Covid-19 pandemic, the deficit reached as high as $3 trillion, 14.9 percent of GDP, a percentage exceeded only during the height of World War II.[15]

Donald Trump mirrored Ronald Reagan in another feature of his presidency. He, too, suffered an attack from a would-be assassin. On October 2, 2020, Trump fell ill with Covid-19, the pandemic virus he had spent so much of 2020 lying about, minimizing its hazards, or even denying them entirely. Fortunately, the medical science he reflexively denigrated provided his team of physicians with what were at the time advanced experimental treatments unavailable to virtually any other person on the planet. These were far superior to the "miracle cures" Trump championed, such as hydroxychloroquine, veterinary Ivermectin, and bleach injections. Trump rapidly recovered and staged, from the Truman Balcony, his own B-picture triumphant return to the White House.

Few events in life could possibly be more heroically victorious than surviving a near-death experience with grace, as Ronald Reagan in fact did. Trump ascended the Truman Balcony; defiantly tore off his surgical mask; and, in a look worthy of Benito Mussolini, scanned the onlookers below. Clearly, Trump hoped something akin to the Reagan post-assassination-attempt magic would rub off on him.

It did not.

Postscript: A jury found John Hinckley, Jr., not guilty by reason of insanity, and he was duly confined to a psychiatric hospital. Most assumed that he would spend the rest of his life immured in St. Elizabeth's, but on July 27, 2016, a federal judge ordered his release into the care of his mother in her Williamsburg, Virginia, home. On June 15, 2022, pursuant to another federal court ruling, Hinckley was released unconditionally and is now walking among us.

James Brady, the one Hinckley victim who had sustained life-altering injuries, became a passionate advocate of federal regulation of handguns. While President Reagan remained a lover of the Second Amendment, in his post-presidency he did support passage of the 1993 Brady Bill (imposing a five-day waiting period before a licensed gun dealer can transfer a handgun to an unlicensed individual) and the 1994 Assault Weapons Ban (prohibiting the manufacture for civilian use of certain semi-automatic weapons deemed assault weapons). The 1994 Assault Weapons Ban expired in 2004 and was not renewed by Congress. Donald Trump acted to strengthen some federal gun control but mostly eased existing restrictions. In a post-presidency appearance at the 2022 NRA convention in Houston, he summarily rejected all gun regulations and, in response to a horrific rash of school shootings, called vaguely for an overhaul of school safety.[16]

CHAPTER 13

PATCO Tamed

"By instinct and experience, I supported unions and the rights of workers to organize and bargain collectively," Ronald Reagan declared in his 1990 memoir.[1] This was true. Ronald Reagan did have a long record as president of the Screen Actors Guild, an AFL-CIO union representing actors in film and television. Reagan's Guild activity began on August 11, 1941, when he attended his first SAG board meeting as an alternate for British actress Heather Angel (best remembered, if at all, for roles in *Peter Pan* and *Alice in Wonderland*). World War II intervened, interrupting Reagan's SAG activity, but in 1947 he was elected to the first of seven presidential terms (1947, 1948, 1949, 1950, 1951, 1959, and 1960).[2] He was, in fact, the only U.S. president to lead a labor union.

Under Reagan, the SAG presidency was no ceremonial sinecure. It was a momentous period in the union's history. SAG enacted its first new contract since 1937; weathered passage of the 1947 Taft-Hartley Act, which generally weakened unions; became involved in the House Committee on Un-American Activities hearings, which brought the infamous blacklist of the McCarthy Era; witnessed the decline of Hollywood film production with the rise of television; was party to the so-called Paramount Decree of 1948, which ushered in the end of the "studio system" (monopolistic domination all aspects of the motion picture industry, including production, distribution, and exhibition); passed the controversial MCA waiver (see Chapter 6); and struggled over residuals (actor payment for filmed television programs). There were also strikes in 1952–1953, 1955, and 1960, some of which were violent.

Reagan described his role in the 1960 strike as "leading [SAG] in its first major strike in history." (The strikes of 1952–1953 and 1955 affected SAG but were not led by the organization.) He was a dedicated strike leader, and yet he took pains not to define the studios as an enemy to labor. As he wrote in 1990:

> Some authors have suggested my work in the Screen Actors Guild fighting
> the studios hurt my film career, as it had hurt some of the early pioneers in the

173

union, but I've never felt any sour grapes about it. To a newspaper columnist who asked, after the 1960 strike, if I thought the union work had hurt my career, I said, "I think it has hurt some, although certainly not in the way that someone says, 'I'm mad at this guy so I won't use him in my pictures.' In all my years with the union, I've never seen any grudges carried deliberately out of the conference room. Any suffering careerwise definitely isn't retaliatory, although there are a lot of people involved in making a motion picture, and you become typecast in their minds on the basis of what they know about you off the screen. They stop thinking of you as an actor. The image they have of you isn't associated with your last role, but with the guy who sat across the conference table, beefing. And that's death!"[3]

Reagan's rise in national politics took place during the 1970s, a decade of economic uncertainty under Nixon, Ford, and Carter. Nixon and Ford brought recession and stagflation, while the Carter years were characterized by continued high inflation compounded by an energy crisis and the Iranian hostage crisis. A global recession closed the decade and continued well into the Reagan administration. During 1974–1979, unemployment was around 5 percent, rising to 7 percent in April 1980 and worsening by the second year of the Reagan presidency, jumping to 10.8 percent late in 1982, the highest rate since the Great Depression.

The economic conditions fostered the ascension of the New Right, to which Reagan most appealed. They were advocates of "traditional" religion, small government, and a "muscular" foreign policy. The New Right ate into the traditional Democratic support from blue-collar workers and their families. Pressured by high unemployment, union membership declined, and more of the working class began identifying with Reagan's pro-business, traditional (that is mythically nostalgic) values. Despite the economic woes of the working class, the majority bought into Reagan's supply-side, trickle-down economic program. Many blue-collar voters followed the GOP's party line in blaming big unions, not Big Business management for job losses and the rise in production costs that sent many jobs overseas.

While Ronald Reagan embraced the Republican Party and, as president, rose to its leadership, he managed to avoid alienating most blue-collar unions by effectively marketing his own small-town Heartland, blue-collar origins as well as his leadership of a union. This values-based mythology was compelling to a few unions, including PATCO (Professional Air Traffic Controllers Organization).

PATCO was established in 1968 and during the recession years of the 1970s was highly successful in strategically employing slowdowns and sick-outs—labor actions stopping short of strikes—to win retirement and retraining benefits for its federal traffic controller membership.

In response to PATCO's endorsement, candidate Reagan wrote to union president Robert Poli in October 1980: "I will take whatever steps are necessary to provide our air traffic controllers with the most modern equipment available, and to adjust staff levels and workdays so they are commensurate with achieving the maximum degree of public safety. I pledge to you that my administration will work very closely with you to bring about a spirit of cooperation between the President and the air traffic controllers."[4]

Armed with a presidential pledge, Poli took PATCO into new contract negotiations with the FAA on February 1981. Poli's chief asks were a thirty-two-hour work week, a $10,000 raise for all PATCO members, and a better retirement package. The cost of all this was $681 million. The FAA countered with $40 million. In rejecting the government's paltry counteroffer, Poli cited a crisis of job-related stress among its members, pointing out that 89 percent of those who left air traffic controller positions in 1981 were either retiring early and seeking medical benefits or walking out of the profession entirely.[5]

Negotiations between PATCO and the FAA broke down, and air traffic controllers walked out on August 3, 1981, over four main grievances:

1. Air traffic controllers' work was undervalued and under-rewarded.

2. The work week was unreasonably long.

3. The FAA's dictatorial approach to supervision and to union-management relations undermined morale and safety.

4. The FAA neglected serious deficiencies in staffing levels and the reliability of obsolescent air traffic control equipment.

The government did not dispute PATCO's grievances but simply asserted that, under the Taft-Hartley Act, the strike was illegal. And it was. PATCO was breaking the law. Poli's high-stakes gamble was that the president, who pledged his support in writing, would nevertheless back the walkout.

President Reagan announced a press conference. Four hours after the commencement of the strike, he entered the Rose Garden with what can best be described as a purposeful stride. In fact, "purposeful stride" could have been a stage direction on a script. He took up his position at the lectern, looked out at the gathered reporters, and said:

This morning at 7 a.m. the union representing those who man America's air traffic control facilities called a strike. This was the culmination of 7 months of negotiations between the Federal Aviation Administration and the union. At one point in these negotiations agreement was reached and signed by both sides, granting a $40 million increase in salaries and benefits. This is twice what other government employees can expect. It was granted in recognition of the difficulties inherent in the work these people perform. Now, however, the union demands are 17 times what had been agreed to—$681 million. This would impose a tax burden on their fellow citizens which is unacceptable.

Not every PATCO controller had walked out. The former SAG president, now commander in chief of the United States, did not denounce those controllers who remained on the job as scabs, but, on the contrary, singled them out for his personal thanks, remarking that they were "helping to get the nation's air system operating safely. In the New York area, for example, four supervisors were scheduled to report for work, and 17 additionally volunteered. At National Airport a traffic controller told a newsperson he had resigned from the union and reported to work because, 'How can I ask my kids to obey the law if I don't?' This is a great tribute to America."

Then the president became more nuanced:

Let me make one thing plain. I respect the right of workers in the private sector to strike. Indeed, as president of my own union, I led the first strike ever called by that union. I guess I'm maybe the first one to ever hold this office who is a lifetime member of an AFL-CIO union. But we cannot compare labor-management relations in the private sector with government. Government cannot close down the assembly line. It has to provide without interruption the protective services which are government's reason for being.

It was in recognition of this that the Congress passed a law forbidding strikes by government employees against the public safety. Let me read the solemn oath taken by each of these employees, a sworn affidavit, when they accepted their jobs: "I am not participating in any strike against the Government of the United States or any agency thereof, and I will not so participate while an employee of the Government of the United States or any agency thereof."

He then issued an ultimatum: "It is for this reason that I must tell those who fail to report for duty this morning they are in violation of the law, and if they do not report for work within 48 hours, they have forfeited their jobs and will be terminated."

At this point a reporter asked if the president if he was "going to order any union members who violate the law to go to jail."

"Well," Reagan answered, "I have some people around here, and maybe I should refer that question to the Attorney General."

"Do you think that they should go to jail, Mr. President, anybody who violates this law?" the reporter pressed.

"I told you what I think should be done. They're terminated."

With this, the attorney general piped in: "Well, as the President has said, striking under these circumstances constitutes a violation of the law, and we intend to initiate in appropriate cases criminal proceedings against those who have violated the law."

"How quickly will you initiate criminal proceedings, Mr. Attorney General?"

"We will initiate those proceedings as soon as we can."

The reporter was dogged: "Today?"

"The process will be underway probably by noon today," the AG replied.

"Are you going to try and fine the union $1 million per day [as provided for by law]?"

"Well, that's the prerogative of the court. In the event that any individuals are found guilty of contempt of a court order, the penalty for that, of course, is imposed by the court."

"How much more is the government prepared to offer the union?", the reporter asked. The Secretary of Transportation held the podium:

> We think we had a very satisfactory offer on the table. It's twice what other Government employees are going to get—11.4 percent. Their demands were so unreasonable there was no spot to negotiate, when you're talking to somebody 17 times away from where you presently are. We do not plan to increase our offer to the union. ... We will not meet with the union as long as they're on strike. When they're off of strike, and assuming that they are not decertified, we will meet with the union and try to negotiate a satisfactory contract.[6]

As he was being wheeled toward the operating room at George Washington University Hospital after having been shot by John Hinckley, Reagan caught sight of all his top aides anxiously waiting for the doctors to save their stricken chief.

"Who's minding the store?", President Reagan asked.

One wonders if he thought to ask this very same question, now that he was about to fire most the nation's air traffic controllers. Asked how things were "going at the airports around the country," the transportation secretary answered. "Relatively, it's going quite well. We're operating somewhat in excess of 50 percent capacity."[7] As if losing nearly half the capacity of all airports constituted "quite well," even "relatively."

"Mr. President," a reporter followed up, "will you delay your trip to California or cancel it if the strike is still on later this week?"

> If any situation should arise that would require my presence here, naturally I will do that. So, that will be a decision that awaits what's going to happen. May I just—because I have to be back in there for another appointment—may I just say one thing on top of this? With all this talk of penalties and everything else, I hope that you'll emphasize, again, the possibility of termination, because I believe that there are a great many of those people—and they're fine people—who have been swept up in this and probably have not really considered the result—the fact that they had taken an oath, the fact that this is now in

violation of the law, as that one supervisor referred to with regard to his children. And I am hoping that they will in a sense remove themselves from the lawbreaker situation by returning to their posts.

I have no way to know whether this had been conveyed to them by their union leaders, who had been informed that this would be the result of a strike.

A reporter asked about the deadline for returning to work. "Forty-eight hours," came the answer.

"Mr. President," the reporter continued, "why have you taken such strong action as your first action? Why not some lesser action at this point?"

"What lesser action can there be? The law is very explicit. They are violating the law. And as I say, we called this to the attention of their leadership. Whether this was conveyed to the membership before they voted to strike, I don't know. But this is one of the reasons why there can be no further negotiation while this situation continues. You can't sit and negotiate with a union that's in violation of the law."[8]

*   *   *

"PATCO was dominated by Vietnam War–era veterans who'd learned air traffic control in the military and were one of a vanishingly small number of unions to endorse Reagan in 1980, thereby scoring one of the greatest own goals in political history," Jon Schwarz wrote in a 2021 article for *The Intercept*. "It's easy to imagine strikers expressing the same sentiments as a Trump voter who famously lamented [almost forty years later], 'I thought he was going to do good things. He's not hurting the people he needs to be hurting.'"[9]

True, the strike violated the letter of the law. Yet government unions had declared approximately twenty-two unauthorized strikes in recent years without incurring penalties. Until Reagan's ultimatum, PATCO members had not considered him an adversary. They were convinced he would see the strike as one against the FAA—a "Big Government" agency and an unfair employer. PATCO did not think Reagan would fail to honor the "historically accepted" guidelines for treatment of illegally striking workers.[10]

In the end, 11,345 controllers were fired and summarily banned from all federal employment for life. The *Encyclopedia of Activism and Social Justice* called it "Undoubtedly the most important federal employee strike in the second half of the 20th century, it is widely regarded as the commencement of virulent attacks on the U.S. labor movement by both private and public sector employers."

During the PATCO strike, some seven thousand flights were

cancelled, which meant that 80 percent of flights were *not* affected. The strike was a failure—PATCO was soon dissolved—and the walkout probably would not have lasted much longer. A combination of some 3,000 supervisors (management personnel, who were not unionized), 2,000 non-striking air traffic controllers, and 900 military air traffic controllers were called up. This left a gap of 5,445 absent controllers.[11]

During Reagan's administration, the average first-year raise for workers in the manufacturing sector fell from 7.2 percent to 1.2 percent. Still, blue-collar support for Reagan in 1980 was founded on a combination of his working-class "get big government off our backs" personal mythology and a kind of operative meme: "When things got in trouble, Republicans could fix them." No blue-collar Reagan supporter said of him what that disillusioned Trump voter later said of Trump: "He's not hurting the people he needs to be hurting." Much as had happened when he ran for governor, a voting bloc of so-called Reagan Democrats emerged, people who crossed party lines in the belief that Reagan supported *their* class, *their* race, *their* values, and *their* religious orientation *and* would do what unions could not do: stop the government from picking *their* pockets.

True, a minority of union members saw the firings for what they were, a declaration of war against unionism in America, and by no less than the only U.S. president who had also been a union president. Reagan's harsh response to an illegal strike by federal government employees was interpreted by many as a federal green light for union busting and, at a minimum, obtaining union concessions such as permitting part-time workers, employee contributions for health care coverage, and reduced pensions. Yet the event also demonstrated the remarkable power of the Reagan mythology in a changing America, where class and race allegiance began to trump economic, ideological, and political party affiliation.

Reagan always relished playing manly roles, and the response to the PATCO strike gave him an opportunity to appear tough as nails. Animated by so-called identity politics—solidarity based on class and race—Trump, whose Secret Service codename was "Mogul," talked tough just like Reagan. Unlike Reagan (Secret Service codename "Rawhide"), Trump rarely acted on his tough talk. But, when he did, he came off not as macho but as mean-spirited or even deliberately sadistic, as in sanctioning the caged separation of immigrant children from their parents or clearing out peaceful protestors in Lafayette Square Park with flash-bang explosions and tear gas deployed by the U.S. Park Police so that he could have his picture taken holding a Bible (at first, upside down) in front of St. John's Church, the so-called Church of the Presidents.

Reagan? Well, they didn't call him "Teflon Ron" for nothing.

University and Labor Archivist at the University of Texas at Arlington Michael Barera wrote:

> PATCO lost the public relations battle ... as it was estimated that the public backed Reagan over the union by nearly a two-to-one margin. Writing in *The Baltimore Sun* in 1991, Michael K. Burns argued that the lack of public support for the strike stemmed from both PATCO's demands being unattainable for most workers in the country and the disruption it caused for summer vacationers. [Gregory] Pardlo opined [in *The New* Yorker] that the strike ultimately became "a fiasco of diminishing morale and failed public relations." At its beginning, though, he noted that PATCO thought that its strike could work if it maintained 100% participation among its rank-and-file members, which it did not. Pardlo also opined that the strike caused the public to suffer "an inconvenience on the magnitude of a gas shortage or a natural disaster," and for that inconvenience, they squarely blamed PATCO.[12]

In a 2006 op ed for *The New York Times,* conservative commentator Ben Stein quoted an uncharacteristically acerbic Warren Buffett: "There's class warfare, all right, but it's my class, the rich class, that's making war, and we're winning."[13] This was as true in 1981 as it was in 2006 and would be in 2017–2020.

* * *

It is easy to dismiss PATCO's endorsement of candidate Ronald Reagan as naivete or wishful thinking. In 2017, labor journalist Sharon Block attributed union member support for Donald Trump to "Jurassic Park–like fantasies" of the reemergence in this non–Establishment candidate of "the species known as the 'pro-union Republican.'" Block ascribed widespread union support of Trump to the "myth of a pro-union Trump":

> Trump teased us with hints of it during the campaign—he was apparently anti-trade, he claimed he would bring back industries with high union density, like manufacturing and coal, and promised a "yuge" infrastructure-spending plan. Union members responded by coming out to vote for him in higher proportions than they have for any Republican presidential candidate since Ronald Reagan in 1984.

Indeed, early in his term, Trump

> continued to fan these fantasies, at least in his rhetoric and during some strategic photo ops. During the first week of his presidency, he held a White House meeting with leaders of several trade unions. He made sure pictures of the meeting in the historic Roosevelt Room were widely shared; he hailed it an "excellent" meeting. In April, he spoke before the North American Building Trades annual convention and promised that, "America's labor leaders will always find an open door with Donald Trump." (Perhaps more foreboding, however, was his early meeting with the heads of some of the country's largest corporations, to whom he promised massive cuts in taxes and regulations.)[14]

The result of Reagan's response to the PATCO strike was literally union busting. PATCO went belly-up. If anything, the harsh reality behind the Trump pro-union myth was even harsher. In Trump's first budget, the Department of Labor's Office of Labor-Management Standards (OLMS), responsible for enforcing requirements that unions and their leaders disclose extensive financial information, received an eight-million-dollar operating budget increase. The National Labor Relations Board (NLRB), on the other hand, tasked with protecting workers' rights to collective bargaining and safeguarding the elections by which workers decide whether or not to unionize, took a $16 million budgetary hit, a 6 percent decrease over its 2017 baseline.[15]

In 2020, the Economic Policy Institute reported:

> Workers are not experiencing democracy in the workplace, and this disenfranchisement is abetting the Trump administration's broader attack on democratic processes in the United States. While nearly half of nonunionized workers say they would like a union in their workplace, a National Labor Relations Board (NLRB) packed with Trump appointees has made it more difficult for workers to exercise their right to elect union representation—a right guaranteed to private-sector workers by the National Labor Relations Act (NLRA).

The Trump NLRB sought to roll back Obama era reforms by

- suspending union elections (citing Covid-19 safety concerns— hardly a top priority for the Trump administration)
- implementing provisions of a "representation case procedures rule" designed to complicate and impeded union elections and provoke litigation
- making it easier for employers to effectively gerrymander the bargaining unit sought by employees, such that eligible voters would be less likely to vote for a union[16]

The CWA (Communication Workers of America) summed up Trump's documented anti-union record by arguing that "he has encouraged freeloaders, made it more difficult to enforce collective bargaining agreements, silenced workers and restricted the freedom to join unions." The CWA also cited Trump-era restrictions on overtime pay, opposition to wage increases, and evisceration of health and safety protections. Contrary to his campaign positions on "America First," Trump (the CWA argued) "has encouraged outsourcing and offshoring." As for the Covid-19 pandemic, which the Trump administration had used as an excuse to suspend union elections, the CWA pointed out that his administration consistently "opposes hazard pay for essential workers, and has given employers a free pass to lower safety standards."[17]

During his administration, Trump found a prime outlet for the indulgence of his imperial passion for executive orders. The National Federation of Federal Employees (NFFE) cited three examples:

Executive Order #13836: Re-open collective bargaining agreements and then rush negotiations

- Directs agencies to renegotiate collective bargaining agreements as soon as possible;
- Sets arbitrary timelines for the negotiation process which, when exceeded, will result in the unilateral imposition of terms by the agencies;
- Establishes a new bureaucracy called "The Labor Relations Group" that will dictate "one-size-fits-all" proposals to agencies engaged in bargaining; and
- Encourages agencies to engage in "take-it-or-leave-it" bargaining tactics inconsistent with agencies' good-faith bargaining obligations.

Executive Order #13837: Hamstring unions' ability to represent workers

- Attempts to prevent union stewards from using official time to aid employees in preparing or pursuing grievances;
- Directs agencies to drastically reduce official time authorizations to 1 hour per bargaining unit employee per year, an attack designed to make it harder for your union to help you; and
- Cuts off access to agency office space for union officials carrying out their representational duties making it harder to help workers.

Executive Order #13839: Fire first, ask questions never

- Encourages agencies to abandon fairness concepts such as progressive discipline process;
- Encourages agencies to tailor different penalties for the same or similar offenses, ignoring established law;
- Directs the Office of Personnel Management to give performance appraisal more weight than seniority when an agency faces a reduction in force, creating great potential for unfairness; and
- Instructs agencies to take away our ability to grieve unfair removals from service or to challenge performance appraisals or awards at all.[18]

Like the trickle-down Reagan administration, the Trump administration missed few opportunities to elevate the power of corporations over labor, and yet the Reagan myth and its Trumpian sequel have proved resilient. Politico put this headline on a report about the 2020 elections, "Rank-and-file union members snub Biden for Trump." Joe Biden spent his political career pitching himself to voters as a genuine "union man," the product of rustbelt Scranton, Pennsylvania, a rustbelt and union poster child town. Union leadership was largely persuaded by the sincerity of Biden's pitch, but it nevertheless persistently failed to sway the rank and file, who remained "firmly in Donald Trump's camp."

As the 2020 campaign season unfolded, Ryan Bennett, an official of a plumbers and pipefitters union local in Coopersville, Michigan, told *Politico* that he was starting to hear complaints from members about Trump's broken promises for organized labor. "They've all seen that none of that has come to fruition," referring to Trump's pledges to bring back manufacturing jobs. "A lot of those members that were in the middle are going to end up on Joe Biden's side." And yet, Mike Knisley, executive secretary-treasurer with the Ohio State Building and Construction Trades Council, told *Politico,* "We haven't moved the needle here." He "estimated that about half of his members voted for Trump in 2016 and will do so again." "Even if given all the information that's been put out there, all the facts—just pick an issue that the president has had his hands in—it doesn't make a difference."[19]

In the end, 57 percent of union households nationwide voted for Joe Biden in 2020, compared with 40 percent for Trump. Yet the national results obscure regional differences. While Biden was helped by union turnout in Michigan and Wisconsin, Ohio and Pennsylvania union voters broke for Trump.[20] Evidence persists that the counterfactual mythology born in the Reagan era remained powerful in the age of Trump, when so many in the working class enthusiastically voted against their own demonstrable economic self-interest. Voter rationality, never a very sturdy commodity, has not been prized by the GOP since the Reagan era. With the advent of Trump, rationality became a will-o'-the-wisp.

CHAPTER 14

Supply-Side Economics:
Under Reagan's Shadow

*"Reagan was this way throughout his life ... before a micro-
phone or on stage he lived in a world of make-believe in which
it was legitimate to invent or alter a story for dramatic or
political purposes"*
— Lou Cannon, *Governor Reagan:*
His Rise to Power

What is "Reaganism," where did it come from, and what is its economic legacy? How did Reaganism shape post–Reagan politics in America? The core answer to these questions is supply-side economics.

The Reagan administration implemented this novel economic theory
hoping to revive an economy battered during the 1970s. That decade was a
period of economic deterioration for the United States as integration into
the rest of the world economy materially increased. Economic stagnation
and growing international competition put pressure on the cost of labor,
government regulation, and corporate taxes. Proponents of supply-side
economics contended that deregulation and tax cuts favoring the wealthy
would unleash new investment and spur economic growth.

The theory behind supply-side economics is generally based on "The
Laffer Curve" named after economist Arthur Laffer, who in the mid–1970s
popularized the notion that tax cuts would increase government revenues
or even pay for themselves. The Laffer Curve is intended to illustrate the
relationship between rates of taxation and the resulting levels of the government's tax revenue. For example, between the extreme tax rates of 0
percent and 100 percent, there is a tax rate that maximizes government tax
revenue as economic activity and taxable income changes in response to
the rate of taxation.

The centerpiece of Reagan's 1981 supply-side tax bill, the Economic
Recovery Tax Act (ERTA), was the largest tax cut in U.S. history. ERTA
phased in 25 percent across-the-board tax cuts and dropped the top

marginal individual tax rate from 70 percent to 50 percent.[1] It's not intuitive, but so-called "across-the-board" tax cuts disproportionally benefit the wealthy. For example, assume a tax system with just two tax rates: 20 percent and 40 percent. Now, assume that both rates are reduced by 50 percent, so that the new bottom rate is 10 percent, and the new top rate is 20 percent. For the lower tax bracket, these tax cuts enable taxpayers to now keep 90 cents rather than 80 cents of each dollar taxed. This represents a 12.5 percent tax cut (10 cents is 12.5 percent of 80 cents). On the other hand, for the higher tax bracket, these tax cuts enable taxpayers to now keep 80 cents rather than 60 cents of each dollar taxed. This represents a 33 percent tax cut (20 cents is 33 percent of 60 cents).[2]

The Democratic Party mostly went along with Reagan's plan to cut taxes and shrink social spending. In anticipation of one of the first votes on Reagan's program in early 1981, Democratic House Speaker Tip O'Neill conceded to his opposition. "I can read Congress. They go with the will of the people, and the will of the people is to go along with the President. I've been in politics a long time. I know when you fight and when you don't."[3]

With regard to implementing this novel (some say radical) economic strategy, calibrating the size of the tax cuts, their associated budget impact and managing negotiations with Congressional leaders, David Stockman, Reagan's budget director, offered a less-than-flattering portrayal of the sixty-nine-year-old newly elected chief executive of the United States: "The problem was that the President did not have great depth of understanding about the tax code. The complexities, intricacies, and mysteries involved in the tax breaks that Congress wanted were simply beyond him. In essence, he didn't understand the link between the federal tax structure and the budget. He could not grasp that to fiddle significantly with the former was to change the numbers in the latter—and for the worse."[4]

Note, an underlying premise of the Laffer Curve theory is that increasing tax rates beyond a certain level is counter-productive to economic growth and limits tax revenue. One can immediately see the appeal of this premise to Reagan. As early as 1965, in his first memoir, *Where's the Rest of Me?* Reagan wrote of his handsome earnings going through the 91 percent marginal tax bracket and that such a process is a "tragic fact of life in this evil day of progressive taxation...."[5]

It is impossible to rationalize the inherent contradiction in Reagan's policy goals between taming the deficit and significantly cutting taxes in terms other than magical thinking. Reagan, who said in his 1981 inaugural address that "for decades we have piled deficit upon deficit, mortgaging our future and our children's future for the temporary convenience of the present," was responsible for enacting the largest tax cut in U.S. history. You may be asking, how does this pencil out?

The 1981 tax cuts did not produce a supply-side miracle. The so-called "Reagan Revolution" was a revolution in name only. Enacting massive tax cuts without an equal reduction in government spending resulted in a fiscal disaster. During Reagan's eight years in office, the U.S. national debt increased from $914 billion to $2.6 trillion.[6] The cumulative national debt under the nation's first thirty-nine presidents more than doubled under its fortieth.[7] Despite Reagan's promise to balance the budget by 1984, he never proposed a balanced budget.

How does one best characterize such a fiscal strategy? If Democrats are saddled with the reputation of "tax and spend," perhaps the Republican moniker should be "spend and borrow."

Reagan's Alice in Wonderland approach to fiscal policy is nicely captured by David Stockman in his recollection of his boss's re-election campaign in 1984, which was epitomized by an instantly iconic political campaign titled "Morning in America." In *The Triumph of Politics*, Stockman writes: "I was appalled by the false promises of the 1984 campaign. Ronald Reagan had been induced by his advisers and his own illusions to embrace one of the most irresponsible platforms of modern times. He had promised, as it were, to alter the laws of arithmetic. No program that had a name or line in the budget would be cut; no taxes would be raised. Yet, the deficit was pronounced intolerable, and it was pledged to be eliminated. This was the essence of unreality."[8]

Reagan's 1984 campaign was foundational not only in firmly establishing the Reagan myth but also in giving birth to the GOP's irrational policy regarding taxes, budget deficits, and the role of government as these were further described by Stockman: "By 1985, only the White House speechwriters carried on a lonely war of words, hurling a stream of presidential rhetoric at a ghostly abstraction called Big Government. The White House itself had surrendered to the political necessities of the welfare state early on. The White House's claims to be serious about cutting the budget had, in fact, become an institutionalized fantasy"[9]

In many economic circles, supply-side economics has become a discredited theory because it exacerbates both federal deficits and income inequality.[10] Economist Paul Krugman has observed that, for the GOP, tax cuts have become more of a political strategy than an economic one.[11] And yet the GOP's institutionalized fantasies live on in the myth of tax magic and a nostalgia for the 1980s as a decade bathed in the soothing balm of the Reagan economy.

In 1980, George H.W. Bush famously described supply-side economics as "voodoo economic policy." He was correct then and is now. Yet supply-side economics is the official doctrine of the Republican Party. Unlike his father, George W. Bush embraced supply-side tax cuts and enacted significant tax cuts as president, quickly turning the Clinton-era balanced budget into a bottomless deficit. "W," as some called him, either did not understand (or perhaps did not want to understand) the arithmetic that Poppy Bush embraced when he spouted the following falsehoods regarding self-financing tax cuts:

- "These [tax] proposals will help stimulate investment and put more people back to work.... That growth will bring the added benefit of higher revenues for the government."[12]
- "Supply-side economics yield additional revenues."[13]
- "One of the interesting things that I hope you realize when it comes to cutting taxes is that tax relief has not only helped our economy, but it's helped the federal budget.... You cut taxes and the tax revenues increase."[14]

Even John McCain got into the act, telling the *National Review* in 2007 that "tax cuts, starting with Kennedy, as we all know, increase revenues."[15]

None of these claims regarding tax cuts is accurate or even remotely true.

*   *   *

Generally, the postwar governing consensus between America's two great political parties was well established and nicely summed up by JFK to Yale University's Class of 1962: "The differences today are usually a matter of degree.... What is at stake today is not some grand warfare of rival ideologies which will sweep the country with passion, but the practical management of a modern economy."[16]

The unraveling of America's postwar governing consensus began with the election of Ronald Wilson Reagan. In the four decades that have passed since he was first elected to the presidency, the myth of Reagan as tax cutter, proponent of cutting government waste, and championing traditional small-town values remains the compelling theme. Since 2000, C-Span has conducted a historian's survey of prior U.S. Presidents each time there has been a change in administrations. In the most recent cycle, 142 historians and professional observers of the presidency participated, in which Ronald Wilson Reagan was ranked #9, right behind John F. Kennedy.[17] Not bad for a former sportscaster from Dixon, Illinois.

Yet, it was Reagan who set America on a course of hyper-capitalism and wholesale industry deregulation. The legacy of Reaganism is all around us: heedless consumption, reduction in the progressivity of the tax code, weakened environmental laws, a war against expertise and government, legitimizing structural budget deficits, and widening economic inequality.

There is a fascinating and grand disconnect between, on the one hand, the policies of the Reagan administration and their enduring impact on the nation and, on the other hand, America's perception of the man under the shadow of the Reagan myth: his sunny optimism, his small-town values, and his "everyman" quality. As Reagan biographer Lou Cannon wrote, "He was the wholesome citizen-hero who inhabits our democratic imagination, an Everyman who was slow to anger but willing to fight for the right and correct wrongdoing when aroused."[18] Cannon continues: the presidency "was a role in a movie … in which homespun American virtue prevails over the wily and devious 'special interests' that rule the nation's capital. Reagan believed in this role, and he was such a good actor that he did not seem to be an actor at all. He seemed even less a politician."[19]

Reagan's speeches brimmed over with bromides about the military hero, the working man, the farmer, the factory worker, and the cop on the corner, and how they all represented the bedrock of America. In his 1981 inaugural address, Reagan spoke of those long-neglected figures as the "men and women who raise our food, patrol our streets, man our mines and factories, teach our children, keep our homes, and heal us when we're sick—professionals, industrialists, shopkeepers, clerks, cabbies, and truck-drivers."[20] In fact, it was the so called "Reagan Democrats" (many of whom wore blue collars), believing that Reagan would fight for them, who made him President in 1981.[21] Therein lies the blinding power of the Reagan myth and the inability of many to recognize his betrayal, whether intended or not, of the middle class and the working people of America.

In reflecting on Reagan, a former western governor, rancher, and avid horse lover, one cannot help but think about the line from *The Man Who Shot Liberty Valance*. In the movie, Senator Stoddard (played by Jimmy Stewart) rises to fame on a story that, in his youth, he had slain an out-law named "Liberty Valance." A reporter who discovers that the story is a hollow legend is confronted with whether to expose the truth or continue to promote the fiction. He resolves his dilemma by declaring, "This is the West, sir. When the legend becomes fact, print the legend."

As Peter Behr of *The Washington Post* wrote in 1988, "The Reagan years have witnessed one of the greatest waves of mergers, takeovers, and corporate restructurings in history, with the tally standing at more than 25,000 deals worth $2 trillion and still rising."[22] To critics, the Reagan years were an enshrinement of the maxim "Greed is good," spoken in the 1987 movie *Wall Street* by Michael Douglas in the role of Gordon Gekko, a Wall Street tycoon and corporate raider.

Reagan was a gifted storyteller and communicator who set out to persuade his audience, not just inform them. In reflecting on the impact of Reagan's presidency, David Gergen, who served as Communications Director in the Reagan White House, wrote that "over time, he [Reagan] converted much of the country to his own views and values." In reflecting on the power of Reagan's messaging skills, Gergen noted, "His more important legacy is how much he changed our minds."[23]

Pause for a moment and reflect upon what David Gergen has written about the fortieth President of the United States. At the core of Reagan's legacy is his ability to convince many Americans that government is the problem; government programs are mismanaged and inherently wasteful; and solutions to our economic difficulties are found exclusively in free markets, deregulation, and cutting taxes.

Importantly, as America was considering whether Reagan deserved a second term in 1984, another gifted storyteller and communicator addressed the nation in a prime-time speech at the 1984 Democratic National Convention. Mario Cuomo, then Governor of New York, spoke to the country in a keynote on behalf of the Democratic presidential nominee, Walter Mondale, Jimmy Carter's vice president. Directly addressing Reagan's well-worn metaphor of America as the "Shining City on the Hill," Cuomo responded that America was actually "more a 'Tale of Two Cities' than it is just a 'Shining City on a Hill.'"[24] Cuomo added, "A shining city is perhaps all the president sees from the portico of the White House and the veranda of his ranch, where everyone seems to be doing well. But there's another city; there's another part to the shiny city; the part where some people can't pay their mortgages ... where students can't afford the education they need, and the middle-class parents watch the dreams they hold for their children evaporate."[25]

In addressing Reagan's embrace of supply-side tax cuts and the growing federal budget deficit, Cuomo remarked, "President Reagan told us from the very beginning that he believed in a kind of social Darwinism. Survival of the fittest. 'Government can't do everything,' we were told. So, it should settle for taking care of the strong and hope that economic ambition and charity will do the rest. Make the rich richer, and what falls from the table will be enough for the middle class and those who are trying desperately to work their way into the middle class."

Regarding the impact of the supply-side tax cuts and growing budget deficit, Cuomo noted, "the President's deficit is a direct and dramatic repudiation of his promise in 1980 to balance the budget by 1983,"[26] and he called the size of the deficit "a mortgage on our children's future that will be paid only in pain and that could bring this nation to its knees."[27]

By all historic accounts, Cuomo's speech was moving and well received.[28] In fact, prior to Bill Clinton's rise in the Democratic party, many wanted Cuomo to run for president. Despite a wonderful effort, Cuomo's 1984 convention speech was no match against the burgeoning Reagan myth and the true skills of the Great Communicator. Later that year, Reagan won the 1984 presidential election in a landslide, carrying forty-nine states.

Before Cuomo's 1984 appeal to Americans to reflect and reconsider the path of the nation, there was a similar appeal from President Jimmy Carter back in 1979. He delivered the much-maligned "malaise speech" during a period of soaring inflation and gasoline rationing. Carter was candid and honest with his fellow citizens:

> In a nation that was proud of hard work, strong families, close-knit communities, and our faith in God, too many of us now tend to worship self-indulgence and consumption. Human identity is no longer defined by what one does, but what one owns. But we've discovered that owning things and consuming things does not satisfy our longing for meaning. We've learned that piling up material goods cannot fill the emptiness of lives which have no confidence or purpose.[29]

Carter's attempt to move the nation in a more thoughtful direction was no match for the Gipper's easy message. Reagan was not selling spirituality, conservation, or the meaning of life. He was selling "having-it-all" tax cuts and, yes indeed, Big Government. In stark contrast to Carter's approach of asking Americans to look beyond personal possessions, Reagan asked "Are you better off than you were four years ago?"[30]

In the wake of Reagan's reelection in 1984, Lance Morrow of *Time* described Reagan's enduring popularity: "Ronald Reagan has a genius for American occasions. He is a Prospero of American memories, a magician who carries a bright, ideal America like a holograph in his mind and projects its image in the air. Reagan, master illusionist, is himself a kind of American dream. Looking at his genial, crinkly face prompts a sense of wonder: How does he pull it off?"[31] Noting Reagan's efforts to rewrite the role of America's post-war government, Lance continued:

> He has set out to reverse the course of American government that was charted by Franklin Roosevelt. If F.D.R. explored the upper limits of what government could do for the individual, Reagan is testing the lower limits. And yet something about Reagan soothes and unites—even though the effects of his programs may repel. He softens the meaner edges of conservatism with populist effusions, reaching outside the rigid framework of ideologies to the pool of shared American experience, to our dreamy nostalgias.[32]

The *New Oxford Dictionary of English* defines nostalgia as "a sentimental longing or wistful affection for the past, typically for a period or place with happy personal associations." The *Handbook on Experimental Existential Psychology* tells us that nostalgia is an emotion that involves reliving one's past, which enables a person to escape present mediocrity by resorting to a *splendid past*.[33]

Donald Trump was not the first presidential candidate to run on the slogan "Make America Great Again." Some four decades earlier, Reagan, in his gauzy, misty-eyed version of America's golden past, trotted out essentially the same slogan: "Let's Make America Great Again." Boiled down, there is substantively no difference. Both are a pull on the powerful psychology of nostalgia, the good old days and the powerful emotions that arise from them. In many ways, Trump rallies are a play on nostalgia. Individuals collectively looking to escape present-day pain, present-day isolation, and America's economic inequalities long to recapture what is perceived as a better version of the nation and perhaps a better version of themselves. Importantly, it is the power of the Reagan myth that blinds the MAGA faithful to the reality that it was Reagan's policies and supply-side tax cuts that have largely created the financial dimension of their predicament.

The New Deal principles of post-war America brought intellect, reason, and government to bear in helping to solve problems of American society. Reaganism, on the other hand, blamed government, income taxes, and regulation for most of the nation's ills, trading postwar realism for blind trust in free markets. Reagan, speaking or writing in various venues, convinced many that those nameless faceless bureaucrats were elitist, incompetent, and intent on limiting freedom of citizens.

The election of Reagan opened an era of mediocrity in government. To a great degree, Reagan's railing about the inefficiencies of government became a self-fulfilling prophesy, as many agencies under GOP administrations were underfunded, understaffed, and lacking in resources. With his claims of reducing the interference of Big Government, Reagan overlooked that the country's prosperity in terms of equal wage growth reached its apex during periods of government activism, which brought a progressive tax code, adequate regulations, and robust labor unions. Based on his false assumptions about the role of government and its proper role in a modern western society, Reagan helped install a new order of vast economic inequality. Indeed, in many ways the seed-corn laid down by Reagan—the myth of rugged individualism, supply-side tax cuts, the celebration of wealth and private markets, and plaintive concerns about government power live on in today's GOP.

*　*　*

Beginning with election of Ronald Reagan, the United States set about redefining itself from a manufacturing nation to a financial economy built on leverage, debt, and some element of speculation. In the *American Prospector*, Kevin Phillips, a former Republican strategist, summarizes the legacy of Reaganism:

In the 1990s ... financial services sprinted ahead of manufacturing as a share
of U.S. GDP. To suggest "bubble and bail" as a description of U.S. economic
policy over the past quarter-century is inelegant but by no means inaccurate.
Obviously, this is not the way to manage a nation passing the peak of its global
power and very much at risk from a reckless financial endgame. The growth
of public and private (consumer, corporate, and financial) debt ... is closely
related to the rise of what the press has belatedly started to call the debt industry. Indeed, most financial-services conglomerates can list debt and credit
instruments (cards, securities, and fees) as their principal products and
services.[34]

While criticizing all administrations since 1980, Philips, despite his
Republican roots, leveled his more severe accusations of irresponsibility
at the GOP:

The Reagan administration and the first Bush administration indulged in
deficit-ridden public finance and reckless lending practices in commercial
banks and savings and loan institutions alike; the bailouts were notorious. The
Clinton administration brought down the federal budget deficit but bailed out
Wall Street repeatedly and abetted the private-debt orgy that nurtured the tech
bubble. The second Bush administration, together with the Greenspan Fed,
encouraged the blowing up of a giant mortgage and housing bubble to replace
the stock-market bubble that imploded in 2000–2001. The Republicans may be
more to blame over five presidential terms than the Democrats were during
just two, but both parties seem to have pursued a common underlying financial mercantilism of bubble and bail. In the process, excessive debt and depen-
dence on finance rather than production has been front and center.[35]

*   *   *

Despite the halcyon portrayal of the 1980s, during the second half of his
second term, Reagan encountered significant political headwinds, and
a majority of the American electorate was unhappy with the state and
direction of the country. A July 1987 *Washington Post*–ABC News poll
reported that 62 percent of Americans thought that the country was on
the wrong track.[36] Then there was "Black Monday." On October 19, 1987,
the global equity markets suffered a sudden and severe crash. This was an
unexpected event and a significant deviation from Reagan's boom economy. Black Monday came in the wake of Congressional investigations of
the Iran-Contra Affair, which brought growing concerns over whether an
aging President Reagan was still up to job.

In the wake of Black Monday, Walter Isaacson of *Time* wrote what
many Americans knew in their bones that "What crashed was more than
just the market. It was the Reagan Illusion: the idea that there could be a
defense buildup and tax cuts without a price, that the country could live
beyond its means indefinitely. The initial Reagan years, with their aura

of tinseled optimism, had restored the nation's tattered pride and the lost sense that leadership was possible in the presidency."[37] Isaacson commented on the growing concerns over Reagan's mental acuity, the spirit and greed of the 1980s, and the fundamental change in the nation's economy under Reagan's eye from manufacturing cars and steel to financial engineering. "But he stayed a term too long," Isaacson wrote.

> As he shouted befuddled Hooverisms over the roar of his helicopter last week or doddered precariously through his press conference, Reagan appeared embarrassingly irrelevant to a reality that he could scarcely comprehend. Now it's the morning after, and the dream of painless prosperity has been punctured. But what a wild binge it was! Speculative fortunes built on junk bonds and stock manipulations helped paper over the cracks in an economy beset by sluggish investment and productivity. Some of the best minds of a generation marched off to make millions as market mavens, embracing the greed-and-glory smugness that suffused both Wall Street and Washington. An economy that was once based on manufacturing might and inventive genius began pursuing wealth through mergers and takeovers and the creation of new "financial instruments." Fortunes were conjured out of thin air by fresh-faced traders who created nothing more than paper—gilded castles in the sky held aloft by red suspenders.[38]

Other writers, such as the *New York Times'* Anthony Lewis, expressed a similar view shortly after the end of Reagan's second term in September 1989:

> "It's morning again in America," the Reagan TV spot said in the 1984 campaign. We were convinced. Now it is the morning after. The reckoning is starting to come in for those eight years. We see that the indulgence in private greed exacted a heavy public cost, one that will burden our children and grandchildren.

In foreshadowing the rise of the right wing, the negative view of government, and lack of compassion for the less fortunate, Lewis wrote, "The intangible costs of the Reagan years to our domestic tranquility are surely greater than what can be measured in dollars. They are the costs of hostility to the role of government, of indulgence toward private greed, of insensitivity to the needs of the weak in our society."[39]

* * *

Cue the Reagan Myth Makers! The Ronald Reagan Legacy Project was formed in 1997 to promote and memorialize the former president. A goal of the Project was—and remains—to name at least one notable public landmark in each U.S. state and all 3,067 counties after Ronald Reagan. Grover Norquist, president of the initiative, is also the founder of Americans for Tax Reform, an organization that seeks to compel all candidates for and incumbents in elective office to make a written commitment to oppose any tax increases. Ever. Hence, these two organizations seek to harmonize the structural underpinnings of the Reagan myth, delivering the country from the darkness of the Carter years and the evils of the federal income tax.

The Reagan Legacy Project website crows, "Reagan's leadership left a resounding impact on the lives of citizens here at home and individuals worldwide. His policies led us out of double-digit inflation, twenty percent plus interest rates, and double-digit unemployment. Abroad, his disdain for communism moved him to set in place policies that would see the Soviet Union fall."[40] The website goes on to paint in simplistic strokes a cultish vision of the Reagan legacy. The Project's enthusiasts obviously fail to see the irony in its goal to name public works after Ronald Reagan, the Great Scorner of public works. It was Paul Volcker, a Jimmy Carter appointee, as head of the Federal Reserve who was primarily responsible for taming inflation through his continuance of high interest rates. Volcker allowed the federal funds rate to rise to 20 percent and, with it, went the interest on home mortgages and everything else.[41] His actions put the economy into a recession and helped Reagan get elected.

The Americans for Tax Reform tax pledge is also simplistic and cultish. There are times in which it is necessary to raise taxes, such as during wars, pandemics, and national emergencies, and to sustain government programs on which citizens depend, such as Social Security and Medicaid. As Supreme Court Associate Justice Oliver Wendell Holmes wrote, "Taxes are what we pay for civilized society."[42]

Reaganism did not change math, although perhaps those operating under the shadow of the Reagan myth have claimed a forty-some-year license to ignore the most basic math and other facts. Haven't they heard? There is no free lunch. If you like Big Government (and who really doesn't?), it's either tax and spend or spend and borrow. The essence of Reaganomics is spend and borrow.

The Reagan "boom" economy of the 1980s was in many ways an illusion. It was built on an irresponsible borrowing binge fueled by the USA credit card that didn't max out even after more than $2 trillion dollars, most of it going to an unprecedented peacetime military build-up combined with the slashing of public spending for the needy. With the help of Mike Deaver, Reagan's Deputy Chief of Staff at the White House, Reagan the actor revolutionized the TV presidency with short scripted events crafted to influence the press and the American people. The packaging and selling of supply-side economics conditioned the public to live beyond its means. It triggered a deficit time bomb.

The residue of Reaganism persists to this day among the GOP faithful: a reluctance to regulate Wall Street, an uncontrollable urge to diminish the world of science and expertise, a bashing of governmental programs as economically harmful and wasteful unfunded tax cuts weighted toward the wealthy. Nevertheless, after four decades of growing economic inequality, unfunded supply-side tax cuts adding trillions to the deficit, years of inadequate investment in government infrastructure needed to boost America's GDP, and market crashes such as George W. Bush's Great Recession of 2008, most voters never manage to focus on the root cause of America's current plight: trickle-down Reaganomics.

✳   ✳   ✳

The Swiss psychiatrist Carl Jung wrote, "Man positively needs general ideas and convictions that will give a meaning to his life and enable him to find his place in the universe."[43] Indeed, we believe that most American people seek meaning, challenge, and purpose in their lives, including a sense of national purpose to address the pressing challenge of their time and lives. Back in January 1961, John F. Kennedy called upon Americans to be larger than themselves, to sacrifice, to give back. This notion is captured by the oft-quoted line from JFK's inaugural address: "ask not what your country can do for you—ask what you can do for your country." This call to public service resonated with what Kennedy called the "new generation of Americans—born in this century, tempered by war, disciplined by a hard and bitter peace, proud of our ancient heritage." An early example of Kennedy's ambition to influence the country's national purpose was the formation of the Peace Corps on March 1, 1961. Later, at a speech at Rice University on September 12, 1962, JFK challenged the nation with the audacious goal of sending a man safely to the moon and returning him safely back to earth: Below is a passage from that speech—

> We choose to go to the moon. We choose to go to the moon in this decade and do the other things, not because they are easy, but because they are hard, because that goal will serve to organize and measure the best of our energies and skills, because that challenge is one that we are willing to accept, one we are unwilling to postpone, and one which we intend to win, and the others, too.[44]

Pay particular attention to the language JFK used. "We choose to go to the moon and do the other things, not because they are easy, but because they are hard." It is the vocabulary and syntax of a grand challenge to a nation, to its collective imagination, to the best of its energies and skills. When was the last time you heard another national leader address the country in like manner? Jimmy Carter came close, but missed nevertheless.

Andrew Bacevich, a professor of history and a retired U.S. Army colonel, wrote in *The Limits of Power: The End of America Exceptionalism*:

> For the United States, the pursuit of freedom, as defined in the age of consumerism, has induced a condition on dependence—on imported goods, on

imported oil and on credit. The chief desire of the American People, whether they admit it or not, is that nothing should disrupt their access to these goods ... the chief aim of the U.S. Government is to satisfy that desire....[45]

How did we get here?

Reagan helped. He downgraded and discredited government and government programs as a legitimate and necessary presence in the lives of Americans. In stark contrast to JFK's clarion call to a national purpose and shared sacrifice, Reagan rejected the notion of shared sacrifice or any harnessing the spirit of Americans to solve the nation's most pressing problems. He encouraged Americans to put self-interest above all.

For Reagan to win in 1980, he had to refute Carter's message of moderation, sacrifice, and energy conservation. Reagan provided his response to Carter on November 13, 1979, when he declared himself a candidate from the presidency. He denounced those "who would have us believe that the United States, like other great civilizations of the past, has reached its zenith of power" and who dared suggest that "we must learn to live with less." Reagan's alternative to self-sacrifice for the collective good was easy and simple, requiring neither sacrifice nor effort of any kind from the citizenry. Just cut federal spending, reduce government waste, fraud, and abuse, and reduce income taxes.[46] In recognition of both an energy crisis and threats to the environment, Jimmy Carter put solar panels on the White House roof and funded federal programs to promote renewable energy sources. Soon after he was inaugurated, President Reagan put an end to solar and wind subsides and removed the solar panels.[47] He told us we could have it all, tax cuts, higher speed limits, and bigger cars. How could he possibly say otherwise? He would have sounded like the man he was looking to defeat in 1980: James Earl Carter, Jr.

As author Will Bunch wrote in *Tear Down This Myth,* "Ronald Reagan had a God-given gift for connecting with the American People, but he abused it. He abused his skill as a Great Communicator on issues of substance, for example preaching the gospel of less government even as the middle class in reality faced a worsening tax bite, but he also abused his power with the broader signals he sent to the nation, that it was possible to have everything without making hard choices."[48]

Yes, it was Reagan, a child of the depression, the son of a shoe salesman from middle America, who led the transformation of the national zeitgeist from "ask not what your country can do for you" to "greed is good." As Bunch further explains, "It was Ronald Reagan and his allies who fanned those flames of indulgence." And it is the keepers of the Reagan myth who whipped them even higher into the dark night of magical thinking in which inconvenient truths—from the ever-growing IOU on the federal debt to the grim forecast of those maligned scientific "doom-and-gloomers."[49]

Americans do not want government to solve every problem, but on a warming planet with eight billion people, there is a rightful place for the role of government to implement policy to make society more just, provide education, fund infrastructure, and protect the health and welfare of all Americans. Such actions must be grounded in objective facts and science.

*   *   *

But ... back to the future....

The GOP politicians compare every Democratic president or presidential contender to Jimmy Carter. They cannot help themselves, given the power of the Reagan myth. By way of calling President Obama weak, Mitt Romney compared him to Jimmy Carter.[50] Now other Republican politicians are doing the same with President Joe Biden. Comparisons between the thirty-ninth president and the forty-sixth have become inescapable. Rep. Jim Jordan (R–Ohio) tweeted that "Joe Biden is the new Jimmy Carter."[51] Sen. Lindsey Graham (R-S.C.) claimed that Biden is "worse than Carter."[52] Never mind that the list of Carter's presidential accomplishments is long. He deregulated the airline industry, doubled the size of the national parks, and initiated the "Camp David" accords and peace agreements between Israel and Egypt.[53] The Biden-Carter comparisons are hardly astute acts of analysis. They are wish-casting. In the pantheon of Reagan mythology, Reagan's Morning in America presidency was preceded by the bleak midnight of the Carter years, with high inflation, humiliation abroad, and economic stagnation. Republicans are always rooting for history to repeat itself.[54]

Speaking of which, the Republican 2022 midterm election platform, titled "Commitment to America," contains more than a few of the Gipper's 1980s hits that never seem to go out of style. The Commitment to America platform includes the following planks—

- Curbing wasteful government spending
- Reducing the national debt
- Enacting pro-growth tax and deregulatory policies
- Eliminating welfare incentives

If Reagan were alive today, this now decades old rinse-and-repeat of Reaganomics might even have the Gipper uttering "Well, there you go again."

But wait, as the TV pitchman says, there's more! Using a factory floor in Monongahela, Pennsylvania, as a backdrop for its unfurling, House Republican leaders, in an effort to take back the majority in November 2022, discussed the GOP's Commitment to America. At the event, then

House Minority Leader Kevin McCarthy said, "On that very first day that we're sworn in, you'll see that it all changes. Because on our very first bill, we're going to repeal 87,000 IRS agents. Our job is to work for you, not go after you."[55] McCarthy was referring to the recently passed Inflation Reduction Act and its funding for IRS operations. Note, U.S. Treasury officials and tax experts say the hires, over the next decade, will mainly replace retiring agents, answer taxpayer questions, and program new equipment. The IRS expects more than 50,000 retirements over the next five years.[56]

Once again, the shadow of Reagan steals over the GOP. Government is the problem, taxes are bad, enforcing the tax laws is really bad, and funding the government is bad. Perhaps someone should mention to Kevin McCarthy that if deficit reduction is truly a priority, properly enforcing the nation's tax laws and maximizing revenue collections are required.

Paul Krugman of the *New York Times* recently addressed the GOP's Commitment to America:

> Its economic program, such as it is, calls for "pro-growth tax and deregulatory policies." No specifics, but this is clearly a call for zombie Reaganomics.
> Why "zombie"? Because we now have four decades' worth of experience showing that deregulation and tax cuts for the rich do not, in fact, produce higher wages and faster economic growth. So the idea that tax cuts are the secret of prosperity should be dead, yet somehow it's still shambling along, eating Republican brains.[57]

As of the writing of this book, the U.S. Treasury Department reported that the America's gross national debt is more than $33 trillion.[58] Recall that when Reagan was elected in 1980, the country's gross national debt was less than $1 trillion. Now, obviously all this red ink is not the fault of Ronald Reagan, but it was Reagan who made the USA dependent on borrowing, normalizing deficits, and living beyond its means. If the GOP won't actually get rid of the "Big Government" it claims to detest—and it won't because voters will not allow it—the only alternative is to borrow because taxes can never be raised. This mortgaging the future is something that presidential *candidate* Reagan would have been mad as hell about.

As the national debt grows, so, too, grows the cost of servicing that debt. And, as interest rates rise, so will that cost. Debt that is high and rising as a percentage of GDP increases federal and private borrowing costs, slows the growth of economic output, and increases interest payments abroad. A growing U.S. debt burden could increase the risk of a fiscal crisis and higher inflation as well as undermine confidence in the U.S. dollar. Servicing the debt crowds out opportunities to invest in other areas of the economy, such as the environment, public health, and education.[59]

The legacy of living in Reagan's America lives on. Nearly each day we are reminded by members of the GOP that we can ignore the rising deficit, tax cuts are the miracle elixir for any economic ill, and rising temperatures on a warming planet are either not happening at all or the science is not proven or it's just all too expensive to address. The notion of a carbon tax is out of the question because it is a tax increase.

These are just some of the reasons why the Reagan myth must be revisited. Though it is a formidable legacy, it is not to be celebrated but overcome.

The economic costs of the Reagan mythology are succinctly summed up by John W. Sloan in *Deconstructing Reagan, Conservative Mythology and America's Fortieth President*: "In deifying Reagan, conservatives have an unhidden agenda—to commit future Republican presidents and Congresses to fulfilling conservative policy preferences. In their eyes, Reagan's policies worked miracles during the 1980s and should continue."[60]

Certainly, we do not disagree that Reagan has been deified by the GOP, which used to be the Party of Lincoln. This deification by the faithful has had a significant adverse impact on both U.S. fiscal and environmental policy. "The economic costs of the Reagan mythology are high because it encourages conservative policy makers to believe in ideologically deduced miracles rather than that which is feasible based on empirically derived probabilities," John W. Sloan writes. "Trust in miracles provides perverse incentives for politicians to avoid confronting painful issues like budget and trade deficits, global warming, the future funding of Social Security and Medicare."[61]

The "shadow" is a concept first coined by Carl Jung to describe those aspects of the personality that we choose to reject and repress—the dark side of a personality. Operating under Reagan's shadow, Sloan writes, the GOP defines "ridged and delusional behavior ... as moral and attempts to forge compromise [as] ... immoral. Reagan's legacy inspires conservatives to champion ideologically based initiatives and condemn both reality-based thinking and pragmatic adjustments. When there is conflict between Reagan's truths and the evidence from math and science, conservatives argue that policy makers should continue Reagan's course and disregard the evidence."[62] Who are you going to believe, the Gipper or your own lyin' eyes?

Carl Jung wrote, "Until you make the unconscious conscious, it will direct your life and you will call it fate." The time has come for America to confront the shadow of Reagan before it is too late.

CHAPTER 15

Imperial Visions

Donald Trump was quick to hire generals, retired or retiring. He named Marine General Jim Mattis secretary of defense, making a point of calling him by the sobriquet the sober Mattis detested, "Mad Dog." He tapped another Marine general, John Kelly, as head of Homeland Security. Army Lieutenant General Mike Flynn was briefly National Security Advisor. He lasted less than a month after the revelation of covert meetings with Russian ambassador Sergey Kislyak and was replaced by Army lieutenant general H.R. McMaster. Retired Army major general Mark S. Inch briefly served as director of the Federal Bureau of Prisons until Governor Ron DeSantis hired him away in 2019 as Secretary of the Florida Department of Corrections. Trump also nominated the distinguished Army chief of staff General Mark Milley as chairman of the Joint Chiefs of Staff.

Trump habitually referred to these warriors as "my generals," but, as journalist Joshua Geltzer wrote in an early 2020 review of Peter Bergen's *Trump and His Generals: The Cost of Chaos,* the bromances never lasted. Geltzer cited an October 2019 Trump tweet, "We train our boys to be killing machines," and went on to observe that the president's "sense of military men and women as 'killing machines' was what drew Trump to populate his cabinet early on with generals like Michael Flynn, John Kelly, James Mattis, and H.R. McMaster. Yet, in some cases sooner and in some cases later, Trump soured on all of them—and they soured on Trump. (The possible exception is Flynn, but he at least soured enough to cooperate extensively with Special Counsel Robert Mueller's investigation.)"[1]

Joshua Geltzer characterized Donald Trump's views on the military as "cartoonish."[2] The president's own military service, as mentioned in Chapter 4, was his education in an upstate New York military-themed combination reform and prep school. Famously—infamously—through the agency of his father, young Donald was able to wangle a medical draft deferment during Vietnam due to a spurious diagnosis of bone spurs.

Trump was hardly alone in not having served. Bill Clinton, Barack Obama, and Joe Biden likewise had no record of military service. But there was a time in American politics, after World War II, when the absence of military service would have been virtually disqualifying for a presidential candidacy. Franklin D. Roosevelt, the president who brought America into and through that war, had been assistant secretary of the navy during World War I. His fifth cousin, Theodore Roosevelt, had held the same post in the run-up to the Spanish-American War of 1898. Against the wishes but with the consent of President William McKinley, TR resigned to raise and lead the volunteer "Rough Riders" in that war. FDR sought Woodrow Wilson's permission to serve as a naval officer in World War I (polio did not strike and disable him until 1921[3]), but Wilson insisted that he was far more important to the war effort as assistant secretary of the navy. FDR's successor, Harry S. Truman, volunteered for service in World War I as an artillery captain and served on the Western Front in France. Dwight D. Eisenhower, Supreme Allied Commander, Europe, during World War II, was the first general officer to become president since James A. Garfield, who was elected in 1880.

Ike's successor, John F. Kennedy, was marketed to voters (legitimately enough) as the heroic skipper of PT-109, who had saved most of his crew after the Japanese destroyer *Amagiri* hit and severed the plywood torpedo boat during the night of August 2, 1943, in waters off the Solomon Islands. Lyndon B. Johnson, who assumed the presidency after JFK's assassination, had joined the Naval Reserve in 1940 while serving in the House of Representatives and on December 10, 1941, three days after Pearl Harbor, was called to active duty with the rank of lieutenant commander. Initially assigned to inspect shipyards in Texas, he was later tapped by President Roosevelt for service with a three-man team assigned to report directly to the president on conditions in the Southwest Pacific. LBJ volunteered to fly as an observer on a bombing mission over New Guinea. His B-26, however, turned back before reaching its objective. Johnson and others claimed the bombers were attacked by enemy aircraft and his plane, having developed engine trouble, was forced to abort. Others reported that the aircraft, having developed generator trouble, turned back before even encountering the enemy. Either way, Johnson, a mere observer, was nominated by General MacArthur for a Silver Star. (MacArthur, it is well known, was hopeful of getting much-needed congressional funding for his underserved theater of the war.) LBJ wore the civilian lapel pin representing his military decoration for the rest of his life.[4]

When Johnson bowed out of reelection contention in 1968 amid the divisive disasters of the Vietnam War and a faltering economy, Richard Nixon defeated Hubert Humphrey to become the thirty-seventh president of the United States. A Quaker by birth and upbringing, though never observant himself, Nixon could have obtained an exemption from service on religious grounds or a deferment because he was a federal employee, working in the Office of Price Administration. Instead, he applied for a naval commission and was appointed a lieutenant junior grade in the U.S. Naval Reserve in June 1942. Assigned to command the small Naval Air Station Ottumwa in Iowa, he sought sea duty, was promoted to lieutenant, and served as a logistics officer in the South Pacific. It was a desk job in a war zone, and he not only continued in logistical and personnel functions through the end of the war but also continued to serve in the Naval Reserve until 1966, when he retired with the rank of commander.

Another World War II naval officer, Vice President Gerald R. Ford, succeeded Nixon after the president resigned in disgrace on August 9, 1974. Ford served in the Pacific as a gunnery officer on the aircraft carrier USS *Monterey* and was decorated for his combat service. His successor, Jimmy Carter, graduated from the Naval Academy at Annapolis in 1946, too late for service in World War II but had the distinction of serving under Captain (later Admiral) Hyman Rickover in the navy's fledgling nuclear submarine program.

As discussed earlier, Ronald Reagan, who defeated Carter in 1980, served in the U.S. Army and then the Army Air Corps in World War II, not in a combat role but, in Hollywood, making motion pictures for the war effort—informational films, propaganda films, and many, many training films. In most of these, he played men in uniform. The work did not require that he lay his life on the line, but it did entail significant sacrifice. It disrupted his film career, taking him out of the public limelight for four years. His upward trajectory never resumed, and he failed to graduate from B-level popularity to stardom in major motion pictures. Still, his experience in film during the war kept him close to the war and the American military. His concept of patriotism, like that of many who served, was bound up in the idea of the righteousness of American military might and its power to save the world. This was a vision largely shared by all the presidents who came to office having served.

Reagan's vice president and former rival, George H.W. Bush, succeeded his boss and is the last president to have served in World War II—in his case, as the youngest aviator in the World War II navy, flying fifty-eight combat missions and narrowly escaping death when he was shot down in the Pacific, bailed out over the ocean, and was rescued by the U.S. submarine *Finback*.[5] Awarded the Distinguished Flying Cross, Bush was profoundly affected by his close brush with mortality. "Why had I been spared and what did God have for me?"[6] Some degree of this sense of obligation to live a meaningful life in service to others or one's country is common in the presidents who served in the military during the World War II era.

All of the post–World War II presidents, Ronald Reagan included, stand in stark contrast to the forty-fifth, which their own GOP enabled, empowered, and ultimately embraced. Donald Trump has been casually diagnosed by many pundits as exhibiting "malignant narcissism" and "narcissistic personality disorder." His niece, Mary L. Trump, PhD, a clinical psychologist by training and profession, wrote that she had "no problem calling Donald a narcissist," observing that "he meets all nine criteria in the *Diagnostic and Statistical Manual of Mental Disorders* (DSM-5)," cautioning, however, that "the label gets us only so far." She suggests that her uncle "also meets the criteria for antisocial personality disorder, which in its most severe form is generally considered sociopathy but can also refer to chronic criminality, arrogance, and disregard for the rights of others." She adds by way of "comorbidity," dependent personality disorder ("hallmarks ... include an inability to make decisions or take responsibility, discomfort with being alone, and going to excessive lengths to obtain support from others"). She suspects a "long undiagnosed learning disability that for decades has interfered with his ability to process information," not to mention a "substance- (in this case caffeine-) induced sleep disorder" caused or exacerbated by drinking "upward of twelve Diet Cokes a day."[7]

Maybe. Or maybe Trump is a selfish opportunist without empathy or a moral compass and with a propensity to take without earning or asking, as when he took government documents, including many marked Top Secret, with him to Mar-a-Lago after he left office in 2021, railing "against attempts by the National Archives and Records Administration (NARA) to retrieve [them], saying 'it's not theirs, it's mine.'"[8]

And who can erase the image of the newly inaugurated president as he "put his right hand on the right arm of Montenegro Prime Minister Dusko Markovic and pushed himself ahead as NATO leaders walked inside the alliance's new headquarters and prepared for a group photo"? The Montenegro newspaper *Vijesti* observed, "It seems Donald Trump did not want that anyone overshadows his presence at the [NATO] summit," while "Balkan websites ran headlines such as 'America First' and 'Where do you think you are going?'"[9]

Donald Trump did campaign on the slogan "America First," appropriating a phrase one would have thought had been rendered forever toxic by its linkage to the infamous pro-appeasement and even pro–Nazi "America First Committee," which functioned as an American isolationist pressure group opposed to U.S. entry into World War II. Doubtless Trump, profoundly ignorant of history, was unaware of the America First Committee, though he clearly shared its philosophy. For him, we suspect, "America First" was merely a projection of his own all-consuming geocentricism onto the nation.

* * *

American presidential elections are rarely decided on issues of foreign policy. "Are you better off today than you were four years ago?" Reagan asked the American electorate in one debate with incumbent Jimmy Carter. More than most rhetorical questions, it was brilliant, broaching as it did the domestic issue on everyone's mind—the economy. But Reagan also dared to ask in that debate, "Is America as respected throughout the world as it was? Do you feel that … we're as strong as we were four years ago?"[10] With this, he gave foreign policy a popular urgency almost as insistent as the question of the economy. More significantly, in raising the issue of international *respect,* he made imperialism a popular imperative.

World War II was brought to an end in its Pacific and Asian theater with the atomic bombing of Hiroshima and Nagasaki in August 1945. The United States had won a race against Nazi Germany to weaponize nuclear energy. In using that energy against Japan, America inaugurated the "Atomic Age," in which the prospect of total war now meant the prospect of total annihilation. This became an all too real possibility when, on August 29, 1949, the Soviet Union ended the U.S. monopoly on nuclear weapons by detonating its first atomic bomb, which the American intelligence officials dubbed Joe-1 (after Joseph Stalin). Three years earlier, on February 9, 1946, Stalin made a widely quoted speech, in which he declared that communism and capitalism were fundamentally incompatible, drawing the conclusion that another war was therefore inevitable. Stalin used this as the springboard for his announcement of a new five-year plan, in which weapons production would be tripled, whereas the consumer goods the average Soviet citizen had begun to clamor for would have to "wait on rearmament." He became even more specific: the war with the West would come in the 1950s, by which time (he assured his audience) the United States and other capitalist powers would be in the grip of a new Great Depression.

To call Stalin's speech provocative was a pale understatement. Supreme Court Associate Justice William O. Douglas, probably the most liberal voice in Washington at the time, pronounced it the "Declaration of World War III." Albert Einstein once commented on the prospect of World War III: "I do not know with what weapons World War III will be fought," he purportedly said, "but World War IV will be fought with sticks and stones."[11]

On March 5, 1946, Britain's World War II prime minister, Winston Churchill, spoke at Westminster College in Truman's home state of Missouri:

From Stettin in the Baltic to Trieste in the Adriatic an iron curtain has descended across the Continent. Behind that line lie all the capitals of the ancient states of Central and Eastern Europe. Warsaw, Berlin, Prague, Vienna, Budapest, Belgrade, Bucharest and Sofia, all these famous cities and the populations around them lie in what I must call the Soviet sphere, and all are subject in one form or another, not only to Soviet influence but to a very high and, in some cases, increasing measure of control from Moscow. Athens alone—Greece with its immortal glories—is free to decide its future at an election under British, American and French observation. The Russian-dominated Polish Government has been encouraged to make enormous and wrongful inroads upon Germany, and mass expulsions of millions of Germans on a scale grievous and undreamed-of are now taking place. The Communist parties, which were very small in all these Eastern States of Europe, have been raised to pre-eminence and power far beyond their numbers and are seeking everywhere to obtain totalitarian control. Police governments are prevailing in nearly every case, and so far, except in Czechoslovakia, there is no true democracy.[12]

Churchill was brutally blunt about the sharp division at the "Iron Curtain" between democracy on the one side and Soviet communism on the other. Moreover, within a few months of Churchill's speech, that "Iron Curtain" was assuming physical shape as the Soviets and the Western powers militarized their frontiers. The most visible manifestation was the militarized border between West Germany and Soviet-controlled East Germany. Soon, a wall would divide West Berlin from East Berlin.

Harry Truman and others in the West saw the Iron Curtain as important but also recognized that Stalin had visions of extending Soviet influence worldwide. U.S. diplomat George F. Kennan served as deputy head of the U.S. mission in Moscow from July 1944 to April 1946. As his term of service was about to end, Kennan drafted a cable to Truman's secretary of state, James Byrnes. At more than 5,300 words, it was appropriately dubbed the "Long Telegram," though it was actually a remarkably concise set of proposals for a strategy to structure U.S.-Soviet diplomatic relations going forward. Kennan rejected the classical Marxist explanation of communist expansion—that the communist revolution would not be complete until all the world's states had been replaced by a global union of the working class—and suggested that Stalin's aggressive expansionism partook more of what he called "the traditional and instinctive Russian sense of insecurity." True, Marx had theorized that capitalism and communism were fundamentally incompatible, that, in the end, the world was too small to contain both systems. Yet Kennan doubted Stalin truly believed this. He argued that the Soviet dictator used it as a convenient theory because he needed the vision of a world in which every non-communist country was an enemy. This would legitimate and perpetuate his own totalitarian regime. Out of fear, the Soviet people would worship him and make any sacrifice he called for.

To counter Soviet expansion without triggering a new world war, Kennan proposed what came to be called the containment policy. He explained this in an article he published under the pseudonym "X" in the journal *Foreign Affairs,* titled "The Sources of Soviet Conduct." He wrote, "Soviet pressure against the free institutions of the Western world [could] be contained by the adroit and vigilant application of counterforce at a series of constantly shifting geographical and political points, corresponding to the shifts and manoeuvers of Soviet policy." The pressure of Soviet expansionism could be "contained," but not defeated outright or quickly; nor could it be "charmed or talked out of existence." Still, Kennan argued, there would be a victory at the end. If the United States could maintain containment, footing the bill for years of a globally demanding economic and military policy, the Soviet economy and the structure of the ruling Soviet Communist Party would be subjected to prolonged strain, which would yield one of two results: "either the break-up or the gradual mellowing of Soviet power."[13] Thus began the Cold War, a combination of economic and cultural initiatives and proxy wars, in which the West confronted the Soviets via the smaller third-party nations in which the forces of democracy and communism directly and violently contended.

*   *   *

Ronald Reagan took office after some four decades of Cold War and containment had worn down the Soviet Union, even as that nation, together with "Communist" China, continued to build their nuclear and thermonuclear arsenals. Impatient with the slow grinding of the containment policy, Reagan sharply turned his own foreign policy on a radical redefinition of America's stance toward the USSR. If he had grown weary of the Cold War, he felt certain that this fatigue was shared by many of his fellow Americans.

In 1972, the Nixon administration had negotiated with the Soviets the highly successful SALT (Strategic Arms Limitation Treaty), which limited a wide variety of nuclear weapons. Talks resumed almost immediately after SALT-I was ratified that year by both nations. The talks failed to achieve any new breakthroughs, but by 1979, both the United States and Soviet Union were eager to resume. Many in the American leadership and electorate feared that the Soviets were leaping ahead in the arms race. For their part, the Soviets were looking for a way to blunt the effect of an increasingly close relationship between the United States and China. In June 1979, President Carter and Soviet premier Leonid Brezhnev signed a SALT-II agreement, which established numerical equality between the two nations in terms of nuclear weapons delivery systems. In truth, the treaty was something of a fig leaf, doing little to stop or even slow the arms race.

Yet it met with unrelenting criticism from the American right wing, which claimed that SALT-II was a capitulation to the Soviets. Debate dragged on in U.S. Congress, but when, in December 1979, the Soviets invaded Afghanistan, President Carter unilaterally withdrew the treaty from the Senate in January 1980. SALT-II thus remained signed but unratified— though both nations agreed to respect the substance of the agreement until new arms negotiations could take place.

Almost immediately after taking office, Ronald Reagan argued that SALT-II was a mistaken concession at a time when, he was convinced, the Soviets were economically far weaker than the U.S. intelligence community reported. Far from the United States agreeing to nuclear arms *limitation*, Reagan told *The Washington Post*, the time was ripe for a strategic arms "buildup."[14] He believed that if the United States spent lavishly on a military buildup, the Soviets would be obliged to keep up and thereby spend themselves into defeat and, quite possibly, dissolution.

Reagan did not look at the situation dispassionately. He did not simply want to end the Cold War. He believed with all his being that the Soviet Union was an "evil empire," as he called it in his celebrated speech of March 8, 1983, "the focus of evil in the modern world."[15] It was a speech that thrilled as many Americans as it terrified. Reagan's most ardent supporters were exhilarated by this strongman side of their president, even though spending the Evil Empire into dissolution promised to overwhelm Reagan's cornerstone opposition to deficit spending and Big Government. President Reagan rationalized the cognitive dissonance of this dilemma by declaring to his advisors that "Defense is not a budget issue. You spend what you need."[16]

And so, they did, creating the biggest peacetime defense budget in American history, culminating in the Strategic Defense Initiative (SDI)— the "Star Wars" project, an enterprise intended to end the "MAD" (mutually assured destruction) thermonuclear deterrence policy that had defined the Cold War since 1947. SDI, Reagan assured the American electorate, would be capable of shooting down incoming nuclear missiles. A feat likened to shooting a bullet with another bullet, it was, in fact, a massive boondoggle that was probably never expected to work—but that would serve as an act of geopolitical jiujitsu, trapping the Soviets into spending themselves quite literally into economic collapse.

Boondoggle it was. A gift to the defense industry it was. And yet, it worked—not as a successful SDI system but as a kind of thermonuclear potlatch, in which the over-extended and very brittle Soviet economy buckled and began to crumble under the burden of an arms race that had turned into a race to the bottom of the cookie jar.

* * *

In whatever way SDI may have functioned as a bloodless weapon in the Cold War, it definitely forged an alliance between the Executive Branch and what another Republican, Dwight D. Eisenhower, Supreme Allied Commander turned United States president, had warned against in his farewell address:

> In the councils of government, we must guard against the acquisition of unwarranted influence, whether sought or unsought, by the military-industrial complex. The potential for the disastrous rise of misplaced power exists and will persist. We must never let the weight of this combination endanger our liberties or democratic processes. We should take nothing for granted. Only an alert and knowledgeable citizenry can compel the proper meshing of the huge industrial and military machinery of defense with our peaceful methods and goals, so that security and liberty may prosper together.[17]

Reagan had no problem with the military-industrial complex and the big spending of Big Government it called for. For the period 1982–1986, Reagan proposed military spending of $1.341 trillion, some $6,000 for every man, woman, and child in the United States.[18] In 1980, the Carter defense budget represented 4.9 percent of GDP. In 1988, under Reagan, it rose to 5.8 percent of GDP.[19] President Trump's America First stance was not initially conducive to military spending, though he did relish displays of military might and was envious of totalitarian leaders such as Kim Jong-un and Vladimir Putin, who reveled in staging military parades. After being hosted in Paris by President Emmanuel Macron in 2018, Trump was giddy over the spectacle of a Bastille Day parade. "We're going to have to try to top it," Trump declared.[20] He proposed a budget of $92 million for the 2018 parade, but the plan was scuttled when the cost was leaked to the public. The parade finally did happen in 2019 but at a "rough total" cost of "only" $5.4 million.[21]

Reagan made a much more expensive spectacle with SDI, but it did produce results—not as a kinetic weapon system but as a means of breaking the Evil Empire's bank. Trump burned up money in 2019 on a much more modest display—a parade, complete with tanks—that made little impression on the public but did gratify him personally. At the front end of his presidency, when he was still president elect, Trump had used the whole U.S nuclear/thermonuclear arsenal as a prop in a pissing contest with Kim Jong-un, who had welcomed New Year's 2017 with a speech he wanted the whole world to hear. Kim announced that North Korea was in the "last stage" of preparations to test-fire an inter-continental ballistic missile (ICBM), the ultimate superpower weapon. In response, Trump, who always wanted to be seen and heard, took to his favorite social media platform, Twitter: "North Korea just stated it is in the final stages of developing a nuclear weapon capable of reaching parts of the U.S.," he tweeted. "It won't happen!"[22] (For the record, it *did* happen—on Trump's watch.)

With this exchange, a new Korean War broke out. It was a war of words more suited to the schoolyard than to the global stage. Trump hurled threats of "fire and fury" and lifted an Elton John song title from 1972 to mock Kim as "Rocket Man." The North Korean dictator shot back by denouncing Trump as a "mentally deranged US dotard" (the more literal translation was roughly "old man lunatic"). As the barbs (such as they were) continued to fly back and forth, Russia's foreign minister, Sergey Lavrov, compared the reciprocal posturing of Trump and Kim to "what happens when children in a kindergarten start fighting and no-one can stop them," failing to note that kindergarteners don't have nukes.[23] Exactly a year later, New Year's 2018, when Kim taunted Trump again, the president tweeted, "North Korean Leader Kim Jong Un just stated that the 'Nuclear Button is on his desk at all times.' Will someone from his depleted and food starved regime please inform him that I too have a Nuclear Button, but it is a much bigger & more powerful one than his, and my Button works!"[24]

The mine-is-bigger-than-yours military bravado Trump exhibited belied the fact that, under him, defense spending was comparable to the Obama years. In 2017, defense spending was $645.75 billion, 3.31 percent of GDP. It rose to $672.49 billion in 2018, 3.32 percent of GDP, hit $734.34 billion, 3.43 percent of GDP, in 2019, and rose more sharply to $778.23 billion, 3.74 percent of GDP, in 2020.[25] In magnitude of military spending, Donald Trump was no Ronald Reagan. In fact, unlike Reagan, Trump was often contemptuous of the military and did not hide his contempt. When he appeared on CBS News's *Face the Nation* on June 5, 2016, then-presumptive GOP nominee Trump declared that America's generals "don't know much [about ISIS] because they're [meaning the generals] not winning," adding that he knew "more about ISIS than the generals do."[26]

Far worse than disparaging his generals, Trump cancelled a solemn centennial visit to the World War I-era Aisne-Marne American Cemetery near Paris in 2018, blaming heavy rain for the cancellation. "The helicopter couldn't fly," he said. It was a lie.

Trump rejected the idea of the visit because he feared his hair [a complex comb-over] would become disheveled in the rain, and because he did not believe it important to honor American war dead, according to four people with firsthand knowledge of the discussion that day. In a conversation with senior staff members on the morning of the scheduled visit, Trump said, "Why should I go to that cemetery? It's filled with losers." In a separate conversation on the same trip, Trump referred to the more than 1,800 marines who lost their lives at Belleau Wood as "suckers" for getting killed.[27]

It was at the Battle of Belleau Wood (June 1–26, 1918) that the Marines and U.S. Army troops defeated a German breakthrough to Paris, which might have ended World War I with a German victory. Not that Trump knew this, and not that he would have cared had he known. This was of a piece with his infamous disparagement of the heroism of John McCain, a POW in Hanoi for five and a half years: "He's not a war hero. He was a war hero because he was captured. I like people who weren't captured."[28]

* * *

Ronald Reagan's respect for the military was born in World War II, while he was an actor in military movies, but it was both deep and sincere. Nevertheless, he used the military as an instrument for achieving executive policy goals. As narrated in Chapter 4, this happened first in 1983, after more than two hundred U.S. Marines in Beirut, Lebanon, were killed in their sleep on October 23, 1983, by a terrorist truck bomb. During a firestorm of criticism, Reagan, just two days later, launched Operation Urgent Fury, a strategically dubious invasion of the West Indies island nation of Grenada, population 110,000. It is difficult to see it as anything other than a wag-the-dog op.[29]

Far more consequential than the show in Grenada was the Iran-Contra scheme, a gob-smacking instance of presidential overreach. Two related clichés have long dominated American political life: "There are no second acts in American politics" and "No president has a successful second term." As with most clichés, tired though they may be, there is plenty of truth in both. President Reagan was reelected in 1984 with 59 percent of the popular vote over Democratic challenger Walter Mondale's 41 percent; however, the Democrats retained a large majority in the House and, in 1986, took the Senate as well. There was a growing sense among some that the Reagan presidency, from the beginning a rhetorical presidency, now relied too heavily on rhetoric. The "make America great again" message that had worked so well against the Carter "malaise" in 1980 began to ring hollow. Worse, the president often seemed out of touch, his edge seemingly dulled with age.

It was in this context of growing doubt that President Reagan, in November 1986, confirmed reports that the United States had secretly sold arms to Iran, the nation that had held the U.S. embassy staff hostage for 444 days during the Carter administration. After initially denying rumors that the arms sale had been intended to gain the release of U.S. hostages held by terrorists in Lebanon, Reagan later admitted the existence of an arms-for-hostages swap. Hard on the heels of this admission came the revelation from Attorney General Edwin Meese that a portion of the arms profits had been diverted to finance the rightwing Contra rebels fighting against the leftist Sandinista government of Nicaragua. The Reagan administration favored a rightwing rebellion in Nicaragua, but Congress, hoping to avoid a Central American reincarnation of the Vietnam War, specifically barred Contra aid. The diversion of the secret arms profits was therefore a blatantly unconstitutional executive branch usurpation of legislative branch authority, not to mention the will of the people that Democratic majority represented. The affair was variously dubbed the "Iran-Contra scandal" and, more pointedly, "Iran-gate," an unmistakable nod to Watergate, the ruination of Richard Milhous Nixon.

A congressional investigation gradually revealed how, in 1985, an Israeli group had approached National Security Advisor Robert McFarlane with a scheme in which Iran, in exchange for arms, would use NSA influence to free the Lebanon hostages. Secretary of State George Shultz and Secretary of Defense Caspar Weinberger objected to the plan, but (McFarlane testified to Congress) the president agreed to it. That is when U.S. Marine Lieutenant Colonel Oliver (Ollie) North suggested adding the twist by which profits from the sales would be funneled to the Contras. The beauty of the scheme was downright Nixonian: Illegal arms sales produced illegal profits, which (because illegal) would be totally concealed from Congress, which meant that the illicit money could be slipped under the table to the Contras.

In what indeed seemed an eerie replay of Watergate, the congressional investigation climbed the White House ladder, ascending through national security advisors John Poindexter and McFarlane, through CIA Director William J. Casey (who died in May 1987), and up to Defense Secretary Caspar Weinberger. This left one question: Was President Reagan in on the scheme or was he the dupe of rightwing zealots in his administration? Neither answer would be good for the president.

As a result of the congressional inquiry into Iran-gate, North, Poindexter, CIA administrator Clair E. George, and Weinberger were either indicted or indicted and convicted. All the convictions, except Weinberger's, were overturned on appeal, and Weinberger, like the others, was subsequently pardoned by President Reagan's successor, George H.W. Bush. As for Ronald Reagan himself, Iran-gate was biggest of several second-term missteps. He had sleepily bumbled his way through a 1986 summit with Soviet premier Mikhail Gorbachev, and he had watched helplessly as the stock market, in the high times that followed Reagan-era government-is-the-problem deregulation, crashed precipitously in 1987.

Within a single month after the revelation of the Iran-Contra scheme, Reagan's approval rating fell from a celestial 67 percent to an earthly 46 percent. Yet there was never truly serious talk of impeachment. Representative Pat Schroeder, a Colorado Democrat, took to the House floor to denounce the president. "He has been perfecting the Teflon-coated presidency: He sees to it that nothing sticks to him." What did stick, however, was the "Teflon president" label. Schroeder later remarked that the figure of speech came to her while she was frying eggs in her new Teflon-coated non-stick pan. Score one for DuPont de Nemours, Inc.[30]

Although Reagan did survive a rather feeble movement toward impeachment, he was forced to dodge barbed questions about his quite possibly failing mental acuity. By early 1987, Ronald Reagan was in a most unaccustomed position: his back to the wall. On March 4, 1987, he addressed the nation, taking "full responsibility for my own actions and for those of my administration," claiming, however, that his "heart and ... best intentions" told him what he had done was both good and legal, "but the facts and the evidence tell me it is not."[31]

* * *

In the movies heart and intentions always win out over facts and evidence, and Iran-Contra never really became a smoking-gun moment for Ronald Reagan. His poll numbers rose after his March 4 apology speech, as the public clearly *wanted* to forgive him for making a "blunder." And it was in this mood of forgiveness that Americans heard President Reagan at the Berlin Wall on June 12, 1987, call out to the leader of the ailing Soviet Union: "Mr. Gorbachev, tear down this wall!" That speech was a mythic victory crowning fifty years of Cold War—a grinding, anxious sort of war, with neither clear defeats nor unambiguous victories. Months after flirting with vague talk of impeachment and parrying more pointed accusations of encroaching senility, Ronald Reagan had slain the Soviet dragon without so much as having to unsheathe his sword.

In Ronald Reagan, Donald Trump might have seen a model for an "outsider" president who dominated his party, transforming the GOP into the party of Reagan. Whether or not this was Trump's conscious ambition in 2016, he succeeded in emulating Reagan by turning the GOP into the Trump Party. What is more, like Reagan, Trump became a political cult figure.

But he also took a sharp turn away from Reagan. Instead of creating an *imperial* presidency, which, in the Iran-Contra affair, extended to Nixonian transgressions against separation of powers, Trump aspired to an *autocratic* presidency. When the crowd at a 2020 campaign rally chanted in Nixonian fashion "Four more years! Four more years!" Trump asked unsmilingly for twelve.[32]

For Reagan, the imperial presidency had a great deal to do with his leadership of America in the world. He came of age during World War II, in which he served though did not fight, and he witnessed the United

States rise to the position of savior and leader of the free world. When he saw an opportunity to bring the Cold War to the victory toward which it had been headed slowly but surely since the days of Harry Truman and the Containment Policy, Reagan acted both as a world leader and, quite simply, *acted,* reverting to his Hollywood days.

"Mr. Gorbachev," he declaimed, "tear *down* this wall."

Nailed it. And like the efficient journeyman actor that he had been, nailed it in a single take.

Trump, in contrast, became obsessed with *building* a wall to seal off Mexico from the United States and, symbolically, the United States from the rest of the world. In the name of "America First," he withdrew the nation from the *Pax Americana* position of world leadership that had been established in World War II and built upon ever since. The owner of a closely held real estate development firm, Donald Trump strove to reduce the United States to the dimensions of just another real estate deal. Surely, Ronald Reagan could not have imagined Trump's shriveled, selfish, simple-minded ambition as a vision of presidential leadership. Surely, he would not have wished such a diminishment upon an America that he did, finally, love. But it was what he sowed and what his party reaped. Its toxic grain is now baked into our daily bread.

CHAPTER 16

In the Twilight of an Idol, the Chickens Come Home to Roost

"The moral test of government is how it treats those in the dawn of life, the children; those who are in the twilight of life, the aged; and those who are in the shadows of life, the sick, the needy and the handicapped."
—Hubert Humphrey

"The great political temptation of our age is to believe that some charismatic leader, some party, some ideology or some improvement in technology can be substituted for an economy in which millions of individual human beings make their own decisions…. It only takes one man in power with the wrong ideas to ruin an economy, and a nation."
—Ronald Reagan[1]

At a Christian conference in June 2022, Lauren Boebert, the Trumpist representative for Colorado's 3rd congressional district (as of January 3, 2021), declared that Jesus didn't have enough AR-15 rifles to "keep his government from killing him."[2] Boebert made this comment knowing that an AR-15 rifle had been used a month earlier in a school shooting in Uvalde, Texas, which left nineteen students and two teachers dead.

If you are a Christian who attended Sunday school, we can guarantee that you were taught that Jesus was the "lamb of God" and that God's plan was to sacrifice his only son to take away the sins of the world. The Crucifixion of Jesus is the cornerstone of the Christian faith, and, by all historical accounts, Jesus did not defend himself but willingly accepted his cross. Indeed, all Scripture leads up to this pinnacle moment in the history of humanity.

So, where did Boebert get the recipe for her highly idiosyncratic cocktail—definitely shaken, not stirred—of fundamental Christian beliefs and the right to bear AR-15 assault rifles?

In his 1981 inaugural address, Ronald Reagan declared that "government is the problem." Despite his optimistic, affable-bordering-on-aw-shucks everyman demeanor, Reagan turned government-bashing into an art form. The Great Communicator conditioned many in America's body politic to demonize activist government and progressive taxation and glorify unregulated markets. *Consumatum est* became *Caveat emptor*, and we are led to believe through Boebert's reckless rhetoric that Jesus Christ, like Reagan, believed government was the problem. The New Testament, however, is silent on Christ's political platform, though we are told that Jesus advised his followers to "Render to Caesar the things that are Caesar's, and to God the things that are God's," which, as an admonition to pay your taxes, seems to ratify the legitimacy of government—Big Government at that, since Emperor Julius Caesar Augustus Tiberius, who reigned over Rome at the time of Christ's Crucifixion, had most of the known world under his fasces.

Okay. Enough. So, Lauren Boebert flunks Sunday School, political policy, and ancient Roman history. Nothing she says will make the lives of Americans better, but there is a message for the MAGA faithful. Not quite sure what that message is. At its mildest, it simply reiterates Ronald Reagan: *government is the problem*. At its spicier, it seems to say *government is the problem and government will try to kill you*. At its Tabasco sauce Scoville heat units extreme, the message is *Take up arms against the government before its kills you*.

The modern GOP holds gun ownership to be a right enshrined in the Second Amendment of the Constitution, a right not to be infringed, no matter how much blood is spilled in workplaces, classrooms, and other American spaces, public and private. There are more guns in the United States than people. But many of the MAGA faithful don't believe that's anywhere near enough. Some Republican candidates express an adolescent's masturbatory ecstasy in their campaign ads by posing with guns, talking about guns, and shooting guns. This gun fetish has even oozed into holiday greeting cards, in which some GOP politicians pose with spouse and kids, mugging with assault rifles in hand to properly celebrate the birthday of the unarmed Prince of Peace.

Are these guns-at-the-ready poses legitimately about states' rights—that is, federalism? Are they icons of fighting the perceived tyranny of the national government? Is the threat of big government such a problem that going to the ballot box and voting are inadequate to change polices? Is some form of political violence or threats thereof necessary to "preserve freedom"?

Well, frankly, no, no, and no.

Within the simplistic narrative of "government: bad; guns: good" it is important for voters not to lose sight of the substance of the transaction actually taking place here. Instead of seeking a job in the free marketplace, which they unabashedly celebrate, these gun-hugging GOP candidates are running for a federal office, knowing that, if successful, they will be paid by the federal government, provided government healthcare and benefits, furnished with a congressional office, a professional staff, and a budget allowance—all paid for with the federal taxes they claim are too high. You bet your ass, don't tread on me!

Despite Reagan's long-standing rhetoric regarding government over-reach and over-regulation, Reagan benefited from the perks and emol-uments of state and federal office more than just about any other office holder of his era. After leaving state politics and entering the national arena, Reagan, whose showbiz career had guttered into extinction, was a highly paid speaker, receiving some $1 million for speeches and com-mentary in a two-year runup to his 1980 bid for the presidential nomi-nation and election. "He charged savings-and-loan executives $10,000 for one speech. Florida lumber dealers paid him $8,000 for another. The tur-key industry, in turn, scratched up $7,500. Even the Boy Scouts had to be prepared—to pay a fee of $5,000."[3] By 1989, having been bathed in the bap-tismal font of the Oval Office, he set his standard speaking fee at $50,000, and a Japanese corporation paid him $2 million for a pair of speeches that year.[4]

President Harry S Truman left the White House in 1953 with no income from the federal government save his U.S. Army pension of $112.56 a month. He and wife Bess moved back to the Independence, Missouri, house his wife had inherited from her parents. They had no other choice. Yet Truman refused any employment offers "that would commercialize on the prestige and dignity of the presidency," though he did sell the rights to his autobiography for a hefty sum—but this he also considered a labor he owed to history.[5]

The days of Truman are long gone, of course. As of 2014, Bill and Hil-lary Clinton were each charging $200,000 to speak, and ex-president Don-ald Trump expected a fee of $1 million per speech, though the *Washington Post* reported in September 2022 that his paid speeches organizer—which put him on something called the "American Freedom Tour"—was "strug-gling to pay vendors, investors and employees."[6] On November 15, 2022, when Trump, twice impeached and under dark legal clouds, announced his intention to make a third run for the White House the day after the GOP suffered humiliating defeats in midterm elections they were expected to run away with, his small audience began to tire of a rambling speech going more than twice as long as its announced half-hour length. "Olivia Rubin, reporter with ABC News, posted a video on Twitter of the crowd at

Mar-a-Lago. She commented that a crowd 'formed by the exit' of the ball-room and people were trying to leave before Trump finished his speech. She added that 'security won't let them.'"[7]

On February 14, 2018, a gunman killed seventeen and wounded seventeen more at the Marjory Stoneman Douglas High School in Parkland, Florida. Days later, on February 28, Donald Trump "shocked lawmakers from both parties ... during an hour-long televised meeting at the White House in which he voiced support for far stricter gun-control measures than most Republicans appear willing to support. At one point, he accused lawmakers of being 'scared of the NRA.'"[8] He soon backpedaled before turning the bike a full 180 degrees. His administration even reversed an Obama-era rule restricting gun purchases by people deemed by the Social Security Administration to be mentally unable to manage their affairs.[9] By 2022, he was firmly back in the NRA's embrace, speaking—without charge—at a National Rifle Association (NRA) annual meeting in Houston, Texas, on May 28, 2022, just four days after a gunman fatally shot nineteen students and two children and wounded seventeen others at Robb Elementary School in Uvalde, Texas, a four-hour drive from Houston. Donald Trump may or may not have been scared of the NRA, but he sure knew that the organization buttered his bread, having endorsed him in 2016 and 2020, donating $30 million to his 2016 campaign.

While Trump was a new NRA member, President Reagan had been a member "lifelong." He continued to oppose handgun restrictions even after he was shot and nearly killed in March 1981. Early in his administration, he even expressed a desire to shut down the Bureau of Alcohol, Tobacco, and Firearms, the agency charged with enforcing America's gun laws. But ten years later, in March 1991, after he left the White House, he wrote a *New York Times* op-ed supporting the Brady Bill, named after his press secretary, James Brady, who had been grievously wounded and partially paralyzed by one of the bullets would-be assassin John Hinckley intended for Reagan. The Brady Bill imposed a five-day waiting period before a licensed importer, manufacturer, or dealer could sell, deliver, or transfer a handgun to an unlicensed individual. In 1994, Reagan joined two other former presidents, Gerald Ford and Jimmy Carter, in an open letter to members of the House of Representatives urging Congress to pass a ban on the domestic manufacture of military-style assault weapons.[10]

Notably, Reagan's support of gun control legislation came only after his political career had ended. Back in 1980, he had used the Second Amendment as a prop to garner NRA and gun lobby support. He promoted no new significant gun control legislation during his two presidential terms but did sign into law the Firearm Owners Protection Act in 1986, which amended the Gun Control Act of 1968 by repealing parts of the act some studies considered unconstitutional. The 1986 legislation made it easier to transport long rifles domestically, ended federal records-keeping on ammunition sales, and barred the prosecution of anyone passing through jurisdictions with strict gun control while transporting "properly stored" firearms in their vehicle. At the eleventh hour, Rep. William J. Hughes, a New Jersey Democrat, inserted a provision banning ownership of any fully automatic firearms not registered by May 19, 1986.[11] It's not clear whether Reagan was aware of this addition when he signed the law. As for the NRA, despite suffering a bankrupting corruption scandal in 2022, the organization has broadened its focus from gun rights to include other conservative culture war grievances and has increasingly allied itself with the GOP.[12]

On balance, then, the gun-friendly presidency of Ronald Reagan, who was the victim of a failed assassination, helped lay the foundation of the GOP's unbreakable embrace of the NRA, the elevation of the Second Amendment, and the culture of guns. Worse, in the fullness of time, perhaps the allegiance of the GOP to the Second Amendment has become a call to arms, albeit somewhat muted, by some in the elevation of violence as a possible political tool.

*   *   *

Ronald Reagan's second term was tinged with hints of a mind now in age-related decline, and he was possibly snatched from the jaws of impeachment over the Iran-Contra scandal—though they do not seem to have been very toothy jaws. Much like the threat posed by his 1981 gunshot wound—a .22 caliber "Devastator" round lodged in his lung—the danger the Iran-Contra Affair posed to his presidency was deliberately underrated.

The same GOP faithful who minimized the hazards of the president's second term were quick to canonize him after he left office. Relentlessly yet meaninglessly, Republicans had been calling themselves the Party of Lincoln since 1865. After 124 years, they finally had a new patron saint, and within months of Reagan's departure from Washington, federal buildings and public works were beginning to be named in his honor.

On one thing everyone can agree. The Reagan presidency was at least as transformational as FDR's. The difference, of course, was that FDR offered a New Deal, with the federal government as the driver of national movement forward, while Reagan told us that "government is the problem," a brake instead of an engine.

Before Reagan's eight years were up, both the president and his director of the Office of Management and Budget David Stockman learned that most of the American public rather like "Big Government." What they do not like is paying for it. Nevertheless, close to forty years later, the scorn of

Big Government remains the most persistent Reagan myth. Whether we fully realize it or not, we are still living in Reagan's America. The economic cocktail mixed and poured by the Gipper in 1980, one part low tax rates and one part deregulation, is still being served, and the GOP is ordering doubles. It is a drinking game that comes at the expense of meaningful investment in the nation's infrastructure, rebuilding public school systems, public health initiatives, free public college educations, investment in clean energy, funding to combat climate change and rising oceans, not to mention public health and the ability and will to protect the American population against a pandemic disease.

In foreign relations, Ronald Reagan set the stage for a peaceful resolution of the Cold War. Claims that he singlehandedly "won" that fifty-year conflict are grossly distorted and unjustifiable, however. A half-century of "containment" and American global leadership combined with the moral and economic poverty of the Soviet system to make the fall of the USSR inevitable. Ronald Reagan found himself facing low-hanging fruit, and he picked it masterfully, doing so, ultimately, with a generosity that created a productive relationship with Mikhail Gorbachev. At the same time, he was slow to recognize the threats posed by a world no longer neatly divided between two superpowers. He created no foreign policy legacy for that new scenario, except for the squalid and unlawful Iran-Contra affair. There was also the bug-out retreat from Beirut after the deaths of hundreds of Marines, and a wag-the-dog "war" waged in what was at the time the sad little Marxist Caribbean enclave of Grenada.

As for Reagan's domestic policy, the most generous thing that can be said about it is that it was mixed. Importantly, over the course of the past four decades, given the continuation of Reagan's tax policies—lack of progressivity in the tax code and a continuation of supply-side tax cuts by the GOP—this wealth and income gap between the wealthiest and the rest of us is now simply staggering. Under Reagan, the funding of countless government programs intended to benefit the middle class and poor was slashed even as government spending—and borrowing—increased in the absence of adequate tax revenue. The rich were out on the town, armed with Uncle Sam's credit card.

* * *

In his 1980 speech accepting the Republican nomination for his candidacy as president of the United States, Ronald Reagan depicted a nation in deep trouble but said to his audience, "I ask you not simply to 'Trust me,' but to trust your values—our values—and to hold me responsible for living up to them." Writing thirty-six years later about Donald Trump's acceptance speech in *The Atlantic* on July 21, 2016, Yoni Appelbaum noted:

"Donald Trump didn't ask Americans to place their trust in each other or in God, but rather, in Trump." He painted a far darker picture of America than Reagan had, depicting a nation suffering attacks on the police, terrorism run amok, poverty and violence at home, and war and destruction abroad. He told his audience, "I am your voice. I alone can fix it."[13] And in his bleak inaugural address on January 20, 2017, he spoke of a nation of "Mothers and children trapped in poverty in our inner cities, rusted out factories, scattered like tombstones across the landscape of our nation, an education system flush with cash, but which leaves our young and beautiful students deprived of all knowledge, and the crime, and the gangs, and the drugs that have stolen too many lives and robbed our country of so much unrealized potential." He pledged: "This American carnage stops right here and stops right now."[14]

As different as he was in demeanor from Richard Nixon, Ronald Reagan resembled him in being an imperial president. Yet neither Nixon nor Reagan was an autocrat, though they both toed that mark. Trump? He stepped, lead feet and all, right across it. All three men left their mark. Nixon, for all his corrupt self-dealing, left a valuable, even bold, diplomatic legacy. Reagan did not "win" the Cold War, but he did not lose it, either, when he looked forward with the world to that conflict's imminent and triumphant end. In the domestic sphere, Reagan bequeathed his country the name by which his economic policies are still remembered: Reaganomics.

Trump? His diplomatic legacy could be called negligible were it not so destructive. His domestic agenda was chaos and anarchy with a twist of cult worship. His economic legacy lacked any overt policy but was destructive in effect with more supply-side tax cuts in 2017 weighted in favor of the wealthy and further adding to the nation's deficit.

But what of Reaganomics? It did help supply the fertile seeds of a wealth gap instrumental in driving national division not seen since the Civil War. President Reagan had not intended this. Nor had he intended priorities of cultural and religious piety to drown the GOP in a thick coat of sorghum, which drew single-issue voters like flies at the expense of urgent issues and constituent needs.

No, not at all. Reagan had a vision. He saw the power of Hollywood to aggregate eyeballs in front of a silver screen. He reaped the financial—and, ultimately, political—benefit of being an adept journeyman film star capable (as producers say) of putting asses in theater seats. He was the most media-savvy president since JFK and inspired a comparable following with stagecraft and scripted events "produced" by his long-time aide Mike Deaver. In contrast to Kennedy, however, his inspirational message contained not a whisper of collective self-sacrifice. "Ask not what your country can do for you, but what you can do for your country" became "Tell the federal government to get off your back and take its hand out of your pocket." In place of a "New Deal" or a "Great Society," Reagan offered a "shining city on a hill"—a piece of high-end real estate whose apex offered vanishingly small room for occupancy.

Ronald Reagan promised wealth and victory without sacrifice, and yet many Americans remember him as a latter-day George Washington, a man and a president of "character." These people agree with Peggy Noonan, who wrote, in effect, that Reagan's greatest contribution to American political life was character: "*He was a giant.* He was our giant, a giant of history." He was a man of "courage. He always tried to do what he thought was right."[15] Republicans often put him up against Bill Clinton, whose legacy was marred by the Monica Lewinsky affair and a sheaf of pardons he distributed like party favors at the end of his second term. Compared with the Trump administration, the Clinton years seem pure as the driven snow (though they were not). Compared with the mythology of the Reagan administration, Clinton does look pretty shady, but nothing in his eight years ever rose even close to the magnitude of the Iran-Contra affair, in which the president trampled the Constitution by deliberately and covertly thwarting the expressed will of Congress.

As Kyle Longley argues in "When Character Was King? Ronald Reagan and the Issues of Ethics and Morality,"[16] the more relevant character comparison is Reagan versus Carter, not Reagan versus Clinton. Why? Simply because Reagan never ran against Clinton but did run against Carter.

The success of Reagan's candidacy was in part the product of Nixon's Southern Strategy, with Reagan winning a large portion of the evangelical Christian vote. Yet Reagan was not a born-again Christian. Though his mother was what we would today call a fundamentalist Christian, Reagan rarely attended church services. In contrast, Jimmy Carter was a bona fide evangelical, born-again Christian, a church deacon who not only attended services every Sunday but taught Sunday school to boot. More important, he lived a Christian life as Jesus preached it, a life of service to the poor and to the common good—"as ye have done it unto one of the least of these my brethren, ye have done it unto me"—both before and after his presidency. Well into his eighties, Carter was building—and helping to fund—Habitat for Humanity houses. His Carter Center in Atlanta is a vital non-profit institution dedicated to humanitarian and civic service worldwide. Even the Rev. Billy Graham, most often associated with rightwing Republican politics, contrasted Carter with the "many leaders [who] place their religious and moral convictions in a separate compartment and to not think of the implications of their faith on their responsibilities. Jimmy Carter was not like that." He was "a man of faith and sterling integrity."[17]

In the mid–1950s, Carter's faith moved him to oppose the racial seg-regationists of the Southern Citizens' Council in his hometown of Plains, Georgia. As a result, his business was boycotted, and he suffered severe economic loss, but he never looked back. One does not have to accuse Ronald Reagan of racism to acknowledge that he built his presidential campaign, in part, on Nixon's Southern Strategy by launching his 1980 campaign in the town associated with one of the most heinous Ku Klux Klan lynchings of the Civil Rights era. Carter opposed South African apartheid. On September 26, 1986, Ronald Reagan vetoed HR 4868, the Comprehensive Anti-Apartheid Act of 1986. Carter criticized the Soviet Union's human rights abuses, retaliating against these abuses in 1980 with a grain embargo and a boycott of the 1980 Moscow Olympics. He also implemented a human rights policy in Latin America. Later, Jeane Kirk-patrick, Reagan's UN ambassador, criticized Carter for failing to work with authoritarian states that were nevertheless pro–American. Indeed, whereas Carter made human rights the centerpiece of his administration, Reagan failed to establish any humanitarian policy whatsoever let alone a human rights agenda during his two terms.

Ronald Reagan welcomed the anti-abortion/pro-life vote. The ultra-conservative writer Dinesh D'Souza claims that Reagan's "greatest regret was that he was unable to do more as president to protect the lives of the unborn."[18] Indeed, to this day, pro-lifers quote Reagan and invoke him at their rallies and functions as a patron saint. Yet Governor Ronald Reagan signed into law perhaps the nation's most liberal abortion legisla-tion. As president, he appointed two pro-choice Supreme Court justices, and he never publicly embraced the pro-life movement, not even after he left the White House. Most telling, perhaps, is that Reagan makes but a single reference to abortion in his 1990 valedictory autobiography, *An American Life*, a book that runs to 726 pages, nearly a quarter-million words.

Ronald Reagan, as we have argued, was a master of self-mythology, and as William Pemberton wrote, he "kept his Religious Right followers happy through rhetoric and symbolic gestures, rather than through effec-tive action on their agenda."[19] There is a thin line between mythology and fiction and between self-mythologizing and lying. Reagan's supporters cel-ebrate him as a truth teller above all else, but he "often told lies, in private and public, confusing stories he read or movie plots with real events. In addition, a disproportionate number of officials (138 to 190) in his admin-istration, including many close to the president, perpetrated acts that were at the least unethical and often criminal."[20] Reagan's loyalty even to those found guilty of corruption has led one historian to compare his "record of ethical malpractice" to the administrations of Grant and Harding, noting that the number of officials who "were obliged to resign (they were never fired) for illegal or unethical practices" exceeded that of the Grant and Harding administration.[21] Of course, it was Reagan himself who was at the center of the most spectacular instance of corruption—impeachable, to be sure—the Iran-Contra Affair.

Some of Reagan's tall tales were laughable, including one he told to the Congressional Medal of Honor Society in 1983, about a World War II B-17 pilot who refused to bail out of his doomed aircraft because one of his gunners was too badly wounded to survive. "He took the boy's hand and said, 'Never mind, son, we'll ride it down together.' Congressional Medal of Honor, posthumously awarded." Not only is there no record of this Medal of Honor but also there is this disqualifying conundrum: if both men were killed in the crash of the plane, who was there to bear witness and quote the words of the pilot?[22] More troubling was Reagan's claim, made to Israeli prime minister Yitzhak Shamir, that, as an officer in the U.S. Army Signal Corps, he had personally filmed death camps and the horrors of the Holocaust. The problem here is that, during World War II, Reagan never served overseas. He subsequently repeated the story to less a figure than the legendary Holocaust survivor turned "Nazi hunter" Simon Wiesenthal.[23]

∗　∗　∗

As human beings and as chief executives, Ronald Reagan and Donald Trump are, as Reagan ally and admirer Margaret Thatcher might have put it, as "different as chalk and cheese." We find it impossible to imagine Ronald Reagan instigating an attack on the United States Capitol. And yet we are convinced that the Party of Trump found root in the Party of Reagan, and the first toxic fruit it bore was the bloody Sack of the Capitol on January 6, 2021. Ronald Reagan was a storyteller and myth maker, who thought in terms of government as the problem and the Soviet Union as an evil empire. For him, being a lifeguard, a sportscaster, an actor, a union president, a governor, and a president of the United States were all in some degree projections of a self-identity that was a self-mythology. Anything like objective truth was subordinate to it. There were times when truth and mythology clashed—times of intense cognitive dissonance, as, for example, when Reagan refused to believe he was capable of any act of racism because his parents providentially refused to raise him as a racist. Mostly, however, he reconciled myth and fact through storytelling, when, as noted above, he stated that he had shot film of the Nazi death camps—never mind that his military service did not take him to Europe. The point is that he *would* have documented the horrors of the Holocaust if he had had the opportunity. For him, that was truth enough.

The trouble is that there is never "truth enough." A thing is either true, false, or unknown. The "Great Communicator," Reagan continually communicated his self-mythology. He truly believed the lie that was supply-side economics and trickledown. That *he* believed it does not make it true. Former Reagan aide Pat Buchanan observed that "For Ronald Reagan, the world of legend and myth is a real world." Buchanan further noted that "He visits it regularly, and he's a happy man there."[24]

The presidency of Ronald Reagan built into American politics a very high tolerance for mythologies that are often indistinguishable from lies. We do not believe that Ronald Reagan was a malevolent man. We do believe, however, that his most dubious gift to American politics was the license to lie—if lying made for a better story, a more compelling mythology. But did Reagan lie? Biographer Lou Cannon writes of a "serious debate within the White House" over "whether Reagan knew what he was doing when he told a made-up story or whether he had reached a point where he actually could not distinguish films from fact." Substitute "self-mythology" for "films" and you may have a plausible theory. In a political party primed to prefer mythology over reality when the mythology better suits the program of the party, the possibility of the rise of malevolent politicians is multiplied beyond the usual odds. In conditioning America and the Republican Party to a mythic American narrative over his two presidential terms, Reagan also held open the door to mendacity. As president, he saw government as an impediment, and he saw Congress as the embodiment of government. This created a vacuum, which he filled with an imperial presidency.[25]

Thomas Jefferson wrote, "The government you elect is the government you deserve."[26] Over the last four decades, Americans have been conditioned to believe they can have it all. Deep down inside, we all know this is not possible, sustainable, or fair to our children. As owners of the American experiment in self-governance, we must make the effort to be better informed, more mature in our choices of candidates for public office and accept the hard reality that we cannot have both supply-side tax cuts and big government. We can no longer accept the magical thinking that tax cuts pay for themselves and only lip service regarding the need to tame the deficit. No doubt, the Democratic party has been negligent in educating voters in this regard, and to some degree, even embracing the paradox of low taxes and big government.

As of the writing of this book, the American economy resembles the economy of 1979 near the cusp of Reagan's election. Inflation, rising interest rates, and popular concern over the direction of the economy. How will Americans vote as the bill for Reaganomics is coming due?

That USA credit card, with the national debt now more than $33 trillion, must be nearing its limit. What about the tab for continued dependence on cheap gasoline? Catastrophic storms, floods, and unprecedented heat, the result of climate change, remind us of the cost of ignoring proven science and expertise.

When will we stop living in Reagan's America, let alone what is even worse, Trump's America?

It will pass only when both citizens and elected officials regain a sense of humility and national purpose, heeding the call for shared sacrifice and embracing science and objective facts as the basis for policy decisions while paying adequate taxes and embracing the role of government as both a patriotic duty and the price for civilization. President Joe Biden recently observed in a speech at Cuyahoga Community College in Ohio, "from 1948 after the war to 1979, productivity in America grew by 100 percent. We made more things with productivity. You know what the workers' pay grew? By 100 percent. Since 1979, all of that changed. Productivity has grown four times faster than pay has grown. The basic bargain in this country has been broken."[27]

Fortunately, in contrast to Donald Trump, Ronald Reagan was not a vicious man. He was capable of both compassion and a sense of duty. His single most serious transgression, the unconstitutional and therefore autocratic Iran-Contra deception, was bad, but it was of limited scope and duration. Reagan knew that he had done something wrong, and he should have held himself and have been held more accountable for it—not to punish him but to deter others from following his example. For when the politics and party Reagan created came into the grasp of a malignant narcissist incapable of compassion and uninterested in duty, the license to lie became a weapon, and Donald Trump put American democracy to its most severe test since the Civil War. It remains to be seen what the future of Trump himself will be, but we have no way of knowing the poisonously radioactive half-life of Trumpism, through which politics, once the art of the possible, has become the surprisingly banal art of the lie. Perhaps we, as a nation, will choose to reject it.

Chapter Notes

Chapter 1

1. Carolyn Kormann, "From Bats to Human Lungs, the Evolution of a Coronavirus," *The New Yorker* (March 27, 2020), https://www.newyorker.com/science/elements/from-bats-to-human-lungs-the-evolution-of-a-coronavirus.

2. Javier C. Hernández and Sui-Lee Wee, "W.H.O. experts who are investigating the origin of the virus visit a lab in Wuhan," *New York Times* (February 3, 2021), https://www.nytimes.com/2021/02/03/world/asia/who-wuhan-lab.html.

3. The Editorial Board, "A president unfit for a pandemic," *The Boston Globe* (March 30, 2020), https://www.bostonglobe.com/2020/03/30/opinion/president-unfit-pandemic/.

4. Yoni Appelbaum, "'I Alone Can Fix It,'" *The Atlantic* (July 21, 2016), https://www.theatlantic.com/politics/archive/2016/07/trump-rnc-speech-alone-fix-it 492557/.

5. Charles S. Clark, "Deconstructing the Deep State," *Government Executive* (undated), https://www.govexec.com/feature/gov-exec-deconstructing-deep-state/.

6. Ryan Broderick, "Trump's Biggest Supporters Think The Coronavirus Is a Deep State Plot," *BuzzFeedNews* (February 26, 2020), https://www.buzzfeednews.com/article/ryanhatesthis/trump-supporters-coronavirus-deep-state-qanon.

7. Jennifer Steinhauer and Zolan Kanno-Youngs, "Job Vanacies and Inexperience Mar Federal Response to Coronavirus," *The New York Times* (March 26, 2020), https://www.nytimes.com/2020/03/26/us/politics/coronavirus-expertise-trump.html.

8. Cynthia Cox and Krutika Amin, "COVID-19 is the Number One Cause of Death in the U.S. in Early 2021," Health System Tracker (January 28, 2021), https://www.healthsystemtracker.org/brief/covid-19-is-the-number-one-cause-of-death-in-the-u-s-in-early-2021/.

9. "Obama Roasts Donald Trump," YouTube (posted April 28, 2016), https://www.youtube.com/watch?v=HHckZCxdRkA.

10. Ryan Teague Beckwith, "Watch President Obama Troll Donald Trump in 2011," *Time* (August 10, 2015), https://time.com/3991301/donald-trump-barack-obama/.

11. On March 31, 2017, after three lawsuits and lengthy litigation, a federal judge approved a $25 million settlement between then-President Trump and "students who paid for Trump University real estate seminars." (Camila Domonoske, "Judge Approves $25 Million Settlement of Trump University Lawsuit," *NPR: The Two-Way* (March 31, 2017), https://www.npr.org/sections/thetwo-way/2017/03/31/522199535/judge-approves-25-million-settlement-of-trump-university-lawsuit.

12. William Kleinknecht, *The Man Who Sold the World: Ronald Reagan and the Betrayal of Main Street America* (New York: Perseus, 2009), 47.

13. Michael Reagan, "Ronald Reagan's Son Remembers The Day When GE Fired His Dad," *Investor's Business Daily* (February 4, 2011), https://www.investors.com/politics/commentary/ronald-reagans-son-remembers-the-day-when-ge-fired-his-dad/.

14. Jim Wright, *Balance of Power: Presidents and Congress from the Era of*

McCarthy to the Age of Gingrich (Atlanta: Turner Publishing, 1996), 341.

15. Ronald Reagan, First Inaugural Address (January 20, 1981), The Avalon Project, https://avalon.law.yale.edu/20th_century/reagan1.asp.

16. Chris Cameron, "These are the People Who Died in Connection with the Capitol Riot," *The New York Times* (January 5, 2022, updated October 13, 2022), https://www.nytimes.com/2022/01/05/us/politics/jan-6-capitol-deaths.html.

17. CBS News, "CBS News archives: Carter's famous 'malaise' speech," posted on YouTube, July 15, 2011, https://www.youtube.com/watch?v=0tGd_9Tahzw.

18. Bruce Bartlett, "Reagan's Forgotten Tax Record," *Tax Notes* (February 21, 2011).

19. George Packer, "We Are Living in a Failed State," *The Atlantic* (June 2020), https://www.theatlantic.com/magazine/archive/2020/06/underlying-conditions/610261/.

Chapter 2

1. Jim Wright, *Balance of Power: Presidents and Congress from the Era of McCarthy to the Age of Gingrich* (Atlanta: Turner Publishing, 1996), 341.

2. Joe Klein, "Why the 'War President' Is Under Fire," *Time* (February 15, 2004), http://content.time.com/time/nation/article/0,8599,591270,00.html.

3. Ronald Reagan, "Farewell Speech," transcribed in *The New York Times* (January 12, 1989), https://www.nytimes.com/1989/01/12/news/transcript-of-reagan-s-farewell-address-to-american-people.html.

4. "Immigration During Ronald Reagan's Presidency," Boundless blog (April 7, 2017), https://www.boundless.com/blog/reagan/; EEOC, "An Act to Amend the Immigration and Nationality Act to revise and reform the immigration laws, and for other purposes," https://www.eeoc.gov/eeoc/history/35th/thelaw/irca.html.

5. Ronald Reagan, First Inaugural Address (January 20, 1981), The Avalon Project, https://avalon.law.yale.edu/20th_century/reagan1.asp.

6. Ronald Reagan, "A Time for Choosing" (broadcast October 27, 1964), https://www.americanrhetoric.com/speeches/ronaldreaganatimeforchoosing.htm.

7. Robert Blake, *Disraeli* (New York: St. Martin's Press, 1967), 179.

8. C.Ó Gráda and Joel Mokyr, "New developments in Irish Population History 1700–1850," *Economic History Review*, vol. xxxvii, no. 4 (November 1984), pp. 473–488.

9. Sara Goek, "From Ireland to the U.S.: a brief migration history," *The Irish Times* (October 29, 2015), https://www.irishtimes.com/life-and-style/abroad/generation-emigration/from-ireland-to-the-us-a-brief-migration-history-1.2409960.

10. *Ibid.*

11. R. Andrew Pierce, "Notes on the Irish Ancestry of President Ronald Reagan," http://www.wargs.com/articles/reagan.html.

12. Ronan McGreevy, "Ronald Reagan's Irish ancestors found on historical Morpeth Roll," *The Irish Times* (November 20, 2013), https://www.irishtimes.com/culture/heritage/ronald-reagan-s-irish-ancestors-found-on-historic-morpeth-roll-1.1601480.

13. AP, "Ronald Reagan is descendant of Irish high-king," *Daily Kent Stater* (November 12, 1980), https://dks.library.kent.edu/cgi-bin/kentstate?a=d&d=dks19801112-01.2.60.

14. *Ibid.*

15. "Reagan feared Irish roots would damage his career," *Independent* (October 23, 2004), https://www.independent.ie/irish-news/reagan-feared-irish-roots-would-damage-his-career-26225824.html.

16. *Ibid.*

17. David Lehman, ed. *The Oxford Book of American Poetry* (New York: Oxford University Press, 2006), p. 184.

18. Ronald Reagan, "Ronald Reagan: Immigrants recognize the intoxicating power of America," *The Kansas City Star* (July 23, 2019), https://www.kansascity.com/opinion/opn-columns-blogs/syndicated-columnists/article232864812.html.

19. William Kleinknecht, *The Man Who Sold the World: Ronald Reagan and the Betrayal of Main Street America* (New York: Nation Books, 2009), 36.

20. Lou Cannon, *Governor Reagan: His Rise to Power* (New York: Public Affairs, 2003), 11.

21. Many of the details related here of Ronald Reagan's childhood and youth are drawn from *Governor Reagan* by Lou

Cannon, who was one of Reagan's few intimates, especially among members of the press.

22. Kleinknecht, 36.

23. Cannon, 12.

24. Quoted in Cannon, 13.

25. Ronald Reagan and Richard C. Hubler, *Where's the Rest of Me?* (New York: Dell, 1965), 12–13.

26. Reagan and Hubler, 12–13.

27. Reagan and Hubler, 14.

28. Cannon, 14–15.

29. Cannon 15; Ronald Reagan, *An American Life* (New York: Simon & Schuster, 1990), 20.

30. Reagan and Hubler, 20.

31. Dixon State Hospital was opened in 1918 to care for epileptics; it soon also accommodated developmentally disabled persons. It later became Dixon State School and was closed altogether in 1983. See "Dixon State School," https://www.asylumprojects.org/index.php/Dixon_State_School.

32. Cited in Jerry Griswold, "Young Reagan's Reading," *The New York Times Book Review* (August 30, 1981).

33. Mary L. Trump, *Too Much and Never Enough: How My Family Created the World's Most Dangerous Man* (New York: Simon & Schuster, 2020), 49–50.

34. Jeffrey Goldberg, "Trump: Americans Who Died in War Are 'Losers' and 'Suckers,'" *The Atlantic* (September 3, 2020), https://www.theatlantic.com/politics/archive/2020/09/trump-americans-who-died-at-war-are-losers-and-suckers/615997/.

35. Michael Barbaro, "Donald Trump Likens His Schooling to Military Service in Book," *New York Times* (September 8, 2015), https://www.nytimes.com/2015/09/09/us/politics/donald-trump-likens-his-schooling-to-military-service-in-book.html.

36. Mary L. Trump, 72; Lisette Voytko, "Report: UPenn Professor Renews Call for Investigation into Trump's Alleged SAT Cheating," *Forbes* (August 28, 2020), https://www.forbes.com/sites/lisettevoytko/2020/08/28/report-upenn-professor-renews-call-for-investigation-into-trumps-alleged-sat-cheating/?sh=7014dae8256f.

37. David Nakamura, "Trump boasts that he's 'like, really smart' and a 'very

stable genius' amid questions over his mental fitness," *The Washington Post* (January 6, 2018), https://www.washingtonpost.com/news/post-politics/wp/2018/01/06/trump-boasts-that-hes-like-really-smart-and-a-very-stable-genius-amid-questions-over-his-mental-fitness/.

38. Cannon, 18.

39. Windsor Mann, "Trump's lethal aversion to reading," *The Week* (May 21, 2020), https://theweek.com/articles/915606/trumps-lethal-aversion-reading.

40. Material on young Reagan's reading in this paragraph and the next is from Griswold, op. cit. Cannon cites Stephen Vaughn, *Ronald Reagan in Hollywood: Movies and Politics* (New York: Cambridge University Press, 1994), 5–6, as "the best list of Reagan's early reading" (Cannon, 19, note 7).

41. Lou Cannon, "The Truth in Reagan's Humor," *Washington Post* (April 27, 1987), https://www.washingtonpost.com/archive/politics/1987/04/27/the-truth-in-reagans-humor/4540f5ea-45e1-4cf7-a635-28b1ea471234/.

42. Cannon, 22.

43. Mary L. Trump, 138.

44. Mary L. Trump, 198–199.

Chapter 3

1. Patti Davis, *The Way I See It: An Autobiography* (New York: Putnam, 1992), 23.

2. Ronald Reagan, *An American Life: An Enhanced eBook with CBS Video: The Autobiography* (New York: Simon & Schuster. 1990), Kindle Edition, locs. 196–198.

3. Reagan, *An American Life,* locs. 199–201.

4. Reagan, *An American Life,* loc. 199.

5. *Ibid.*

6. *Ibid.*

7. *Ibid.*

8. *Ibid.*

9. *Ibid.*

10. Reagan, *An American Life,* loc. 221.

11. Reagan, *An American Life,* loc. 237.

12. Reagan, *An American Life,* loc. 221.

13. Reagan, *An American Life,* loc. 237.

14. *Ibid.*

15. *Ibid.*

16. Reagan, *An American Life,* loc. 254.

17. NASA Earth Observatory, "'Killer'

Trees? Not Exactly" (September 1–30, 2013), https://earthobservatory.nasa.gov/images/84021/killer-trees-not-exactly.

18. Reagan, *An American Life,* loc. 254.

19. Wikipedia, "Selective Service Act of 1917," National registration days and termination, https://en.wikipedia.org/wiki/Selective_Service_Act_of_1917#:~:text=The%20first%2C%20on%20June%205,old%20after%20June%205%2C%201918.

20. Reagan, *An American Life,* loc. 271.

21. Reagan, *An American Life,* loc. 290.

22. Reagan, *An American Life,* loc. 307.

23. CBS News Chicago, "Chicago Population Lowest Since 1910" (February 15, 2011), https://www.cbsnews.com/chicago/news/census-shows-chicago-population-down-7-percent/#:~:text=The%20last%20Census%20that%20showed,higher%20than%202010%2C%20at%202%2C701%2C705.&text=The%20population%20was%20also%20down,the%20Census%20recorded%202%2C896%2C016%20people; Christopher Manning, "African Americans," *Encyclopedia of Chicago,* http://www.encyclopedia.chicagohistory.org/pages/27.html#:~:text=Steady%20southern%20migration%20raised%20Chicago's,black%20institutions%20for%20racial%20uplift.

24. Reagan, *An American Life,* loc. 307.

25. *Ibid.*

26. Reagan, *An American Life,* loc. 326.

27. Reagan, *An American Life,* locs. 326, 345.

28. Reagan, *An American Life,* loc. 359.

29. Harold Bell Wright, *That Printer of Udell's* (1902; reprint ed., Pelican Publishers, 1996).

30. Reagan, *An American Life,* loc. 405.

31. *Ibid.*

32. Reagan, *An American Life,* loc., 424.

33. Reagan, *An American Life,* loc.435.

34. Reagan, *An American Life,* loc.452.

35. Reagan, *An American Life,* loc.471.

36. Reagan, *An American Life,* loc.491.

37. Reagan, *An American Life,* loc.508.

38. *Ibid.*

39. Reagan, *An American Life,* loc.528.

40. Reagan, *An American Life,* loc. 560.

41. Reagan, *An American Life,* loc.707.

42. Reagan, *An American Life,* loc. 718.

43. Reagan, *An American Life,* loc. 726.

44. Reagan, *An American Life,* loc. 738.

45. Reagan, *An American Life,* loc.756.

46. *Ibid.*

47. Reagan, *An American Life,* loc. 776.

48. *Ibid.*

49. Reagan, *An American Life,* loc. 852.

Chapter 4

1. Ronald Reagan and Richard C. Hubler, *Where's the Rest of Me? Ronald Reagan Tells His Own Story* (New York: Dell, 1965), 59–60.

2. Cannon, *Governor Reagan,* 48.

3. Ronald Reagan Presidential Library & Museum, "Military Service of Ronald Reagan," https://www.reaganlibrary.gov/reagans/ronald-reagan/military-service-ronald-reagan.

4. Richard L. Coe, "The Chimp's a Lot Cuter Than Reagan," *Washington Post* (March 15, 1951), B11.

5. Ted Berkman, "Bonzo comes swinging back," *Christian Science Monitor* (February 19, 1981), https://www.csmonitor.com/1981/0219/021957.html.

6. Wikipedia, "*Bedtime for Bonzo,*" https://en.wikipedia.org/wiki/Bedtime_for_Bonzo.

7. UPI, "The creators of 'Bedtime for Bonzo' wanted Cary Grant," UPI Archives (December 25, 1980), https://www.upi.com/Archives/1980/12/25/The-creators-of-Bedtime-for-Bonzo-wanted-Cary-Grant/4355346568400/.

8. Steven Eder, "Did a Queens Podiatrist Help Donald Trump Avoid Vietnam?" *New York Times* (December 26, 2018), https://www.nytimes.com/2018/12/26/us/politics/trump-vietnam-draft-exemption.html?login=email&auth=login-email; Steve Eder and Dave Philipps, "Donald Trump's Draft Deferments: Four for College, One for Bad Feet," *New York Times* (August 1, 2016), https://www.nytimes.com/2016/08/02/us/politics/donald-trump-draft-record.html.

9. Eder and Philipps, https://www.nytimes.com/2016/08/02/us/politics/donald-trump-draft-record.html.

10. Jonathan Martin and Alan Rappeport, "Donald Trump Says John McCain Is No War Hero, Setting off Another Storm," *New York Times* (July 18, 2015), https://www.nytimes.com/2015/07/19/us/politics/trump-belittles-mccains-war-record.html; Michael Barbaro, "Donald Trump Likens

His Schooling to Military Service in Book," *New York Times* (September 8, 2015), https://www.nytimes.com/2015/09/09/us/politics/donald-trump-likens-his-schooling-to-military-service-in-book.html.

11. Ale Russian, "Trump Boasted of Avoiding STDs While Dating: Vaginas Are 'Landmines … It Is My Personal Vietnam," *People* (October 15, 2016), https://people.com/politics/trump-boasted-of-avoiding-stds-while-dating-vaginas-are-landmines-it-was-my-personal-vietnam/.

12. LBJ Presidential Library, "LBJ's Military Service," https://www.lbjlibrary.org/life-and-legacy/the-man-himself/lbjs-military-service; Julian Borger, "LBJ's medal for valour 'was sham.'" *The Guardian* (July 6, 2001), https://www.theguardian.com/world/2001/jul/06/internationaleducationnews.humanities.

13. Richard Halloran, "Reagan as Military Commander," *New York Times* (July 15, 1984), https://www.nytimes.com/1984/01/15/magazine/reagan-as-military-commander.html.

14. Francis X. Clines, "It Was a Rescue Mission, Reagan Says," *The New York Times* (November 4, 1983), https://www.nytimes.com/1983/11/04/world/it-was-a-rescue-mission-reagan-says.html.

15. Reagan, *Where's the Rest of Me?* 222–223.

16. Reagan, *An American Life,* loc. 1274.

Chapter 5

1. Petula Dvorak, "Jane Wyman as the anti–Ivana Trump," *Chicago Tribune* (October 11, 2017), https://www.chicagotribune.com/opinion/commentary/ct-perspec-flotus-ivana-melania-trump-jane-wyman-1012-20171011-story.html.

2. *Ibid.*

3. Edward M. Yager, *Ronald Reagan's Journey: Democrat to Republican* (New York: Rowman and Littlefield, 2006), 12–15.

4. Mary Beckman, "Did FDR Have Guillain-Barré?" *Science* (October 31, 2003), https://www.science.org/content/article/did-fdr-have-guillain-barr#:~:text=A%20new%20analysis%20of%20Franklin,moved%20up%20to%20his%20neck.

5. Dvorak, https://www.chicago tribune.com/opinion/commentary/ct-perspec-flotus-ivana-melania-trump-jane-wyman-1012-20171011-story.html; Cannon, *Governor Reagan,* 82–83.

6. Lawrence L. Knutson, "Reagan, Communism Met in Hollywood," *AP News* (November 13, 1985), https://apnews.com/article/43e9c90d8177871105953a7c4728a781.

7. Reagan, *Where's the Rest of Me?* 266.

8. Cannon, *Governor Reagan,* 77–78.

9. Reagan, *Where's the Rest of Me?* 268.

10. Cannon, *Governor Reagan,* 77–78.

11. Reagan, *An American Life,* locs. 1448-1450.

12. Reagan, *An American Life,* locs. 1458-1464.

13. John Cogley, *Report on Blacklisting,* I: *Movies* (New York: Fund for the Republic, 1956), 69.

14. Reagan, *An American Life,* locs. 1472-1480.

15. Reagan, *An American Life,* locs. 1522-1525.

16. Reagan, *An American Life,* locs. 1528-1533.

17. Reagan, *Where's the Rest of Me?* 139.

18. This may have been on April 10, 1947; see Peter Schweizer, "Reagan's War: The Epic story of His Forty-Year Struggle and Final Triumph Over Communism," *Washington Post* (October 29, 2020).

19. Reagan, *An American Life,* loc. 1533.

20. Stephen Vaughn, *Ronald Reagan in Hollywood: Movies and Politics* (Cambridge and New York: Cambridge University Press, 1994), 277–78, n. 45.

21. "Hollywood: Unmasking Informant T-10," *Time* (September 9, 1985), http://content.time.com/time/magazine/article/0,9171,959749,00.html; Scott Herhold and Knight-Ridder Newspapers, "Reagan Played Informant Role for FBI in '40s" *Chicago Tribune* (August 25, 1985), https://www.chicagotribune.com/news/ct-xpm-1985-08-26-8502250710-story.html.

22. Herhold, https://www.chicago tribune.com/news/ct-xpm-1985-08-26-8502250710-story.html.

23. Reagan interview with Hedda Hopper, printed in the *Chicago Tribune,* May 18, 1947, G7.

24. Cannon, *Governor Reagan,* 96–99.

25. Lois Romano, "ADA: Optimism Flowing Liberally," *Washington Post*

(March 19, 1983), https://www.washington post.com/archive/lifestyle/1983/03/19/ada-optimism-flowing-liberally/b98809a7-61a4-456c-b37a-b2651b22cf1c/.

26. Cannon, *Governor Reagan*, 83.

27. Thomas F. Brady, "RED PROBE ON IN HOLLYWOOD; Congressional Group Investigates Movie Colony's Politics—Labor Issues Remain Unsettled—'Red Pony' in Production," *New York Times* (May 18, 1947), https://www.nytimes.com/1947/05/18/archives/red-probe-on-in-hollywood-congressional-group-investigates-movie.html.

28. Lee Edwards, *The Essential Ronald Reagan* (Lanham, MD: Rowman and Littlefield Publishers, 2005), 37, 47.

29. Reagan, *Speaking My Mind: Selected Speeches* (New York: Simon & Schuster, 1989), 17–21.

30. CQ Researcher, "Tax Loopholes: Congress and Truman's 1950 Tax Proposals," https://library.cqpress.com/cqresearcher/document.php?id=cqresrre1950020100.

31. Reagan, *Speaking My Mind*, 17–21.

32. *Ibid.*

33. Michael Reagan with Jim Denney, *The City on a Hill: Fulfilling Ronald Reagan's Vision for America* (Nashville: Thomas Nelson Publishers, 1997), 135–36; Reagan testimony, January 27, 1958, p. 1985.

road-conservatism-george-nash.html#%20ftn52.

7. Reagan, *An American Life*, Chapter 18.

8. Nash, https://theimaginative conservative.org/2018/11/ronald-reagan-road-conservatism-george-nash.html#%20ftn52.

9. *Ibid.*

10. *Ibid.*

11. Reagan, *An American Life*, Chapter 18.

12. *Ibid.*

13. Alan Snyder, "Ronald Reagan, Whittaker Chambers, and the Dialogue of Liberty," *Law and Liberty* (March 13. 2012), https://lawliberty.org/ronald-reagan-whittaker-chambers-and-the-dialogue-of-liberty/.

14. Nash, https://theimaginative conservative.org/2018/11/ronald-reagan-road-conservatism-george-nash.html#%20ftn52.

15. Ronald Reagan, commencement address, Eureka College, 1957, https://whatrocks.github.io/commencement-db/1957-ronald-reagan-eureka-college/.

16. Reagan, *An American Life*, loc. 1856.

17. *Ibid.*

18. Reagan, *An American Life*, loc. 1875.

19. *Ibid.*

Chapter 6

1. Information on Reagan's relationship with Wasserman and MCA in this chapter is drawn from Dan E. Moldea, *Dark Victory: Ronald Reagan, MCA, and the Mob* (New York: Penguin, 1987)..

2. Robert McG. Thomas Jr., "Sidney Korshak, 88, Dies; Fabled Fixer for the Chicago Mob," *The New York Times* (January 22, 1996), https://timesmachine.nytimes.com/timesmachine/1996/01/22/090018.html?pageNumber=52.

3. Moldea, 15, 17.

4. Cannon, *Governor Reagan*, 106.

5. Tim Brooks and Earle Marsh, *The Complete Directory of Prime Time Network TV Shows, 1946–Present*, Fifth Edition (New York: Ballantine, 1992), 335.

6. George Nash, "Ronald Reagan's Road to Conservatism," *The Imaginative Conservative*, https://theimaginative conservative.org/2018/11/ronald-reagan-

Chapter 7

1. Reagan, *An American Life*, loc. 1924; Reagan, *"Where's the Rest of Me?"* 297.

2. Reagan, *"Where's the Rest of Me?"* 297.

3. Cannon, *Governor Reagan*, 109.

4. *Ibid.*

5. *Ibid.*

6. Reagan, *"Where's the Rest of Me?"* 306.

7. Cannon, *Governor Reagan*, 110.

8. Reagan, *"Where's the Rest of Me?"* 306.

9. Reagan, *"Where's the Rest of Me?"* 307–308.

10. Reagan, *"Where's the Rest of Me?"* 308; Cannon, *Governor Reagan*, 112–113; Reagan, *An American Life*, loc. 1924.

11. The Ronald Reagan Presidential Library, "Ronald Reagan speaks out on Socialized Medicine," YouTube, https://www.youtube.com/watch?v=AYrlDlrLDSQ.

12. Both quoted in Alan Axelrod, *The Complete Idiot's Guide to the American Presidency* (New York: Alpha, 2009), 186.

13. Ronald Reagan, *An American Life,* 244.

14. Quoted in Dan E. Moldea, "Reagan Was Forgetting 25 Years Ago, as Well," *Washington Post* (March 15, 1987), https://www.washingtonpost.com/archive/opinions/1987/03/15/reagan-was-forgetting-25-years-ago-as-well/53286eb4-4e8e-4156-9e11-f2495192d5c6/.

15. Reagan, *"Where's the Rest of Me?"* 314.

16. Famously, in 1985, when Reagan spoke out against taxes at the American Business Conference, he commandeered the one line from *Dirty Harry* everybody knows: "I have my veto pen drawn and ready for any tax increase that Congress might even think of sending up. And I have only one thing to say to the tax increasers. Go ahead—make my day." (George J. Church, "Go Ahead—Make My Day," *Time* [March 25, 1985], http://www.time.com/time/magazine/article/0%2C9171%2C964091%2C00.html).

17. Reagan, *An American Life,* locs. 1924–1952.

18. *Ibid.*

19. *Ibid.*

20. *Ibid.*

21. George Dunea, MD, "Loyal Davis, Legendary Neurosurgeon (1896–1982)," *Hektoen International* (Summer 2018), https://hekint.org/2018/08/16/loyal-davis-legendary-neurosurgeon-1896-1982/.

22. Cory Franklin, "The other man in Nancy Reagan's life," *Chicago Tribune* (March 8, 2016), https://www.chicagotribune.com/opinion/commentary/ct-nancy-reagan-loyal-davis-stepfather-perspec-0309-20160308-story.html.

23. Reagan, *An American Life,* loc. 1952.

24. *Ibid.*; Reagan did not comment on Goldwater's states' rights opposition to passage of the Civil Rights Act of 1964, though he made no secret about not supporting passage himself. Nevertheless, the following year, Reagan not only declared his support for what had become law of the land but also said that "it must be enforced at gunpoint, if necessary." During his presidency, Reagan compiled a poor record on civil rights, culminating in his veto of the Civil Rights Restoration Act—a veto overridden by Congress. Operationally, it is notable that both the Reagan-era Equal Employment Opportunity Commission and the Department of Justice prosecuted fewer civil rights cases than during the administration of any predecessor.

25. Reagan, *An American Life,* loc. 1952.

26. *Ibid.*

27. Reagan, *An American Life,* loc. 1976.

28. *Ibid.*

29. *Ibid.*

30. Ronald Reagan, "A Time for Choosing Speech," October 27, 1964, https://www.reaganlibrary.gov/reagans/ronald-reagan/time-choosing-speech-october-27-1964.

31. Alan Axelrod, *Full Faith and Credit: The National Debt, Taxes, Spending, and the Bankrupting of America* (New York: Abbeville Press, 2016), 95.

32. Ron Elving, "Trump's Helsinki Bow to Putin Leaves World Wondering: Why?" *NPR* (July 17, 2018), https://www.npr.org/2018/07/17/629601233/trumps-helsinki-bow-to-putin-leaves-world-wondering-whats-up.

33. Thomas Reed, *At the Abyss: An Insider's History of the Cold War* (New York: Ballantine, 2004), 145; The Editors, "Goldwater on the Bomb ..." *New York Times* (August 28, 1964), https://www.nytimes.com/1964/08/28/archives/goldwater-on-the-bomb-.html.

34. Clay F. Richards, "'He did a real job on America,'" UPI (December 9, 1980), https://www.upi.com/Archives/1980/12/09/He-did-a-real-job-on-America/8126345186000/.

Chapter 8

1. Ronald Reagan, *An American Life,* loc. 2033.

2. Constance L. Hays, "Holmes Tuttle, 83; In 'Kitchen Cabinet' That Aided Regan," obituary, *New York Times* (June 17, 1989), https://timesmachine.nytimes.com/timesmachine/1989/06/17/946889.html?pageNumber=29. See also David Leighton, "Street Smarts: Auto Mall Drive," *Arizona Daily Star* (August 3, 2018), https://tucson.com/news/local/street-smarts-auto-mall-drive/article_01c83be2-cc60-5a9b-b4d0-1b3a6b9d8015.html.

3. Ronald Reagan, *An American Life,* loc. 2033.

4. Ronald Reagan, *An American Life,* loc. 2061.

5. *Ibid.*

6. *Ibid.*

7. *Ibid.*

8. *Ibid.*

9. *Ibid.*

10. *Ibid.*

11. Cannon, *Governor Reagan,* 131; Ronald Reagan, "The Republican Party and the Conservative Movement," *National Review* (December 1, 1964).

12. Cannon, *Governor Reagan,*133.

13. Cannon, *Governor Reagan,*135.

14. Cannon, *Governor Reagan,*136.

15. Ronald Reagan, *An American Life,* loc. 2033.

16. Ronald Reagan, *An American Life,* locs. 2061–2091.

17. Ronald Reagan, *An American Life,* loc. 2091.

18. Ronald Reagan, *An American Life,* loc 2098.

19. *Ibid.*

20. Lou Cannon, "Ronald Reagan: Life Before the Presidency," UVA: Miller Center, https://millercenter.org/president/reagan/life-before-the-presidency.

21. Cannon, *Governor Reagan,* 592.

22. Cannon, *Governor Reagan,*175.

23. Lawrence E. Davies, "Reagan Submits Tax Increases; Rise Would Top $800 Million," *New York Times* (March 9, 1967), https://timesmachine.nytimes.com/timesmachine/1967/03/09/issue.html.

24. "Reagan Affirms Anti-Abortion Stand," *The New York Times* (February 8, 1976), https://timesmachine.nytimes.com/timesmachine/1967/08/29/issue.html. https://www.nytimes.com/1976/02/08/archives/reagan-affirms-antiabortion-stand.html.

25. "Reagan Aide Resigns, Raising Speculation on '68," *The New York Times* (August 29, 1967), https://www.nytimes.com/1967/08/29/archives/reagan-aide-resigns-raising-speculation-on-68-possibility-seen-that.html.

26. Kitty Kelley, *Nancy Reagan: The Unauthorized Biography* (New York: Simon & Schuster, 2011), 337.

27. Lou Cannon, "Reagan Staff: Old-Time California Aides to Play Important Roles," *Washington Post* (November 6, 1980), https://www.washingtonpost.com/archive/politics/1980/11/06/reagan-staff-old-time-california-aides-to-play-important-roles/746f2d60-aa9f-49b1-8a14-46591bb38d0c/.

28. Lou Cannon, "Why Nancy Reagan Didn't Want Ronald to Run for a Second Term," *Politico* (March 7, 2016), https://www.politico.com/magazine/story/2016/03/nancy-reagan-ronald-reagan-second-term-213704/.

29. Joan Didion, "Many Mansions" (1977), in Joan Didion, *We Tell Ourselves Stories in Order to Live: Collected Nonfiction* (New York: Knopf, 2006), 227–231.

30. "Reagan Foes Fail in Recall Effort," *The New York Times* (August 2, 1968), https://timesmachine.nytimes.com/timesmachine/1968/08/02/91234204.html?pageNumber=20.

31. Governor Reagan wanted the condemned man, Robert Lee Massie, to testify at the trial of his accomplice. The stay had unintended consequences when the death sentence was overturned in 1972 after the U.S. Supreme Court's decision in *Furman v. Georgia* (408 U.S. 238) invalidated all death penalty schemes in the nation. Resentenced to life imprisonment in 1972, Massie was paroled in 1978 and committed another murder the following year, having pleaded guilty. That plea was overturned, however, because his lawyer had not consented to it. Retried in 1989, Massie received his third death sentence, which was carried out in 2001.

32. *Governor's Gallery*, Ronald Reagan, Budgets, https://governors.library.ca.gov/33-Reagan.html.

33. "California Proposition 1, Taxing and Spending Powers Initiative (1973)," *BallotPedia*, https://ballotpedia.org/California_Proposition_1,_Taxing_and_Spending_Powers_Initiative_(1973).

34. Jackson K. Putnam, "Governor Reagan: A Reappraisal," *California History* (2006), 24–45.

Chapter 9

1. John Meroney, "Ron Reagan: Growing Up as the Son of a President—and a Movie Star," *Atlantic*, January 18, 2011.

2. Sarah Mervosh and Niraj Chokshi, "Reagan Called Africans 'Monkeys' in Call with Nixon, Tape Reveals," *The New York Times* (July 31, 2019), https://www.nytimes.com/2019/07/31/us/politics/

ronald-reagan-richard-nixon-racist. html.

3. *Ibid.*

4. Reagan, *An American Life,* locs. 5898–5899.

5. PBS, *Bill Moyers Journal,* Transcript, November 7, 2008, https://www.pbs.org/ moyers/journal/11072008/transcript3.html.

6. Robert L. Coate, "Reagan's Racism Seen Underneath Ambiguous Talk," *Los Angeles Sentinel* (November 9, 1967).

7. The reference to "jungles" is in Jeremy D. Mayer, "Reagan and Race: Prophet of Color Blindness, Baiter of the Backlash," in Kyle Longley et al., *Deconstructing Reagan: Conservative Mythology and America's Fortieth President* (Armonk, NE: M.E. Sharpe 2007), 76; the reference to "jungle" is in John Ehrenberg, *White Nationalism and the Republican Party, Toward Minority Rule in America* (New York: Routledge, 2022) p. 45.

8. Reagan quoted in Daniel S. Lucks, *Reconsidering Reagan: Racism, Republicans, and the Road to Trump* (Boston: Beacon Press, 2020), 11; Ronald Reagan, Taped announcement on candidacy for Governor, January 4, 1966, https://www. americanrhetoric.com/speeches/ ronaldreagancalgovcandidacy.htm.

9. Cannon, *Governor Reagan,* 142.

10. *Ibid.*

11. Jeremy D. Mayer, "Reagan and Race: Prophet of Color Blindness, Baiter of Backlash," in Kyle Longley et al., *Deconstructing Reagan: Conservative Mythology and America's Fortieth President* (Armonk, NE: M. E. Sharpe, 2007), 72–73.

12. Kiron K. Skinner et al., *Reagan: A Life in Letters* (New York: Free Press, 2003), 335.

13. Mayer, *Running on Race,* 165.

14. Mayer, "Reagan and Race," 75.

15. Mayer, *Running on Race,* 85.

16. Gillian Brockell, "She was stereotyped as 'the welfare queen.' The truth was more disturbing, a new book says," *Washington Post* (May 21, 2019), https://www. washingtonpost.com/history/2019/05/21/ she-was-stereotyped-welfare-queen-truth-was-more-disturbing-new-book-says/.

17. Frank Rich, "Ronald Reagan Was Once Donald Trump," *New York Magazine* (June 1, 2016), https://nymag.com/ intelligencer/2016/05/ronald-reagan-was-once-donald-trump.html.

18. Daniel S. Lucks, *Reconsidering Reagan: Racism, Republicans, and the Road to Trump* (Boston: Beacon Press, 2020), 121.

19. Jon Nordheimer, "Reagan Is Picking His Florida Spots," *The New York Times* (February 5, 1976), https://www.nytimes. com/1976/02/05/archives/reagan-is-picking-his-florida-spots.html.

20. Daniel S. Lucks, "The GOP can't escape Trump without letting go of Reagan," *The Washington Post* (February 22, 2021), https://www.washingtonpost.com/ outlook/2021/02/22/gop-cant-escape-trump-without-letting-go-reagan/.

21. Malcolm D. MacDougall, *We Almost Made It* (New York: Crown, 1977), 48; "Test of Governor Ronald Reagan's Nationwide Television Address, NBC," March 31, 1976 (Cited in Mayer, "Reagan on Race," 78); Mayer, *Running on Race,* 134–136.

22. Mayer, "Reagan on Race," 79.

23. Martin Schram and others, "Reagan Beats a Retreat on Klan Remark," *Washington Post* (September 3, 1980), https:// www.washingtonpost.com/archive/ politics/1980/09/03/reagan-beats-a-retreat-on-klan-remark/dcd581f5-435e-419f-9216-25d98dbcf859/.

24. Mayer, "Reagan and Race," 80.

25. Mayer, "Reagan and Race," 87.

26. Jonathan Mahler and Steve Eder, "'No Vacancies' for Blacks: How Donald Trump Got His Start, and Was First Accused of Bias," *New York Times* (August 27, 2016), https://www.nytimes.com/2016/08/28/ us/politics/donald-trump-housing-race. html. During Trump's presidential campaign, a 1927 *New York Times* story mentioning the arrest of Fred Trump at a KKK Rally was interpreted as proof of the senior Trump's membership in the Klan. The reporting, in fact, is inconclusive at best. See Kim LaCapria, "Was Donald Trump's Father Arrested at a KKK Rally?" *Snopes* (February 28, 2016), https://www.snopes.com/fact-check/donald-trump-father-kkk-1927/.

27. Jan Ransom, "Trump Will Not Apologize for Calling for Death Penalty Over Central Park Five," *New York Times* (June 18, 2019), https://www.nytimes.com/ 2019/06/18/nyregion/central-park-five-trump.html/.

28. Ransom, https://www.nytimes. com/2019/06/18/nyregion/central-park-five-trump.html/.

29. Stephen Collinson and Jeremy

Diamond, "Trump finally admits it: 'President Barack Obama was born in the United States,'" CNN Politics (September 16, 2016), https://www.cnn.com/2016/09/15/politics/donald-trump-obama-birther-united-states.

30. Michelle Ye Hee Lee, "Donald Trump's false comment connecting Mexican immigrants and crime," *Washington Post* (July 8, 2015), https://www.washingtonpost.com/news/fact-checker/wp/2015/07/08/donald-trumps-false-comments-connecting-mexican-immigrants-and-crime/.

31. Eugene Scott, "Trump's most insulting—and violent—language is often reserved for immigrants," *Washington Post* (October 2, 2019), https://www.washingtonpost.com/politics/2019/10/02/trumps-most-insulting-violent-language-is-often-reserved-immigrants/.

32. Victoria M. Massie, "Donald Trump's 'inner city' has nothing to do with where black people live," *Vox* (October 20, 2016), https://www.vox.com/identities/2016/9/28/13074046/trump-presidential-debate-inner-city.

Chapter 10

1. Fiscal Year 2021, Historic Tables, Budget of U.S. Government.

2. PolitiFact, "Ronald Reagan understood to make a deal he would propose both spending cuts and tax increases," Angie Drobnic Holan, April 4, 2012; Bloomberg, "The Mostly Forgotten Tax Increases of 1982–1993," Justin Fox, December 15, 2017; Tax Notes, February 21, 2011, "Reagan's Forgotten Tax Record," Bruce Bartlett.

3. Committee for a Responsible Federal Budget, Post-State of the Union Fact Check Roundup, February 2, 2018.

4. Gerald F. Seib, *We Should Have Seen It Coming*, 37.

5. David Weigel, "Pawlenty: Bush Tax Cuts 'Didn't Fully Serve Their Intended Purposes,'" *Slate*, June 12, 2011. Arthur Laffer, one of the godfathers of supply-side economics, wrote, "It is reasonable to conclude that each of the proposed 10 percent reductions in tax rates, would, in terms of overall tax revenues, be self-financing in less than two years" Arthur Laffer. "Government Exactions and Revenue Deficiencies." *Cato Journal* 1:1 (1981), 1–21.

6. "Recession Economics," *New York Review of Books*, Volume 29, Number 1 (4 February 1982); https://www.nybooks.com/articles/1982/02/04/recession-economics/?printpage=true.

7. Committee for a Responsible Federal Budget, "Tax Cuts Don't Pay for Themselves" (October 4, 2017), https://www.crfb.org/papers/tax-cuts-dont-pay-themselves.

8. Edward Cowan, "Reagan's 3-Year, 25% Cut in Tax Rate Voted by Wide Margins in the House and Senate," *New York Times* (July 30, 1981), https://www.nytimes.com/1981/07/30/business/reagan-s-3-year-25-cut-in-tax-rate-voted-by-wide-margins-in-the-house-and-senate.html.

9. Ronald Reagan, Remarks on Signing the Tax Reform Act of 1986 (October 22, 1986), The American Presidency Project, https://www.presidency.ucsb.edu/documents/remarks-signing-the-tax-reform-act-1986.

10. *Your World with Neil Cavuto*, April 27, 2010, https://archive.org/details/FOXNEWS_20101227_210000_Your_World_With_Neil_Cavuto.

11. Fox News Sunday, September 18, 2011, https://www.imdb.com/title/tt2059719/.

12. Rick Scott, Rescue America-11 Point Plan, https://rescueamerica.com/12-point-plan/. See also press release of Senator Rick Scott, September 15, 2021: "I will NOT let Florida taxpayers' foot the bill to bail out blue states from their own failed policies. We need to call this out for what it is: pure and unadulterated systemic socialism from Biden and the Democrats. I won't stand for it and will keep fighting every day to defeat the big government, high tax and debt-boosting plans of socialist liberals in Washington," https://www.rickscott.senate.gov/2021/9/sen-rick-scott-democrats-socialist-agenda-tax-increases-will-kill-the-american-dream.

13. Richard Fry, "The Pace of Boomer retirements has accelerated in the past year," Pew Research Center (November 9, 2020), https://www.pewresearch.org/fact-tank/2020/11/09/the-pace-of-boomer-retirements-has-accelerated-in-the-past-year/.

14. *Fortune* Staff, "The Shrinking of the Middle Class," *Fortune Magazine* (January 1, 2019), https://fortune.com/longform/shrinking-middle-class/.

15. Michael Grunwald, "Paul Ryan's Legacy of Red Ink," *Politico* (April 11, 2018), https://www.politico.com/magazine/tory/2018/04/11/paul-ryan-legacy-record-budget-red-ink/.

16. Ronald Reagan, Announcement for Presidential Candidacy, November 13, 1979, UVA/Miller Center, https://millercenter.org/the-presidency/presidential-speeches/november-13-1979-announcement-presidential-candidacy. A version of the announcement was provided on video, which played for the former actor's communication skills.

17. Ronald Reagan, Address before a joint session of Congress on the Program for Economic Recovery, February 18, 1981, https://www.presidency.ucsb.edu/documents/address-before-joint-session-the-congress-the-program-for-economic-recovery-0.

18. Ronald Reagan, State of the Union Address, February 6, 1985, https://www.reaganfoundation.org/ronald-reagan/reagan-quotes-speeches/state-of-the-union-3/.

19. Ronald Reagan, Inaugural Address, January 20, 1981, https://www.presidency.ucsb.edu/documents/inaugural-address-11.

20. Doyle McManus and Douglas Jehl, "The Pluses, Minuses: Reagan Era: What Will History Say." *Los Angeles Times* (August 21, 1988), https://www.latimes.com/archives/la-xpm-1988-08-21-mn-1150-story.html.

21. William Greider, "The Education of David Stockman," *The Atlantic* (December, 1981), https://www.theatlantic.com/magazine/archive/1981/12/the-education-of-david-stockman/305760/.

22. David Stockman, *The Triumph of Politics: Why the Reagan Revolution Failed* (New York: Harper & Row, 1985), 9.

23. Lou Cannon, *President Reagan: The Role of a Lifetime* (New York: Public Affairs, 2000), 7.

24. Joe Davidson, "Reagan's complicated legacy for federal workers," *Washington Post* (February 8, 2011), https://www.washingtonpost.com/local/despite-reagans-actions-government-workforce-grew-in-his-tenure/2011/02/07/ABuzkZF_story.html; Congressional Budget Office, "The Budget and Economic Outlook: 2018 to 2028" (April 9, 2018),https://www.cbo.gov/publication/53651; FRED, "Shares of gross domestic product: Government expenditures and gross investment: Federal," https://fred.stlouisfed.org/graph/?g=kakV.

25. Cannon, *President Reagan: The Role of a Lifetime*, 6. The national debt was nearly tripled to $2.684 trillion. The United States, once the world's great creditor nation had become a debtor under Reagan's watch. See also FRED, "Federal Debt Held by the Public," August 22, 2022, https://fred.stlouisfed.org/graph/?g=k977.

26. "The Democratic Fisc: The White House budget office offers a scorecard on Obamanomics," *Wall Street Journal* (July 26, 2010), https://www.wsj.com/articles/SB10001424052748703995104575389430430274968; U.S. Federal; Deficit as Percentage of GDP by Year, http://www.multpl.com/u-s-federal-deficit-percent/table.

27. Bill Fay, "Timeline of U.S. Federal Debt Since Independence Day 1776," Debt.Org (October 12, 2021), https://www.debt.org/faqs/united-states-federal-debt-timeline/.

28. Peter G. Peterson Foundation, "What Is the National Debt Costing Us?" https://www.pgpf.org/national-debt-clock#what-is-it-costing-us.

29. *Ibid.*

30. Bill Clinton, "The New Covenant: Responsibility and Rebuilding the American Community," Georgetown University, October 23, 1991, https://digital.tcl.sc.edu/digital/collection/p17173coll40/id/474.

31. Bill Clinton, State of the Union Address, January 23, 1996, https://clintonwhitehouse4.archives.gov/WH/New/other/sotu.html.

32. Thomas Piketty, *Capital in the Twenty-First Century* (Cambridge: Belknap Press of Harvard University Press, 2014), 650.

33. Thomas Piketty, *A Brief History of Equality* (Cambridge: Belknap Press of Harvard University Press, 2022), 135–137.

34. Trends in the Distribution of Family Wealth, 1989 to 2019, Congressional Budget Office, September, 2022; https://www.cbo.gov/system/files/2022-09/57598-family-wealth.pdf.

35. Juliana Menasce Horowitz, Ruth Iglelnik, and Rakesh Kochhar, "Views of economic inequality," Pew Research Center (January 9, 2020), https://www.

pewresearch.org/social-trends/2020/
01/09/views-of-economic-inequality/.

36. David Hope and Julian Limberg, "The Economic Consequences of
Major Tax Cuts for the Rich," *Socio-Economic Review*, 20:2 (April 2022), 539–
559. https://academic.oup.com/ser/
article/20/2/539/6500315.

37. Piketty, *Capital in the Twenty-First
Century*, 656.

38. Kathryn A. Edwards and Carter C.
Price, "A $2.5 Trillion Question: What If
Incomes Grew Like GDP Did?" Rand Corporation, the Rand Blog (October 6, 2020),
https://www.rand.org/blog/2020/10/a-25-
trillion-question-what-if-incomes-grew-
like-gdp.html. See also, "Tax Cuts Don't
Pay For Themselves," Committee for a
Responsible Federal Budget (October 4,
2017), https://www.crfb.org/papers/tax-
cuts-dont-pay-themselves.

39. *Ibid.*

40. Thomas Piketty, *Capital in the
Twenty-First Century*, 660.

Chapter 11

1. John F. Kennedy, Commencement
Address at Yale University (June 11, 1962),
https://www.jfklibrary.org/asset-viewer/
archives/JFKWHA/1962/JFKWHA-104/
JFKWHA-104.

2. Sen. Rand Paul interview with Sean
Hannity, Fox News, April 7, 2015, https://
finance.yahoo.com/news/rand-paul-
just-summed-2016-220013618.html?
guccounter=1&guce_referrer=
aHR0cHM6Ly93d3cuZZ29vZ2xl
LmNvbS8&guce_referrer_sig=-
AQAAAFxIscrTpJZN-ftwx2gc4IQVf0E
pnH3vPg3uzu5GnCm7WqyHR8rrZM
9liE0g73rwUWx8nxAkOxBP5ozIHdK
2vgJsOTQyoQEqqm8O3a-5MOGjvzX-
FxfgkTAZDQEUaMCToBxlOA6zhE_4P_
1qp30685btTLSHa4Av9ahxTIXOwvj.

3. Art Laffer interview on Fox Business, *Cavuto: Coast to Coast* (September
21, 2017).

4. Kate Davidson, "Treasury Secretary
Steven Mnuchin: GOP Tax Plan Would
More Than Offset Its Cost," *Wall Street
Journal* (September 28, 2017), https://
www.wsj.com/articles/treasury-secretary-
steven-mnuchin-gop-tax-plan-would-
more-than-offset-its-cost-1506626980.

5. Statements of Paul Ryan on the floor
of the House of Representatives, December 19, 2017, https://www.congress.gov/
congressional-record/volume-163/issue-
207/senate-section/article/S8088-2.

6. *Ibid.*

7. Tweet of Donald J. Trump, October
2, 2016, https://www.presidency.ucsb.edu/
documents/tweets-october-2-2016.

8. Federal Reserve Economic Data—All
Employees Total Non-Farm, https://fred.
stlouisfed.org/series/PAYEMS.

9. *Ibid.*

10. Bruce Bartlett, "The 1981 Tax Cut
After 30 Years: What Happened to Revenues?" *Tax Notes* (August 8, 2011), https://
papers.ssrn.com/sol3/papers.cfm?
abstract_id=1906654.

11. *Ibid.*

12. Department of the Treasury, "Revenue Effects of Major Tax Bills, OTA
Working Paper 81" (September 2006),
chrome-extension://efaidnbmnnnibpcajp-
cglclefindmkaj/https://home.treasury.gov/
system/files/131/WP-81.pdf.

13. Glenn Kessler, "Rand Paul's claim
that Reagan's tax cuts produced 'more revenue' and 'tens of millions of jobs,'" *Washington Post* (April 10, 2015), https://www.
washingtonpost.com/news/fact-checker/
wp/2015/04/10/rand-pauls-claim-that-
reagans-tax-cuts-produced-more-
revenue-and-tens-of-millions-of-jobs/.

14. Bartlett, "The 1981 Tax Cut After 30
Years: What Happened to Revenues?"

15. Bruce Bartlett, "I helped create the
GOP tax myth. Trump is wrong: Tax Cuts
don't equal growth," *Washington Post*
(September 28, 2017), https://www.wash
ingtonpost.com/news/posteverything/
wp/2017/09/28/i-helped-create-the-gop-
tax-myth-trump-is-wrong-tax-cuts-dont-
equal-growth/.

16. Joel Slemrod, "Income Creation or
Income Shifting? Behavioral Responses to
the Tax Reform Act of 1986," *American Economics Review* 85, no. 2 (May 1995), 175–
180, https://www.jstor.org/stable/2117914.

17. Tax Rates and Economic Growth,
Congressional Research Service, Janu-
ary 2, 2014; https://sgp.fas.org/crs/misc/
R42111.pdf.

18. George H. W. Bush, Speech at the
Republican National Convention, New
Orleans (August 18, 1988), https://www.
youtube.com/watch?v=AdVSqSNHhVo.

19. Pat Buchanan: "Is Trump the heir to Reagan?" *Sioux City Journal* (October 25, 2017), https://buchanan.org/blog/knives-come-christie-5983.

20. Gerald F. Seib, *We Should Have Seen It Coming: From Reagan to Trump—A Front-Row Seat to a Political Revolution* (New York: Random House, 2021), 95.

21. Remarks by George W. Bush in Tax Cut Bill Signing Ceremony (June 7, 2001), https://georgewbush-whitehouse.archives.gov/news/releases/2001/06/20010607.html.

22. The White House, "Table 14.3—Total Government Expenditures as Percentages of GDP: 1948–2021," https://www.whitehouse.gov/omb/budget/historical-tables/.

23. FRED, "All Employees, Total Nonfarm (PAYEMS)," https://fred.stlouisfed.org/series/PAYEMS.

24. WSJ Staff, "Bush on Jobs: The Worst Track Record on Record," *Wall Street Journal* (January 9, 2009), https://www.wsj.com/articles/BL-REB-2534; FRED, https://fred.stlouisfed.org; FRED, "All Employees, Total Nonfarm (PAYEMS), https://fred.stlouisfed.org/series/PAYEMS.

25. Congressional Budget Office, "The Budget and Economic Outlook: Fiscal Years 2009 to 2019," https://www.cbo.gov/publication/41753.

26. Donald J. Trump on Tax Reform, St. Charles, Missouri (November 29, 2017), https://factba.se/transcript/donald-trump-speech-tax-reform-st-charles-missouri-november-29-2017.

27. Tax Policy Center, "Distributional Analysis of the Tax Cuts and Jobs Act As Passed by the Senate Finance Committee" (November 20, 2017), https://www.taxpolicycenter.org/publications/distributional-analysis-tax-cuts-and-jobs-act-passed-senate-finance-committee.

28. *The Tax Policy Center's Briefing Book,* https://www.taxpolicycenter.org/briefing-book/how-did-tcja-affect-federal-budget-outlook.

29. Allan Sloan and Cezary Podkul, "Trump's most enduring legacy could be the historic rise in national debt," *Washington Post* (January 14, 2001), https://www.washingtonpost.com/business/2021/01/14/trump-legacy-national-debt-increasee/.

30. Bob Woodward and Robert Costa, "Transcript: Donald Trump interview with Bob Woodward and Robert Costa,

Washington Post (April 2, 2016), https://www.washingtonpost.com/news/post-politics/wp/2016/04/02/transcript-donald-trump-interview-with-bob-woodward-and-robert-costa/.

31. Justin Fox, "GDP Growth Under Trump Was the Worst Since Hoover," *Bloomberg* (August 2, 2021), https://www.bloomberg.com/opinion/articles/2021-08-02/trump-s-gdp-growth-was-the-worst-since-the-great-depression.

32. Pat Garofalo, "Hoisted: Flashback: In 1993, GOP Warned That Clinton's Tax Plan Would 'Kill Jobs,' 'Kill The Current Recovery,'" Grasping Reality by Brad DeLong, https://www.bradford-delong.com/2017/09/flashback-in-1993-gop-warned-that-clintons-tax-plan-would-kill-jobs-kill-the-current-recovery-thinkprog.html.

33. Congressional Record, 1993, pg. H1355, https://www.govinfo.gov/app/collection/crecb/_crecb/Volume%20139%20(1993).

34. Congressional Record, 1993, pg. H2949, https://www.govinfo.gov/app/collection/crecb/_crecb/Volume%20139%20(1993).

35. Bruce Bartlett, "I helped create the GOP tax myth. Trump is wrong: Tax Cuts don't equal growth," https://www.washingtonpost.com/news/post-everything/wp/2017/09/28/i-helped-create-the-gop-tax-myth-trump-is-wrong-tax-cuts-dont-equal-growth/.

36. Chuck Jones, "Obama had more stock market records than Trump," *Forbes Magazine* (January 14, 2020), forbes.com/sites/chuckjones/2020/01/14/Obama had more stock market records than trump.

37. FRED, FRED Graph, https://fred.stlouisfed.org/graph/?graph_id=272846&rn=4677; Meg Kelly, "The 'Trump economy' vs. the 'Obama economy,'" *Washington Post* (September 18, 2018), phttps://www.washingtonpost.com/politics/2018/09/18/trump-economy-versus-obama-economy.

38. Alan S. Blinder and Mark W. Watson, "Presidents and the U.S. Economy: An Economic Exploration, *American Economic Review*, 2016, 106(4), 1015–1045, chrome-extension://efaidnbmnnnibpca-jpcglclefindmkaj/https://www.princeton.edu/~mwatson/papers/Presidents_AER_2016.pdf.

39. John Maggs, "Corporate profits' big climb," *Politico* (October 28, 2010), https://www.politico.com/story/2010/10/corporate-profits-big-climb-044268.

40. Yun Li, "This is now the longest U.S. economic expansion in history," CNBC (July 2, 2019), https://www.cnbc.com/2019/07/02/this-is-now-the-longest-us-economic-expansion-in-history.html.

41. Elena Holodny, "The top 0.1% of American households hold the same amount of wealth as the bottom 90%, *Business Insider* (October 23, 2017), https://www.businessinsider.com/americas-top-01-households-hold-same-amount-of-wealth-as-bottom-90-2017-10.

42. The Distribution of Household Income, 2019, Congressional Budget Office, November, 2022. https://www.cbo.gov/publication/58781#:~:text=7%20Before%20means%2Dtested%20transfers,%2423%2C200%20per%20household%2C%20on%20average.

43. Piketty, *Capital in the Twenty-First Century*, 367.

44. *Ibid.*, 368.

45. *Ibid.*, 369.

46. *Ibid.*, 371.

47. *Ibid.*, 373.

48. *Ibid.*, 373.

49. *Ibid.*, 373.

50. *Ibid.*, 373.

51. Alan Sherter, "Nearly 40% of Americans can't cover a surprise $400 expense," *CBS NEWS Money Watch* (May 23, 2019), https://www.cbsnews.com/news/nearly-40-of-americans-cant-cover-a-surprise-400-expense/.

52. Piketty, *Capital in the Twenty-First Century*, 648.

53. *Ibid.*, 655.

54. *Ibid.*, 662.

55. "Constitutional Convention. Remarks on the Term of Office for Members of the Second Branch of the Legislature, [26 June 1787]," Founders Online, National Archives, https://founders.archives.gov/documents/Hamilton/01-04-02-0108. (Original source: *The Papers of Alexander Hamilton*, vol. 4, January 1787–May 1788, ed. Harold C. Syrett [New York: Columbia University Press, 1962], 218–220.)

56. John F. Kennedy, Inaugural Address (January 20, 1961), https://www.archives.gov/milestone-documents/president-john-f-kennedys-inaugural-address#:~:text=On%20January%2020%2C%201961%2C%20President,survival%20and%20success%20of%20liberty.%22.

57. Jean-Jacques Rousseau, *The Essential Rousseau: The Social Contract, Discourse on the Origin of Inequality, Discourse on the Arts and Sciences, The Creed of a Savoyard Priest* (New York: New American Library, 1974).

Chapter 12

1. Ronald Reagan, "Republican National Convention Address" (August 19, 1976), https://www.americanrhetoric.com/speeches/ronaldreagan1976rnc.htm.

2. *Ibid.*

3. Associated Press, "Quotations: The Words of Gerald Ford," *The New York Times* (December 27, 2006), https://www.nytimes.com/2006/12/27/washington/28fordquotescnd.html.

4. Ronald Reagan, "Republican National Convention Address" (August 19, 1976), https://www.americanrhetoric.com/speeches/ronaldreagan1976rnc.htm.

5. *Ibid.*

6. *Ibid.*

7. Ronald Reagan, "Looking Out a Window," January 27, 1978, in Kiron K. Skinner, Annelise Anderson, and Martin Anderson, *Reagan, in His Own Hand* (New York: Touchstone, 2001), 18–19.

8. *Ibid.*

9. "Reagan-Carter Oct. 28, 1980 Debate—'There You Go Again,'" YouTube (September 25, 2012), https://www.youtube.com/watch?v=qN7gDRjTNf4; "Ronald Reagan on 'There You Go Again'; Other Notable Debate Moments," *PBS News Hour*, YouTube (Feb 3, 2011), https://www.youtube.com/watch?v=T43EzCUtSwQ.

10. Ronald Reagan, "Ronald Reagan Speaks Out against Socialized Medicine (1961)," *American Rhetoric Online Speech Bank*, https://www.americanrhetoric.com/speeches/ronaldreagansocializedmedicine.htm.

11. Lynn Rosellini, "Glittering Festivities Usher in Reagan Era," *The New York Times* (January 21, 1981), https://www.nytimes.com/1981/01/21/us/glittering-festivities-usher-in-reagan-era.html.

12. Principal sources for the Hinckley assassination attempt include Joseph

B. Treaster, "A Life That Started Out with Much Promise Took Reclusive and Hostile Path," *The New York Times* (April 1, 1981), https://www.nytimes.com/1981/04/01/us/a-life-that-started-out-with-much-promise-took-reclusive-and-hostile-path.html and Del Quentin Wilber, *Rawhide Down: The Near Assassination of Ronald Reagan* (New York: Henry Holt, 2011).

13. Reagan, *An American Life*, locs. 3796-3801.

14. Barry Sussman, "Shooting Gives Reagan Boost in Popularity," *Washington Post* (April 2, 1981), https://www.washingtonpost.com/archive/politics/1981/04/02/shooting-gives-reagan-boost-in-popularity/9515e340-f295-42e7-89c4-c96ed0ab7a44/.

15. Daniel Funke, "Here's how the deficit performed under Republican and Democratic presidents, from Reagan to Trump," *PolitiFact* (July 29, 2019), https://www.politifact.com/factchecks/2019/jul/29/tweets/republican-presidents-democrats-contribute-deficit/; Brian Riedl, "Trump's Fiscal Legacy: A Comprehensive Overview of Spending, Taxes, and Deficits," *Manhattan Institute* (May 12, 2022), https://www.manhattan-institute.org/trumps-fiscal-legacy.

16. Andrew Zhang, "Addressing NRA in Houston, Donald Trump rejects gun regulations and calls for school safety overhaul," *The Texas Tribune* (May 27, 2022), https://www.texastribune.org/2022/05/27/donald-trump-nra-houston/.

Chapter 13

1. Reagan, *An American Life: An Enhanced eBook with CBS Video: The Autobiography,* Kindle Ed., loc. 4074.

2. SAG-AFTRA, "About: Our History," https://www.sagaftra.org/about/our-history.

3. Reagan, *An American Life: An Enhanced eBook with CBS Video: The Autobiography,* Kindle Ed., loc. 1837–1844.

4. Steven E. Dumin, "The Professional Air Traffic Controllers Strike: A Retrospective Analysis," Embry-Riddle Aeronautical University, order no. EP31097 (1994).

5. This paragraph and those that follow are based on these sources: Michael Barera, "The 1981 PATCO Strike," UTA Libraries Blog (September 2, 2021), https://libraries.uta.edu/news-events/blog/1981-patco-strike; Jon Schwarz, "The Murder of the U.S. Middle Class Began 40 Years Ago This Week," *The Intercept* (August 6, 2021), https://theintercept.com/2021/08/06/middle-class-reagan-patco-strike/.

6. "Ronald Reagan's ultimatum to striking air traffic controllers" (August 3, 1981), Wikisource, https://en.wikisource.org/wiki/Ronald_Reagan%27s_ultimatum_to_striking_air_traffic_controllers.

7. "Who's Minding the Store?" *New York Times* (April 1, 1981), https://www.nytimes.com/1981/04/01/opinion/who-s-minding-the-store.html.

8. Ronald Reagan's ultimatum to striking air traffic controllers" (August 3, 1981), Wikisource, https://en.wikisource.org/wiki/Ronald_Reagan%27s_ultimatum_to_striking_air_traffic_controllers.

9. Schwarz, "The Murder of the U.S. Middle Class Began 40 Years Ago This Week," https://theintercept.com/2021/08/06/middle-class-reagan-patco-strike/.

10. *Ibid.*

11. Barera, "The 1981 PATCO Strike," https://libraries.uta.edu/news-events/blog/1981-patco-strike.

12. *Ibid.*

13. Ben Stein, "In Class Warfare, Guess Which Class Is Winning," *New York Times* (November 26, 2006), https://www.nytimes.com/2006/11/26/business/yourmoney/26every.html/.

14. Sharon Block, "The Myth of a Pro-Union Trump," *Democracy: A Journal of Ideas* (May 24, 2017), https://democracyjournal.org/briefing-book/the-myth-of-a-pro-union-trump/.

15. *Ibid.*

16. Celine McNicholas and Margaret Poydock, "The Trump administration's attacks on workplace union voting rights forewarned of the broader threats to voting rights in the upcoming election," *Economic Policy Institute Report* (October 21, 2020), https://www.epi.org/publication/the-trump-administrations-attacks-on-workplace-union-voting-rights-forewarned-of-the-broader-threats-to-voting-rights-in-the-upcoming-election/.

17. CWA, "Trump's Anti-Worker Record," https://cwa-union.org/trumps-anti-worker-record.

18. NFFE, "President Trump's Union Busting Executive Orders: What You Need

to Know," *NFFE News*, https://nffe.org/nffe_ news/president-trumps-union-busting-executive-orders-what-you-need-to-know/.

19. Holly Otterbein and Megan Cassella, "Rank-and-file union members snub Biden for Trump," *Politico* (September 22, 2020), https://www.politico.com/news/2020/09/22/donald-trump-union-support-snub-joe-biden-418329.

20. Ian Kulgren and Jim Rowley, "Union Workers Weren't a Lock for Biden. Here's Why That Matters," *Bloomberg Law* (November 10, 2020), https://news.bloomberglaw.com/daily-labor-report/union-workers-werent-a-lock-for-biden-heres-why-that-matters.

Chapter 14

1. Revenue Effects of Major Tax Bills, United Stated Depart of Treasury Working Paper; https://home.treasury.gov/system/files/131/WP-81.pdf.

2. Chye-Ching Huang, "Why Uniform, Across-the-Board Cuts in Tax Rates Disproportionately Benefit Those with the Highest Incomes (June 8, 2012), https://www.cbpp.org/research/why-uniform-across-the-board-cuts-in-tax-rates-disproportionately-benefit-those-with-the.

3. David Stockman, *The Triumph of Politics: Why the Reagan Revolution Failed* (New York: Harper & Row, 1985) pg. 174.

4. *Ibid.*, pg. 235.

5. Ronald Reagan, *Where's the Rest of Me?* 245.

6. John W. Sloan, *Deconstructing Reagan, The Economic Costs of the Reagan Mythology* (New York: Routledge, 2007), 52.

7. *Ibid.*

8. David A. Stockman, *The Triumph of Politics, Why the Reagan Revolution Failed* (New York: Harper & Row, 1985), 380.

9. *Ibid.*

10. Peter R. Orszag and William G. Gale, "Bush's Tax-Cut Plan Slashes Growth," Brookings (May 9, 2003), https://www.brookings.edu/opinions/bushs-tax-cut-plan-slashes-growth; Martin Feldstein, "Supply Side Economics: Old Truths and New Claims," National Bureau of Economic Research NBER Working Paper Series (January 1986), https://www.nber.org/papers/w1792.pdf.

11. Paul Krugman, "The Tax-Cut Zombies," *New York Times* (December 23, 2005), https://www.nytimes.com/2005/12/23/opinion/the-taxcut-zombies.html.

12. George W. Bush, "Remarks Following a Cabinet Meeting and an Exchange from Reporters," American Presidency Project, Nov. 13, 2002.

13. George W. Bush, "The President's News Conference," American Presidency Project, September 20, 2007, https://www.presidency.ucsb.edu/documents/the-presidents-news-conference-1135.

14. George W. Bush, "Remarks to the Business and Industry Association of New Hampshire in Manchester, New Hampshire," American Presidency Project, February 8, 2006, https://www.govinfo.gov/app/details/PPP-2006-book1/PPP-2006-book1-doc-pg200.

15. Bruce Bartlett, "How Supply-Side Economics Trickled Down," *The New York Times* (April 6, 2007), https://www.nytimes.com/2007/04/06/opinion/06bartlett.html.

16. John F. Kennedy, Commencement Address at Yale University, June 11, 1962, https://www.jfklibrary.org/archives/other-resources/john-f-kennedy-speeches/yale-university-19620611.

17. C-Span, Presidential Historians Survey 2021, https://www.c-span.org/presidentsurvey2021.

18. Cannon, *President Reagan: The Role of a Lifetime*, 23.

19. *Ibid.*

20. Ronald Reagan, Inaugural Address, January 20, 1981, https://www.reaganlibrary.gov/archives/speech/inaugural-address-1981.

21. Carl Hulse, "The 40th President: The Democrats; How Reagan Forced Foes to Reinvent Party," *The New York Times* (June 10, 2004), https://www.nytimes.com/2004/06/10/us/the-40th-president-the-democrats-how-reagan-forced-foes-to-reinvent-party.html.

22. Peter Behr, "Wave of Mergers, Takeovers Is Part of the Reagan Legacy," *Washington Post* (October 30, 1988), https://www.washingtonpost.com/archive/business/1988/10/30/wave-of-mergers-takeovers-is-a-part-of-reagan-legacy/e90598c2-628d-40fe-b9c6-a621e298671d/.

23. David Gergen, "Ronald Reagan's Most Important Legacy," *U.S. News & World Report* (January 9, 1989).

24. Mario Cuomo, 1984 Democratic Convention Keynote Address (July 16, 1984), https://www.c-span.org/video/?323534-1/mario-cuomo-1984-democratic-national-convention-keynote-speech.

25. *Ibid.*

26. *Ibid.*

27. *Ibid.*

28. https://www.nytimes.com/2016/07/28/nyregion/a-torrent-of-praise-for-mario-cuomos-1984-democratic-convention-speech.html.

29. Jesse McKinley, "A Torrent of Praise for Mario Cuomo's 1984 Democratic Convention Speech," *The New York Times* (July 27, 2016), https://slate.com/news-and-politics/2021/10/jimmy-carter-energy-crisis-malaise-speech-biden-supply-chain.html.

30. Bret Schulte, "Ronald Reagan v. Jimmy Carter: 'Are You Better Off Than You Were Four Years Ago?'" *U.S. News & World Report* (January 17, 2008), https://www.usnews.com/news/articles/2008/01/17/the-actor-and-the-detail-man.

31. Lance Morrow, "Yankee Doodle Magic" *Time* (July 7, 1986), https://content.time.com/time/magazine/article/0,9171,961668,00.html.

32. *Ibid.*

33. Jeff Greenberg, ed., *Handbook of Experimental Existential Psychology* (New York: The Guilford Press, 2004), Chapter 13, pp. 2016 and 2013.

34. Kevin Phillips, "Bubble and Bail," *The American Prospect* (April 18, 2008), https://prospect.org/features/bubble-bail/.

35. *Ibid.*

36. David Hoffman, "Confidence in Reagan on Deficit Declines; Poll Find Greater Trust in Congressional Democrats to handle Red-Ink Problem," *Washington Post* (July 2, 1987), https://www.washingtonpost.com/archive/politics/1987/07/02/confidence-in-reagan-on-deficit-declines/97abcd2d-4c66-4694-8009-87c1405eb261/.

37. Walter Isaacson, "After the Fall," *Time* (November 2, 1987), https://content.time.com/time/magazine/article/0,9171,965864,00.html.

38. *Ibid.*

39. Anthony Lewis, "Abroad at Home; The Cost of Reagan," *The New York Times* (September 7, 1989), https://www.nytimes.com/1989/09/07/opinion/abroad-at-home-the-cost-of-reagan.html.

40. Americans For Tax Reform, "About the Ronald Reagan Legacy Project" (June 18, 2010), https://www.atr.org/ronald-reagan-legacy-project-a4499/.

41. Patti Domm, "When Volcker ruled the Fed, 'people thought they'd never buy a home again,'" CNBC (December 9, 2019), https://www.cnbc.com/2019/12/09/when-volcker-ruled-fed-people-thought-theyd-never-buy-a-home-again.html.

42. *Compañía General de Tabacos de Filipinas v. Collector of Internal Revenue* (Decided November 21, 1927), LII Legal Information Institute, https://www.law.cornell.edu/supremecourt/text/275/87.

43. C. G. Jung, *The Collected Works,* Sir Herbert Read, ed. (East Sussex, UK: Routledge & Kegan Paul, 1953–1991), paragraph 564, p. 8096, https://books.google.com/books?id=9eY4CQAAQBAJ&pg=PA8096&lpg=PA8096&dq=Man+positively+needs+general+ideas+and+convictions+that+will+give+a+meaning+to+his+life+and+enable+him+to+find+his+place+in+the+universe&source=bl&ots=7we24DWSP4&sig=ACfU3U0muwoZorL3nK0GMNY0yz7d8_rpGA&hl=en&sa=X&ved=2ahUKEwjv1MPa5s77AhWamIQIHd99DBkQ6AF6BAgDEAM#v=onepage&q=Man%20positively%20needs%20general%20ideas%20and%20convictions%20that%20will%20give%20a%20meaning%20to%20his%20life%20and%20enable%20him%20to%20find%20his%20place%20in%20the%20universe&f=false.

44. John F. Kennedy, Address at Rice University on the Nation's Space Effort (September 12, 1962), https://www.jfklibrary.org/learn/about-jfk/historic-speeches/address-at-rice-university-on-the-nations-space-effort.

45. Andrew J. Bacevich, *The Limits of Power* (New York: Metropolitan Books, 2008), 173.

46. Ronald Reagan, Announcement for Presidential Candidacy, 1979, https://www.reaganlibrary.gov/archives/speech/ronald-reagans-announcement-presidential-candidacy-1979.

47. Associated Press, "White House Will Not Replace Solar Water-Heating System," *The New York Times* (August 24, 1986), https://www.nytimes.com/1986/08/24/us/white-house-will-not-replace-solar-water-heating-system.html; Special to the *New York Times,* "Reagan Proposals

Detail Further Trims in Budget," *The New York Times* (March 11, 1981), https://www.nytimes.com/1981/03/11/us/reagan-proposals-detail-further-trims-in-budget.html.

48. Will Bunch, *Tear Down This Myth* (New York: Free Press, 2009), 224.

49. *Ibid.*, 225.

50. Robert Pastor, "Column: Is Obama like Carter as Romney Says?" *USA Today* (November 1, 2012), https://www.usatoday.com/story/opinion/2012/11/01/obama-romney-carter-presidential-election/1674099/.

51. Tweet of Jim Jordan, May 11, 2021.

52. Tweet of Lindsey Graham, November 11, 2021.

53. Jonathan Alter, "Joe Biden is no Jimmy Carter. He should wish he was," *Washington Post* (January 14, 2022), https://www.washingtonpost.com/outlook/2022/01/14/jimmy-carter-biden-comparisons/.

54. Joel Mathis, "Republicans really, really want Biden to be the new Jimmy Carter," *YahooNews* (August 30, 2021), https://news.yahoo.com/republicans-really-really-want-biden-091858717.html.

55. Jory Heckman, "House GOP leaders vow to undo $80B to rebuild IRS if party regains majority," Federal News Network (September 23, 2022), https://federalnewsnetwork.com/budget/2022/09/house-gop-leaders-vow-to-undo-80b-to-rebuild-irs-if-party-regains-majority/.

56. David Lawder, "The new IRS employees: An 'army' or harmless programmers?" Reuters (August 19, 2022), https://www.reuters.com/world/us/republicans-call-it-an-army-irs-hires-will-replace-retirees-do-it-says-treasury-2022-08-19/.

57. Paul Krugman, "Why Zombie Reaganomics Still Rules the G.O.P.," *The New York Times* (September 26, 2022), https://www.nytimes.com/2022/09/26/opinion/gop-economic-policy.html/.

58. "What is the national debt?" FiscalData.Treasury.gov, https://fiscaldata.treasury.gov/americas-finance-guide/national-debt/.

59. Congressional Budget Office, "The 2021 Long-Term Budget Outlook," https://www.cbo.gov/publication/57038#_idTextAnchor001.

60. John W. Sloan, "The Economic Costs of the Reagan Mythology," in *Deconstructing Reagan* (Armonk, NY: M. E. Sharpe, 2007), 67–68.

61. *Ibid.*, 69.

62. *Ibid.*, 69.

Chapter 15

1. Joshua Geltzer, "Trump Loved 'His Generals'—Until He Got to Know Them," *Just Security* (January 2, 2020), https://www.justsecurity.org/67884/trump-loved-his-generals-until-he-got-to-know-them/. The book under review was Peter Bergen's *Trump and His Generals: The Cost of Chaos* (New York: Penguin Press, 2019).

2. *Ibid.*

3. Polio was and remains the consensus diagnosis; however, a 2003 study published in *Journal of Medical Biography* (November 1) argues that his paralytic affliction was more likely Guillain-Barré syndrome. Mary Beckman, "Did FDR Have Guillain-Barré?" *Science* (October 31, 2003), https://www.science.org/content/article/did-fdr-have-guillain-barr.

4. Julian Borger, "LBJ's medal for valour 'was sham,'" *The Guardian* (July 6, 2001), https://www.theguardian.com/world/2001/jul/06/internationaleducationnews.humanities.

5. Remarkably, young Bush's rescue is recorded on film: The Bush Library, "George Bush Rescued at Sea by the USS Finback—02 June 1992," YouTube, https://www.google.com/search?q=rescue+of+George+H.+W.+Bush+by+Finback&rlz=1C1CHZN_enUS1015US1015&oq=rescue+of+George+H.+W.+Bush+by+Finback&aqs=chrome..69i57j33i16012.12768j0j4&sourceid=chrome&ie=UTF-8.

6. Gary S. Smith, "The Faith of George HW Bush," *The Christian Post* (June 26, 2017), https://www.christianpost.com/news/the-faith-of-george-h-w-bush.html.

7. Mary L. Trump, *Too Much and Never Enough: How My Family Created the World's Most Dangerous Man* (New York: Simon & Schuster, 2020), 12–13.

8. Mia Jankowicz, "Trump resisted requests to return stash of documents at Mar-a-Lago, saying 'it's not theirs, it's mine,' NYT reports," *Business Insider* (August 17, 2022), https://www.businessinsider.

com/trump-on-documents-sought-nara-not-theirs-mine-nyt-2022-8.

9. Associated Press, "Trump pushes aside Montenegro leader—who calls it natural," *AP News* (May 25, 2017), https://apnews.com/article/donald-trump-us-news-ap-top-news-international-news-dusko-markovic-60dfbc344f7f482d95af53531aec6841. The video may be found on YouTube, "Trump pushes past Montenegro's PM—BBC News," https://www.youtube.com/watch?v=vIdrTSjzGKY. Markovic himself seemed unoffended: ""It didn't really register," he told reporters. "I just saw reactions about it on social networks. It is simply a harmless situation."

10. Carter-Reagan Debate, October 28, 1980, https://millercenter.org/the-presidency/presidential-speeches/october-28-1980-debate-ronald-reagan.

11. Dan Evon, "Did Albert Einstein Say World War IV Will Be Fought 'With Sticks and Stones'?" *Snopes* (April 16, 2018), https://www.snopes.com/fact-check/einstein-world-war-iv-sticks-stones/.

12. Winston Churchill, "Sinews of Peace, 1946," https://www.national churchillmuseum.org/sinews-of-peace-iron-curtain-speech.html.

13. X (George F. Kennan), "The Sources of Soviet Conduct," *Foreign Affairs* (July 1947), https://www.foreignaffairs.com/articles/russian-federation/1947-07-01/sources-soviet-conduct.

14. David Hoffman, "Reagan Calls SALT II Dead," *Washington Post* (June 13, 1986), https://www.washingtonpost.com/archive/politics/1986/06/13/reagan-calls-salt-ii-dead/b0f19d98-7d94-453f-8cb0-4cecd2f493b9/.

15. Ronald Reagan, "Evil Empire Speech" (March 8, 1982), https://voicesof democracy.umd.edu/reagan-evil-empire-speech-text/.

16. Ronald Reagan, "Address to the Nation on Defense and National Security" (March 23, 1983), https://www.reagan library.gov/archives/speech/address-nation-defense-and-national-security.

17. C-SPAN, "President Dwight Eisenhower Farewell Address," https://www.c-span.org/video/?15026-1/president-dwight-eisenhower-farewell-address.

18. James R. Anderson, "Bankrupting America: The Impact of President Reagan's Military Budget," *International Journal of Health Services* 11, no. 4 (1981), 623–629, https://www.jstor.org/stable/45130983.

19. Alan Axelrod, *Full Faith and Credit: The National Debt, Taxes, Spending, and the Bankrupting of America* (New York: Abbeville Press, 2016), 126.

20. Danielle Diaz, "Trump suggests U.S. will have military parade on July," CNN (September 19, 2017), https://www.cnn.com/2017/09/19/politics/donald-trump-emmannuel-macron-white-house-parade-bastille-day/index.html; Tina Nguyen, "Trump Channels Inner Kim Jong Un, Orders Giant Military Parade," *Vanity Fair* (February 7, 2018), https://www.vanityfair.com/news/2018/02/trump-wants-military-parade.

21. Adam Taylor, "Trump's July 4 military parade is a celebration of himself," *The Washington Post* (July 4, 2019), https://www.washingtonpost.com/world/2019/07/04/trumps-july-military-parade-is-celebration-himself/; Ellen Knickmeyer, "Rough total for Trump's July Fourth extravaganza: $5.5M." AP News (July 11, 2019).

22. Melanie Zanona, "Trump on North Korea missile threat: 'It won't happen,'" *The Hill* (January 2, 2017), https://thehill.com/homenews/administration/312428-trump-on-north-korea-missile-threat-it-wont-happen.

23. NBC News, "Lavrov Derides Trump Kim 'Kindergarten Fight,'" NBC News (September 22, 2017), https://www.nbc news.com/video/lavrov-derides-kindergarten-fight-between-trump-and-kim-1052924995934.

24. Max Greenwood, "Trump: I have a 'much bigger' button than Kim Jong Un," *The Hill* (January 2, 2022), https://thehill.com/homenews/administration/367149-trump-i-have-a-much-bigger-button-than-kim-jong-un/.

25. https://www.macrotrends.net/countries/USA/united-states/military-spending-defense-budget.

26. CBS News, *Face the Nation*, https://www.cbsnews.com/video/trump-u-s-generals-dont-know-much-about-isis/.

27. Jeffrey Goldberg, "Trump: American Who Died in War 'Losers' and 'Suckers,'" *The Atlantic* (September 3, 2020), https://www.theatlantic.com/politics/archive/2020/09/trump-americans-who-died-at-war-are-losers-and-suckers/615997/.

28. Chris Cillizza, "The awful reality

that Donald Trump's repeated attacks on John McCain prove," CNN Politics (March 19, 2019), https://www.cnn.com/2019/03/19/politics/donald-trump-john-mccain-dead.

29. *Wag the Dog* was a 1997 movie in which a fabricated war is used to distract attention from a presidential scandal. Ever since, *wag the dog* has been used to describe a political move used to divert attention from something of greater importance to something of lesser importance.

30. "Teflon president," *Taegan Goddard's Political Dictionary,* https://politicaldictionary.com/words/teflon-president/.

31. Ronald Reagan, "March 4, 1987: Address to the Nation on Iran-Contra," Miller Center, https://millercenter.org/the-presidency/presidential-speeches/march-4-1987-address-nation-iran-contra.

32. E. J. Dionne Jr., "Trump's '12 more years' shout shows what he has in common with autocrats," *Washington Post* (August 24, 2020), https://www.washingtonpost.com/opinions/2020/08/24/republicans-are-one-man-party/.

Chapter 16

1. Quoted by Joan Alker, "Children in the Dawn and Shadows of Life Should Be a Top Priority in Budget Talks," *Georgetown University Health Policy Institute* (January 14, 2011), https://ccf.georgetown.edu/2011/07/14/children_in_the_dawn_and_shadows_of_life_should_be_a_top_priority_in_budget_talks/; Ronald Reagan, quoted in "Excerpts from President's Speech to National Association of Evangelicals," *New York Times* (March 9, 1983), https://www.nytimes.com/1983/03/09/us/excerpts-from-president-s-speech-to-national-association-of-evangelicals.html.

2. Chloe Folmar, "Boebert: Jesus didn't have enough AR-15s to 'keep his government from killing him,'" *The Hill* (June 17, 2022), https://thehill.com/homenews/house/3528049-boebert-jesus-didnt-have-enough-ar-15s-to-keep-his-government-from-killing-him/.

3. Brooks Jackson and Jerry Lauer, "Reagan Got $1 Million for Speeches, Commentary in 2 Years," *Washington Post* (July 1, 1980), https://www.washingtonpost.com/archive/politics/1980/07/01/reagan-got-1-million-for-speeches-commentary-in-2-years/34d88553-09cb-4442-be4c-2736e9c56ea4/.

4. *Ibid.*; "Ronald Reagan's $2-Million Speaking Fee," *Los Angeles Times* (November 4, 1989), https://www.latimes.com/archives/la-xpm-1989-11-04-fi-149-story.html.

5. The editors, "Harry Truman's obsolete integrity," *The New York Times* (March 2, 2007), https://www.nytimes.com/2007/03/02/opinion/02iht-edjacoby.4775315.html.

6. *Ibid.*; Scott Wilson, "In Demand: Washington's Highest (and Lowest) Speaking Fees," ABC News (July 14, 2014), https://abcnews.go.com/Politics/washingtons-highest-lowest-speaking-fees/story?id=24551590; Josh Dawsey and Isaac Arnsdorf, "Trump's paid-speeches organizer is struggling financially," *Washington Post* (September 29, 2022), https://www.washingtonpost.com/politics/2022/09/29/trump-speeches-bankruptcy-vendors/.

7. Jenni Fink and Kaitlin Lewis, "Did Mar-a-Lago Crowd Try to Leave While Trump Was Speaking?" *Newsweek* (November 16, 2022), https://www.newsweek.com/did-mar-lago-crowd-try-leave-while-trump-was-speaking-1759909.

8. David Nakamura, "White House softens tone on gun-control measures after Trump meets with NRA," *Washington Post* (March 2, 2018), https://www.washingtonpost.com/news/post-politics/wp/2018/03/02/white-house-softens-tone-on-gun-control-measures-after-trump-meets-with-nra/.

9. Matt Pearce, "Trump and Biden on guns: Far apart on policy and perspective," *Los Angeles Times* (August 19, 2020), https://www.latimes.com/politics/story/2020-08-19/trump-biden-gun-policy.

10. Peter Weber, "How Ronald Reagan learned to love gun control," *The Week* (December 3, 2015), https://theweek.com/articles/582926/how-ronald-reagan-learned-love-gun-control; Ian Shapira, "Before Trump's wild shifts on the NRA, Ronald Reagan took on the gun lobby," *Washington Post* (March 2, 2018), https://www.washingtonpost.com/news/retropolis/wp/2018/03/02/before-trump-defied-the-nra-ronald-reagan-took-on-the-gun-lobby/.

11. Ben Garrett, "Gun Rights Under President Ronald Reagan," *ThoughtCo.* (October 24, 2019), https://www.thoughtco.com/gun-rights-under-president-ronald-reagan-721343.

12. Isaac Arnsdorf, "Trump, Cruz join NRA leaders in defiant response to Uvalde shooting," *The Washington Post* (May 27, 2022), https://www.washingtonpost.com/politics/2022/05/27/trump-cruz-nra-speech-uvalde/.

13. https://www.theatlantic.com/politics/archive/2016/07/trump-rnc-speech-alone-fix-it/492557/.

14. *Politico* Staff, "Full text: 2017 Donald Trump inauguration speech transcript," *Politico* (January 1, 2017), https://www.politico.com/story/2017/01/full-text-donald-trump-inauguration-speech-transcript-233907.

15. Peggy Noonan, *When Character Was King: A Story of Ronald Reagan* (New York: Viking, 2003), 248–249.

16. Much of the discussion that follows comparing Reagan with Carter is based on Kyle Longley, "When Character Was King? Ronald Reagan and the Issues of Ethics and Morality," in Kyle Longley et al., *Deconstructing Reagan: Conservative Mythology and America's Fortieth President* (Armonk, NY: M.E. Sharpe, 2007), 90–119.

17. Billy Graham, *Just as I Am* (New York: HarperCollins, 1997), 589–590.

18. Dinesh D'Souza, *Ronald Reagan: How an Ordinary Man Became an Extraordinary Leader* (New York: Free Press, 1997), 212.

19. William Pemberton, *Exit with Honor: The Life and Presidency of Ronald Reagan* (Armonk, NY: M.E. Sharpe, 1998), 137.

20. Longley, 104.

21. Wilbur Edel, *The Reagan Presidency: An Actor's Finest Performance* (New York: Hippocrene Books, 1992), 296.

22. *Ibid.*

23. Longley, 105.

24. Steven V. Roberts, "Return to the Land of the Gipper," *The New York Times* (March 9, 1988).

25. Lou Cannon, *President Reagan: The Role of a Lifetime* (New York: Public Affairs, 2000), 40.

26. Thomas Jefferson cited by Voice of the People, "Readers sound off on Election Day," *New York Daily News* (November 6, 2018), https://www.nydailynews.com/opinion/ny-letter-nov6-20181104-story.html.

27. Remarks of President Biden, Cuyahoga Community College, Cleveland, Ohio May 27, 2001.

Bibliography

Americans For Tax Reform. "About the Ronald Reagan Legacy Project" (June 18, 2010). https://www.atr.org/ronald-reagan-legacy-project-a4499/.

Anderson, James R. "Bankrupting America: The Impact of President Reagan's Military Budget." *International Journal of Health Services* 11, no. 4 (1981), 623–629. https://www.jstor.org/stable/45130983.

Appelbaum, Yoni. "'I Alone Can Fix It.'" *The Atlantic* (July 21, 2016). https://www.theatlantic.com/politics/archive/2016/07/trump-rnc-speech-alone-fix-it/492557/.

Arnsdorf, Isaac. "Trump, Cruz join NRA leaders in defiant response to Uvalde shooting." *The Washington Post* (May 27, 2022). https://www.washingtonpost.com/politics/2022/05/27/trump-cruz-nra-speech-uvalde/.

Associated Press. "Ronald Reagan is descendant of Irish high-king." *Daily Kent Stater* (November 12, 1980). https://dks.library.kent.edu/cgi-bin/kentstate?a=d&d=dks19801112-01.2.60.

Associated Press. "Trump pushes aside Montenegro leader—who calls it natural." *AP News* (May 25, 2017). https://apnews.com/article/donald-trump-us-news-ap-top-news-international-news-dusko-markovic-60dfbc344f7f482d95af5353laec6841.

Associated Press. "White House Will Not Replace Solar Water-Heating System." *The New York Times* (August 24, 1986). https://www.nytimes.com/1986/08/24/us/white-house-will-not-replace-solar-water-heating-system.html.

Axelrod, Alan. *The Complete Idiot's Guide to the American Presidency*. New York: Alpha, 2009.

Axelrod, Alan. *Full Faith and Credit: The National Debt, Taxes, Spending, and the Bankrupting of America*. New York: Abbeville Press, 2016.

Bacevich, Andrew J. *The Limits of Power: The End of American Exceptionalism*. New York: Metropolitan Books, 2008.

Balitzer, Alfred, ed. *A Time for Choosing: The Speeches of Ronald Reagan 1961–1982*. Chicago: Regnery Gateway, 1983.

Barbaro, Michael. "Donald Trump Likens His Schooling to Military Service in Book." *New York Times* (September 8, 2015). https://www.nytimes.com/2015/09/09/us/politics/donald-trump-likens-his-schooling-to-military-service-in-book.html.

Barera, Michael. "The 1981 PATCO Strike." UTA Libraries Blog (September 2, 2021), https://libraries.uta.edu/news-events/blog/1981-patco-strike.

Barlett, Donald L., and James B. Steele. *America: What Went Wrong? The Crisis Deepens*. Traverse City, MI: Mission Point Press, 2020.

Bartlett, Bruce. "How Supply-Side Economics Trickled Down." *The New York Times* (April 6, 2007). https://www.nytimes.com/2007/04/06/opinion/06bartlett.html.

Bartlett, Bruce. "I helped create the GOP tax myth. Trump is wrong: Tax Cuts don't equal growth." *Washington Post* (September 28, 2017). https://www.washingtonpost.com/news/posteverything/wp/2017/09/28/i-helped-create-the-gop-tax-myth-trump-is-wrong-tax-cuts-dont-equal-growth/.

Bartlett, Bruce. "The 1981 Tax Cut After

30 Years: What Happened to Revenues?" *Tax Notes* (August 8, 2011). https://papers.ssrn.com/sol3/papers.cfm?abstract_id=1906654.

Bartlett, Bruce. "Reagan's Forgotten Tax Record." *Tax Notes* (February 21, 2011).

Bartlett, Bruce R. *Reaganomics, Supply-Side Economics in Action*. New York: Quill, 1981.

Beckwith, Ryan Teague. "Watch President Obama Troll Donald Trump in 2011." *Time* (August 10, 2015). https://time.com/3991301/donald-trump-barack-obama/.

Behr, Peter. "Wave of Mergers, Takeovers Is Part of the Reagan Legacy." *Washington Post* (October 30, 1988). https://www.washingtonpost.com/archive/business/1988/10/30/wave-of-mergers-takeovers-is-a-part-of-reagan-legacy/e90598c2-628d-40fe-b9c6-a621e298671d/.

Bergen, Peter. *Trump and His Generals: The Cost of Chaos*. New York: Penguin Press, 2019.

Berkman, Ted. "Bonzo comes swinging back." *Christian Science Monitor* (February 19, 1981). https://www.csmonitor.com/1981/0219/021957.html.

Berman, Larry, ed. *Looking Back on the Reagan Presidency*. Baltimore: Johns Hopkins University Press, 1990.

Biden, Joseph R. "Remarks of President Biden, Cuyahoga Community College, Cleveland, Ohio May 27, 2001."

Blair, Gwenda. *The Trumps: Three Generations That Built an Empire*. New York: Simon & Schuster, 2000.

Blinder, Alan S., and Mark W. Watson. "Presidents and the US Economy: An Economic Exploration." *American Economic Review* (2016), 106(4), 1015–1045. https://www.aeaweb.org/articles?id=10.1257/aer.20140913.

Block, Sharon. "The Myth of a Pro-Union Trump." *Democracy: A Journal of Ideas* (May 24, 2017). https://democracyjournal.org/briefing-book/the-myth-of-a-pro-union-trump/.

Borger, Julian. "LBJ's medal for valour 'was sham.'" *The Guardian* (July 6, 2001). https://www.theguardian.com/world/2001/jul/06/internationaleducationnews.humanities.

Brady, Thomas F. "Red Probe on in Hollywood: Congressional Group Investigates Movie Colony's Politics—Labor Issues Remain Unsettled—'Red Pony' in Production." *New York Times* (May 18, 1947). https://www.nytimes.com/1947/05/18/archives/red-probe-on-in-hollywood-congressional-group-investigates-movie.html.

Brands, H. W. *Reagan: The Life*. New York: Doubleday, 2015.

Brinkley, Douglas, ed. *The Notes: Ronald Reagan's Private Collection of Stories and Wisdom*. New York: Harper, 2011.

Brinkley, Douglas, ed. *The Reagan Diaries*. New York: HarperCollins, 2007.

Brockell, Gillian. "She was stereotyped as 'the welfare queen.' The truth was more disturbing, a new book says." *Washington Post* (May 21, 2019). https://www.washingtonpost.com/history/2019/05/21/she-was-stereotyped-welfare-queen-truth-was-more-disturbing-new-book-says/.

Broderick, Ryan. "Trump's Biggest Supporters Think the Coronavirus Is a Deep State Plot." *BuzzFeedNews* (February 26, 2020). https://www.buzzfeednews.com/article/ryanhatesthis/trump-supporters-coronavirus-deep-state-qanon.

Brownlee, W. Elliot, and Hugh Davis Graham, eds. *The Reagan Presidency: Pragmatic Conservatism and Its Legacies*. Lawrence: University Press of Kansas, 2003.

Buchanan, Pat. "Is Trump the Heir to Reagan?" *Sioux City Journal* (October 25, 2017). https://buchanan.org/blog/knives-come-christie-5983.

Bunch, Will. *Tear Down This Myth: The Right-Wing Distortion of the Reagan Legacy*. New York: Free Press, 2009.

Busch, Andrew. *Reagan's Victory: The Presidential Election of 1980 and the Rise of the Right*. Lawrence: University Press of Kansas, 2005.

Bush, George H. W. Speech at the Republican National Convention, New Orleans (August 18, 1988). https://www.youtube.com/watch?v=AdVSqSNHhVo.

Bush, George W. Remarks Following a Cabinet Meeting and an Exchange from Reporters (November 13, 2002). American Presidency Project.

Bush, George W. Remarks in Tax Cut Bill Signing Ceremony (June 7, 2001). https://georgewbush-whitehouse.archives.gov/news/releases/2001/06/20010607.html.

Bush, George W. Remarks to the Business and Industry Association of New Hampshire in Manchester, New Hampshire (February 8, 2006). American Presidency Project. https://www.govinfo. gov/app/details/PPP-2006-book1/PPP-2006-book1-doc-pg200.

Bush, George W. The President's News Conference. American Presidency Project (September 20, 2007). https://www. presidency.ucsb.edu/documents/the-presidents-news-conference-1135.

C-Span. Presidential Historians Survey 2021. https://www.c-span.org/president survey2021.

Cameron, Chris. "These Are the People Who Died in Connection with the Capitol Riot." *New York Times* (January 5, 2022, updated October 13, 2022). https:// www.nytimes.com/2022/01/05/us/ politics/jan-6-capitol-deaths.html.

Cannon, Lou. *Governor Reagan: His Rise to Power*. New York: Public Affairs, 2003.

Cannon, Lou. *President Reagan: The Role of a Lifetime*. New York: Simon & Schuster, 2000.

Cannon, Lou. *Reagan*. New York: G.P. Putnam's Sons, 1982.

Cannon, Lou. "Reagan Staff: Old-Time California Aides to Play Important Roles," *Washington Post* (November 6, 1980), https://www.washingtonpost. com/archive/politics/1980/11/06/ reagan-staff-old-time-california-aides-to-play-important-roles/746f2d60-aa9f-49b1-8a14-46591bb38d0c/.

Cannon, Lou. *Ronald Reagan: The Presidential Portfolio: A History Illustrated from the Collection of the Ronald Reagan Library and Museum*. New York: Public Affairs, 2001.

Cannon, Lou. "The Truth in Reagan's Humor." *Washington Post* (April 27, 1987), https://www.washingtonpost. com/archive/politics/1987/04/27/the-truth-in-reagans-humor/4540f5ea-45e1-4cf7-a635-28b1ea471234/.

Cannon, Lou. "Why Nancy Reagan Didn't Want Ronald to Run for a Second Term." *Politico* (March 7, 2016). https://www. politico.com/magazine/story/2016/03/ nancy-reagan-ronald-reagan-second-term-213704/.

Carter-Reagan Debate. October 28, 1980. Miller Center. https://millercenter.org/ the-presidency/presidential-speeches/ october-28-1980-debate-ronald-reagan.

CBS News. "CBS News archives: Carter's famous 'malaise speech.'" Posted on YouTube, July 15, 2011. https://www. youtube.com/watch?v=0tGd_9Tahzw.

Chait, Jonathan. *The Big Con: Crackpot Economics and the Fleecing of America*. New York: Houghton Mifflin Company, 2007.

Church, George J. "Go Ahead—Make My Day." *Time* (March 25, 1985). http:/www. time.com/time/magazine/article/0% 2C9171%2C964091%2C00.html.

Cillizza, Chris. "The Awful Reality That Donald Trump's Repeated Attacks on John McCain Prove." CNN Politics (March 19, 2019). https://www.cnn.com/ 2019/03/19/politics/donald-trump-john-mccain-dead.

Clark, Charles S. "Deconstructing the Deep State." *Government Executive* (undated). https://www.govexec.com/ feature/gov-exec-deconstructing-deep-state/.

Clines, Francis X. "It Was a Rescue Mission, Reagan Says." *The New York Times* (November 4, 1983). https://www. nytimes.com/1983/11/04/world/it-was-a-rescue-mission-reagan-says.html.

Clinton, Bill. "The New Covenant: Responsibility and Rebuilding the American Community." Speech at Georgetown University (October 23, 1991). https:// digital.tcl.sc.edu/digital/collection/ p17173coll40/id/474.

Clinton, Bill. State of the Union Address (January 23, 1996). https://clinton whitehouse4.archives.gov/WH/New/ other/sotu.html.

Coate, Robert L. "Reagan's Racism Seen Underneath Ambiguous Talk." *Los Angeles Sentinel* (November 9, 1967).

Coe, Richard L. "The Chimp's a Lot Cuter Than Reagan." *Washington Post* (March 15, 1951), B11.

Cogley, John. *Report on Blacklisting, I: Movies*. New York: Fund for the Republic, 1956.

Collinson, Stephen, and Jeremy Diamond. "Trump Finally Admits It: 'President Barack Obama Was Born in the United States.'" CNN Politics (September 16, 2016). https://www.cnn.com/2016/09/15/ politics/donald-trump-obama-birther-united-states.

Committee for a Responsible Federal Budget. "Tax Cuts Don't Pay for Themselves (October 4, 2017). https://www.crfb.org/papers/tax-cuts-dont-pay-themselves.

Congressional Budget Office. "Trends in the Distribution of Family Wealth, 1989 to 2019" (September 2022). https://www.cbo.gov/system/files/2022-09/57598-family-wealth.pdf.

Cowan, Edward. "Reagan's 3-Year, 25% Cut in Tax Rate Voted by Wide Margins in the House and Senate." *New York Times* (July 30, 1981). https://www.nytimes.com/1981/07/30/business/reagan-s-3-year-25-cut-in-tax-rate-voted-by-wide-margins-in-the-house-and-senate.html.

Cuomo, Mario. "1984 Democratic Convention Keynote Address" (July 16, 1984). https://www.c-span.org/video/?323534-1/mario-cuomo-1984-democratic-national-convention-keynote-speech.

CWA. "Trump's Anti-Worker Record." https://cwa-union.org/trumps-anti-worker-record.

Davidson, Joe. "Reagan's complicated legacy for federal workers." *Washington Post* (February 8, 2011). https://www.washingtonpost.com/local/despite-reagans-actions-government-workforce-grew-in-his-tenure/2011/02/07/ABuzkZF_story.html.

Davidson, Kate. "Treasury Secretary Steven Mnuchin: GOP Tax Plan Would More Than Offset Its Cost." *Wall Street Journal* (September 28, 2017). https://www.wsj.com/articles/treasury-secretary-steven-mnuchin-gop-tax-plan-would-more-than-offset-its-cost-1506626980.

Davies, Lawrence E. "Reagan Submits Tax Increases; Rise Would Top $800 Million. *New York Times* (March 9, 1967). https://timesmachine.nytimes.com/timesmachine/1967/03/09/issue.html.

Davis, Patti. *The Way I See It: An Autobiography.* New York: Putnam, 1992.

Dawsey, Josh, and Isaac Arnsdorf. "Trump's paid-speeches organizer is struggling financially." *Washington Post* (September 29, 2022). https://www.washingtonpost.com/politics/2022/09/29/trump-speeches-bankruptcy-vendors/.

Deaver, Michael R. *Behind the Scenes.* New York: William Morrow & Company, 1987.

Deaver, Michael R. *A Different Drummer:* *My Thirty Years with Ronald Reagan.* New York: HarperCollins, 2001.

"The Democratic Fisc: The White House budget office offers a scorecard on Obamanomics." *Wall Street Journal* (July 26, 2010). https://www.wsj.com/articles/SB10001424052748703995104575389430430274968.

Diaz, Danielle. "Trump suggests US will have military parade on July." CNN (September 19, 2017). https://www.cnn.com/2017/09/19/politics/donald-trump-emmannuel-macron-white-house-parade-bastille-day/index.html.

Didion, Joan. "Many Mansions" (1977). In Joan Didion, *We Tell Ourselves Stories in Order to Live: Collected Nonfiction,* 227–231. New York: Knopf, 2006.

Dionne, E.J., Jr. "Trump's '12 more years' shout shows what he has in common with autocrats." *Washington Post* (August 24, 2020). https://www.washingtonpost.com/opinions/2020/08/24/republicans-are-one-man-party/.

Domm, Patti. "When Volcker ruled the Fed, 'people thought they'd never buy a home again.'" CNBC (December 9, 2019). https://www.cnbc.com/2019/12/09/when-volcker-ruled-fed-people-thought-theyd-never-buy-a-home-again.html.

Domonoske, Camila. "Judge Approves $25 Million Settlement of Trump University Lawsuit." *NPR: The Two-Way* (March 31, 2017). https://www.npr.org/sections/thetwo-way/2017/03/31/522199535/judge-approves-25-million-settlement-of-trump-university-lawsuit.

D'Souza, Dinesh. *Ronald Reagan: How an Ordinary Man Became an Extraordinary Leader.* New York: Free Press, 1997.

Dunea, George, MD. "Loyal Davis, Legendary Neurosurgeon (1896–1982)." *Hektoen International* (Summer 2018). https://hekint.org/2018/08/16/loyal-davis-legendary-neurosurgeon-1896-1982/.

Durnin, Steven E. "The Professional Air Traffic Controllers Strike: A Retrospective Analysis." Embry-Riddle Aeronautical University, order no. EP31097 (1994).

Dvorak, Petula. "Jane Wyman as the anti–Ivana Trump." *Chicago Tribune* (October 11, 2017). https://www.chicagotribune.com/opinion/commentary/ct-perspec-flotus-ivana-melania-trump-jane-wyman-1012-20171011-story.html.

Edel, Wilbur. *The Reagan Presidency: An Actor's Finest Performance.* New York: Hippocrene Books, 1992.

Eder, Steven. "Did a Queens Podiatrist Help Donald Trump Avoid Vietnam?" *New York Times* (December 26, 2018). https://www.nytimes.com/2018/12/26/us/politics/trump-vietnam-draft-exemption.html?login=email&auth=login-email.

Eder, Steven, and Dave Philipps. "Donald Trump's Draft Deferments: Four for College, One for Bad Feet." *New York Times* (August 1, 2016). https://www.nytimes.com/2016/08/02/us/politics/donald-trump-draft-record.html.

Editorial Board. "A president unfit for a pandemic." *The Boston Globe* (March 30, 2020). https://www.bostonglobe.com/2020/03/30/opinion/president-unfit-pandemic/.

Edwards, Kathryn A., and Carter C. Price. "A $2.5 Trillion Question: What If Incomes Grew Like GDP Did?" Rand Blog (October 6, 2020). https://www.rand.org/blog/2020/10/a-25-trillion-question-what-if-incomes-grew-like-gdp.html.

Edwards, Lee. *The Essential Ronald Reagan.* Lanham, MD: Rowman and Littlefield Publishers, 2005.

Elving, Ron. "Trump's Helsinki Bow to Putin Leaves World Wondering: Why?" NPR (July 17, 2018). https://www.npr.org/2018/07/17/629601233/trumps-helsinki-bow-to-putin-leaves-world-wondering-whats-up.

Evans, Thomas W. *The Education of Ronald Reagan: The General Electric Years and the Untold Story of His Conversion to Conservatism.* New York: Columbia University Press, 2006.

Feldstein, Martin. "Supply Side Economics: Old Truths and New Claims." National Bureau of Economic Research NBER Working Paper Series (January 1986). https://www.nber.org/papers/w1792.pdf.

Fink, Jenni, and Kaitlin Lewis. "Did Mar-a-Lago Crowd Try to Leave While Trump Was Speaking?" *Newsweek* (November 16, 2022). https://www.newsweek.com/did-mar-lago-crowd-try-to-leave-while-trump-was-speaking-1759909.

Fitzgerald, Frances. *Way Out There in the Blue: Reagan, Star Wars, and the End of the Cold War.* New York: Simon & Schuster, 2000.

Folmar, Chloe. "Boebert: Jesus didn't have enough AR-15s to 'keep his government from killing him.'" *The Hill* (June 17, 2022). https://thehill.com/homenews/house/3528049-boebert-jesus-didnt-have-enough-ar-15s-to-keep-his-government-from-killing-him/.

Fortune staff. "The Shrinking of the Middle Class." *Fortune Magazine* (January 1, 2019). https://fortune.com/longform/shrinking-middle-class/.

Fox, Justin. "GDP Growth Under Trump Was the Worst Since Hoover." *Bloomberg* (August 2, 2021). https://www.bloomberg.com/opinion/articles/2021-08-02/trump-s-gdp-growth-was-the-worst-since-the-great-depression.

Fox, Justin. "The Mostly Forgotten Tax Increases of 1982–1993." *Bloomberg* (December 15, 2017).

Franklin, Cory. "The other man in Nancy Reagan's life." *Chicago Tribune* (March 8, 2016). https://www.chicagotribune.com/opinion/commentary/ct-nancy-reagan-loyal-davis-stepfather-perspec-0309-20160308-story.html.

Funke, Daniel. "Here's how the deficit performed under Republican and Democratic presidents, from Reagan to Trump." *PolitiFact* (July 29, 2019). https://www.politifact.com/factchecks/2019/jul/29/tweets/republican-presidents-democrats-contribute-deficit/.

Garrett, Ben. "Gun Rights Under President Ronald Reagan." *ThoughtCo.* (October 24, 2019). https://www.thoughtco.com/gun-rights-under-president-ronald-reagan-721343.

Geltzer, Joshua. "Trump Loved 'His Generals'—Until He Got to Know Them." *Just Security* (January 2, 2020). https://www.justsecurity.org/67884/trump-loved-his-generals-until-he-got-to-know-them/.

Gergen, David. "Ronald Reagan's Most Important Legacy." *U.S. News & World Report* (January 9, 1989).

Goldberg, Jeffrey. "Trump: American Who Died in War 'Losers' and 'Suckers.'" *The Atlantic* (September 3, 2020). https://www.theatlantic.com/politics/archive/2020/09/trump-americans-who-died-at-war-are-losers-and-suckers/615997/.

Graham, Billy. *Just as I Am*. New York: HarperCollins, 1997.

Greenwood, Max. "Trump: I have a 'much bigger' button than Kim Jong Un." *The Hill* (January 2, 2022). https://thehill.com/homenews/administration/367149-trump-i-have-a-much-bigger-button-than-kim-jong-un/.

Greider, William. "The Education of David Stockman." *The Atlantic* (December 1981). https://www.theatlantic.com/magazine/archive/1981/12/the-education-of-david-stockman/305760/.

Griswold, Jerry. "Young Reagan's Reading." *The New York Times Book Review* (August 30, 1981).

Grunwald, Michael. "Paul Ryan's Legacy of Red Ink." *Politico* (April 11, 2018). https://www.politico.com/magazine/tory/2018/04/11/paul-ryan-legacy-record-budget-red-ink/.

Haberman, Maggie. *Confidence Man: The Making of Donald Trump and the Breaking of America*. New York: Penguin, 2022.

Hacker, Jacob S. *The Great Risk Shift: The New Economic Insecurity and the Decline of the American Dream*. New York: Oxford University Press, 2008.

Halloran, Richard. "Reagan as Military Commander." *New York Times* (July 15, 1984). https://www.nytimes.com/1984/01/15/magazine/reagan-as-military-commander.html.

Hanson, Victor David. *The Case for Trump*. New York: Basic Books, 2019.

Hays, Constance L. "Holmes Tuttle, 83; In 'Kitchen Cabinet' That Aided Reagan" (obituary). *New York Times* (June 17, 1989). https://timesmachine.nytimes.com/timesmachine/1989/06/17/946889.html?pageNumber=29.

Heckman, Jory. "House GOP leaders vow to undo $80B to rebuild IRS if party regains majority." Federal News Network (September 23, 2022). https://federalnewsnetwork.com/budget/2022/09/house-gop-leaders-vow-to-undo-80b-to-rebuild-irs-if-party-regains-majority/.

Herhold, Scott, and Knight-Ridder Newspapers. "Reagan Played Informant Role for FBI in '40s." *Chicago Tribune* (August 25, 1985). https://www.chicagotribune.com/news/ct-xpm-1985-08-26-8502250710-story.html.

Hoffman, David. "Confidence in Reagan on Deficit Declines; Poll Find Greater Trust in Congressional Democrats to handle Red-Ink Problem." *Washington Post* (July 2, 1987). https://www.washingtonpost.com/archive/politics/1987/07/02/confidence-in-reagan-on-deficit-declines/97abcd2d-4c66-4694-8009-87c1405eb261/.

Hoffman, David. "Reagan Calls SALT II Dead." *Washington Post* (June 13, 1986). https://www.washingtonpost.com/archive/politics/1986/06/13/reagan-calls-salt-ii-dead/b0f19d98-7d94-453f-8cb0-4cecd2f493b9/.

Holan, Angie Drobnic. "Ronald Reagan understood 'to make a deal he would propose both spending cuts and tax increases.'" *PolitiFact* (April 4, 2012). https://www.politifact.com/factchecks/2012/apr/04/barack-obama/ronald-reagan-understood-make-deal-he-would-have-p/.

Holodny, Elena. "The top 0.1% of American households hold the same amount of wealth as the bottom 90%." *Business Insider* (October 23, 2017). https://www.businessinsider.com/americas-top-01-households-hold-same-amount-of-wealth-as-bottom-90-2017-10.

Hope, David, and Julian Limberg. "The Economic Consequences of Major Tax Cuts for the Rich." *Socio-Economic Review*, 20:2 (April 2022), 539–559. https://academic.oup.com/ser/article/20/2/539/6500315.

Horowitz, Juliana Menasce, Ruth Iglelnik, and Rakesh Kochhar. "2. Views of economic inequality." Pew Research Center (January 9, 2020). https://www.pewresearch.org/social-trends/2020/01/09/views-of-economic-inequality.

Hulse, Carl. "The 40th President: The Democrats; How Reagan Forced Foes to Reinvent Party." *The New York Times* (June 10, 2004). https://www.nytimes.com/2004/06/10/us/the-40th-president-the-democrats-how-reagan-forced-foes-to-reinvent-party.html.

Isaacson, Walter. "After the Fall." *Time* (November 2, 1987). https://content.time.com/time/magazine/article/0,9171,965864,00.html.

Jackson, Brooks, and Jerry Lauer. "Reagan Got $1 Million for Speeches, Commentary in 2 Years." *Washington Post* (July

1, 1980). https://www.washingtonpost.com/archive/politics/1980/07/01/reagan-got-1-million-for-speeches-commentary-in-2-years/34d88553-09cb-4442-be4c-2736e9c56ea4/.

Jankowicz, Mia. "Trump resisted requests to return stash of documents at Mar-a-Lago, saying 'it's not theirs, it's mine,' NYT reports." *Business Insider* (August 17, 2022). https://www.businessinsider.com/trump-on-documents-sought-nara-not-theirs-mine-nyt-2022-8.

Johns, Andrew L., ed. *A Companion to Ronald Reagan.* Chichester, West Sussex, UK: Wiley Blackwell, 2015.

Jones, Chuck. "Obama had more stock market records than Trump." *Forbes Magazine* (January 14, 2020). forbes.com/sites/chuckjones/2020/01/14/Obama had more stock market records than trump.

Jung, C.G. *The Collected Works.* East Sussex, UK: Routledge & Kegan Paul, 1953–1991.

Kelley, Kitty. *Nancy Reagan: The Unauthorized Biography.* New York: Simon & Schuster, 2011.

Kelly, Meg. "The 'Trump economy' vs. the 'Obama economy.'" *Washington Post* (September 18, 2018). https://www.washingtonpost.com/politics/2018/09/18/trump-economy-versus-obama-economy.

Kennedy, John F. Address at Rice University on the Nation's Space Effort (September 12, 1962). https://www.jfklibrary.org/learn/about-jfk/historic-speeches/address-at-rice-university-on-the-nations-space-effort.

Kennedy, John F. Commencement Address at Yale University (June 11, 1962). https://www.jfklibrary.org/archives/other-resources/john-f-kennedy-speeches/yale-university-19620611.

Kennedy, John F. Inaugural Address (January 20, 1961). https://www.archives.gov/milestone-documents/president-john-f-kennedys-inaugural-address#:~:text=On%20January%2020%2C%201961%2C%20President,survival%20and%20success%20of%20liberty.%22.

Kessler, Glenn. "Rand Paul's claim that Reagan's tax cuts produced 'more revenue' and 'tens of millions of jobs.'" *Washington Post* (April 10, 2015). https://www.washingtonpost.com/news/fact-checker/wp/2015/04/10/rand-pauls-claim-that-reagans-tax-cuts-produced-more-revenue-and-tens-of-millions-of-jobs/.

Kiely, Eugene, Brooks Jackson, Brea Jones, D'Angelo Gore, Lori Robertson, and Robert Farley. "Trump's Final Numbers," FactCheck.org (October 8, 2021), https://www.factcheck.org/2021/10/trumps-final-numbers/.

Kleinknecht, William. *The Man Who Sold the World: Ronald Reagan and the Betrayal of Main Street America.* New York: Perseus, 2009.

Knickmeyer, Ellen. "Rough total for Trump's July Fourth extravaganza: $5.5M." AP News (July 11, 2019).

Knutson, Lawrence L. "Reagan, Communism Met in Hollywood." AP News (November 13, 1985). https://apnews.com/article/43e9c90d8177871105953a7c4728a781.

Krugman, Paul. "The Tax-Cut Zombies." *The New York Times* (December 23, 2005). https://www.nytimes.com/2005/12/23/opinion/the-taxcut-zombies.html.

Krugman, Paul. "Why Zombie Reaganomics Still Rules the G.O.P." *The New York Times* (September 26, 2022). https://www.nytimes.com/2022/09/26/opinion/gop-economic-policy.html/.

LaCapria, Kim. "Was Donald Trump's Father Arrested at a KKK Rally?" *Snopes* (February 28, 2016). https://www.snopes.com/fact-check/donald-trump-father-kkk-1927/.

Laffer, Art. Interview on Fox Business, *Cavuto: Coast to Coast* (September 21, 2017).

Lawder, David. "The new IRS employees: An 'army' or harmless programmers?" Reuters (August 19, 2022). https://www.reuters.com/world/us/republicans-call-it-an-army-irs-hires-will-replace-retirees-do-it-says-treasury-2022-08-19/.

LBJ Presidential Library. "LBJ's Military Service." https://www.lbjlibrary.org/life-and-legacy/the-man-himself/lbjs-military-service.

Lee, Michelle Ye Hee. "Donald Trump's false comment connecting Mexican immigrants and crime." *Washington Post* (July 8, 2015). https://www.washingtonpost.com/news/fact-checker/wp/2015/07/08/donald-trumps-false-comments-connecting-mexican-immigrants-and-crime/.

Leighton, David. "Street Smarts: Auto Mall Drive." *Arizona Daily Star* (August 3, 2018). https://tucson.com/news/local/street-smarts-auto-mall-drive/article_01c83be2-cc60-5a9b-b4d0-1b3a6b9d8015.html.

Leonnig, Carol, and Philip Rucker. *I Alone Can Fix It: Donald J. Trump's Catastrophic Final Year.* New York: Penguin, 2021.

Lewis, Anthony. "Abroad at Home: The Cost of Reagan." *The New York Times* (September 7, 1989). https://www.nytimes.com/1989/09/07/opinion/abroad-at-home-the-cost-of-reagan.html.

Longley, Kyle. "When Character Was King? Ronald Reagan and the Issues of Ethics and Morality." In Kyle Longley et al., 90–119.

Longley, Kyle, Jeremy D. Mayer, Michael Schaller, and John W. Sloan. *Deconstructing Reagan: Conservative Mythology and America's Fortieth President.* Armonk, NY: M.E. Sharpe, 2007.

Lord, Jeffrey. *What America Needs: The Case for Trump.* Washington, D.C.: Regnery, 2016.

Lucks, Daniel S. "The GOP can't escape Trump without letting go of Reagan." *The Washington Post* (February 22, 2021). https://www.washingtonpost.com/outlook/2021/02/22/gop-cant-escape-trump-without-letting-go-reagan/.

Lucks, Daniel S. *Reconsidering Reagan, Racism, Republicans, and the Road to Trump.* Boston: Beacon Press, 2020.

MacDougall, Malcolm D. *We Almost Made It.* New York: Crown, 1977.

Maggs, John. "Corporate profits' big climb." *Politico* (October 28, 2010). https://www.politico.com/story/2010/10/corporate-profits-big-climb-044268.

Mahler, Jonathan, and Steven Eder. "'No Vacancies' for Blacks: How Donald Trump Got His Start, and Was First Accused of Bias." *New York Times* (August 27, 2016). https://www.nytimes.com/2016/08/28/us/politics/donald-trump-housing-race.html.

Mann, Windsor. "Trump's lethal aversion to reading." *The Week* (May 21, 2020). https://theweek.com/articles/915606/trumps-lethal-aversion-reading.

Martin, Jonathan, and Alan Rappeport. "Donald Trump Says John McCain Is No War Hero, Setting off Another Storm." *New York Times* (July 18, 2015). https://www.nytimes.com/2015/07/19/us/politics/trump-belittles-mccains-war-record.html.

Massie, Victoria M. "Donald Trump's 'inner city' has nothing to do with where black people live." *Vox* (October 20, 2016). https://www.vox.com/identities/2016/9/28/13074046/trump-presidential-debate-inner-city.

Mayer, Jeremy D. "Reagan and Race: Prophet of Color Blindness, Baiter of Backlash," in Kyle Longley et al., *Deconstructing Reagan: Conservative Mythology and America's Fortieth President.* Armonk, NY: M. E. Sharpe, 2007, 70–89.

Mayer, Jeremy D. *Running on Race: Racial Politics in Presidential Campaigns, 1960–2000.* New York: Random House, 2002.

McGreevy, Ronan. "Ronald Reagan's Irish ancestors found on historical Morpeth Roll." *The Irish Times* (November 20, 2013). https://www.irishtimes.com/culture/heritage/ronald-reagan-s-irish-ancestors-found-on-historic-morpeth-roll-1.1601480.

McKinley, Jesse. "A Torrent of Praise for Mario Cuomo's 1984 Democratic Convention Speech." *The New York Times* (July 27, 2016). https://slate.com/news-and-politics/2021/10/jimmy-carter-energy-crisis-malaise-speech-biden-supply-chain.html.

McManus, Doyle, and Douglas Jehl. "The Pluses, Minuses: Reagan Era: What Will History Say." *Los Angeles Times* (August 21, 1988). https://www.latimes.com/archives/la-xpm-1988-08-21-mn-1150-story.html.

McNicholas, Celine, and Margaret Poydock. "The Trump administrations attacks on workplace union voting rights forewarned of the broader threats to voting rights in the upcoming election." *Economic Policy Institute Report* (October 21, 2020). https://www.epi.org/publication/the-trump-administrations-attacks-on-workplace-union-voting-rights-forewarned-of-the-broader-threats-to-voting-rights-in-the-upcoming-election/.

Meroney, John. "Ron Reagan: Growing Up

as the Son of a President—and a Movie Star." *Atlantic* (January 18, 2011).

Mervosh, Sarah, and Niraj Chokshi. "Reagan Called Africans 'Monkeys' in Call with Nixon, Tape Reveals." *The New York Times* (July 31, 2019). https://www.nytimes.com/2019/07/31/us/politics/ronald-reagan-richard-nixon-racist.html.

Metz, Allan. *Ronald Reagan: A Bibliography.* Lanham, MD: Scarecrow Press, 2008.

Moldea, Dan E. *Dark Victory: Ronald Reagan, MCA, and the Mob.* New York: Penguin, 1987.

Moldea, Dan E. "Reagan Was Forgetting 25 Years Ago, as Well." *Washington Post* (March 15, 1987). https://www.washingtonpost.com/archive/opinions/1987/03/15/reagan-was-forgetting-25-years-ago-as-well/53286eb4-4e8e-4156-9e11-f2495192d5c6/.

Morris, Edmund. *Dutch.* New York: Random House, 1999).

Morrow, Lance. "Yankee Doodle Magic." *Time* (July 7, 1986). https://content.time.com/time/magazine/article/0,9171,961668,00.html.

Nakamura, David. "Trump boasts that he's 'like, really smart' and a 'very stable genius' amid questions over his mental fitness." *The Washington Post* (January 6, 2018). https://www.washingtonpost.com/news/post-politics/wp/2018/01/06/trump-boasts-that-hes-like-really-smart-and-a-very-stable-genius-amid-questions-over-his-mental-fitness/.

Nakamura, David. "White House softens tone on gun-control measures after Trump meets with NRA." *Washington Post* (March 2, 2018). https://www.washingtonpost.com/news/post-politics/wp/2018/03/02/white-house-softens-tone-on-gun-control-measures-after-trump-meets-with-nra/.

Nash, George. "Ronald Reagan's Road to Conservatism." *The Imaginative Conservative.* https://theimaginativeconservative.org/2018/11/ronald-reagan-road-conservatism-george-nash.html#%20ftn52.

NBC News. "Lavrov Derides Trump Kim 'Kindergarten Fight.'" NBC News (September 22, 2017). https://www.nbcnews.com/video/lavrov-derides-kindergarten-fight-between-trump-and-kim-1052924995934.

NFFE. "President Trump's Union Busting Executive Orders: What You Need to Know." *NFFE News.* https://nffe.org/nffe_news/president-trumps-union-busting-executive-orders-what-you-need-to-know/.

Nguyen, Tina. "Trump Channels Inner Kim Jong Un, Orders Giant Military Parade." *Vanity Fair* (February 7, 2018). https://www.vanityfair.com/news/2018/02/trump-wants-military-parade.

Niskanen, William A. *Reaganomics: An Insider's Account of the Polices and the People.* New York: Oxford University Press, 1988.

Noonan, Peggy. *When Character Was King: A Story of Ronald Reagan.* New York: Viking, 2003.

Nordheimer, Jon. "Reagan Is Picking His Florida Spots." *The New York Times* (February 5, 1976). https://www.nytimes.com/1976/02/05/archives/reagan-is-picking-his-florida-spots.html.

"Obama Roasts Donald Trump." YouTube (posted April 28, 2016). https://www.youtube.com/watch?v=HHckZCxdRkA.

O'Brien, Timothy L. *TrumpNation: The Art of Being the Donald.* New York: Warner Books, 2005.

Otterbein, Holly, and Megan Cassella. "Rank-and-file union members snub Biden for Trump." *Politico* (September 22, 2020). https://www.politico.com/news/2020/09/22/donald-trump-union-support-snub-joe-biden-418329.

Packer, George. "We are Living in a Failed State." *The Atlantic* (June 2020). https://www.theatlantic.com/magazine/archive/2020/06/underlying-conditions/610261/.

PBS. *Bill Moyers Journal.* Transcript (November 7, 2008). https://www.pbs.org/moyers/journal/11072008/transcript3.html.

Pearce, Matt. "Trump and Biden on Guns: Far Apart on Policy and Perspective." *Los Angeles Times* (August 19, 2020). https://www.latimes.com/politics/story/2020-08-19/trump-biden-gun-policy.

Pemberton, William E. *Exit with Honor: The Life and Presidency of Ronald Reagan.* Armonk, NY: M.E. Sharpe, 1997.

Perlstein, Rick. *The Invisible Bridge: The Fall of Nixon and the Rise of Reagan.* New York: Simon & Schuster, 2014.

Perlstein, Rick. *Reaganland: America's Right Turn 1976–1980*. New York: Simon & Schuster, 2020.

Peter G. Peterson Foundation. "What Is the National Debt Costing Us?" https://www.pgpf.org/national-debt-clock#-what-is-it-costing-us.

Phillips, Kevin. "Bubble and Bail." *The American Prospect* (April 18, 2008). https://prospect.org/features/bubble-bail/.

Pierce, R. Andrew. "Notes on the Irish Ancestry of President Ronald Reagan." http://www.wargs.com/articles/reagan.html.

Piketty, Thomas. *A Brief History of Equality*. Cambridge: Belknap Press of Harvard University Press, 2022.

Piketty, Thomas. *Capital in the Twenty-First Century*. Cambridge: Belknap Press of Harvard University Press, 2013.

Politico Staff. "Full text: 2017 Donald Trump Inauguration Speech Transcript." *Politico* (January 1, 2017). https://www.politico.com/story/2017/01/full-text-donald-trump-inauguration-speech-transcript-233907.

Public Papers of the Presidents: Ronald Reagan, 1981–1989. Washington, D.C.: U. S. Government Printing Office, 1982–1991.

Putnam, Jackson K. "Governor Reagan: A Reappraisal." *California History* (2006), 24–45.

Ransom, Jan. "Trump Will Not Apologize for Calling for Death Penalty Over Central Park Five." *New York Times* (June 18, 2019). https://www.nytimes.com/2019/06/18/nyregion/central-park-five-trump.html/.

Rappeport, Alan, and Jim Tankersley. "U.S. National Debt Tops $31 Trillion for First Time." *The New York Times* (October 4, 2022). https://www.nytimes.com/2022/10/04/business/national-debt.html.

Reagan, Michael. "Ronald Reagan's Son Remembers the Day When GE Fired His Dad." *Investor's Business Daily* (February 4, 2011). https://www.investors.com/politics/commentary/ronald-reagans-son-remembers-the-day-when-ge-fired-his-dad/.

Reagan, Michael, with Jim Denney. *The City on a Hill: Fulfilling Ronald Reagan's Vision for America*. Nashville: Thomas Nelson Publishers, 1997.

Reagan, Ronald. "Address before a joint session of Congress on the Program for Economic Recovery" (February 18, 1981). https://www.presidency.ucsb.edu/documents/address-before-joint-session-the-congress-the-program-for-economic-recovery-0.

Reagan, Ronald. Address to the Nation on Defense and National Security (March 23, 1983). https://www.reaganlibrary.gov/archives/speech/address-nation-defense-and-national-security.

Reagan, Ronald. *An American Life: An Enhanced eBook with CBS Video: The Autobiography*. New York: Simon & Schuster. 1990.

Reagan, Ronald. Announcement for Presidential Candidacy (November 13, 1979). UVA/Miller Center. https://millercenter.org/the-presidency/presidential-speeches/november-13-1979-announcement-presidential-candidacy.

Reagan, Ronald, Commencement Address, Eureka College (1957). https://whatrocks.github.io/commencement-db/1957-ronald-reagan-eureka-college/.

Reagan, Ronald. "Evil Empire Speech" (March 8, 1982). https://voicesofdemocracy.umd.edu/reagan-evil-empire-speech-text/.

Reagan, Ronald. Farewell Speech. *The New York Times* (January 12, 1989). https://www.nytimes.com/1989/01/12/news/transcript-of-reagan-s-farewell-address-to-american-people.html.

Reagan, Ronald. Inaugural Address (January 20, 1981). https://www.reaganlibrary.gov/archives/speech/inaugural-address-1981.

Reagan, Ronald. "Looking Out a Window" (January 27, 1978). In Skinner et al., 18–19.

Reagan, Ronald. "March 4, 1987: Address to the Nation on Iran-Contra." Miller Center. https://millercenter.org/the-presidency/presidential-speeches/march-4-1987-address-nation-iran-contra.

Reagan, Ronald. Quoted in "Excerpts from President's Speech to National Association of Evangelicals." *The New York Times* (March 9, 1983). https://www.nytimes.com/1983/03/09/us/excerpts-from-president-s-speech-to-national-association-of-evangelicals.html.

Reagan, Ronald. Remarks on Signing the

Tax Reform Act of 1986 (October 22, 1986). The American Presidency Project. https://www.presidency.ucsb.edu/documents/remarks-signing-the-tax-reform-act-1986.

Reagan, Ronald. "Republican National Convention Address" (August 19, 1976). https://www.americanrhetoric.com/speeches/ronaldreagan1976rnc.htm.

Reagan, Ronald. "The Republican Party and the Conservative Movement." *National Review* (December 1, 1964).

Reagan, Ronald. "Ronald Reagan: Immigrants recognize the intoxicating power of America." *The Kansas City Star* (July 23, 2019). https://www.kansascity.com/opinion/opn-columns-blogs/syndicated-columnists/article232864812.html.

Reagan, Ronald. *Ronald Reagan Speaks Out against Socialized Medicine* (1961). *American Rhetoric Online Speech Bank.* https://www.americanrhetoric.com/speeches/ronaldreagansocializedmedicine.htm.

Reagan, Ronald. "Ronald Reagan's ultimatum to striking air traffic controllers" (August 3, 1981). Wikisource. https://en.wikisource.org/wiki/Ronald_Reagan%27s_ultimatum_to_striking_air_traffic_controllers.

Reagan, Ronald. *Speaking My Mind: Selected Speeches.* New York: Simon & Schuster, 1989.

Reagan, Ronald. State of the Union Address (February 6, 1985). https://www.reaganfoundation.org/ronald-reagan/reagan-quotes-speeches/state-of-the-union-3/.

Reagan, Ronald. "A Time for Choosing" (October 27, 1964). https://www.reaganlibrary.gov/reagans/ronald-reagan/time-choosing-speech-october-27-1964.

Reagan, Ronald, and Richard C. Hubler. *Where's the Rest of Me? Ronald Reagan Tells His Own Story.* New York: Dell, 1965.

"Reagan Affirms Anti-Abortion Stand." *The New York Times* (February 8, 1976). www.nytimes.com/1976/02/08/archives/reagan-affirms-antiabortion-stand.html.

"Reagan Aide Resigns, Raising Speculation on '68." *The New York Times* (August 29, 1967). https://www.nytimes.com/1967/08/29/archives/reagan-aide-resigns-raising-speculation-on-68-possibility-seen-that.html.

"Reagan-Carter Debate Oct. 28, 1980— 'There You Go Again.'" YouTube (September 25, 2012). https://www.youtube.com/watch?v=qN7gDRjTNf4.

"Reagan feared Irish roots would damage his career." *Independent* (October 23, 2004). https://www.independent.ie/irish-news/reagan-feared-irish-roots-would-damage-his-career-26225824.html.

"Reagan Foes Fail in Recall Effort." *The New York Times* (August 2, 1968). https://timesmachine.nytimes.com/timesmachine/1968/08/02/91234204.html?pageNumber=20.

Reagan interview with Hedda Hopper. *Chicago Tribune* (May 18, 1947), G7.

"Reagan Proposals Detail Further Trims in Budget." *The New York Times* (March 11, 1981). https://www.nytimes.com/1981/03/11/us/reagan-proposals-detail-further-trims-in-budget.html.

"Recession Economics." *New York Review of Books,* 29:1 (4 February 1982). https://www.nybooks.com/articles/1982/02/04/recession-economics/?printpage=true.

Reed, Thomas. *At the Abyss: An Insider's History of the Cold War.* New York: Ballantine, 2004.

Reeves, Richard. *President Reagan: The Triumph of Imagination.* New York: Simon & Schuster, 2005.

Rich, Frank. "Ronald Reagan Was Once Donald Trump." *New York Magazine* (June 1, 2016). https://nymag.com/intelligencer/2016/05/ronald-reagan-was-once-donald-trump.html.

Richards, Clay F. "'He did a real job on America.'" UPI (December 9, 1980). https://www.upi.com/Archives/1980/12/09/He-did-a-real-job-on-America/8126345186000/.

Riedl, Brian. "Trump's Fiscal Legacy: A Comprehensive Overview of Spending, Taxes, and Deficits." *Manhattan Institute* (May 12, 2022). https://www.manhattan-institute.org/trumps-fiscal-legacy.

"Ronald Reagan on 'There You Go Again'; Other Notable Debate Moments." *PBS NewsHour.* YouTube (February 3, 2011). https://www.youtube.com/watch?v=T43EzCUtSwQ.

Ronald Reagan Presidential Library.

"Ronald Reagan speaks out on Socialized Medicine." YouTube, https://www.youtube.com/watch?v=AYrlDlrLDSQ.

Ronald Reagan Presidential Library & Museum. "Military Service of Ronald Reagan." https://www.reaganlibrary.gov/reagans/ronald-reagan/military-service-ronald-reagan.

Rosellini, Lynn. "Glittering Festivities Usher in Reagan Era." *The New York Times* (January 21, 1981). https://www.nytimes.com/1981/01/21/us/glittering-festivities-usher-in-reagan-era.html.

Rossinow, Douglas C. *The Reagan Era: A History of the 1980s.* New York: Columbia University Press, 2015.

Rucker, Philip, and Carol Leonnig. *A Very Stable Genius: Donald J. Trump's Testing of America.* New York: Penguin, 2020.

Russian, Ale. "Trump Boasted of Avoiding STDs While Dating: Vaginas Are 'Landmines … It Is My Personal Vietnam.'" *People* (October 15, 2016). https://people.com/politics/trump-boasted-of-avoiding-stds-while-dating-vaginas-are-landmines-it-was-my-personal-vietnam/.

Sayler, James, comp. *Presidents of the United States—Their Written Measure: A Bibliography.* Washington, D.C.: Library of Congress, 1996.

Schlafly, Phyllis, with Ed Martin and Brett M. Decker. *The Conservative Case for Trump.* Washington, D.C.: Regnery, 2016.

Schmidt, Michael S. *Donald Trump v. The United States.* New York: Random House, 2020.

Schram, Martin, et al. "Reagan Beats a Retreat on Klan Remark." *Washington Post* (September 3, 1980). https://www.washingtonpost.com/archive/politics/1980/09/03/reagan-beats-a-retreat-on-klan-remark/dcd581f5-435e-419f-9216-25d98dbcf859/.

Schulte, Bret. "Ronald Reagan v. Jimmy Carter: 'Are You Better Off Than You Were Four Years Ago?'" *U.S. News & World Report* (January 17, 2008). https://www.usnews.com/news/articles/2008/01/17/the-actor-and-the-detail-man.

Schwarz, Jon. "The Murder of the U.S. Middle Class Began 40 Years Ago This Week." *The Intercept* (August 6, 2021). https://theintercept.com/2021/08/06/middle-class-reagan-patco-strike/.

Schweizer, Peter. "Reagan's War: The Epic story of His Forty-Year Struggle and Final Triumph Over Communism." *Washington Post* (October 29, 2020).

Scott, Eugene. "Trump's most insulting—and violent—language is often reserved for immigrants." *Washington Post* (October 2, 2019). https://www.washingtonpost.com/politics/2019/10/02/trumps-most-insulting-violent-language-is-often-reserved-immigrants/.

Seib, Gerald F. *We Should Have Seen It Coming: From Reagan to Trump—A Front-Row Seat to a Political Revolution.* New York: Random House, 2021.

Shapira, Ian. "Before Trump's wild shifts on the NRA, Ronald Reagan took on the gun lobby." *Washington Post* (March 2, 2018). https://www.washingtonpost.com/news/retropolis/wp/2018/03/02/before-trump-defied-the-nra-ronald-reagan-took-on-the-gun-lobby/.

Skinner, Kiron K., Annelise Anderson and Martin Anderson, eds. *Reagan: A Life in Letters.* New York: Free Press, 2003.

Slemrod, Joel B. "Income Creation or Income Shifting? Behavioral Responses to the Tax Reform Act of 1986." *American Economics Review* 85, no. 2 (May 1995). https://www.jstor.org/stable/2117914.

Slemrod, Joel B., ed. *Does Atlas Shrug?* New York: Russell Sage Foundation, 2000.

Sloan, John W. "The Economic Costs of the Reagan Mythology." In Longley et al. *Deconstructing Reagan,* 41–69.

Sloan, John W. *The Reagan Effect: Economics and Presidential Leadership.* Lawrence: University Press of Kansas, 1999.

Smith, Gary S. "The Faith of George H.W. Bush." *The Christian Post* (June 26, 2017). https://www.christianpost.com/news/the-faith-of-george-h-w-bush.html.

Snyder, Alan. "Ronald Reagan, Whittaker Chambers, and the Dialogue of Liberty," *Law & Liberty* (March 13, 2012), https://lawliberty.org/ronald-reagan-whittaker-chambers-and-the-dialogue-of-liberty/.

Stein, Ben. "In Class Warfare, Guess Which Class Is Winning." *New York Times* (November 26, 2006). https://www.nytimes.com/2006/11/26/business/yourmoney/26every.html/.

Steinhauer, Jennifer, and Zolan Kanno-Youngs. "Job Vacancies and Inexperience

Mar Federal Response to Coronavirus." *The New York Times* (March 26, 2020). https://www.nytimes.com/2020/03/26/us/politics/coronavirus-expertise-trump.html.

Stockman, David. *The Triumph of Politics: Why the Reagan Revolution Failed.* New York: Harper & Row, 1985.

Sussman, Barry. "Shooting Gives Reagan Boost in Popularity." *Washington Post* (April 2, 1981). https://www.washingtonpost.com/archive/politics/1981/04/02/shooting-gives-reagan-boost-in-popularity/9515e340-f295-42e7-89c4-c96ed0ab7a44/.

"Tax Cuts Don't Pay For Themselves." Committee for a Responsible Federal Budget (October 4, 2017). https://www.crfb.org/papers/tax-cuts-dont-pay-themselves.

Tax Policy Center. "Distributional Analysis of the Tax Cuts and Jobs Act as Passed by the Senate Finance Committee" (November 20, 2017). https://www.taxpolicycenter.org/publications/distributional-analysis-tax-cuts-and-jobs-act-passed-senate-finance-committee.

Tax Policy Center. *The Tax Policy Center's Briefing Book.* https://www.taxpolicycenter.org/briefing-book/how-did-tcja-affect-federal-budget-outlook.

Taylor, Adam. "Trump's July 4 military parade is a celebration of himself." *Washington Post* (July 4, 2019). https://www.washingtonpost.com/world/2019/07/04/trumps-july-4-military-parade-is-celebration-himself/.

Tempalski, Jerry. "Revenue Effects of Major Tax Bills, OTA Working Paper 81." Department of the Treasury Office of Tax Analysis (September 2006).

Thomas, Robert McG., Jr. "Sidney Korshak, 88, Dies; Fabled Fixer for the Chicago Mob." *The New York Times* (January 22, 1996). https://timesmachine.nytimes.com/timesmachine/1996/01/22/090018.html?pageNumber=52.

Treaster, Joseph B. "A Life That Started Out with Much Promise Took Reclusive and Hostile Path." *The New York Times* (April 1, 1981). https://www.nytimes.com/1981/04/01/us/a-life-that-started-out-with-much-promise-took-reclusive-and-hostile-path.html.

Trump, Donald J. "Donald J. Trump on Tax Reform." St. Charles, Missouri (November 29, 2017). https://factba.se/transcript/donald-trump-speech-tax-reform-st-charles-missouri-november-29-2017.

Trump, Donald J. Tweet (October 2, 2016). https://www.presidency.ucsb.edu/documents/tweets-october-2-2016.

Trump, Donald J., with Tony Schwartz. *Trump: The Art of the Deal.* New York: Random House, 1987.

Trump, Mary L. *Too Much and Never Enough: How My Family Created the World's Most Dangerous Man.* New York: Simon & Schuster, 2020.

UPI. "The creators of 'Bedtime for Bonzo' wanted Cary Grant." UPI Archives (December 25, 1980). https://www.upi.com/Archives/1980/12/25/The-creators-of-Bedtime-for-Bonzo-wanted-Cary-Grant/4355346568400/.

Vaughn, Stephen. *Ronald Reagan in Hollywood: Movies and Politics.* New York: Cambridge University Press, 1994.

Voytko, Lisette. "Report: UPenn Professor Renews Call for Investigation into Trump's Alleged SAT Cheating." *Forbes* (August 28, 2020). https://www.forbes.com/sites/lisettevoytko/2020/08/28/report-upenn-professor-renews-call-for-investigation-into-trumps-alleged-sat-cheating/?sh=7014dae8256f.

Weber, Peter. "How Ronald Reagan learned to love gun control." *The Week* (December 3, 2015). https://theweek.com/articles/582926/how-ronald-reagan-learned-love-gun-control.

Weisberg, Jacob. *Ronald Reagan.* New York: Times Books, 2016.

The White House, "Table 14.3—Total Government Expenditures as Percentages of GDP: 1948–2021, https://www.whitehouse.gov/omb/budget historical-tables/.

"Who's Minding the Store?" *The New York Times* (April 1, 1981). https://www.nytimes.com/1981/04/01/opinion/whos-minding-the-store.html.

Wikipedia. *"Bedtime for Bonzo."* https://en.wikipedia.org/wiki/Bedtime_for_Bonzo.

Wilber, Del Quentin. *Rawhide Down: The Near Assassination of Ronald Reagan.* New York: Henry Holt, 2011.

Woodward, Bob. *Fear: Trump in the White House.* New York: Simon & Schuster, 2018.

Woodward, Bob, and Robert Costa. "Transcript: Donald Trump interview with Bob Woodward and Robert Costa." *Washington Post* (April 2, 2016). https://www.washingtonpost.com/news/post-politics/wp/2016/04/02/transcript-donald-trump-interview-with-bob-woodward-and-robert-costa/.

Wright, Harold Bell. *That Printer of Udell's* (1902; reprint ed., Pelican Publishers, 1996).

Wright, Jim. *Balance of Power: Presidents and Congress from the Era of McCarthy to the Age of Gingrich*. Atlanta: Turner Publishing, 1996.

WSJ Staff. "Bush on Jobs: The Worst Track Record on Record." *Wall Street Journal* (January 9, 2009). https://www.wsj.com/articles/BL-REB-2534.

"X" (George F. Kennan). "The Sources of Soviet Conduct." *Foreign Affairs* (July 1947). https://www.foreignaffairs.com/articles/russian-federation/1947-07-01/sources-soviet-conduct.

Yager, Edward M. *Ronald Reagan's Journey: Democrat to Republican*. New York: Rowman and Littlefield, 2006.

Yergin, Daniel, and Joseph Stanislaw. *The Commanding Heights: The Battle for the World Economy*. New York: Free Press, 2002.

Yun Li. "This is now the longest US economic expansion in history." CNBC (July 2, 2019). https://www.cnbc.com/2019/07/02/this-is-now-the-longest-us-economic-expansion-in-history.html.

Zanona, Melanie. "Trump on North Korea missile threat: 'It won't happen.'" *The Hill* (January 2, 2017). https://thehill.com/homenews/administration/312428-trump-on-north-korea-missile-threat-it-wont-happen.

Zhang, Andrew. "Addressing NRA in Houston, Donald Trump rejects gun regulations and calls for school safety overhaul." *The Texas Tribune* (May 27, 2022). https://www.texastribune.org/2022/05/27/donald-trump-nra-houston/.

Index